A HISTORY OF HAWORTH

A history of Haworth

from earliest times

MICHAEL BAUMBER

A History of Haworth

Copyright © Michael Baumber, 2009

First published in 2009 by
Carnegie Publishing Ltd
Chatsworth Road,
Lancaster LA1 4SL
www.carnegiepublishing.com

British Library Cataloguing-in-Publication data
A catalogue record for this book is available from the British Library

ISBN 978-1-85936-156-6   *hardback*

Designed, typeset and originated by Carnegie Publishing
Printed and bound by Cromwell Press Group, Trowbridge

Contents

Preface and acknowledgements

The subject of this book is the chapelry or township of Haworth, covering not just Haworth itself but also the hamlets of Near and Far Oxenhope and Stanbury. There are practical reasons for this choice. To write a continuous history of any of the four in isolation, before the sixteenth century, would be difficult because information is so sparse. Even when the available material becomes more extensive it is often hard to distinguish what applies to each hamlet. This is particularly the case with the inventories which are the basis of the first two sections of chapter 6. However, using the old administrative divisions creates a difficulty of its own, because their boundaries often followed streams and this had the effect of splitting valleys in two. This is a particular problem in considering the textile industry. Ponden and Springhead mills are technically on the Oakworth side of the river Worth and the original Lee Syke mill, with the exception of the boiler house, was in Bingley parish but the omission of these from discussion of the Haworth textile industry in chapters 7, 9, 12 and 17 would have distorted them completely. Lees and Crossroads provide a different conundrum. They are clearly outside Haworth, but they were added to the Haworth UDC in 1894 so issues such as the sewage controversy in chapter 13 and the free library farce in chapter 15 cannot be understood without their inclusion. Consequently I have largely omitted Lees and Crossroads material from before 1894, but included it after that date.

Considering the chapelry as a whole in any case has its advantages. One of the besetting sins of most village history writing is the belief that the community concerned can be understood by looking at its buildings and institutions in isolation from larger places near by. In the Worth valley there is an undercurrent of resentment in Oxenhope and Stanbury at the prominence given to Haworth village by what might be termed 'the Brontë industry', which churns out books practically every year. The benefits which accrue from comparing and contrasting the fortunes of the four hamlets instead of studying them in isolation are apparent in practically every chapter.

What is true of the relationship between Stanbury and Oxenhope on the one hand and Haworth on the other is also that between Haworth and the world outside. I have tried to place the Haworth experience within this wider context wherever possible, though but there has to be a limit, since otherwise local history would cease to be local.

The problem is particularly acute where Haworth formed part of a larger administrative unit. From 1837 to 1929, for example, it was within the Keighley and Bingley Poor Law Union which twice made the national headlines. The first was what Disraeli called 'the great Mott case' of 1842, involving conditions at the Keighley workhouse, and the second the notorious anti-smallpox vaccination campaign of the 1870s. These were really pieces of Keighley's history, for the Haworth poor were consigned to Bingley workhouse (not to Keighley) and the three Haworth guardians consistently supported compulsory vaccination and were not involved with the events which led to the jailing of those Keighley guardians who defied the law as it then stood.

A book needs an organising principle, or otherwise it becomes just a jumble of unrelated facts. The principle I have adopted is the history of Haworth's textile industry from its medieval beginnings through to its twentieth-century collapse. Examination of the development of communications dovetails neatly with these changes, as does Haworth's governmental history. Haworth started out as part of the manor of Bradford but steadily acquired more administrative freedom, reaching its greatest independence at the height of the textile boom in the 1860s. After 1914 there was a parallel decline which saw Haworth absorbed first of all by Keighley and then back into Bradford. The religious and social history of the township is also closely bound up with its economic fortunes, so it is possible to describe the career of William Grimshaw and the fortunes of the Brontë family quite naturally within the format chosen. Brontë addicts will find much to interest them, particularly in chapters 9–11, but they should not ignore other parts of the book – notably the strange case of Henry Casson in chapter 5, the destruction of the Brontë church and the free library controversy in chapter 15, and the foundation of the Brontë Society in chapter 19. The way in which textiles, administrative independence, the churches and chapels, the co-operative society and the characteristic leisure pursuits all collapsed together is strikingly brought out by chapters 17 and 18.

Some issues were more difficult to treat within the chosen framework. Agriculture was never very important and once the link with textiles was broken, when all the processes went into the mills, finding a logical place to put it proved difficult. Concentration on textiles tends to cast a shadow over other minor industries. This is particularly the case with stone quarrying. Animated discussions with my readers has modified my original rather dismissive attitude but those who feel that I am still underrating its importance should turn to the appropriate parts of the books of Reg Hindley and Steve Wood for a more detailed consideration. Another striking feature of the Worth valley is its reservoirs. I have little to say about them because they were constructed by specialist gangs of navvies, few of whom came from Haworth, and they served the needs of Bradford and Keighley rather than the local area, so they are only discussed in relation to their impact on Haworth water problems and when they swallowed mills. Yet they are arguably the most enduring local monuments to the industrial revolution, whose other artefacts are passing from the scene. Primary education falls into the scheme naturally but Haworth was not important enough to boast a secondary school. To include people who achieved academic distinction has thus called for some ingenuity and there is not much space for celebrating those who left Haworth and made their careers elsewhere. There is one exception. No account of any British community in the twentieth century would be complete if it did not mention the two world wars. Chapter 16 covers the experiences of Haworth men outside Haworth and all over the world, experiences which many of them sadly did not survive.

I take this opportunity to thank all those who have helped in the production of this book, in particular the staffs of the archives and libraries in which I have worked and who have proved unfailingly helpful and supportive. Naming them all would be very difficult. I have been working on this book for 12 years and some of the material was collected as long as 40 years ago, so many have moved on, some have retired and others, such as David James, have alas died. May I also thank all those individuals who have allowed family photographs to be used. I have also benefited from discussions and information from many people over the years but two stand out. I am indebted to the researches of Robin Greenwood into his family, the Haworth textile industry and the Baptist churches in Haworth, the various volumes of which and their updates still make my shelves groan. The debates we have had over the manor of Oxenhope and Haworth's perpetual curates during the Civil Wars and the Interregnum have also been most helpful and he has ferreted out family photographs for me. I have benefited greatly from my association with Steve Wood. His editions of the Haworth tithe apportionment and the Babbage Report, his compilation of Haworth trade directories and the year books of the Haworth UDC have put all Haworth researchers in his debt. We collaborated in securing copies of the Royal Commission on Historical Monuments reports into Haworth mills from Swindon and his persistence was largely responsible for the unearthing of the rate assessment books in the basement of Keighley Town Hall. His collection of digitised photographs must also be the first stop for anyone wanting illustrations for a book on the area. I remember with gratitude the times I have sat on his sofa and discussed Haworth history and many other topics as well. Robin, Steve and Reg Hindley also read the manuscript for me and made many valuable comments. Any errors which may remain are my responsibility not theirs.

Finally may I thank my editor, Dr Alan Crosby, for knocking the book into shape, and everyone at Carnegie for all the hard work they have put in.

Michael Baumber
Sutton-in-Craven
October 2009

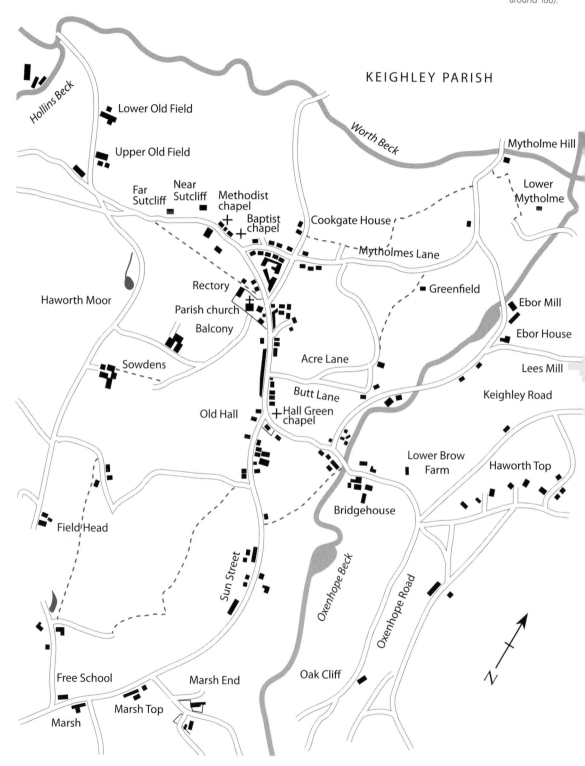

Haworth as it was around 1867.

KEIGHLEY PARISH

Hollins Beck

Worth Beck

Lower Old Field

Mytholme Hill

Upper Old Field

Lower Mytholme

Far Sutcliff

Near Sutcliff

Methodist chapel

Baptist chapel

Cookgate House

Mytholmes Lane

Haworth Moor

Rectory

Greenfield

Parish church

Ebor Mill

Balcony

Ebor House

Sowdens

Acre Lane

Lees Mill

Keighley Road

Old Hall

Butt Lane

Hall Green chapel

Lower Brow Farm

Haworth Top

Field Head

Bridgehouse

Sun Street

Oxenhope Beck

Oxenhope Road

Free School

Marsh End

Oak Cliff

Marsh Top

N

Marsh

The Haworth area before the
Norman Conquest

The history of the Haworth area, as of so many other places, only emerges into a bright light during the Middle Ages. Before then the lack of documentary or physical evidence makes it very much harder to piece together a coherent story. For thousands of years before the Anglo-Saxon period almost nothing is known, apart from brief glimpses and tantalising fragments. This presents the historian with a major challenge, for we strongly suspect that, for example, the pre-Roman inhabitants of the area played an active role in modifying the landscape and changing their environment. This notion – that our forebears have been agents for landscape change for millennia rather than just centuries – has lately emerged as one of the most significant themes in landscape history, and in some parts of England it is possible to find tangible and identifiable evidence to support it. Here, however, the landscape has not been the subject of serious investigation by archaeologists and others, and we have little in the way of detailed written records until only nine hundred years ago – which might seem a long time, but is just a few moments in the long span of human endeavour in these islands. For this reason the first part of this book covers a huge timespan and is, unavoidably, based on the very limited evidence available to us for the long centuries before the history of this fascinating and beautiful area comes into the daylight.

Earliest settlements

The first people to colonise the Haworth area are thought to have arrived from the Continent about 15,000 years ago, after the end of the Ice Age. Evidence has been found at Nab Water of the presence of these Mesolithic peoples. There were three separate archaeological excavations between 1930 and 1970, in which 1154 artefacts were collected from three linked sites, among them 64 blades, 27 microliths (tiny flints) and 14 scrapers. Their style suggests a connection with the Maglemosian culture of Belgium. The flint cores had been prepared from small water-rolled pebbles from the beaches of east Yorkshire and Lincolnshire. Nab Water, therefore, appears to have been a regular camp site for a group of hunter-gatherers who wintered on the coast but came into the hills to hunt during the late summer and autumn months. They made flint implements at the site, and the scrapers indicate that they may have cleaned the skins of the animals they killed, in order to make clothing.

The implements were buried under a layer of peat, but in Mesolithic times much of the hill country around Haworth was tree-covered and the hunters would have taken woodland animals such as red deer, roe deer, pig, elk and auroch. Fur-bearing animals such as beaver, pine martin, fox, wild cat and badger would also have been caught. The heathland and woodlands were probably exploited for food plants such as nuts and berries. The absence of axe heads among the tools suggests that there was no systematic felling of trees, so the camp site was perhaps just above the tree line.[1]

During the Neolithic period, which saw the first domestication of animals and arable agriculture, farmers preferred the more fertile and easily worked land on lower valley sides, and no traces of occupation from this period have been identified in the chapelry. There was a new influx of colonisers during the Bronze Age (around 1500 BC). They penetrated up the Ribble valley and settled much of the highland region. Examples of

'On Crow Hill, the loftiest eminence in the chapelry, 1,500 feet above the level of the sea, is a cromlech, evidently Druidical, consisting of one flat stone weighing about six tons, placed horizontally upon two huge upright blocks, now half embedded in the heather' (from Lewis's Topographical Dictionary, 7th edition, 1848). The Alcomden Stones are now thought to be a fortuitous assemblage of stones, probably glacial erratics.

their barbed and tanged arrowheads were found in 1837 on Keighley Moor, south of the Aire, and at Burnt Moor and Middle Moor Hill on Stanbury Moor. There is a Bronze Age barrow on Armshaw Low and there may be another at Silver Hill beyond Stanbury.[2]

In Emily Brontë's *Wuthering Heights*, Catherine accuses Nellie Dean of 'gathering elf bolts to hurt our heifers'. The folk-term 'elf bolts' was applied to Neolithic and Bronze Age arrowheads, and some commentators have assumed that they were common around Haworth. In fact finds of this nature are very rare. Emily could have heard about them in tales her father told about Ireland or when she spent some time teaching in the Halifax area, where Bronze Age remains are more thickly spread. There, Bronze Age barrows and stone circles have been identified, while urns and arrowheads have been found at different times.[3] In the later Bronze Age the weather became colder and wetter, making the continuance of settled agriculture more difficult, and by 600 BC much of the Haworth area was probably deserted. During the half-millennium before the Roman Conquest there was a further wave of settlement, as this part of northern England came under the control of a Celtic people, the Brigantes, who possessed knowledge of ironworking, but specific evidence for the Haworth area during the Brigantian period is ambiguous. The early historians of the district, John James and Horsfall Turner, thought that Oakenden (i.e. Alcomden) Stones on Stanbury Moor were a cromlech (stone burial chamber) 'consisting of one flat stone, weight about six tons, placed horizontally upon two upright blocks, now half embedded in the heather', and attributed the site to the Druids, but they are now regarded as a fortuitous assembly of completely natural rocks.[4]

The Brigantes were subjugated by the Romans between AD 69 and 74, but no Roman sites in this area have been found.[5] Two military roads skirted the chapelry, but did not cross it. One ran from York and Ilkley via Elslack to Ribchester and the Lancashire coast, while the other started from Manchester and ran via Littleborough and Blackstone Edge, entering the Keighley area a little to the west of Cullingworth Gate. From there it traversed Harden Moor, crossed the Aire near Marley and reached Ilkley by way of Rombalds Moor.[6] The extensive earthwork at Catstones on Harden Moor, close to the latter road, and concentrations of flint arrowheads along parts of it, has led to speculation that the Romans encountered stiff resistance in the Haworth area. The evidence for such an interpretation is tenuous. The Catstones earthwork is difficult to date and may have been late Roman, while another possibility is that the enclosure was simply a cattle pound. Certainly, no archaeological trace of fighting has been found.[7]

The Roman occupation came to an end in the early fifth century AD. In the Pennines their departure was followed by almost two centuries of rule by British tribes of Celtic origin. There were several 'regiones' or small kingdoms. From the poems of Taliesin we know that Cumbria was covered by the kingdom of Rheged. Further south, occupying parts of south and west Yorkshire, was the kingdom of Elmet. Information about what lay in between is difficult to come by, but later political divisions suggest the existence of a third small kingdom called Craven which covered some of north Lancashire as well as present day Craven.[8] There is uncertainty about where its southern borders lay. One theory, relying on the Domesday Book, draws the boundary some distance south of the river Worth, which would place Haworth in Craven.[9] Others, however, suggest that the chapelry was in Elmet. A widespread assumption is that the border ran along the river Worth, because this formed the boundary of the later deanery of Craven. An alternative hypothesis would make the northern boundary of Elmet correspond to the spread of '-*ley*' names in west and north Yorkshire. They signify clearings in woodland, and Elmet appears to have been protected from Saxon conquest for many decades because the newcomers found fighting in wooded country difficult. If this theory is correct the boundary with Craven would have lain north of Bradley and Cononley. Perhaps this was Elmet's frontier at its largest extent, with the Worth boundary representing a later stage when Saxon pressure drove the Britons back down the Aire valley.[10]

One post-Roman settlement was in the hamlet of Stanbury (which means 'settlement at the foot of a stone hill where there was a fort').[11] There, earthworks have been identified which could have provided protection against cattle rustlers. The inhabitants would probably have been involved in transhumance, whereby animals were grazed on summer pastures in the hills and then driven down to the lowlands for the winter. Just west of the present village air photographs and phosphate sampling

> seem to show a large rectangular enclosure approximately 0.4 hectares (1 acre) in size, well laid out with rectangular corners. Within the enclosure there appear to be a number of structures including a large rectangular building while to the west there appear to be several overlapping enclosures, possibly indicating more than one phase of construction and so an extended period of occupation of the site.

The structures lay within two fields named Eccles and Top Eccles in the 1852–53 tithe survey. The element '*eccles*' in a place or field name is often taken to be from the British word for a church, which derives from the Latin '*ecclesia*'. This has led to the suggestion that the fields marked the site of an early Christian church.

Field names are subject to frequent change, so we must be very cautious in this interpretation. The Haworth township rating valuation for 1838 names them as Upper, Middle and Lower *Aightalls*, as does a Stanbury valuation of 1813 and 1814 at the Cliffe Castle Museum in Keighley. The fields were part of property bought for the support of the perpetual curate of Haworth in 1558 and the 1672 glebe terrier includes the entry, 'in the occupation of widdow Mitchell of Stanbury in Haworth aforesaid and her sons … one close called Aughtalls joyning to the said high way'. The highway was the road to Colne and the field was almost certainly Top Eccles, so we must conclude that there is no reliable evidence for an early church in Stanbury and that 'Eccles' is in fact a late corruption of the name 'Aightalls'. If there *was* an early British church in the area it was probably on the other side of the Worth in Laycock, which lay within the old manor of Exley (still remembered in the place-name Exley Head between Oakworth and Keighley). Exley is a corruption of *Ecclesay* which more reliably denotes an early church.[12] The suggestion that '-*ley*' names mark the extent of the northern boundary of Elmet fits with this since the local distribution of '*eccles*' sites seems to approximate to that kingdom.

Stanbury from Oldfield. Croft field names suggest that the village extended further down this slope in medieval times so that the other or 'Sun' side could be used for crops. The 'eccles' fields, once thought to be the site of an early medieval church, are on the far right. The photograph also illustrates the difficulties Oldfield children would have experienced getting to school in Stanbury.

BY COURTESY OF IAN PALMER

From Northumbria to the Norman Conquest

During the sixth century the Angles and Saxons established their supremacy over the coastal districts of Northumberland, Durham and the East Riding, forming the two states of Bernicia and Deira, which subsequently joined to form the great kingdom of Northumbria. In a battle fought in about 600 the English defeated the Britons near Catterick. The result was the collapse of Craven as a separate entity and the isolation of Rheged from Elmet. The next step, an attack on Elmet, was only a matter of time. In 616 Edwin of Northumbria conquered the British kingdom. The elimination of effective British opposition did not end the fighting. War broke out between Northumbria and another Anglo-Saxon kingdom, Mercia, which covered a large part of the Midlands. In 632 Edwin was defeated and killed by Cadwallon of Gwynedd and Penda of Mercia. The Mercians then annexed a large part of Elmet. Place name evidence suggests that Mercian influence was strong in the wapentakes of Agbrigg and Morley, where the names ending in '-*bury*' (such as Almondbury and Dewsbury) are thought to be of Mercian origin. There are no references to Stanbury, which is another such name, until about

1200 but it seems reasonable to suppose that there was a small English settlement within the hamlet by the middle of the seventh century, and the two races may well have lived side by side for some time.[13]

Mercian control proved to be very brief and by 660, at the latest, Stanbury was again within Northumbrian territory. The English began to arrive in greater numbers, making clearings in the forest and on the lower ground creating settlements, such as Keighley and Bingley, whose names end in '-*ley*' ('a clearing'). Soon dependent farms with names ending in '-*ton*' (for example, Sutton, Steeton and Morton), were founded. On the higher ground other colonisation took place and here the typical suffix was '-*worth*' ('an enclosure') as in Hainworth, Oakworth and Haworth.

After 800 there were also Scandinavian settlers in the area, their presence being indicated by a series of place-names of Norse origin. Most of the major settlements retained their English names, but a substantial number of smaller places have names containing Scandinavian elements. This may possibly indicate the actual geographical pattern of settlement or it may simply be that the numbers of Scandinavian settlers were insufficient to influence the well-established names of larger places. Thus places such as Haworth and Stanbury have English names, but in Oxenhope ('the valley of oxen'),

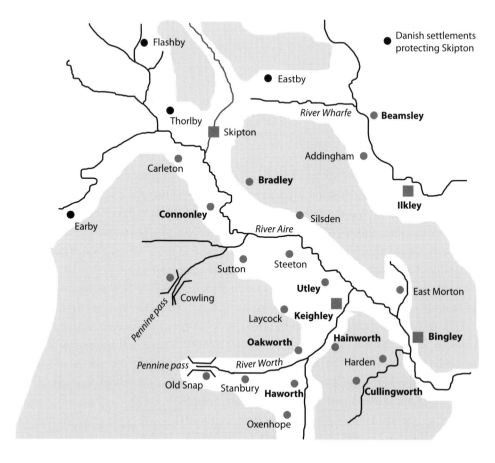

Upper Airedale before the Norman Conquest. Place-names ending in -*ley* and -*worth* are in bold type.

where there were numerous individual farms, these smaller settlements often have the Scandinavian suffix '-house' (-hus) as in Moorhouse, Roydhouse and Hillhouse. However, we must be cautious because the names were not recorded before the twelfth century and in some instances, such as 'Roydhouse', the name itself may well not have been coined until after the Norman Conquest. Scandinavian words such as 'beck' are quite common in the district, suggesting that the newcomers influenced the dialect of local people.

After the incorporation of most of the north into the kingdom of England, which emerged in the middle of the ninth century, a major headache for the king's local representatives, the earls of Northumbria, was the continuation of Viking raids from the east and west, as well as the growing threat of incursions southwards by the Britons of Strathclyde and their successors, the Scots. According to one theory Siward, who was earl from 1035 to 1055, tried to strengthen the area by planting groups of Danish settlers at strategic places in the Pennines. One of these was perhaps Skipton, which controlled the entrance to both the Aire and Wharfe valleys and is surrounded by a distinctive group of Danish place names ending in -by, such as Eastby, Thorlby, Flasby and Earby.[14] Most names in the surrounding area are either English or Norse.

We have little direct information about the way land-holding evolved in pre-Conquest times, primarily because written documentation is very scarce, but we can try to reconstruct the pattern from examples of later survivals. English Northumbria appears to have consisted originally of a series of multiple estates, large areas of territory under the control of a single lord but including many separate communities. It can be shown that these formed the basis of the later hundreds or wapentakes, the medieval adminis-trative divisions of the area, but comparison with Welsh thirteenth-century evidence suggests that the English themselves inherited these multiple estates from their British predecessors. This means that the pattern may well have been very ancient indeed, perhaps predating the Roman period. With the passage of time the ownership of multiple estates was gradually fragmented or extensively modified, but the boundaries of the hundreds and wapentakes survived into the nineteenth century. Land-holdings owned by the king or the church stood a greater chance of retaining their integrity.[15]

One such survival was the vast royal manor of Wakefield, which included the chapelry of Haworth. The typical Welsh estate had two subdivisions, known as 'commotes', usually separated by either a wood or a river. The ancient manor of Wakefield seems to have followed that model, as it included the two wapentakes of Agbrigg and Morley. In principle, the *caput*, or head settlement, of a multiple estate would be situated in the lowland area but relatively close to the higher ground. Around the *caput* would be the main arable farming areas, while the waste (the rough grazing) and the summer pasture would be in the uplands. Transhumance appears to have been widespread in the north of England in the Anglo-Saxon period, though it was clearly becoming less significant by the time of the Norman Conquest. Grazing on the uplands from May onwards helped to conserve the lowland pastures for the winter months.[16]

Another feature of the Celtic system was that the king's manor was typically in one commote and the principal church in the other. Sometime in the seventh century a minster

CLARO

CRAVEN

AINSTY

SKYRACK

Stanbury

Leeds

BARKSTON ASH

Haworth   Bradford

Oxenhope

OSGOLDCROSS

Dewsbury

Pontefract

TICKHILL

MORLEY

Wakefield

AGBRIGG

STAINCROSS

STRAFFORTH

Manor of Wakefield

Boundary of the Honour of Pontefract

church was established at Dewsbury, acting as the focus of religious administration for the whole area. Wakefield was situated in Agbrigg wapentake and Dewsbury in Morley, thus reinforcing the similarity with the Celtic pattern. The extent of Dewsbury's influence can be gauged from the fact that its daughter churches included Wakefield, Kirkburton, Kirkheaton, Huddersfield, Almondbury, Thornhill and Bradford, all of which were still contributing to its expenses in the late Middle Ages.[17] Here, as was often the case in northern England, a site of British Christianity (as at Exley in Laycock) was abandoned by the Anglo-Saxons who chose to site their own church some distance away. Part of an early stone cross of Anglian design (and dating perhaps from the ninth century) was found in a field at the aptly named Cross Farm in Stanbury, but older beliefs survived parallel with the new faith, and the pagan symbolism of the Norsemen represented a further complicating factor before their adoption of Christianity. Thus, on the edge of the moor, set between two streams, lies Ponden Kirk, an impressive gritstone crag with a fissure in it. Tradition stated that couples who managed to scramble through the gap would be married within the year, perhaps a dim memory of the ancient form of betrothal among the Norse known as Odin's wedding.[18]

Lords and manors 2
in medieval Haworth

The greatest upheaval of the early medieval period, here as anywhere else in England, was the Norman Conquest. In the years immediately after his victory at Hastings in 1066 William concentrated his attention on the south but a major northern uprising in 1069 forced him to attend to that part of the kingdom. In a campaign known as 'the Harrying of the North' he crushed the opposition and his army ravaged through Yorkshire and adjacent counties, its passage marked by massacres and the destruction of villages.[1] In the Domesday Survey, commissioned by William at Christmas 1085, large parts of Yorkshire were described as 'waste' and many vills were registered as uninhabited, while Haworth is not even mentioned. Most early commentators linked this to the effects of the harrying, so Haworth could have been destroyed when William's men pursued their opponents into the hills. Recent analysis has thrown doubt on this explanation, suggesting that 'waste' was a generic term for uncultivated land, whether the cause was military action or simply its unsuitability, so perhaps Haworth was omitted for that reason.[2] Many of the vills listed as uninhabited were in Craven, but it is possible that the omission of places such as Haworth was nothing more than casual coverage, in which a detailed assessment was not made because this was a less-organised district (which would also account for the poor quality of Domesday entries elsewhere in north-west England).[3]

To ensure that there should be no repeat of the rebellious behaviour of 1069–70 William created a series of military fiefdoms or honours, each based on a well-defended castle. Among them was the honour of Pontefract, which included the old 'multiple estate' of Wakefield. At first the honour was administered from Tanshelf (near Pontefract) but by 1089 a large fortified castle had been erected at Pontefract itself and this formed the administrative centre from that time onwards. When the honour was founded the economic outlook was poor, since whatever the significance of the word 'waste' there can be little doubt that the 'harrying' had had a catastrophic effect on the economy of the Pennines. Law and order must have broken down and there would have been nowhere safe to take cattle and sheep during the winter – in 1086 almost the whole of the wapentakes of Agbrigg and Morley was described as waste. No church was listed even for Bradford, but this may have been because the Domesday Survey was essentially a taxation return, and local churches may have been for some reason exempt, though. W.E. Wightman suggested, in his mapping of the honour of Pontefract under its first lord, Robert de Lacy, that they did exist by 1086.[4]

The economically active part of the honour appears largely confined to the immediate vicinity of Pontefract and Wakefield. Both showed a peculiarity which has led to considerable comment, for they had more ploughs than the size of the local population would suggest was appropriate.[5] One possible explanation is that they were centres from which recolonisation of the uplands was taking place. The last years of the eleventh century saw an expansion of the land under cultivation as de Lacy granted out manors to knights in his train in return for military service. By the time of the death of William Rufus the tide of economic development was flowing up Airedale. In 1100 a new honour was founded based on Skipton, and in 1102 Robert de Lacy, who was also sheriff of Yorkshire, obtained a grant of Bowland and Blackburnshire across the Pennines.

Robert de Lacy rashly supported the abortive rising of Robert of Normandy and Henry I deprived him of Pontefract, which was given to Hugh de la Val. After de la Val's death the estate passed to William Maltravers, who had married his widow,[6] but a generation later Henry de Lacy proved to be one of Henry II's strongest supporters and regained the estate which his father had lost. His importance can be gauged by his apparent immunity from the king's decrees. Henry II was worried about the appearance of 'overmighty subjects' and attempted to limit the number of knights any one magnate might have to 60, but in 1166 Henry de Lacy has 80 knights, and more were to be created before the end of the century. Haworth and Stanbury were part of the honour of Pontefract in 1086,[7] but it is unclear whether they were also part of the manor of Bradford at this time. The Domesday Survey records that one Gamel had 1500 acres in the manor. Combe Hill Cross, which lies on the road to Colne, west of Stanbury, is known locally as Camel Cross, which may be a corruption of Gamel and so indicate the limit of his land. This is suggestive but the settlement history analysed in the later part of the chapter paints a more complicated picture.

Robert de Lacy and his successors also held the honour of Clitheroe, which lay on the other side of the Pennines and occupied a large part of Blackburnshire. The centre was the small castle at Clitheroe. The two honours were connected by a road known

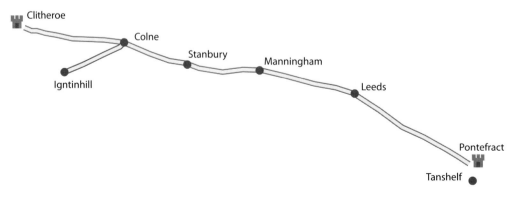

The route of Clitheroegate, the road that linked the honours of Clitheroe and Pontefract.

as Clitheroegate which ran from Pontefract via Leeds and Bradford through Haworth, Stanbury and Colne to Ightenhill and Clitheroe. The importance of the chapelry of Haworth in the Middle Ages was largely due to its location on this important artery, but its relative remoteness meant that it was one of the last parts of the district to experience economic expansion. It is possible that a series of planned villages, including Haworth and Stanbury, were established along the road, each with an adequate water supply and enough arable land to support its inhabitants. These formed bases from which the hinterland could be colonised. Canon Dixon claimed that there was a church at Haworth as early as 1137 but he did not give his source. All we can say for certain is that by 1200 the four hamlets of Haworth, Far Oxenhope, Near Oxenhope and Stanbury had come into existence. Each was estimated to have four bovates of cultivable land and was valued at one-sixteenth of a knight's fee. Stanbury continued to be held in demesne (that is, farmed directly by the lord) throughout the Middle Ages but the other three were granted out to lesser landowners.

Feudal land-holdings in medieval Haworth

Though the records are fragmentary and often open to more than one interpretation, we have glimpses of the way in which the land-holding patterns evolved between the late twelfth and the late fifteenth centuries. It is a very complex story, involving the frequent transfer of control over one or more of the four components of the chapelry. There appear to have been four main phases in this process. The first covers roughly 60 years from around 1180 to 1240 and represents the original sub-infeudation of Haworth (that is, the granting of land by a superior lord to lesser lords). Between 1177 and 1193 Robert de Lacy II granted to Hugh de Horton land worth a third of a knight's fee in Horton and Clayton.[8] Hugh must also have gained some interest in Haworth, because about the same time Thomas, son of Hugh de Horton, gave to St Mary of Woodkirk and the canons of St Oswald (Nostell priory) 'half a bovate of land in Aldworth [Haworth] being the western part of a bovate which Richard, son of Eda, holds of the donor'.[9] The grant implies that Thomas was lord of the manor and Richard his tenant.

The part played by settlers from Clayton in the colonisation of Oxenhope indicates that Horton influence was at work there too. Somewhere about 1200 Alexander, son of Sveinn de Clayton, granted to the canons of Nostell Priory a bovate of land which he held and another bovate held by Wulfgeat, the whole comprising an eighth of the vill of Haworth. Further grants by John, son of Alan de Baildon, and Elias de Oxenhope indicated that the land given to Nostell lay east of the stream now known as Rag Clough Beck, which places it in Far Oxenhope. Consequently, the four bovates which were described in 1302/3 as being held by William de Clayton were located there.[10] The same lands were listed under Clayton in the 1342 extent of the manor of Bradford.[11] In 1302/3 four other bovates, which must have been in Near Oxenhope, were held by William de Heaton. At the time Heaton was a separate manor and Clayton a sub-manor of the manor of Bolton.

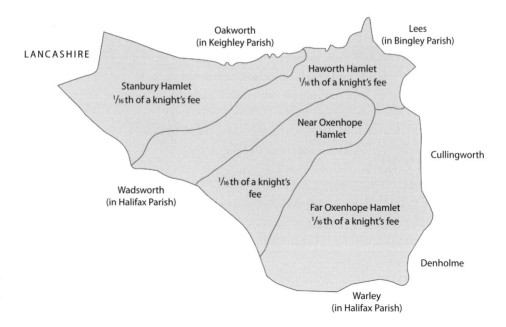

Oakworth
(in Keighley Parish)

Lees
(in Bingley Parish)

LANCASHIRE

Haworth Hamlet
$\frac{1}{16}$th of a knight's fee

Stanbury Hamlet
$\frac{1}{16}$th of a knight's fee

Near Oxenhope
Hamlet

Cullingworth

$\frac{1}{16}$th of a knight's fee

Wadsworth
(in Halifax Parish)

Far Oxenhope Hamlet
$\frac{1}{16}$th of a knight's fee

Denholme

Warley
(in Halifax Parish)

The Chapelry
and Township
of Haworth.

The process of sub-infeudation could be reversed, because in some circumstances, such as rebellion, the feudal overlord could resume his rights. In the second phase, during the remainder of the thirteenth century, the de Lacys made a determined effort to regain the rights they had granted away. Hugh de Horton II had no direct issue and the de Lacys were able to transfer his rights in Horton and the chapelry of Haworth to their manor of Bradford. At an inquisition held in 1277 the jurors testified that, during the rule of Edmund de Lacy and his widow Alice, Clayton, Thornton, Allerton and Heaton had been annexed to the liberty of Bradford. In addition Henry de Lacy, earl of Lincoln, the then holder of the manor of Bradford, had added Wyke and Bolling. Thornton, Heaton and Bolling had originally also been independent manors. Clayton was part of the manor of Bolton before coming into the possession of Hugh de Horton and Allerton had belonged to Thornton. Stanbury was held in demesne by the de Lacys, Haworth had been controlled by the de Hortons, Far Oxenhope had been colonised by Clayton and Near Oxenhope by Heaton, and now in 1277 all four hamlets of the township were part of the manor of Bradford. The consolidation of this territory in the hands of the de Lacys was emphasised at the beginning of the fourteenth century when a manor house was built for their use at Bradford.[12]

Henry de Lacy died in 1311 leaving only a daughter, Alice. In 1296 she had married Thomas, earl of Lancaster, the first nephew of Edward I. This meant that most of the vast de Lacy inheritance passed to him on her father's death, but the manor of Bradford formed part of the dower of de Lacy's widow, Joan, for her lifetime. She married a second time, to Nicholas d'Audley, and the *Nominum Villarum* of 1316 lists Manningham and Haworth as two places from which he was expected to raise men. Joan died in 1319 and the manor of Bradford then passed to Thomas of Lancaster, her son-in-law. He rebelled

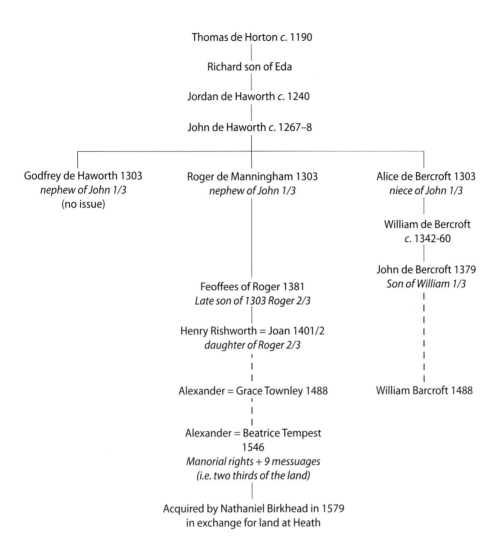

Thomas de Horton *c.* 1190

Richard son of Eda

Jordan de Haworth *c.* 1240

John de Haworth *c.* 1267–8

Godfrey de Haworth 1303
nephew of John 1/3
(no issue)

Roger de Manningham 1303
nephew of John 1/3

Alice de Bercroft 1303
niece of John 1/3

William de Bercroft
c. 1342-60

John de Bercroft 1379
Son of William 1/3

Feoffees of Roger 1381
Late son of 1303 Roger 2/3

Henry Rishworth = Joan 1401/2
daughter of Roger 2/3

Alexander = Grace Townley 1488

William Barcroft 1488

Alexander = Beatrice Tempest
1546
Manorial rights + 9 messuages
(i.e. two thirds of the land)

Acquired by Nathaniel Birkhead in 1579
in exchange for land at Heath

against his cousin Edward II but was defeated at Boroughbridge in 1322 and executed. Whether any Haworth men were at the battle is unknown, but the manor of Bradford was seized by the Crown along with the rest of the earl's estates, and was subsequently given to Philippa of Hainault, the wife of Edward III, as part of her dower.[13]

The resumption of direct control by the lord proved a failure. During the third stage, covering the first half of the fourteenth century, the consolidation of territory in one holding was gradually dismantled. The manor house at Bradford was abandoned by Nicholas d'Audley and in 1342 it was shown that Thornton, Bolling and Heaton had reasserted their independence, though leaving their satellites (Allerton, Wyke and Clayton) within Bradford's liberties.[14] The de Horton family failed to regain its interest in the hamlet of Haworth, having lost its chance a century earlier. An agreement concluded with the prior of Nostell sometime between 1209 and 1240 shows Jordan de Haworth, son of the Richard mentioned earlier, already acting on behalf of the

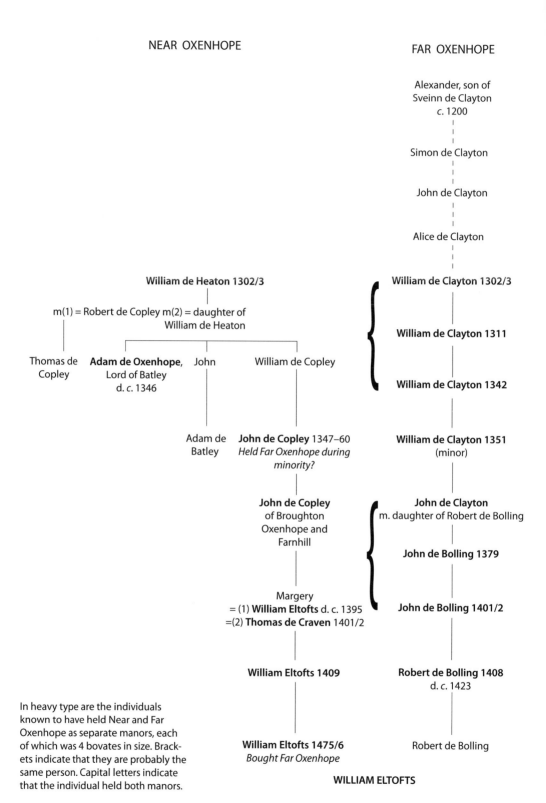

NEAR OXENHOPE

FAR OXENHOPE

Alexander, son of
Sveinn de Clayton
c. 1200

Simon de Clayton

John de Clayton

Alice de Clayton

William de Heaton 1302/3

William de Clayton 1302/3

m(1) = Robert de Copley m(2) = daughter of
William de Heaton

William de Clayton 1311

Thomas de
Copley

Adam de Oxenhope,
Lord of Batley
d. *c.* 1346

John

William de Copley

William de Clayton 1342

Adam de
Batley

John de Copley 1347–60
*Held Far Oxenhope during
minority?*

William de Clayton 1351
(minor)

John de Copley
of Broughton
Oxenhope and
Farnhill

John de Clayton
m. daughter of Robert de Bolling

John de Bolling 1379

Margery
= (1) **William Eltofts** d. c. 1395
=(2) **Thomas de Craven** 1401/2

John de Bolling 1401/2

William Eltofts 1409

Robert de Bolling 1408
d. *c.* 1423

In heavy type are the individuals
known to have held Near and Far
Oxenhope as separate manors, each
of which was 4 bovates in size. Brack-
ets indicate that they are probably the
same person. Capital letters indicate
that the individual held both manors.

William Eltofts 1475/6
Bought Far Oxenhope

Robert de Bolling

WILLIAM ELTOFTS

inhabitants of Haworth hamlet without any reference to the Hortons. In 1267–68, when the reclamation policy was at its height, John de Haworth took Thomas de Copley to court in order to obtain the dower of his wife, Amicis (who appears to have been Thomas's sister) without apparently seeking the permission of any lord.[15] By 1300 Haworth was a recognised sub-manor of the manor of Bradford. John's lands were divided between Godfrey de Haworth, Roger de Manningham and Alice de Bercroft, who were holding them in 1303 and were probably his nephews and niece. Godfrey seems to have died childless because in 1342 Roger de Manningham held two-thirds of the lordship of Haworth and William de Bercroft one third.[16]

As we have seen, Bradford acquired control of Far Oxenhope with Clayton and Near Oxenhope with Heaton. Although the Crown subsequently gave up Heaton in Queen Philippa's time, the area continued to be linked with Clayton.[17] The 1342 extent referred to Adam de Oxenhope, lord of Batley and a member of the prominent de Copley family, as holding four oxgangs of land in Oxenhope by the service of one-sixteenth of a knight's fee and paying 4s. yearly.[18] His father, Robert de Copley, married twice. Thomas, his son by his first marriage, inherited his Copley lands while Adam, his son by his second marriage, acquired Batley and the oxgangs in Oxenhope. A 1339 grant of land to Adam del Holme indicates that the oxgangs were in Near Oxenhope, so they must have been those originally held by William de Heaton.[19]

Adam de Oxenhope died around 1346 without issue and his lands in Batley and Oxenhope were divided between the children of his deceased brothers, John and William.[20] John's son, another Adam, inherited the Batley lands and William's son, John, got Near Oxenhope. In 1347 John, son of William de Copley acknowledged the overlordship of the manor of Bradford, stating that he held one messuage (a piece of land with a house on it), four bovates of land, and a half-share in a mill.[21] Four years later, in 1351, John de Copley is again mentioned in the court rolls, claiming land in Oxenhope by the service of the eighth part of a knight's fee, which implies that he now held Far Oxenhope as well as Near Oxenhope.[22] He had not inherited Far Oxenhope but had bought the rights, though he did not hold them for long because in 1361 Robert de Bolling was holding the hamlet on behalf of the heir of John son of William de Clayton.[23] The 1351 entry says that part of John de Copley's homage was for 'foreign service' which suggests that he was fighting in Edward III's army in France. William de Clayton was a minor and Copley may have been using both Oxenhopes to finance his campaigns until William came of age. Copley died shortly after 1360, and Far Oxenhope reverted to Clayton, reinforcing the separation of the two Oxenhopes.

The fourth stage covers the remainder of the Middle Ages, though information about the development of the chapelry is sparse and difficult to interpret. In 1342 the manor of Bradford passed from Queen Philippa to Henry, earl of Lancaster, and in 1351 the earldom was elevated to a duchy. Henry died in 1361, leaving two daughters who divided the property of the duchy between them. Bradford was among the manors assigned to Blanche, wife of John of Gaunt, who became duke of Lancaster in his wife's right. Gaunt died in 1388 and when his son became king in 1399, as Henry IV, the vast possessions of the duchy fell in to the Crown. Bradford was to remain Crown property until the early seventeenth century.

Stanbury remained part of the Bradford demesne throughout the period, but at Haworth there was continued change. Roger de Manningham was dead by the time of the 1379 poll tax and in 1381 his two-thirds of the Haworth manor was in the hands of trustees, so presumably he had no male heir. William de Bercroft died in 1360 and his third share passed to his son John, who was listed in the 1379 poll tax. In 1401/2 the land in Manningham and Haworth was held jointly by Joan, widow of Henry Rishworth (and probably the daughter of Roger de Manningham) and John Bercroft. Some 25 years later the holders were John Rishworth, son of Henry and Joan, and John Bercroft.[24] The next information comes from 1488. John Rishworth's son, Alexander, was about to marry Grace, daughter of Laurence Towneley. Her father wanted to be quite certain what Alexander would inherit, so John executed a deed conveying his property to trustees for his son but reserving the use to himself of all of it for his life, except Whiteroyd, which was to be Grace's jointure.[25] Originally the land in each of the four hamlets seems to have been divided into thirteen messuages, making a total of 52 properties (see Chapter 4). Sixteenth-century evidence shows that Rishworth owned nine messuages out of the original thirteen in Haworth hamlet, so William Barcroft, who is named among the trustees, probably still had the other four. Alexander was followed by a second John and in 1546, when his son, another Alexander, married Beatrice, the daughter of Nicholas Tempest of Tong, no Barcroft is mentioned in the deed.[26] By this time extensive changes were in progress and the Barcroft share may have become freehold (see Chapter 5).

After the death of John de Copley, Near Oxenhope passed to another John de Copley, usually described as of Broughton, Oxenhope and Farnhill. His only surviving issue was a daughter, Margery, who married William Eltofts. William was dead by 1395 and left a son, another William. In 1401/2, as William was not yet of age, his four bovates were held by Thomas de Craven, his stepfather. Seven years later William had come into his inheritance and his tenure of the same land is recorded later in the fifteenth century.[27] Far Oxenhope had passed into the hands of the Bolling family around 1361. A Robert de Bolling held the four bovates in 1401/2 and the family probably still had them in 1409, when Thomas de Craven had only the four in Near Oxenhope, but later in the century the position changed. In 1475/76 William Eltofts held half the vill of Oxenhope 'of Robert Bolling, as of his manor of Clayton'. Near Oxenhope had been a sub-manor of Bradford, not Clayton, so this implies that Eltofts had now combined Far Oxenhope with his Manor of Near Oxenhope. Exactly when this took place is not clear, but it was probably during the Wars of the Roses, when Robert Bolling supported Henry VI and in 1461, after the accession of Edward IV, was deprived of his lands. They seem to have been returned to him shortly afterwards but he was not formally pardoned until 1472.[28] Pardons were expensive to obtain and he may have sold Far Oxenhope in order to raise the necessary funds. Oxenhope remained one manor from this time forward and was still in the hands of the Eltofts family in the sixteenth century.

One of the distinctive features of Haworth are the many ginnels which run through to Main Street from Croft Street.

PHOTOGRAPH: CARNEGIE, 2009

3   Fourteenth-century Haworth

The manorial economy at its height

Evidence from nineteenth-century tithe maps and other relatively recent sources gives us some idea of the form of settlement in the area by the early fourteenth century. Across upland Britain there were two main types: nucleated villages, and dispersed settlement where communities comprised scattered farms and cottages. Locally, Haworth and Stanbury approximate to the first type, the two Oxenhopes to the second.

Communications were poor and trade relatively undeveloped, so every community had to provide for its own needs, and in the Pennines each family had to grow its own crops. Haworth, a nucleated village, developed its own open field system in which there were separate arable strips in a large unenclosed area. Part of one of the open fields, on the higher slopes of the Worth valley north of the village, survived as late as 1853. In 1891 Horsfall Turner, writing in the *Yorkshire County Magazine*, maintained that this 'Townfield' was divided into 13 'gates' or 'deals' (doles = allotments of common land), each a little less than an acre, and Clifford Whone could still identify many of them in

West Lane from the 1852–53 Tithe Map showing the strips in the Townfield. These were still visible in 1937. (Map based upon work by Steven Wood.)

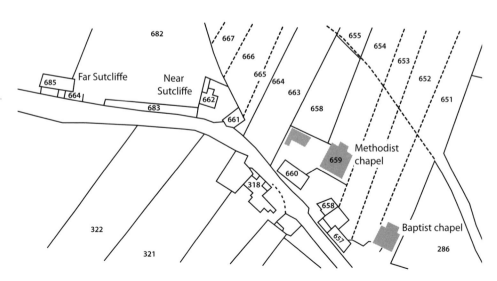

18

The townfield photographed from Oakworth. The low winter sun highlights the medieval furrows in the old townfield. As late as 1937 Clifford Whone was able to locate all the doles, but recent building now means that much of the parts adjoining West Lane have now disappeared. There is still considerable debate as to whether the land on the other side of West Lane behind the church was a separate field in medieval times or simply an extension of this one.

1937.[1] Some are visible even today, though recent development beside the Baptist chapel means that they can no longer be seen from West Lane. The long narrow fields on the opposite side of West Lane, called Far Long Roods, Near Long Roods and Harker Butts, which are typical open field names, indicate that there was a second field (or perhaps a continuation of the first field). There are signs of more open field land on Mytholmes Lane, with Longlands and New Croft (which was arable even in 1853) on the north and a field called Flatt on the south side. This arable land may have extended from Mytholmes Lane to the east of and below Main Street, where the bypass now is, before terminating at Butt Field, bounded by the present Butt Lane.

Down by Bridgehouse Beck there was a stinted common called Mill Hey. This was an area of grazing, where only the tenants or owners of strips in the open fields could pasture their animals, usually in proportion to the area of land they worked. A 1716 lease of Mill Hill Farm describes the occupier as having 'three Cowgates or grass feeding for three cows as well winter as summer in a parcel of woody ground known as Mill Hey'. The undated agreement between Jordan, son of Richard de Haworth, and the prior of Nostell, mentioned in chapter 2, appears to relate to a division of land on the east side of Bridgehouse Beck.[2] The northern half was reserved for the use of the inhabitants of Haworth and the southern for the priory tenants in what is now Far Oxenhope. Each had half of Hawkcliffe Wood, which served to mark the boundary.

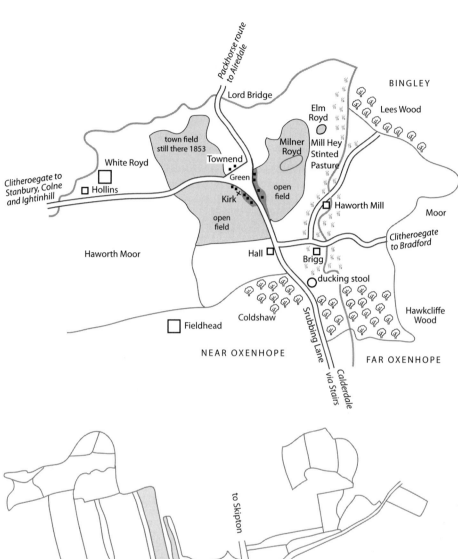

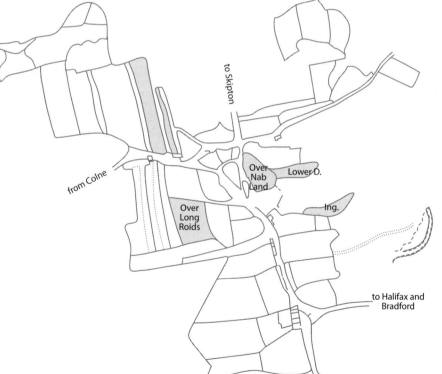

ABOVE

Fourteenth-
century
Haworth.

RIGHT

Estate map,
1769, showing
the Cross Inn
lands.

At the northern end Lees Wood was deemed to be outside Haworth and Jordan was forbidden to cut wood there. Lees remained separate until added to Haworth under the 1894 Local Government Act.

Some farms on the higher land may have used the common pastures only during the winter. Even in the nineteenth century Balcony and Dalemoor farms had summering fields. Sheep would generally be kept in pasture during the winter but turned onto the moorland during the summer. Most of Haworth was a compact hamlet but there were insufficient moorland rights for four bovates within it, so the subdivision included a strip of moorland between the hamlets of Near Oxenhope and Stanbury. The date at which the grass began to grow in spring was vital for the wellbeing of the animals, since fodder ran out. Consequently holly, which was available at least a month before the new grass, was a valuable feedstuff for sheep and cattle. Very few upland townships were without their 'Hollins' or 'Hollings' farm and Haworth was no exception.

Woodland was also important and was carefully managed. The timber provided building wood; the undergrowth, charcoal for the smith and fuel for heating; and acorns and mast gave foraging for pigs. The distribution of tree references in the field names suggests that by 1400 the higher parts of Haworth were above the tree line. The woodland was on the lower slopes by Bridgehouse Beck, resulting in conflicting interests. The word 'hey' means land which was originally covered with trees, so Mill Hey, the common pasture, was cleared woodland. Lord Wood fringed the Worth between Lord Lane and Mytholmes Lane and the tithe map marks Fall Wood on the east side of Bridgehouse Beck. However, by 1400 on the west side all woodland had probably gone between Ebor and the later Woodlands estate. The only wood surviving on higher ground was Coldshaw, which formed the boundary between the Haworth and Near Oxenhope hamlets. The small extent of the remaining woodland made moorland rights even more important. Stone dug there provided a substitute for timber in building, and peat was more significant as a fuel.

As the population grew more land was brought into cultivation to satisfy its needs. One indication is the name Fieldhead Farm, on the edge of the original open fields, while some extra land was provided by cutting down trees and 'stubbing' out the roots. The existence of Stubbing Farm on the edge of the later Woodlands estate shows that medieval encroachments were being made on Coldshaw. Another sign of medieval colonisation of marginal land is the place-name element 'rode' or 'royd'. This relates to new land brought into cultivation in the twelfth and thirteenth centuries, and in Haworth the tithe map shows a field called Milner Royd, adjacent to the open field at the back of Mytholmes Lane; Elm Royd near the junction with Ebor Lane; and White Royd near Hollins Farm. In the original settlement nine of the thirteen farms were probably in the main village and four outside it. Hollins has already been mentioned, while the Bradford court rolls also list 'henry atte Halle', 'Adam del Brige' and 'Robert de Woodhous'. Stubbing and Fieldhead were later developments.

Eighteenth-century land-owning patterns reflected the earlier open field arrangements. An indenture for 1714 showed that attached to Greenfield Farm were nearby fields called

This old photograph shows where the old medieval smithy was sited. The farm is now submerged below the waters of Lower Laithe Reservoir, which was opened in the 1920s. The photograph was taken from the south, looking over the valley to Stanbury village, which can be seen on the skyline.

Croft and Milner Royd; 'the mean Ing at nabland' in the open field area east of the village ('*ing*' meaning a riverside meadow); 'Arcock but' and 'Longroods bottom' in the field to the west; and the 'upper end of Longroods in the Townfield'. A 1769 estate plan shows that the behind Cross Inn Farm were Over and Lower Nablands, with Over Long Roods behind the church and two strips in the Townfield.[3] The 1714 indenture and the 1769 plan suggest that Haworth may have had a fully fledged three-field system at the height of the Middle Ages. One of the requirements for such a system was that the fields were of approximately the same size, which does appear to be the case, but caution must be exercised for the classic system of the English Midlands did not operate in the Pennines, where rainfall was high and the growing season short. Crop rotation and fallow periods were far less likely to be practised, and wheat, the staple of the south, was rare in the north. Eighteenth-century inventories suggest that although some wheat was grown, even then the main crop was oats.[4]

Stanbury village was on an east–west axis, and examination of the present street shows that all but one of the pre-nineteenth-century buildings lie on the north side. This allowed the maximum extent of the south-facing slopes to be used for cultivation. The 1853 tithe map also shows crofts further down the valley side, but without buildings, implying that the medieval village was once more extensive. The field names suggest a more irregular arrangement than at Haworth, with the remains of four arable fields, the West, Great, North and Sun Fields. The 1342 extent of the manor of Bradford records that the whole community held a certain pasture called 'Swyntilgrene'.[5] No surviving deed refers to it and all knowledge of its location has now been lost. As at Haworth, there was a growth in population during the thirteenth century. The original wooded area was more extensive. Thus, the field name Lower Riddings, next to the Great Field, indicates land which was originally tree-covered; this may have been the *royd* land held by Robert Smith in 1342.[6] The farm names Bully Trees and Buckley Green, and the field names Upper and Lower Hey (adjoining Buckley Green) and Shaw Top nearby at the back of Hob Hill, suggest that at one time the higher slopes were also wooded.

The name Buckley Green indicates that there were deer in the hamlet when the farm was named. By 1300 the area was better known for its rabbits (or *coneys*) which were regarded as a delicacy in the medieval period. Under feudal law the right to kill beasts and fowls of the warren – hares, coneys, pheasants and partridges – could only be granted by the king. Edmund de Lacy received such a grant in 1251 from Henry III, and had a warren at Stanbury. Its site is marked by Coneygarths Farm, with its significant name, and the five 'croft' fields marked on the 1853 tithe map just south of the farm were the location of the warren. The existence of Royd Hall farm on one side and the Hey fields on the other suggests that the area west of Hob Hill was being developed around the time that free warren was granted.[7] Stanbury developed as a nucleated village but there were two other settlements within the hamlet. In the Bradford court rolls there are many references to Oldsnap, where there seem to have been two farms in the fourteenth century, and tenants are also mentioned at Oldfield which was then part of Stanbury but is now in Haworth. Smithbank is also mentioned though its age is uncertain.

At Near Oxenhope no regular system of fields can be identified. The western end of the hamlet may not have been settled until comparatively late, because there are no references to the Stairs area in the Bradford court rolls. Part of the eastern end was a marsh, which gave rise to the present names Marsh, Upper Marsh and Marsh End. Peat was being cut there as late as 1760. The best land seems to have lain in a crescent along its margin, from Fieldhead through Old Oxenhope to North Ives. References to doles in eighteenth-century deeds from Moorhouse suggest that the settlement may have had medieval common fields. The name Mouldgreave perhaps indicates the site of the hamlet's woodland, 'greave' being a variant of the word 'grove'.[8] Far Oxenhope was also a community of dispersed farms. Field names which indicate arable land enable us to identify a number of them: Whicker Flatt, near the present Lowertown; Flatt Field at Uppertown; and Longlands on West Shaw Lane. Roydhouse was probably a thirteenth-century offshoot and there are open field names at Far Isle. In addition the court rolls refer to a farm at Haley and an individual living at Bank. The farm name Gate or Yate probably indicates access to common or moorland.

The four hamlets were part of the parish of Bradford and there was a chapel at Haworth. In a 1951 lecture Canon Dixon asserted that it was there in 1137 and 'was probably much older', while in 1954 he claimed that there had probably been a church for a thousand years.[9] Unfortunately he gave no evidence with which to support his claim but it is not in dispute that the archbishop of York issued a monition in 1317 instructing that the chaplain of Haworth be paid what had been due from 'ancient times'. An entry in the archbishop's register for 1320 shows that he received 20s. a year out of the rectory of Bradford, two and a half marks from the vicar, and a mark from the inhabitants of Haworth.[10]

The chaplain's income was increased by the founding of a chantry within the existing building by Adam de Copley of Batley, who left a messuage, 7 acres of land and an annual rent charge of 20s. to the curate, on condition that he celebrated divine service daily in the chapel of St Michael and All Angels at Haworth for the sake of the souls of Adam, his wife Jane, his ancestors Thomas de Thornton and his wife Ellen, all those whose goods he had ill gotten, and all the faithful departed. The chantry was founded in 1338 after an inquest established that the king's interest would not be damaged.[11]

The inscription *ora pro bono statu autest(?) tod* on the fifteenth-century church tower refers to this chantry, which may have been sited in the tower chamber when a new chapel was built in 1488.

Each manor had its own cornmill. That at Haworth was on Bridgehouse Beck and its location is marked by the names Mill Hill and Mill Hey. In 1356 John, son of Simon del Leghs, fell into the machinery and was killed. Oxenhope mill lay near the site of the present railway station. In 1347 John de Copley rendered homage to the lord of the manor of Bradford for, among other things, a 'moiety' of Oxenhope Mill. Henry de Allerton was the miller in 1361.[12] Stanbury was part of the demesne of the manor of Bradford and its inhabitants should have ground their corn at Bradford mill. In 1344 they were cited before the manor court for failing to pay their mulcture (fees for milling, due to the lord). They proved recalcitrant and in 1345 an order was issued to distrain their goods. The case suggests that they had begun to grind locally and that the lessee of the Bradford mill was losing income. There were other minor industries in the area – in 1346, for example, Robert Smith was charged with digging coal at Stanbury without the lord's permission. He was the local blacksmith and his forge was at Smithbank. Another artisan who makes his appearance is Robert le Couper, who lived at Oldsnap.[13]

Life in medieval Haworth

The legal cases which came before the Bradford manorial court give glimpses of the lives of the men and women of medieval Haworth. Three of the four hamlets had their own courts which dealt with land transfers but the manor of Bradford had many other liberties. The subordinate lords had to make their fealty to the steward of the manor, as did those who had special grants. In 1361, for instance, Thomas, prior of Nostell, came before William de Fyneholme and John de Northland at Bradford, to depose that he held 'divers' lands in Oxenhope of William de Clayton in pure and perpetual alms.[14] Cases might involve disputes or the need to guarantee legal rights. In 1363, on the death of Henry atte Halle of Haworth, his widow asked for the right to administer his messuage and four acres until their daughter Margery, who was only three years old, came of age. The lord had the theoretical right to dictate who the daughters of his bondmen should marry. This was commuted to a fine, so in return for a payment of 13s. 4d. Alice was allowed to say whom Margery should marry. The girl was evidently more important than Amicia, daughter of Amicia of Stanbury, who bought the right to marry whom she pleased for only 2d.![15] Disputes about status were also within the view of the court. In 1354 Margaret, wife of John de Woodhous of Haworth, was given until the next court to acquit herself of the charge that she was the maidservant of Henry de Allerton and withdrew her service before her time had expired. The following year the court gave leave for Roger, son of Roger of Manningham, to buy the freedom of his wife, Cecilia, a bondwoman, for half a mark (6s. 8d.).[16]

Every year there was a long list of brewers whose beer did not come up to the specified standard. John atte Kirk and Alice atte Kirk, possibly husband and wife, are the Haworth defaulters most frequently named. The quality of the beer must have caused considerable trouble because the Haworth beer tasters themselves were fined in 1343 and again in 1347 for failing to present defaulters.[17] Other cases concerned failure to honour contracts or pay debts. In 1340 Jone de Haword brought an action against Adam de Heaton for non-payment of 7s. 4d., while in the same year Adam Noteboom was permitted to distrain the goods of Adam de Haworth, who had paid neither the 40d. for which he was bound, nor the 12d. fine imposed by the court. In 1347 Robert de Northeves stood as a pledge for Robert de Kigheley, who owed Thomas the Chaplain 7s. 6d. for a cow, and in 1353 John de Denholme and Roger de Stanbury admitted that they owed Master Robert de Baldock, vicar of Bradford, 8s. 11d. for tithes of sheaves bought from him in 1349. In 1361 Henry de Whitacres sued William de Birle for failure to repair his iron plough parts or return them.[18]

Serious cases of theft were few. In 1348 the court had to deal with a steer and a heifer stolen from Saltonstall by unknown thieves, driven to Oxenhope and left there, while in 1354 William de Wilsden was fined for stealing four swarms of bees from William de Whiteacres. More common were cases concerning stray animals, as in 1351 when a young red ox was found loose in Oxenhope. If an animal was not claimed within a year and a day it could be sold – in 1361 a stray black horse was sold for 4s. and the following year Richard Butler paid a similar amount for a stag found straying at Haworth.[19] More serious than theft were cases of trespass, because this often affected both animals and crops. In 1347 John de Denholme, William del' Oldfield, Roger son of Jordan and John Atcockson admitted that they damaged the corn of Robert Smith of Stanbury by turning their cattle into it, and were fined 5d. William, son of Roger de Stanbiri, was found guilty in 1357 of failing to maintain his hedges properly, so that his animals trod down and ate the corn of Roger Fairegh. In 1360 John atte Kirk, our brewing acquaintance, was fined 3s. for using his dogs to chase sixty sheep belonging to William de Bercroft.

Rights of way could also cause trouble. The following year John Dughti was presented for making a wagon path across the meadows at the upper end of Haley, whereas the following year Thomas Holmes was cited for obstructing two paths with ditches in Old Oxenhope and Coldshaw.[20] The court only dealt with cases of assault when injury was caused enough to 'draw blood'. When Agnes, wife of Adam Fyn, set upon Alice, wife of Adam de Haword, and almost strangled her, because Alice had accused her of stealing their corn, the case was treated as one of trespass, not one of assault. A typical entry is that of a 1346 case concerning Robert Ficher of Haworth, who drew blood from Robert Rudde, and John, son of Thomas of Heton, who in turn drew blood from Ficher. Similarly in 1354 John, son of Jordan of Stanbury, drew blood from Andrew Ack of Stanbury.[21]

In medieval systems of justice, cases were always considered from the viewpoint of the lord – the question was whether his tenants, goods or land had been reduced in value, not who was strictly guilty of the offence. If damage had occurred an appropriate fine had to be paid in recompense. This attitude could lead to what we would regard as blatant injustice. In sexual cases the man had to pay a fine if assault was proved, but the woman always had to pay, whether consenting or not, because by losing her virginity, she was of less value to her lord. In 1343 Margaret de Oldsnap had to pay 6d. because she had been deflowered, the small size of the fine suggesting that she did not consent, whereas in contrast in 1355 Cecilia de la More had her goods distrained to force her to pay a fine of 3s., the large sum perhaps indicating that this was not rape.[22]

The most sensational assault case concerned John Abbot of Oldsnap. In 1352 he was found guilty of assaulting Margery of Oldsnap and was fined 6d. The next year he was fined 2s. for a number of different trespasses and in 1354 the same sum because his beasts depastured the corn of Roger Fairegh and broke and pressed down his hedges, though he was acquitted of similar charges brought against him by Margery. He and Fairegh had also threatened each other with violence. They were ordered to keep the peace and find sureties for £10. At some point during 1354 or early the next year Abbot appears to have violated Agnes and Magota, the daughters of Roger de Oldsnap, because both of them were ordered to pay their 'leyrwite' in 1356. In 1355 he assaulted Roger Fairegh and his sureties became liable for the £10, but the fine was reduced to 20s. because they were all poor bondmen and quite unable to pay. This appears to have been the last straw for Abbot's victims because the next court, later in the year, heard that Richard Old Thomlinson of Keighley, John son of Thomas Maud, and Hugh de Sugden came to Haworth at Michaelmas, where they assaulted John Abbot, beat, wounded and ill-treated him to the shedding of blood. They were fined 40d. Abbot seems to have been so badly injured that he died, because the next year William Frer, his brother, claimed his messuage and eight acres of land as next of kin.[23]

Troubled times

The Abbot case was the only serious affray in Haworth during the 25 years covered by the first three volumes of the Bradford court roll transcripts, suggesting that Haworth was relatively free of strife, but that was not true of England generally. Violence was endemic and travelling any distance was fraught with danger. Wild and desolate places harboured outlaws who preyed on unwary wayfarers. In 1260 Andrew Kay of Haworth was among three men captured and detained in prison in Lancashire for the murder of one William Ball.[24] In bad times many of the principal lords were forced to discharge their followers, who then resorted to robbery and violence as a means of making a living. The Lacys provided elaborate protection for the transport of money and goods between the Honours of Clitheroe and Pontefract. One of the reasons they retained Manningham and Stanbury in demesne was to use them as staging posts, the remains of earthworks at Oldsnap perhaps indicating the site of their 'halfway house'. The 1342 extent of the manor of Bradford records arrangements which might date right to the original sub-infeudation. Among the labour services of John Riens of Manningham was the requirement that, 'he shall carry the lord's victuals with one horse and one man from Bradford to Haworth, and from Haworth to Colne and thence to Ightenhill, receiving at each town 4d'. The same obligation was imposed on all fifteen bond tenements, so that a considerable body of men could be raised if it became necessary. A similar condition was imposed on the bondmen of Stanbury: Jordan Johnson, with his neighbours, was to 'carry the lord's victuals 8 miles from Haworth to Colne, receiving 40d., or to Ightynhyll, receiving ½ mark'.[25]

The most famous outlaw of them all was the mythical Robin Hood. None of the stories mentions Haworth directly but they are thought to have been composed in the households of the Lacys and their successors, the dukes of Lancaster, and may have beguiled many a long evening for servants charged with carrying money, food and goods along Clitheroegate between Ightenhill and Pontefract.[26] Early nineteenth-century maps mark three small wells near Ponden Kirk which were associated with Robin Hood. Halliwell Sutcliffe embroidered the story by naming them after Robin, Little John and Will Scarlett.[27] By that time they were covered with peat and it is unlikely that they are of early provenance, but the Robin Hood well on the road near Combe Cross is a different matter and may have been used in the Middle Ages to water horses on the way across the Pennines. Perhaps the name was given to it by men such as Jordan Johnson and John Riens as they yarned around their fires late into the night.

The early fourteenth century also saw a rise in political strife. After the English defeat at Bannockburn in 1314 there were repeated raids by the Scots into northern

England. In 1318 and 1319 Wharfedale was devastated and the Scots penetrated into Airedale, where Bingley and Bradford were sacked. Haworth may have been saved from their attentions by its location higher up in the Pennines.[28] The township was on the fringes of other tumults – the previous chapter described the rebellion of Thomas of Lancaster which led to Haworth becoming part of the dower of Philippa of Hainault, the wife of Edward III.[29]

The general sense of insecurity was heightened by worsening economic conditions. There is overwhelming evidence to show that by the end of the thirteenth century the growth in the population of England was straining agricultural resources to the limit. The situation was exacerbated by deteriorating weather conditions, and by 1320 famine was an ever-present threat. Ian Kershaw's study of the accounts of Bolton Priory, which had extensive lands in Airedale, shows how receipts reached a peak in 1295 and fell steadily thereafter. Periodic shortages became common and sometimes the bad conditions were nation-wide, the years 1315–16 being particularly bad not only in England but throughout Europe. The effect of the downturn can be gauged from the income of the Bradford living, which halved between 1292 and 1318: an entry in the register of Archbishop Greenfield for 1315 instructs one of his officials not to molest the rector for non-residence. Conditions improved during the 1320s but the living did not recover its earlier value until 1342.[30]

The terrible conditions of the reign of Edward II were still fresh in the memory when the country was hit by an even worse calamity – the Black Death of 1349–51. The proportion of the population which died is difficult to estimate. Current thinking puts the figure at around 50 per cent for the country as a whole. We have no information about mortality in Haworth and the two Oxenhopes but for Stanbury, which was still held in demesne, land transfers recorded in the court rolls can be used as a rough guide. Nothing happened in 1349 (when 17 tenements changed hands in Bradford itself) but during 1350 six of the thirteen tenements that had been listed in 1342, with a total of 3 bovates of land, changed hands. Five of the six entries state that the previous owner was dead. If we add a bovate of land each for Oldsnap and Oldfield to the original four bovates, half the land changed hands within a year, with a casualty rate of 46 per cent among the occupiers. Though nothing would ever again approach the severity of 1349–51, plague returned periodically until the middle of the seventeenth century – in 1359, for example, William Bull was recorded as dying of it.[31]

The effects of the Black Death were felt throughout the community. For a time the manorial administration ceased to function, and in 1357 Thomas de Copley alleged that ever since 1351 Robert Smith of Stanburi, John son of Jordan, Roger de la More, Robert son of William, Roger son of Jordan, John son of Adam, John de Denholm, Henry de Whiteacres and Adam, son of Richard, had been cutting down hazel and oak belonging to him in Oxenhope, which he valued at a total of 60s. As late as 1361 Henry de Allerton was complaining that Elias de Northeves had been depasturing his meadows for three years and his corn for eight.[32] The manor court was able to catch up with such cases eventually but in another way its authority was never completely re-established. In 1347 Robert de Northeves appeared before the court as a pledge for Robert de Kigheley, who owed Thomas the Chaplain 7s. 6d. for a cow. By the time the Black Death was over, Thomas had been replaced as chaplain by William: he may have been one of the victims himself. In 1354 Roger de Manningham brought a plea of trespass against William the Chaplain but was unable to prosecute it because William 'could not be found within the lordship of the lord nor had he anything by which he could be distrained'. His behaviour apparently caused a breakdown in the church services, for the court recommended that the property of Matilda Stubbynge be distrained to force her 'to answer the Lord Duke concerninge one booke of the chapel of Haworth' which she has detained. William, proving a will o' the wisp, was replaced the next year by Nicholas, who was registered as buying a stray colt.[33]

William was far from the only inhabitant who could not be located. The dramatic fall in population left many tenements vacant and the surviving bondmen found themselves in the pleasant position of being able to play off one lord against another. We do not have details for Haworth or the Oxenhopes but in Stanbury the manorial lord had great difficulty in getting the bondmen to stay. Some of the runaways were persuaded to return when offered a better tenement, but the usual outcome was that after the payment of a fine (called 'chevage') a man was allowed to stay in his new location.[34] A minority got away scot-free: thus, Roger, son of William del Marsh, was reported in 1355 to be dwelling with John Vavasor but before the Bradford manor steward could apprehend him he moved to live with John of Bradley and by 1360 was reported to be 'somewhere in Craven'.[35] The system was broken beyond repair.

4　The collapse of manorial authority

The beginning of commercial cloth production

In the high Middle Ages, and until the early fifteenth century, the making of better-quality cloth in Yorkshire was concentrated on the city of York and the town of Beverley. That does not mean that cloth was made nowhere else, for wool was spun and cloth was woven in practically every district where a pastoral economy predominated, but most of the cloth was made for the purely local market and was of poor quality. In Airedale there are early references to weavers at Skipton, and in the manor of Bradford a considerable amount of textile production was already undertaken by 1300. In 1311, for example, a fulling mill at Bradford was said to be worth £1 a year, a large sum for those times, and even the chaplain dabbled in cloth-making.[1] The famine of 1315–17 and the Scottish invasion shortly afterwards had a disastrous effect. Even in 1342, over twenty years later, the trade had not recovered and the value of the mill had fallen to 8s. a year. The decline was compounded by the effects of the Black Death of 1349, and in 1354 the mill was let for a mere 3s. 4d.[2]

When the recovery came the pattern of cloth-production was very much altered. The traditional centres lost their status, and important new districts emerged. There is a consensus that the decay of the cloth trade in Beverley and York was, in considerable measure, due to over-regulation by the town guilds, exacerbated by restrictions on entry to the guilds and by heavy taxation. There is, however, much less agreement as to why cloth-making began to flourish in some parts of the county outside York and Beverley, but not in others. Perhaps the most impressive change was the rise of the Halifax district, which was not even registered separately in the aulnage [wool tax] accounts in 1395 but was second in the county list in 1473–75.[3] No later accounts survive to chart progress, but the rise of Halifax clearly continued and by the 1520s its clothiers had become the dominant element in the Yorkshire wool textile industry.

There are no references to the production of cloth in the chapelry of Haworth during the later fourteenth century, though the surname of one local man, William Tailleur, suggests that he, or his forebears, were known for making garments. Apart from some spinning, which almost always goes unrecorded, the main contribution of the area to the growing textile business may well have been the production of raw wool. In the mid-fourteenth century William de Bercroft had 60 sheep on the moor, and his son John was much the richest man in the chapelry in 1379. He was described as 'merchant' and the commodity he traded in was almost certainly wool. It also seems likely that the lands of Nostell Priory in Oxenhope were used to pasture sheep.

The fifteenth century yields just one very ambiguous piece of information. The government had become increasingly worried about the low standard of cloth produced in the north, one of the complaints being that the fabric was overstretched by excessive tentering. This was the practice of putting cloth over frames and stretching it (fixing it to the frame by tenterhooks). It was essential, to reduce subsequent shrinkage, but if done to excess it loosened and weakened the weave of the cloth itself. In 1483 parliament passed an act which forbade tentering indoors and ordered that instead each village was to have a public tenter ground, where the amount of stretching could be checked.[4] The Haworth tithe map, surveyed at the end of the 1840s, shows an Upper and Lower Tenter Croft on the steep ground between Bridgehouse and the point where the old road to Bradford crosses the one from Lees to Hebden Bridge at Brow Top. There is another Tenter Croft on the Far Oxenhope map at Gate near Lowertown. But we have to remember that this information dates from 1852–53 and so the tenter ground could be much later than 1483.

The first certain information of the presence of the cloth trade is from as late as 1556, when in his will Richard Pighells bequeathed to his mother 'iii yeards of whit carsye or els ii yeards of watchet' and to his son, Henry, a pair of looms, plus half a sum of £5 for five white 'carseys' [kerseys] that Anthony Holmes owed him.[5] Other inventories, or manor court rolls, which might possibly supply us with more information are wanting for this period, but indirect evidence suggests strongly that the real progress of the chapelry from obscurity to the fringes of textile prosperity began earlier, during the reign of Henry VIII. This can be charted from the national taxation returns, which are known as lay subsidies. Those paying tax did so on so many tenths of the value of their lands or fifteenths of their goods, which ever was the larger. The most suitable for analysis are the returns of 1524, 1545 and 1546, although they cannot be directly compared because the minimum level at which people became liable to pay tax was £5 in 1524 and 1546, but only £1 in 1545. In addition there was an estimated inflation of around 30 per cent between 1524 and 1546. There may even be pitfalls in comparing different places within the same return. Richard Hoyle showed, in his examination of Craven, that the commissioners in west Craven used a completely different system of assessment from those in the east.[6] However, assuming that the commissioners for the wapentake of Morley adopted a consistent attitude to all the townships within their area, it should be possible to show where Haworth stood in relation to upper Calderdale (see Table 1).[7]

In 1524 the £16 total value of Haworth's assessment puts it well below the poorest of the nine townships in upper Calderdale. By 1545 Haworth had risen to eighth place and possibly seventh, only to fall back to ninth in 1546. There is no parallel with the

1524				1545				1546			
rank	township	no.	amount	rank	township	no.	amount	rank	township	no.	amount
1	Wadsworth	27	£175	1	Sowerby	129	£715	1	Sowerby	81	£581
2	Halifax	28	£148	2	Warley	78	£510	2	Warley	47	£353
3	Sowerby	22	£132	3	Halifax	74	£414	3	Halifax	43	£343
4	Warley	28	£88	4	Wadsworth	52	£226	4	Wadsworth	40	£203
5	Stansfield	13	£64	5	Midgley	40	£169	5	Midgley	26	£146
6	Midgley	15	£61	6	Heptonstall	127	£137	6	Heptonstall	21	£103
7	Erringden	5	£58	7	Stansfield*			7	Stansfield	18	£99
8	Heptonstall	11	£38	8	Haworth	73	£104	8	Erringden	12	£51
9	Langfield	4	£25	9	Erringden	23	£94	9	Haworth	14	£51
10	Haworth	8	£16	10	Langfield	16	£46	10	Langfield	6	£27

Notes: * There are no statistics for Stansfield in 1545: its position is estimated.

No. = number of people recorded as paying tax (in 1545 at £1 or more, in other years £5 or more).

Amount = total amount of tax paid by township.

very dramatic growth which characterised Sowerby or Warley, but one striking feature is that in 1545 there were 73 taxpayers, only one less than in Halifax. The difference between the townships was more to do with the amount paid by each individual. In that year five of the Haworth assessments are unreadable but of the remaining 68, some 47 were assessed at the minimum level of 20s. and paid a penny in tax – in other words, the majority of the Haworth taxpayers were at the bottom end of the scale. In the mid-1540s, as in 1379, there was just one really wealthy man. This time it was Edmund Binns, whose goods were assessed at £9, which was not only greater than anyone in the Haworth area, but more than anyone in Bradford. Barnard's Survey of 1577 suggests that further economic progress was made in the middle decades of the century.[8] It gives figures for Sowerby of 2s. and Halifax 1s. 2d, placing Haworth (with 8d.) as seventh in the ranking. However, Heptonstall is then combined with Erringden, and if they had been separate (as in 1545–46) Haworth would actually have been sixth.

Population pressure, subdivision and enclosure

There can be little doubt that the improvement in Haworth's fortunes was due to the cloth trade, but why should this have happened significantly later than in neighbouring Calderdale? One factor may have been population pressure. Most larger property holders had enough land to satisfy their needs, either by direct exploitation or by deriving the rent income from leasing-out land. They did not have to produce cloth for sale in order to supplement the income from farming and land. The cloth-makers therefore tended to be the lesser men, those with smallholdings which were insufficient to make them independent – indeed, Herbert Heaton showed that the weavers at Skipton were mainly cottars. Cloth-making was most likely to revive or expand in areas where the population recovered relatively quickly from crisis, or grew rapidly through natural increase. Everyone was affected by the famine of 1315–16 and the Black Death, while the Bradford area had another bad visitation of plague in 1379. Airedale suffered badly in the Scottish incursions of 1318–19 but they did not reach upper Calderdale, and the district seems to have enjoyed a similar immunity when the reign of Richard II brought renewed instability and another Scottish invasion in 1380, during which Bradford was sacked.[9]

A second factor very relevant to the expansion of cloth-making was the subletting and subdivision of holdings. In the early Middle Ages local lords tried to maintain the size of properties at a level which would support a farming family. As long as the lord followed such a policy the tenants had enough to live on without having to supplement their incomes, but as time passed many manorial lords relaxed these policies in response to population pressure. A leaseholder had to raise money for his rent in addition to providing for his family, but smaller properties could not provide enough income from farming to satisfy both demands, so subtenants had to produce cloth and sell it for cash in order to make ends meet.

Calculating population levels is very difficult. In 1342 there were 13 tenements at Stanbury, suggesting a total of 52 in the chapelry as a whole. At the 1379 poll tax 40 individuals in the township paid, which implies that the population had not yet returned to the pre-Black Death figure, which in turn may have been less than at the end of the thirteenth century.[10] An examination of the very fragmentary Bradford court rolls which have survived for the early fifteenth century shows that three land transfers took place in Stanbury in 1421. Each involved a tenement containing a *bovate*, or 12 acres, of land. Yet all the transfers listed in the earlier rolls between 1338 and 1363 involved less than half a bovate, which suggests that there was no pressure on land in Stanbury in 1421 and probably none in the rest of the township either.[11] Towards the end of the fifteenth century the population began to increase again and by the later part of the reign of Henry VIII it had passed its earlier medieval peak – in 1545, 73 individuals paid tax in Haworth township, and while the first list of tenants in the Haworth manor court list, in 1581, names 48 people, by 1612 the number had risen to 61. There were more households living in Haworth hamlet in 1581 than in the whole township in 1379, and the population pressure which was already apparent in 1545 had become a very significant factor by the end of Elizabeth's reign.[12]

Surname evidence shows that the increase in the population involved two main elements. First, there was expansion among families whose names already appear in the township in the fourteenth century, noted in either the Bradford court rolls or the 1379 poll tax returns. The author's database shows that between the 1513 muster list (for the Flodden campaign) and 1558 there were 52 references to the name *Pighells* (modern Pickles), which means a piece of enclosed ground and is thought to have originated in the chapelry.[13] No fewer than eight of them appear in the 1545 subsidy. There are also 31 references to *Binns* (a 'binn' was a manger, but the farm High Binns in Oxenhope may have been the centre from which the family proliferated). Six were important enough to figure in the 1545 subsidy. Other families with medieval roots in the township were the Holmes of Old Oxenhope and the Dicksons or Dixons – a well-established Stanbury family. Smith is a very common surname, held at an early date by many people who were not blacksmiths though that is the origin of the name. However, the families of this name living in Stanbury in the fourteenth and sixteenth centuries were indeed the local blacksmiths, so they were almost certainly related. The connection between the de la More family of the fourteenth century and the sixteenth-century Mores or Moores of Oxenhope is less secure.

The second element consisted of families apparently from outside the township but already settled there by the time of the Flodden muster.[14] All the most important ones came from the south, suggesting that the Haworth textile industry was an offshoot of that of Calderdale. There are 29 references to Shackletons, with ten of them (including four women) in the 1545 subsidy. They appear to have originated at Shackleton in Wadsworth and migrated over the ridge to Haworth. Next come the Mitchells (25). Their origins are difficult to pin down because the name is a patronymic but the consensus is that the Haworth ones also came from the upper Calder valley. Even more important were the Rishworths or Rushworths (24). Henry Rishworth of Coley inherited the manor in the early fifteenth century and most of those with the same name were his relatives. The Aikroyds or Akeroyds (14) (modern Ackroyd), were another Wadsworth family, while the Horsfalls (14) started at Todmorden from where they expanded through Heptonstall and Wadsworth to Haworth. Finally there were the Midgleys (13) who were already established in Midgley, Erringden and Wadsworth when they first appear in Haworth. The flow of incomers apparently slackened after 1513 but the pattern of migration from

Map of the hamlet of Stanbury in the late sixteenth and early seventeenth centuries, showing the earliest known dates of individual farms and houses.

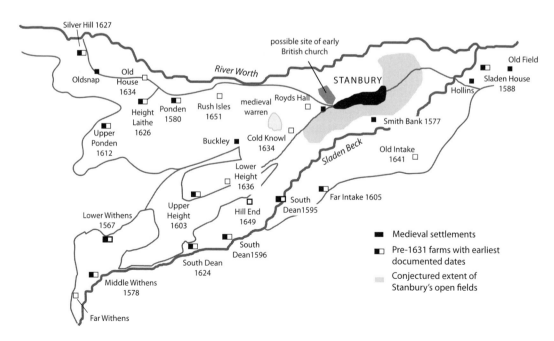

the south persisted. The Toothills are associated with Raistrick, the Denes or Deanes with Sowerby, Warley and Midgley. The Sutcliffes were another Wadsworth family. The Pearsons are thought to have originated in Hartshead and the Ogdens to have come from Rochdale by way of Sowerby.

The reign of Elizabeth brought changes in the ranking but the general pattern remained largely unchanged. The Pighells and the Binns continued to multiply, but the latter lost their social pre-eminence with the death of Edmund Binns at the beginning of Elizabeth's reign, and were overtaken by the Mitchells. Other families in decline by the late sixteenth century were the Akeroyds, Shackletons and Toothills. The Sutcliffes and Briggs steadily increased in importance and two names from an earlier period began to make a stronger showing. The 1379 poll tax lists a Jacobus Scott. He may well have been related to the Batley family of that name, coming to the township when Adam de Oxenhope, lord of Batley, acquired the manor of Near Oxenhope. References to them in the fifteenth and sixteenth centuries are not sparse, but by the seventeenth century the Scotts were one of the most influential families in Oxenhope and they figure importantly in the next chapter.

Another family which took time to become established was the Heatons. They are first mentioned in 1513, when Wilfrid Heaton was granted two acres of land on the south side of Oldsnap. William Shackleton, in his manuscript history of the Heatons of Ponden, believed that they, like so many others, came into the township from Calderdale and he associates them by inference with the Shackletons of Wadsworth. George Redmonds, on the other hand, thinks they were an offshoot of the Bradford Heatons. Wilfrid's wife was Ann Tempest, and it is tempting to see a link with the Tempests of Tong. Shackleton, however, is undoubtedly right in rejecting any direct link with the William de Heaton, whose property passed to Adam de Oxenhope. There is no evidence of any residence in the township prior to 1513.[15] The humble nature of the family's origins is demonstrated by the Flodden muster of 1513. The wealthiest men in the township brought to the muster a horse and an arquebus, and the middling sort, an arquebus. Humfrey Heaton, perhaps the son of Wilfrid, could only produce a bill.[16] Wilfrid Heaton paid at the lowest level in the 1545 subsidy and when the family was next troubled by the taxman in 1597 it was through Robert Heaton of the younger Ponden branch. No less significant is that none of the Heatons produced a pedigree during the heraldic visitations of the sixteenth and seventeenth centuries. Emily Brontë may have picked up a version of their obscure origins. On 29 April 1585 Wilfrid and Anne Heaton and William Earnshaw were each admitted to 'a moiety of a messuage with 30 acres of land and one acre of meadow and pasture called Holnsnap [sic]'. The Earnshaws soon disappeared but their memory perhaps lingered among the inhabitants when the history of Oldsnap was remembered, leading Emily to attach the name to her fictitious family. In fact the Earnshaws seem to have passed their interest to Christopher Binns, not to the Heatons, and it was from Henry Binns that the family eventually acquired the rest of the property.[17]

There were also new names. That with the most references is Hartley (41), a name which is recorded in Calderdale as early as 1297 although by the time it appears in Haworth there were several possible sources on either side of the Pennines. The Bentleys of Oxenhope and Stanbury, and the Crabtrees of Stanbury are both associated with Calderdale. Indeed, by 1660 the Bentleys had gone back there, leaving only the name 'Bentley Hey' in Far Oxenhope as a memorial of their century's residence in the township. The Clayton family, on the other hand, probably came from Bradford; the Fether family seem to have originated in Bingley; and the Sowdens moved up the valley from Keighley. No families of any note came from the north and only one, the Nutters (who were prominent in Pendle) from the west.

Subletting was one way of coping with an increasing population. Another was enclosure. In the textile districts of the Pennines enclosure of common land, including upland waste, was very extensive and important during the sixteenth and early seventeenth centuries. In one sense it signalled the end of the self-sufficient economy, for instead of growing subsistence crops on a few open field strips, the farmer-cum-weaver had a piece of enclosed land on which he kept a few animals and grew some oats for his family. He, and other members of the household, made cloth which was sold for cash, to buy what he could not produce himself. This combination of small-scale farming and domestic production is known to economic historians as a 'dual economy' system. Enclosure of the upland margins and lower moorlands was a key element in the social and economic change during this time. It took two forms. Sometimes the land was already in use as arable common field, divided into unfenced strips. On enclosure, each tenant received a block of land which was in proportion to the extent of the strips he originally held in the open fields plus an allocation of the stinted common. The other way was to enclose land direct from the moor and the waste, parcelling it out into large fields or nibbling away at the fringes with small irregular new closes.

In Haworth the open fields remained more or less intact, one of them still surviving as late as 1853, while the stinted common, known as Mill Hey, lasted until at least 1714. The

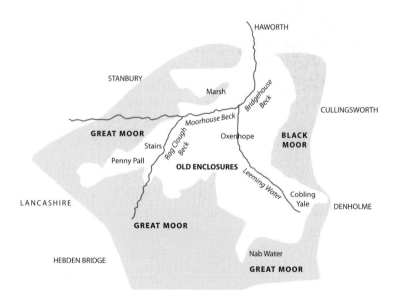

The Oxenhope Enclosure Award. Although the original map this illustration is taken from is dated 1779 it actually shows the situation c.1740 (see Chapter 7). All the old enclosures were before 1740. Most date from the seventeenth century and some from the second half of the sixteenth century. All the parliamentary enclosure did was complete a movement which had begun over two hundred years earlier by enclosing the moors and Near Oxenhope Marsh.

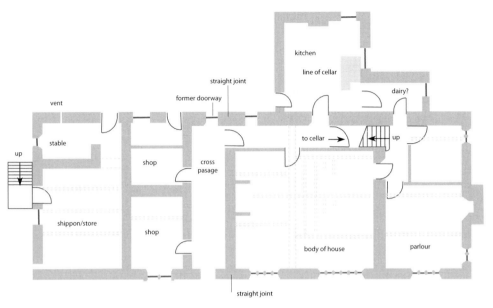

kitchen

line of cellar

straight joint

former doorway

dairy?

vent

to cellar →

up

stable

up

shop

cross
pasage

shippon/store

shop

body of house

parlour

straight joint

PONDEN HALL, (THE THRUSHCROSS GRANGE OF "WUTHERING HEIGHTS.")

Ponden Hall probably dates from 1634, but we know that there was an earlier house on the site because there is evidence of the Heaton family having lived there from at least as early as 1542; they occupied the hall until 1898. For details of its construction see p.38. The alterations of 1801 described on p.94 were to the 'low' end on the left. Access to the pedimented door was by the gate in the wall, and the door can be glimpsed through the trees.

extent of early enclosure was comparatively small, for the medieval village had a mere 13 tenements and in 1579 only three more, which gave stability to the pattern of landholdings. Evidence of continuity comes from a recent examination of Townend Farm. Under the early seventeenth-century house there is a medieval hearth, and the remains of a medieval cruck-framed house have also been identified.[18] One of the farms with enclosed fields, Hall, also dated from the Middle Ages. There was some enclosure from the moor but the opportunities were apparently limited. In Stanbury, on the other hand, the open fields disappeared altogether and by the early seventeenth century extensive encroachments were taking place on the moor. In the two Oxenhopes the vast majority of the cultivable land, even in the Middle Ages, was in separate farms rather than commonly managed systems. The area under occupation was rapidly extended – in the thirteenth century there were 26 tenements but by the late sixteenth in excess of 40.

Charting the expansion of enclosure into the moorland areas is difficult because we have to rely on information from deeds. For Stanbury there is a reference to Withens in 1567 (probably the Lower Withens farm), Middle Withens in 1578, and South Dean in 1595. Confirmation that the Sladen valley was being developed comes from the Haworth manor court rolls, which show that a number of the tenants living in Stanbury paid small rents to pasture animals on the strip of common land, belonging to Haworth, separating Stanbury from Near Oxenhope. There were complaints in 1584 and 1593 that John Pighells of South Dean was driving the cattle and sheep of his neighbours off the Haworth common. By 1597 the pressure had intensified to the point that John and Richard Pighells and Robert Clayton, all of Stanbury, were fined 3s. 4d. each for this offence.[19] Further up the Worth, a branch of the Heaton family was developing the Ponden valley. There is dispute about which of their two houses, Old House or Ponden Hall, was built first. The inscription over the door at Ponden Hall is ambiguous: William Shackleton interpreted it as meaning that the Hall was built around 1580 and the Old House in 1634, but logically it should be the other way round.[20] It is more likely that the whole inscription relates to Ponden Hall itself, the 'new' house being the 1801 extension and the 'old' one the earlier part of 1634. An examination of Ponden Hall has revealed reused materials which indicate a pre-1600 thatched structure with aisles and collar rafters, or alternatively a long house. This would fit well with the general development of the area and with evidence which places the Heatons at Ponden as early as 1542.[21] Most of the other first references to farms are from the early seventeenth century: Height in 1603, Height Laithe in 1626, Silver Hill 1627, Ponden Old House 1634 and Hill End c.1640.

There is a similar pattern in Oxenhope. Most places named earlier than the mid-seventeenth century (such as West Shaw 1545, High Binns 1576, Mouldgreave 1588, and Roydhouse 1598) could have been in occupation continuously since the fourteenth century. For example, Sawood is first mentioned in 1600, Hillhouse in 1624 and Sawood Nab in 1636. During their examination of farm buildings at High Bradley in the neighbouring parish of Kildwick, Alison Armstrong and Arnold Pacey found that each early seventeenth-century farmhouse was built on the foundations of one dateable to at least a century earlier.[22] The evidence from Ponden suggests that thorough exploration would reveal a similar pattern in Stanbury and Oxenhope, matching the population expansion of the early sixteenth century already noted. The survival of deeds is somewhat random and they did not appear in considerable numbers until land became freehold. That process only began in the middle of the sixteenth century and was not complete until around 1640.

The rise of the yeoman freeholder

The upper Calder valley may have forged ahead in textile production because of its distinctive local forms of land tenure. Information about tenurial customs is scarce, but R. C. M. Thornes considered that landlord control was particularly lax in the manor of Wakefield. If that was so, tenants in some of the sub-manors may have established their right to customary rents at an early stage and a fixed entry fine (that is, the payment made on taking over a tenancy). The manor directly administered four of the nine townships in upper Calderdale: Sowerby, Warley, Erringden and Langfield.[23] In Sowerby and Warley most land had originally been held in bondage but in the course of time had become copyhold (i.e. a manorial tenancy). It is significant that these two were the main cloth-making townships. Information about the manor of Bradford is lacking so we must rely on indirect evidence. From the mid-fifteenth century Bradford was regularly leased to syndicates of businessmen, who collected the rents and kept any money above the value of the lease. This is referred to as a 'farm'. Edward IV adopted a liberal approach. The town's market, originally granted in 1295, had lapsed but the trustees were allowed to revive and conduct it toll-free. This attracted trade to the town and contributed towards wider economic growth. Bradford began to appear separately in the aulnage (cloth tax) accounts. Under Henry VII the inhabitants became embroiled in court cases when the Crown tried to increase the value of the farm, which may initially have limited the scope of the cloth trade,[24] but by the middle of the sixteenth century such tactics were becoming counter-productive. In many places the tenants managed to establish copyhold rights, which allowed them to limit the amount paid in fines and to insist on a customary rent. During the middle and later sixteenth century there was rapid inflation and many manorial lords, their economic base undermined, were forced to sell land for a cash sum. We can follow this process in Haworth and Oxenhope.

In Haworth, for example, Alexander Rishworth appears to have inherited the manor with 12 messuages. In 1562 he sold one messuage and lands to Hugh More. There were three more sales in the next decade: in 1576 a messuage was passed to William Haldsworth and Matthew Usher; another went to William Banyster and John Battie in 1577; and in 1579 a third, to John Thorpe and Richard Shefeld.[25] In 1579 Rishworth disposed of the manor itself to Martin Birkhead, in return for property at Heath near Halifax. At that time the manor was stated to consist of 8 messuages, 8 cottages and a watermill with lands in Haworth, Oxenhope and Horton.[26] There was then a lull. Neither Martin nor his widow made any land sales, but his son Nathaniel inherited the manor and estate and decided to dispose of his assets. In 1612 he sold two messuages, two cottages and land in Haworth to Robert Smithe, Edward Holmes, Christopher Totehill and George Taylor.[27] The remaining six messuages went in the Michaelmas term of 1618 – four, with the water cornmill, to Christopher Mitchell, Michael Pighills and Robert Byns. Two more went to Adam Wright, Thomas Horsfall and Richard Smyth. The last sale, which may well have been the Hall farm, was to John Scott and Christopher Sowden.[28]

The change in Oxenhope began later than in Haworth but was swifter. In 1587 Edmund Eltofts decided to sell out. He put on the market 50 messuages with lands at Oxenhope, Morton and Helwick,[29] but died before the transaction was completed. However, in 1589 his son Thomas sold 22 messuages to a syndicate of eight men (Christopher Bentley, Anthony Holmes, John Cosin, Richard Driver, Thomas Fether, Roger Foulds, Thomas Scott and Nicholas Whitaker),[30] who in some cases were buying on behalf of other members of their family. The Fethers, for example, acquired four messuages. In 1592 the remaining 28 properties were each sold to the sitting tenant.[31] There is some confusion over the transfer of the manor of Oxenhope. In 1587 Edmund Eltofts apparently passed the manorial rights and one remaining messuage, together with moorland and pasture, to Stephen Tempest and Christopher Mychell.[32] Yet, in 1618 Thomas Eltoft was still described as lord of the manor of Oxenhope, in the inquisition post mortem of Christopher Holmes of Old Oxenhope, so the earlier transfer may well have been a mortgage which was subsequently redeemed.[33] The manor seems finally to have left Eltoft's possession sometime before 1629, because in that year Edmund Slater was described as lord of the manor by a panel of inhabitants who gave evidence in connection with the Stanbury sale described below.[34]

Stanbury tenants had to wait a little longer to acquire their property. The Crown had continued the policy of leasing the manor of Bradford to tax farmers who paid a rent in return. During the reign of Elizabeth the farm was held by Robert Dudley, earl of Leicester. James I continued the policy, leasing the manor to successive syndicates of businessmen, but Charles I was soon in a more serious financial predicament and by 1628 was selling Crown lands to make ends meet. By letters patent of 9 September 1628 the manor of Bradford was sold to a syndicate of London merchants led by Edward Ditchfield, subject to a yearly rent of £35 4s. 6½d. Less than a year later they resold the manor, subject to the same yearly rent, to a group of local inhabitants headed by John Okell, vicar of Bradford.[35] Robert Heaton of Ponden was one of the group appointed on 20 September 1629 as 'our true and Lawfull Atturney ... to treate, Compounde and agree with his maiesties Commissioners for the infranchising of our Copiehold estates in our severall Lands and Tenements'.[36] There was then a delay, Sir John Bennett claimed that many of the encroachments on the moor came within an earlier grant to him of a 30 year lease of all 'concealed' lands in the duchy of Lancaster.[37] Five tenants, Wilfrid Heaton, Thomas Smith, Christopher Dickson, William Pighells and Samuel Taylor, appear to have become impatient and concluded their own bargains with the Bradford syndicate.[38] The remainder were covered by a deed of conveyance of 12 April 1631.

John Okell and others conveyed to Robert Heaton and John Midgley the elder all the copyhold lands in Stanbury, and Heaton in turn sold out to the tenants of the copyhold land, turning it into freehold.[39] As a result all the land in Stanbury became freehold, as in Oxenhope, but with one major difference. Whereas in Oxenhope the lord of the manor retained his rights over the moors and wastes, in Stanbury the moorlands and waste were divided between the newly enfranchised freeholders in proportion to the land they already possessed.

From this time onwards the manor courts had no control over the disposal of freehold land, although in Haworth, where open fields remained, it retained the residual authority to impose fines on individuals for trespass, knocking down fences, or confining animals in the pinfold. Courts continued to be held in Oxenhope from time to time until the

Townend Farm is a sixteenth-century farmhouse standing in North Street which may be on the site of an earlier medieval building. In the old photograph (*below, left*), the cross-wing can be clearly seen on the left. The entry to the modern passage is on the right. The end gable is rare in this area, being more typical of houses around Colne, which suggests that it was built by the Nutter family. They were clothiers, and their name is the only one recorded in Haworth as originating around Colne.

© KEIGHLEY LIBRARY, THE JONAS BRADLEY COLLECTION; PHOTOGRAPH: CARNEGIE, 2009

enclosure act of 1779 extinguished most of the remaining rights over the moors and waste. There is no information for Stanbury, but if the courts of the manor of Bradford continued to meet they would simply have exacted fines for the transfer of land, since no open fields remained. Real authority had passed to the vestry which controlled church affairs, roads, the poor law, and law and order. The vestry was ultimately responsible to quarter sessions, not to the manor court. By the end of the eighteenth century the costs involved in holding the courts far exceeded their income and they were abandoned.

From the early seventeenth century, therefore, a new class of small freeholders, engaged in farming and weaving, had emerged. They manufactured woollen pieces which were collected and taken to Halifax market by the clothiers. Between 1611 and 1620 there are wills for four men who described themselves as clothiers – Christopher Scott, Alexander Hartley, Thomas Foster and William Nutter – and between 1621 and 1630 three more (William Naylor, Christopher Mitchell and Richard Pighells). There were only two during the 1630s, Edward Fether and William Bynnes, but five in the Civil War period – John Emott alias Scott, William Deane, William Bynnes, John Bynnes and Joseph Emott.[40] In some cases the wills show businesses passing between members of the same family, as with the two Richard Pighells, or three members of the Bynes family. Alexander Hartley, William Deane and William Nutter all appear in the Haworth rentals, while Christopher Mitchell lived at Stanbury and the rest operated in Oxenhope. Nutter may well have been the builder of Townend Farm. His family was the only one in the western quarter identifiable as incomers. A recent examination of Townend has shown it to have a hall and cross-wing plan, with a cross passage against the east gable, a type of plan which appears in a small group of buildings across the county boundary around Colne, but nowhere else.[41] Some of the other clothiers can be located more precisely. The second Richard Pighells lived at Mouldgreave, while documents in the Brigg collection provide details about William Pighells, clothier, of Stanbury. He purchased the property in November 1614, and was almost certainly same man who was mentioned in a marriage settlement of July 1633, when he was described as son and heir of Richard Pighells of Stanbury. An indenture of June 1639 shows that John Bynes was living at Sawood.[42]

Lists compiled solely from wills are fallible because there was little consistency in the descriptions of the status of individuals. Thus, the will of Robert Heaton III describes him as a yeoman but his inventory made on 16 March 1640/41 refers to wool of various types worth £33 4s. 2d.; yarn at £6 10s. 0d.; cards, wheels and two pairs of looms, and thirteen 'carsey' pieces worth £23 18s. 0d. This inventory includes a greater quantity of textile material and equipment than any other from either Keighley or Haworth,[43] so it is clear that 'yeoman' is a label of status, not occupation. It is not clear how long the Heatons had been so heavily engaged in the textile trade, but the inventory of Robert Heaton II (1626), which lists debts due to the testator, suggests that the family had already built up a considerable financial base. In any event, for all these families the period of prosperity was brief, for a trade depression in the 1630s was followed by civil war, with all the dislocation that war brings in its train.

From Reformation to revolution 5

The Reformation and its aftermath

The economic transformation outlined in the last chapter was paralleled by the widespread religious and political changes during and after the Reformation. The personal beliefs of local people were challenged, and they had to adapt to new structures in society itself. The religious preambles to Haworth wills imply that there was continuing loyalty to Catholicism, though we must be cautious with such evidence because the wording could reflect the attitude of the person who wrote the will rather than that of the testator. The earliest Haworth wills were made at the start of the 1530s, when Alexander Emmott was the priest at the chapel. He left in 1531 or 1532 and was replaced by Stephen Smith, who remained until 1543.[1] During their time all the wills but one include the standard reference to the Virgin Mary. Thus, William Horsfall commended his soul 'to God almightye to our ladye saincte marye and to all the saintes in heven'.[2] The exception is Thomas Jenkinson, whose will (12 July 1543) has a more Protestant style – he bequeathed his soul to 'almightie god trustinge by the meritts of Christe passyon that I have and shall have cleane Remission of all my sinnes'.[3]

Stephen Smith was succeeded in 1544 by Arthur Rawling, who stayed until 1578. The wording of local wills suggests that he adapted his beliefs to the various changes in national policy. From 1544 to 1548 the wills with religious preambles follow the Roman Catholic form, but in 1549–53, when the government of Edward VI pushed the country vigorously towards Protestantism, the preambles to Haworth wills closely resemble that of Thomas Jenkinson. There are only three wills from the reign of Mary I, when Catholicism was restored, but each includes references to the Virgin Mary. Following the accession of Elizabeth in 1558 a new religious settlement created the form of the Church of England, combining Protestant beliefs with some of the ritual of the Catholic service. Local wills reflect this ambivalence, as the elaborate preambles of the previous decades were replaced by the simple statement that the testator committed his or her soul 'unto almightie god my maker and redeemer'.

Later in Elizabeth's reign the rise of a new and more radical element in the Church of England, soon labelled 'Puritanism', was reflected in the changing wording of wills.

Ground
plan of the
seventeenth-
century
Haworth
Chapel,
reconstructed
from the
Faculty for
the Grimshaw
extensions.
The south
side is largely
conjectural.

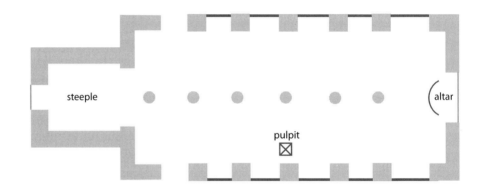

In this area the new styles appear in about 1580. The standard form was that used in the will of Thomas Mitchell of Stanbury, dated 20 May 1580. He commended his soul 'into thandes of almightie god, my creator, trustinge to be saved by the death and passion of Jesus Christ, my redeemer'.[4] Some testators went further: in his will of 13 September 1589 John Brigg asked that his body be interred 'in the church yeard of Haworth aforesaid among the bodies of the faithfull there buried trusting with them to have a joyful resurrection'.[5] The typically Presbyterian doctrine of personal election is absent and a significant minority after 1620 have no reference to a churchyard burial. In some cases the omission may have been because the will maker did not really care but in others it was clearly not accidental. The will of William Naylor, dated 4 June 1623, was composed with great care. After an elaborate preamble in which he comended his soul to Almighty God, Jesus Christ and all the saints in heaven, he instructed that his body be committed 'to the earth whereof it was made hopeing that the same shall have a joyful resurrection at the last day'. The wording of John Stansfield's 1629 will is very similar, though shorter.'[6] The following table suggests that Puritan beliefs had become dominant by 1640, though as always we must accept that the wording is not an infallible guide to belief. Of the 109 wills 47 show some evidence of Puritan beliefs and from the 1620s onwards they are the majority.

decade	Protestant*	soul†	body‡	none §	total
1581–1590	6	4	1	0	11
1591–1600	19	0	3	0	22
1601–1610	11	1	7	1	20
1611–1620	12	5	4	3	24
1621–1630	5	3	12	2	22
1631–1640	2	1	6	3	10
TOTAL	55	14	33	9	109

* wills with a largely neutral protestant beginning.
† wills that only refer to the redemption of the soul.
‡ wills that mention physical resurrection.
§ wills that have no preamble.

The Reformation brought other changes. A new church appears to have been built in 1488,[7] and in 1557 John Rishworth left 16d. to pay for the insertion of glass windows,[8] but in 1584 Christopher Hargreaves of Oxenhope bequeathed 20s. towards 'the buildinge of Haworthe Church when it should be enlarged', and the following year Christopher Mitchell of Haworth gave a similar sum 'if done within twenty years'.[9] There is no contemporary evidence of rebuilding, but in 1664 Christopher Hutchinson of Stanbury, whose memories of Haworth went back 74 years, deposed that 'about 60 years agoe the Church of Haworthe being old and likely to fall the same was pulled down & rebuilt at the proper costs and charges of the inhabitants of Haworth, Stanbury, higher Oxnop, & lower Oxnop'.[10] We know little else, though in 1955 Christies sold a communion cup, dated to 1593, which had apparently come from Haworth. Canon Dixon did not know when it came into the church's possession and thought that it had originally been a drinking or stirrup cup.[11]

Paying the chaplain was a problem. Among the first victims of the second phase of the Reformation, under Edward VI, were the chantry chapels, where masses were said to the souls of dead benefactors, a practice which was forbidden from 1549. The abolition of the chantry at Haworth deprived the chapel of a major source of income, and despite a certificate from the Commissioners of the Duchy of Lancaster stating that the church was seven miles from Bradford 'and therefore most meet to continue for divine service and the administration of the sacraments' no alternative was made available. Bradford could not help, for although that living was worth £70 per annum the vicar only received £20, the rest being in the hands of the rector, whose position was held by a lay patron, the College of Leicester.[12]

For ten years the chaplain, Arthur Rawling, seems to have lived on ad hoc payments but after the accession of Elizabeth it was realised that a more permanent arrangement had to be devised. The wealthier inhabitants clubbed together and raised £36, with which Andrew Heaton of Oldsnap and Christopher Holmes of Old Oxenhope bought five farms in Stanbury. These were transferred to trustees who became responsible for collecting the rents and paying them to the minister.[13] Haworth was still part of the parish of Bradford, so the appointment of the 'perpetual curate' remained the responsibility of the vicar, but the trustees were empowered to reject any nominee whom they disliked. Nevertheless, Rawling's successor, Thomas Lane, was committed to prison in 1580 on a charge of recusancy (that is, being a crypto-Catholic), which suggests that all was not well.[14] Whether the trustees helped his fall from grace is unclear, but there seem to have been no more disputes from then until the Civil War. Lane appears to have been followed by William Parkinson, though the only evidence of his presence is his witnessing three wills. The next perpetual curate was Adam Wright, who was probably ordained at York in 1592 and had spent a year at Elland.[15] By 1603 he was living in Haworth, where he witnessed the will of Nicholas Dickson of Stanbury on 9 November, but he did not apparently become perpetual curate until 1607. He is likely to have been the Adam Wright who bought a messuage from Birkhead in 1618, but there is doubt about his status, for although the 1603 will calls him 'clerk', Archbishop

These communion wine flagons are associated with William Grimshaw because they are dated to 1742. The beaker type chalice of 1613 and the 1659 bible on which they are resting are reminders of the early Stuart church.

Neile's visitation of 1632 described him disapprovingly as merely a 'deacon'.[16] Neither Bradford nor Haworth took any notice of the comment. John Okell, vicar of Bradford, was a staunch puritan and ignored the archbishop's strictures whenever he could, and Wright remained perpetual curate of Haworth at least until the beginning of the Civil War.

The church continued to be a drain on the finances of the community. In 1636 the trustees rather belatedly discovered that the church farms were not included in the bargain which made Stanbury all freehold, and they had to levy a rate on the entire chapelry in order to rectify the position.[17] Tithes were still payable to Bradford and the following year another rate was imposed to buy out the great tithes on the 'new lands', those enclosed during the sixteenth and early seventeenth centuries. The tithes had been put up for sale by the lay-rector of Bradford, Sir John Maynard, and were valued at £200.[18] Over the years such purchases proved to be excellent bargains, but the two levies so close together must have made both the Crown and the Church very unpopular.

Sermons were central to the Puritan concept of church services, so their clergy had to be capable preachers. There was a desperate shortage of qualified ministers and great stress was laid on training. All over the country grammar schools were endowed which were designed to teach boys to read and write English, and those thought to be suitable would then learn the Latin and Greek necessary for university entrance. In 1638 Christopher Scott, rector of Chastleton, Oxfordshire, left an annuity of £18 for the support of a schoolmaster at Haworth.[19] It seems that, on the initiative of his brother, John Scott of Hillhouse, a schoolhouse had already built in anticipation of the benefaction.[20] The building still stands on the 'Schoolhirst' in Near Oxenhope. Scott specified that the master should be a graduate of either Oxford or Cambridge and that preference should be given to his own relatives. He had in mind that the position should go to George, son of John Bentley, for whom he provided £20 for a period of seven years to maintain himself at the university. He also left 100 marks (£66 13s. 4d.) towards the support of an able minister at Haworth 'who will be obliged to preach the word', which suggests that Wright was not regarded as adequate.

Old Haworth Free School. In this context 'Haworth' should be understood as the township, not the hamlet, because the school building stands in Marsh in Near Oxenhope and it was endowed by the Rev. Christopher Scott, rector of Chastleton, Oxfordshire, in 1638. He was the brother of John Scott of Hillhouse, Oxenhope. The aim was to prepare boys for entry to Oxford and Cambridge by teaching 'grammar', i.e. Latin and Greek. In practice the subjects in demand were English and Arithmetic. An attempt to revive the classical curriculum in the nineteenth century was a failure, and the school was dissolved in 1886, the endowments being used to provide scholarships to neighbouring schools, principally the boys' Trade and Grammar School and the girls' Drake and Tonson School, both in Keighley.

© KEIGHLEY LIBRARY

The Civil Wars and the Interregnum

The political crisis of the late 1630s, including two wars between the English and the Scots, steadily worsened until in September 1642 the king raised his standard against parliament at Nottingham. The situation in the West Riding was confused. A substantial majority of the gentry supported the king but the area nonetheless proved to be solidly parliamentarian because in many places, as in Haworth, power had passed from the manorial lords to the yeoman freeholders who were strongly opposed to the king. In the previous decades a few local landowners had paid fines rather than accept forced knighthoods (a favoured royal means of raising revenue) but only John Scott, Robert Heaton and Samuel Rishworth were rich enough to be affected and even they paid at the lowest rate of £10.[21] The Crown sought other ways to maintain its income: there is no evidence about local reactions to ship money, but there is evidence of anger about other devices. In Stanbury, for example, the tenants believed they had bought their freeholds from the Crown but a document in the Heaton papers shows that as late as 1640 they were being dunned for copyhold fines which had allegedly not been paid on lands inherited before the 1632 agreement.[22] Furthermore, everyone involved in the cloth trade had been annoyed by royal exactions. Clarendon wrote that 'Leeds, Halifax and Bradford, three very populous and rich towns – depending wholly on the clothiers, naturally maligned the gentry'. A test of allegiance was whether individuals signed the 1642 'Protestation', by which they undertook to uphold the liberties of parliament and the true Protestant faith. The Bradford churchwardens commented that, 'There are none within the several parishes, Townships and Hamlets within these schedules that have refused to take the protestacon.'[23]

In the autumn of 1642 and spring of 1643 the parliamentarians under Sir Thomas Fairfax proved more than a match for the Yorkshire Royalists, but when the Marquis of Newcastle marched south with a compact and well disciplined army of 6,000 men to join the local cavaliers, the parliamentarians found themselves outnumbered and were defeated at Adwalton Moor in June 1643. Strenuous efforts were made to raise both money and men, and in May 1643 the commissioners appointed by Fairfax were hard at work in Haworth.[24] The battle had serious consequences for Haworth, for about this time John Scott's son, John junior, disappeared and he may have been killed in the battle. The Scott property passed to his daughter, Mary, who had married John Ramsden of Crowstone.[25] Another mysterious death was that of Michael Heaton. Legend has it that, fleeing from the battle, he blundered into a bog and was drowned. For the next year the whole area was open to attack and in January 1644 a detachment of royalist cavalry, under the command of Sir Richard Tancred of Whixley, burned Haworth to the ground. Tancred was an officer in the royalist garrison at Halifax,[26] and his men seem to have been stationed temporarily at Keighley during that very hard winter. Thereafter the focus of conflict moved elsewhere, but a local sequel is the curious story of Henry Casson.

According to William Shackleton in his *History of the Heatons of Ponden House*, in 1651 Henry Casson married Ann Heaton, widow of Michael Heaton of Ponden, by whom he had a son John. Shackleton alleges that Casson did everything he could to ensure that John should succeed to the Heaton estate instead of Robert, Ann's son by her first husband. As evidence of his malign influence, Shackleton points to the failure of the couple to obtain letters of administration for the estate until 1662, 19 years after Michael's decease, and the spiteful way in which Casson forced Robert to pay him for his father's furniture when the strategy failed. He suggested that Emily Brontë, who would have heard the story when visiting Ponden, modelled Heathcliff on Casson. The idea was elaborated by Mabel Edgerley in 1945 (though she later modified some of her views) and Mary Butterfield in 1979, and repeated more recently by Peggy Hewitt. It was alleged that Casson, as constable of Haworth in 1643, had been responsible for the arrest of Andrew Heaton of Oldsnap as a royalist and the murder of Michael Heaton by throwing his body into a bog.

What really happened? For eight years after the death of Michael Heaton (sometime between May and September 1643) his widow Ann administered the Ponden estate at Stanbury on behalf of her young son, Robert. In 1651 she remarried to Henry Casson,[27] who was from West Ardsley in the parish of Rothwell near Wakefield.[28] There is no evidence for his presence in Stanbury before 1651 – indeed, his absence from the 1636 list of freeholders, the Protestation returns of 1642,[29] and the returns for the levy ordered by Fairfax in 1643,[30] show that he cannot have been living in the chapelry before 1645 at the earliest. We can therefore eliminate any involvement in the arrest of Andrew Heaton or the death of Michael.

On the surface the marriage appears not to have been in Mrs Heaton's interest. Her original marriage settlement had provided that in the event of her husband dying before her, she would be entitled to half the income from his property for so long as she remained a widow, provided she had at least one child, but if she remarried she would only get her widow's third. However, closer examination reveals that she was born Ann Scarborough and a letter from her family's attorney, Robert Parker of Extwistle, suggests that the marriage articles were signed in a hurry. The half income was not in fact secured, so she would only have a third of the income by right whether she remarried or not.[31] At the time of Michael Heaton's death, they had two young children – a daughter, Mary, aged two, and a son, Robert, less than a year old. Michael Heaton died intestate and the usual course would have been to apply for letters of administration for his property. Such arrangements often gave the care of male children to a male relative, rather than the widow, or appointed a 'supervisor'. By not applying for administration Ann could retain control of her son and enjoy the *entire* income of the estate. For eight years she maintained her independence but by 1650 the need for security was paramount. She executed a deed securing two messuages in Cowling to her daughter, and then remarried to a Henry Casson to avoid losing Robert to one or other of her late husband's brothers.[32, 33]

The alliance with Casson may have had its roots in local politics. A William Casson was living in the 'Great House' at Kildwick Grange in 1614, and he may well have been Henry's uncle.[34] The house had been built by John Coates, father of Roger Coates, the most important republican in the area. The link with Henry's family may have been reactivated when Coates served with the regiment of John Bright of Badsworth in the Wakefield area during the war. His wife, Rosamund, came from Glusburn in Kildwick parish, as did Ann Heaton. Rosamund probably knew Ann, and Coates might have indicated through his wife that if Ann Heaton married Henry Casson she could expect the protection of the new government. Casson certainly supported the Commonwealth, for in 1651 he took the declaration imposed on everyone who wished to hold office.[35] The couple had two sons. John was born probably in 1651 or 1652, as he was given part of a messuage at Uppertown, Oxenhope, in 1673 which suggests that he reached his 21st birthday in that year. Henry was apprenticed to the Stanbury blacksmith on 1 January 1671/72 and since the usual age of apprenticeship was 15 or 16 he was probably born in 1656 or 1657.[36]

Therefore, Ann Heaton was responsible for the delay in seeking administration, not Casson as Shackleton alleged. The oft-cited incident in February 1664 when Casson made Robert pay for his father's furniture is similarly based on misunderstanding. In his 1641 will Robert had left to his son Michael, one great cupboard and one great table excepted, 'any other of his goods or so much thereof as he would have, paying for them after according to the rate of the appraisement thereof'. His mother and stepfather were therefore treating Robert as she and Michael had been treated by his grandfather. Making sure that her daughter got what was due to her and her son by her first marriage succeeded to an unimpaired estate were the aims of her second marriage, to Casson, and they were triumphantly achieved. Mary received her portion of £100 promptly on her 21st birthday in November 1662,[37] while Robert succeeded to an undivided inheritance in February 1664 without any difficulty.[38]

A postcard view of the Old Hall, Haworth. This is a fairly typical early seventeenth-century gentry house. It was probably built on the site of an earlier building by John Scott after the sales described on p.40. From him it descended to his daughter Mary, who married John Ramsden of Crowstone. From the Ramsdens it passed to the Fawkes and then to the Hawksworth family. The Emmotts did not own any land in Haworth until 1746. The building is now a restaurant.

© STEPHEN HULME

The later stories casting Casson in the role of Heathcliff in *Wuthering Heights* had a number of possible sources. After the Restoration the Heatons may have wanted to distance themselves from a man whose republican antecedents were an embarrassment; or to distract attention from the Earnshaw connection mentioned in chapter 3; or there could have been jealousies between the two branches of the family. In 1685 Henry Casson junior married Martha Dean at Keighley and in 1687 they had a daughter, Elizabeth. For most of his life he lived at Causey Foot, working as a blacksmith. He died in 1736 and was buried in Illingworth churchyard.[39] John was more of a problem. He too may have moved to Halifax parish (a John Casson also lived at Causey Foot) but he later returned to Stanbury and in 1691 badgered Robert Heaton into making a will itemising what he intended to leave him. Eventually in 1710 he signed a quitclaim renouncing all further interest in the Heaton estate.[40] It would seem that Casson has been traduced, and did not fit the Heathcliff mould at all … yet novelists make imaginative use of what they are told, so elements of the Casson story could still have found their way into *Wuthering Heights*.

Local changes during the Civil Wars and Interregnum reflected the national pattern. On the death of Adam Wright, sometime in the early 1640s, John Aldcroft became perpetual curate. Eleven Haworth wills were proved during the 1640s, four of them referring to churchyard burials which suggest that Aldcroft was a moderate, but his successor, Robert Towne, was a very different man. Towne was certainly at Haworth by 1650 and could have arrived as early as 1648.[41] Oliver Heywood later described him as the 'famous Antinomian, who writ some books; he was the best scholar and soberest man of that judgment in the country, but something unsound in principles'.[42]

Neither Puritan Anglicans nor Presbyterians would have any truck with 'antinomian' views, which put more value on individual inspiration and free grace than on scriptural authority. Towne himself vehemently denied that he was an antinomian, claiming that he thought scriptural law paramount, but he was an advocate of free grace.[43] Towne's influence extended far outside Haworth. 'Exercises' – days devoted to preaching and prayer – were held in the Halifax area in 1651 and 1653 and were attended by 'both Mr Townes', the other one being John, minister of Kildwick from 1646 to 1659.[44] In 1653 Robert Towne moved to Elland which, although also a chapelry, was a more prestigious appointment. The move may have been influenced by other considerations, for he had come to Haworth at a time when the living of Bradford was vacant. By 1653 the high tide of radical politics and religion had passed and the new vicar of Bradford was a conservative Presbyterian, Jonas Waterhouse, who may have questioned the legitimacy of Towne's induction. Elland was safely outside his jurisdiction in the parish of Halifax.

Towne's successor was Edmund Garforth,[45] whose moderate mainstream stance may have disappointed those who preferred the more inspirational aspects of Towne's pastorate. These men must have proved receptive to William Dewsbury and Thomas Stubbs, the first Quaker missionaries in the area, 'who came from Ives-Delves in Warley' in 1653. They 'declared the truth about Stanbury and Christopher Smith received them'.[46] He was the eldest son of Robert Smith, the Stanbury blacksmith. The tradition that meetings were held in a small upper room of the house at Horton Croft as early as 1655 is the result of confusion,[47] for 1655 was when land for a Quaker graveyard was purchased. Christopher Smith himself appears to have lived at Clough Bank farm near Laycock, which the Quaker minute book shows was the location of the meeting.[48] By 1660 there was a solid core of Quakers in Stanbury, based on the Smith and Clayton families.

The Restoration

On the restoration of the monarchy in May 1660 the Church of England was also re-established. Many ministers appointed during the Commonwealth were removed from office, either at once or under legislation of 1662 designed to purge the Church of its Puritan elements. At Haworth, Edmund Garforth resigned in August 1660 to become vicar of Gargrave. His successor, John Collier, may have been a younger son of the Rev. Jeremiah Collier, headmaster of Bradford Grammar School at the time of his death in 1635. John graduated from Trinity College, Cambridge in 1646 and became a schoolmaster, becoming headmaster of Ermysted's Grammar School, Skipton, from 1656 and possibly as early as 1654. In September 1660 he was reordained by John Brammall, an itinerant Irish bishop, and in November was inducted to the Haworth living after a hearing established that none of the earlier perpetual curates was still alive, except Towne, and he had moved voluntarily.[49] In 1662, when the Act of Uniformity required all ministers to accept the Book of Common Prayer in its entirety, a fifth of them refused

One of the older houses in the village, with a datestone of 1671.

PHOTOGRAPH: CARNEGIE, 2009

and were ejected, but Collier conformed and remained until his death in 1675. He was succeeded by Edmund Moore, who had been ejected from Baildon in 1662 but later conformed and was reinstated. After a brief period as curate of Coley he came to Haworth and stayed until he died in 1684. His successor, Richard Margerison, was still in place at the time of the 1688 Glorious Revolution.[50]

One result of the 1662 Act of Uniformity was the emergence of groups of religious dissenters, who resisted official attempts to suppress them. Many ejected ministers continued to preach in the houses of sympathisers and in 1672 Charles II issued his first Declaration of Indulgence, aimed at providing some degree of toleration for Roman Catholics but also allowing Protestant dissenters to apply for licences for meeting houses. In that year Haworth was visited by the famous Presbyterian divine, Oliver Heywood, who had been ejected from Coley in 1662. He was unimpressed and wrote in his diary that it was 'an ignorant and prophane place'. On a later visit he commented unfavourably on the rushbearing ceremony, when 'multitudes of people meet, feast, drink, play and commit many outrages in revellings, rantings, ridings without any fear of restraint'.[51] Haworth was not really receptive to Heywood's strict version of nonconformity. Old Robert Towne resigned from Elland in 1657, staying there until 1661, but he may then have returned to Haworth, since he was buried in the churchyard in 1664.[52] His less dogmatic views may still have had adherents within the chapelry.

The Quakers attracted most hostility from the Anglican authorities because they were incapable of keeping their heads down. At the 1662 visitation John Pighells, Christopher Smith, Jonas Smith, William Clayton senior, John Clayton, Robert Clayton, John Jessop and William Clayton junior were presented for failing to attend church and sent for punishment to the Halifax House of Correction.[53] In 1666 an almost identical group is listed among those who had not attended church for a month or upwards.[54] Christopher Smith and Jonas Smith were presented again for the same offence in 1667.[55] They head yet another list of non-attenders in 1669, which also included Joseph Smith, William Clayton junior, John Pighells and three new names – John Tayler, Jonas Turner and Nathan Heaton.[56] In 1674 Christopher and Jonas were presented for burying their dead in the

Quaker graveyard at Stanbury, while they and their wives Mary and Susanna, together with Joseph Smith and Mary his wife, William Clayton and his wife Sarah, and Jonathan Pighells, were also presented for failure to attend church and take the sacrament.[57]

The swift collapse of Charles II's policy of toleration led to renewed persecution of all nonconformists, reaching a peak in the early 1680s. In 1682 and 1684 the same core of families appear – Christopher Smith, William Clayton, their wives, John Smith, and Richard Crabtree were prosecuted for not coming to church or paying their church dues; John Pighells and Matthew Naylor for not coming to church and Jonadab Widdop for not coming and bringing his child with him.[58] All this indicates that persecution was having no effect whatsoever.[59] Under James II, a Roman Catholic, a consensus grew among Anglicans that toleration ought to be conceded to dissenters but not to Roman Catholics. When James was forced to abdicate in 1688, and was succeeded by William III and Mary II as joint monarchs, parliament legalised worship for dissenters in licensed meeting houses.

Though religious dissent and toleration were central issues during those troubled times, many in the chapelry were more interested in separation of a different kind. In 1650 the Commonwealth government ordered a comprehensive survey of church property, with a view to redistributing the assets in a more equitable fashion … It was recommended that Haworth should be removed from Bradford and made into a separate parish. No action ensued, so on 23 November 1657 the people of Haworth presented a petition to the trustees for the maintenance of ministers asking that they 'would be pleased to grant an order of summons for the Churchwardens of Bradford aforesaid to show cause why the said Chappelry should not be made a district parish of itself or take such other course for the separateing of the said Chappell from the said parish Church'.[60] The order was granted, but opposition from Bradford, and the political turmoil of the late 1650s, meant that it was not put into effect, and after the Restoration the Church of England refused to accept the validity of orders such as that. The status quo was unaltered and for the next two centuries the uneasy and often overtly hostile relationship between Haworth and Bradford continued.

During the Civil War, Bradford parish church had been seriously damaged and thereafter the building had been seriously neglected. In 1663 the vicar and churchwardens laid a church rate of £200 to repair and refurbish it, requiring £40 as Haworth's share.[61] No other year before 1700 showed a total of more than £12 and the usual figure was £6. Not unnaturally there was furious opposition from Haworth, local refusal to pay being based on the unsustainable assertion that the chapelry had never been part of the parish of Bradford. The 1657 petition was based on the clear premise that Haworth was within the parish of Bradford. The case was lost and the ecclesiastical court ordered Haworth to pay its rate annually for the repair and maintenance of the nave and churchyard at Bradford. Opposition still continued over the proportion Haworth was expected to pay. Another verdict before the court in 1679 supported the contention of the Bradford churchwardens that 'It is the ancient custom in the parish of Bradford thus to proportion the church lay. First that the chapelry of Haworth pay a fifth part of the whole sume; then Bradford towne a third part of the remaining sume; and the rest equally divided according to the churchwardens of the several towns of Thornton, Heaton-cum-Clayton, Allerton-cum-Wilsden, Great and Little Horton, Wibsey and Bierley, Shipley, Manningham, Bolling, Eccleshill.'[62] Issues of principle, such as scriptural authority, personal election and free grace, had given way to arguments over who should pay for church repairs. This was not the only indication that the religious enthusiasm of the beginning of the century was waning. The introductions to the wills degenerate into identical mechanical formulae, making it pointless to attempt to deduce the makers' beliefs.

A dispute among the school trustees in 1683 (which gives us valuable information about its early history) points in the same direction. In 1683 there were eleven trustees under the terms of the will of Christopher Scott. Of these John Ramsden of Crowstone, husband of Scott's niece Mary, had two votes. The first master was Abraham Padgett, brother of Ambrose Padgett of Wildgreave Head.[63] He appears to have undertaken to resign when George Bentley was qualified, and duly did so, but Bentley proved negligent and was removed. The order of the masters who followed Bentley is difficult to establish. Richard Brown was appointed on 26 January 1656/57[64] but it is not clear whether a Mr Rakes, who is mentioned in depositions, came before or after him because the chronology is confused. A Mr Murgatroyd stayed nine years, but John Collier was relicensed to teach shortly before he became perpetual curate in November 1660.

At least two of these men, Rakes and Murgatroyd, were not university graduates, and there are indications that the salary was too small to attract a highly qualified man. In 1667 Collier was still the schoolmaster,[65] but he was removed for 'insufficiency' in 1673, not long before his death, so the double role may have become too much for him. There were two applicants for the job. One, Mr Ramsden, was an MA and came with the recommendation of Richard Hook, vicar of Halifax, and the other was Timothy Pollard, who was not a graduate but had worked as a tutor in a gentleman's family in Lancashire and could teach both Greek and Latin. Ramsden was probably a distant relation of the founder and he had the required degree, but the trustees chose Pollard. There was a debt of £20 relating to a barn on the school land. The trustees wished to pay it off, and offered Pollard the post at £14 a year until the debt was extinguished and after that at the full rate of £18. Pollard accepted, but once the money was paid off some of the trustees tried to remove him, alleging that he was incompetent and also unqualified under the terms of the founder's will. They sought to replace him with James Roberts, who they claimed was related to the testator and had degrees from both Oxford and Cambridge. An ecclesiastical court found in favour of Pollard after discovering that Roberts was only a very distant relative of Scott and, though he had lived in Oxford and Cambridge, he had attended Glasgow University, where he had quarrelled with his tutor after two years and then gone off to Aberdeen! The judge was doubtless correct, but the fact that the trustees considered paying off the debt more important than appointing a graduate who could train a future generation of preaching ministers (the aim of Christopher Scott) suggests that they were remiss and out of sympathy with the founder's intentions. Times had certainly changed.

The dual economy   6

The dual economy   6

Earning a living

Gentry influence in Haworth was weak even before the decline of the manorial system, and by the end of the seventeenth century only four families qualified for that status. Among them were the Gawkrogers of Cook Gate, a Sowerby family who came to Haworth shortly after the Restoration. Richard Gawkroger, probably the son of Timothy, was perpetual curate during the last decade of the seventeenth century and John Gawkroger was the schoolmaster in the early years of the eighteenth.[1] Cook Gate was later acquired by the Midgleys, whose main holdings were at Oldfield. In 1671 Joseph Midgley had bought the manorial rights, such as they were, from Nicholas Bladen, grandson of Nathaniel Birkhead.[2] By 1666 the largest landowner in Haworth hamlet was John Ramsden, who had inherited the Scott property and lived at what is now called Emmott Old Hall. He added to it by buying Butt farm from Richard Mitchell in 1646 and more land from John Smith in 1659.[3] Ramsden found that the chapelry was a poor prospect for someone trying to improve his status and, though the family did not sell out, his son Joseph went to live at Stead Hall, Burley, which he had acquired through his wife.[4] The Holmes family of Old Oxenhope behaved in a similar fashion. By the later seventeenth century the main branch could live on the rents of the farms they owned but the 1704 poor rate shows that although John Holmes paid on five messuages in Oxenhope he was actually living at Yeadon.[5] Apart from these four the only person of 'private means' was Richard Pollard at Hob Hill, a bachelor with property in Bradford.[6] Everyone else was directly involved in farming, trade or industry.

A picture of Haworth can be formed from the study of inventories, of which a hundred survive for the period 1689 to 1740. They have to be interpreted with care since, for example, some of the shortest inventories belong to the most prosperous testators, perhaps because they had already given up their farm or business and were living with a relative. More importantly, they do not include real estate, so land and other fixed assets are not included. Nonetheless, they are a rich and rewarding source of information. Only 53 of the inventories list sufficient agricultural goods to suggest that the testator was still actively farming, and for most of these the valuations of goods are quite small:

34 (57.4 per cent) had values between £12 and £29; 11 (27.5 per cent) £30–£49; 5 (9.4 per cent) £50–£99; and only three (5.7 per cent) over £100. Those belonged to George Taylor of Stanbury, John Crabtree of Withins, and William Rishworth of Mouldgreave. In contrast, the inventories for the Ainsty of York, a lowland agricultural district, show that of 67 compiled in 1720–22, 34 per cent were over £100 in value.

Farming in Haworth was primarily pastoral. Cattle predominated and they are mentioned in every inventory valued at more than £12. Sheep were much less important but they were noted in all farms with access to open moorland, while every larger inventory included horses maintained as draught or pack animals. Some mention pigs, one includes geese, and another has a hive of bees. Fowls are not listed but they were present in most barnyards. Only three inventories list a bull – those of George Taylor (£120), John Crabtree (£103), and Robert Heaton of Ponden (£93).[7] Many of the smaller farmers would do as the father of the Keighley diarist, William Shackleton, did and take his cows to be put to a wealthier neighbour's bull. An alternative was to buy cows, which were about to calve or had just done so, from Craven dealers. The beasts could be kept a couple of years for their milk and then slaughtered for market. Many of the calves produced in this way were steers, not heifers, so fattening cattle for sale developed as a sideline. The largest farms had oxen for ploughing. Although agriculturists claimed that oxen were less efficient than horses, they could be slaughtered for meat once they had exhausted their usefulness as draught animals. George Taylor had six oxen, eight

Cookgate is often referred to as the 'manor house' because it was occupied for a short time by the Midgley family. None of its other owners or tenants was manorial lords of Haworth. The Rev. John Richardson lived there until the parsonage was completed in 1778.

© F. SHUTTLEWORTH

Emmott Old Hall is so called because it was inherited by the family from the Ramsdens in 1746, but there is no evidence that they ever lived there. The building itself dates from the seventeenth century and is a fine example of the fenestration of the period. It is now an inn.

cattle including a bull, and 66 sheep; John Crabtree had cattle valued at £33 including an ox and a bull, together with sheep worth £40; and William Rishworth did not have a bull but had four cows and six oxen valued at £33 and sheep worth £7.[8]

Possession of farming equipment distinguished the more prosperous from the lesser men. The larger farms all had at least one plough, a harrow, and carts used to collect crops, spread manure and fetch peat. Most of those with valuations over £50 had a plough, but only half of those worth £30–£49, and just two of those under £30. Harrows are present in most inventories down to £30, but only half of those under £30. This suggests that many farmers bought their wheat and oats, and a few may not have harvested their own hay either. Few inventories mention sickles, and scythes were only just coming into use.

Analysis of inventories suggests that a farmer needed around £30 worth of crops, animals and equipment for his holding to be viable, but even those who had that degree of wealth usually had another occupation. George Taylor of Stanbury, who died in 1694 with £47 of agricultural goods, had five geldings which carried the malt, used in making beer, that he bought and sold throughout the township. John Smith of Stanbury (£28) was the local blacksmith. Lesser men such as John Hey of Sawood or Richard Whitfield of Haworth Brow made up the shortfall on their farms by working as a shoemaker and a tailor respectively.[9] These were the exceptions, for most supplemented their farming incomes by participating in the textile trade. Only three of the inventories with agricultural goods over £30 have no textile equipment in them, suggesting strongly that money made from the cloth trade was being used to create viable farms, although

This house was built by the Taylor family in 1753. In addition to their textile business, they traded in malt. The Taylors were not lords of the manor (a modern invention designed to make money from gullible Americans). It is the second house from the right and has a frontage resembling those of Bridgehouse, Cookgate and the Parsonage.

involvement in textiles was not confined to those who needed the money to make ends meet.

The largest farmers were not necessarily those with most investment in the cloth trade, and it is clear that the most important men were those whose inventories included substantial amounts of cloth. At Halifax market they sold the cloth which had been produced by their neighbours, but normally themselves took part in the manufacturing process as well. Halifax was not the only market. Surviving receipts of the Tillotson family of Mouldgreave, covering the years 1716–21, show them supplying a York merchant.[10] At his death in 1693 Timothy Pighells of Stanbury, clothier, had wool, yarn and cloth worth £60, together with an unspecified number of looms, warping wough, and spinning wheels. George Taylor's son, another George, married Timothy's daughter, abandoned malting and took over the cloth business. When he died in 1702 he had wool, yarn and cloth worth £60 and three pairs of looms with other unidentified equipment. The Oxenhope clothiers did not work on such a scale. John Binns (died 1719) had wool, yarn and cloth worth £16, and two pairs of looms. The 1697 inventory of Barnard Hartley includes wool, yarn, three pieces, a pair of looms, warping wough and three spinning wheels, but they were worth only £9 altogether In contrast, his son, Michael Hartley of High Binns (died 1720) had wool, yarn and cloth worth £36 but no equipment, suggesting that he had abandoned production in order to concentrate on trading in finished cloth. He was buying the wool, distributing it to the spinners, taking in the yarn, putting it out to the weavers, and finally collecting the cloth for sale at Halifax. The family had become notably more prosperous: Barnard had £39 of agricultural goods and £19 due in debts, but Michael had £53 worth of farming equipment and £119 due. There were also cloth-producers who employed others, but who sold their cloth to clothiers and did not participate in the marketing of the finished product. Examples include William Rishworth of Mouldgreave, Robert Heaton of Ponden, and John Fether of West Shaw, each of whom had three looms with other equipment.[11] There were family firms, where a single pair of looms was operated by the husband but spinning equipment such as cards and wheels were used by other members of the household to produce the yarn. John Heaton of Oldsnap, who died in 1700, was the most prosperous of this group, although he further supplemented his earnings by dealing in slates and had accumulated £81 worth of agricultural goods. His son, another John, abandoned the slate-dealing and had only £60 worth of agricultural goods by the time of his death in 1708.[12] Others in this category included Caleb Heaton and Sarah Wright of Haworth, Timothy Holmes of Stanbury, William Sagar the elder of Westcrofthead, and William Ogden of South Nab.[13]

The 'Manor House', Stanbury. Built in 1753, this was for a long time the home of the Taylor family, who were clothiers and dealers in malt in the seventeenth century, later becoming woolstaplers (wool dealers). The name of the house is misleading because there was no manor of Stanbury, with the village being held as a demesne of the Manor of Bradford until the manor was sold and all the land became freehold.

PHOTOGRAPH: CARNEGIE, 2009

Before 1700 the cloth produced within the township was almost exclusively woollen kersey pieces, sometimes known as 'northern whites' because they were sent to market undyed. There was then a shift towards the production of serges, a much lighter worsted cloth. Woollen kerseys were made with short staple wool, prepared by the use of cards best suited to the nimble fingers of women or children. Worsted serges needed long staple wool combed into parallel strands with iron combs periodically heated in a large pot. Only full-grown men could handle them. The earliest reference to combs is in the inventory of John Rawson of Silver Hill (1702). He also had a pair of looms and other unspecified textile equipment, suggesting that he was involved in all the production stages. Many families did not have enough adult males for both combing and weaving,[14] so there were specialist combers who supplied spinners with combed tops and then collected the yarn, often over a wide area. In the remarkable 1735 inventory of Adam Wright of Haworth are listed 18lbs of combed tops, three pairs of old combs, two seats and a comb pot, three stones of wool, a warping mill, rings and bobbins, scales and weights, soap, spun warp and weft; 132 tops out for spinning at Kildwick and 55 at home, 12 pieces of weft and 14 warps, with a total value of £33 1s. Robert Craven, also of Haworth, worked on a somewhat lesser scale. In June 1739 he had 'a piece' of a firkin of soap, 11 lbs of wool, 2 stones of Britch wool and a pair of combs, warping mill and rings, some wool, some charcoal, a washing tub, combed wool, warps and wefts, valued at £15 3s.[15]

How they lived

The hearth tax of 1666 lists 158 households within the township of Haworth. Of these 122 (77 per cent) paid for one hearth and 25 (14 per cent) two hearths, leaving only 11 properties with three or more hearths. The largest house had six hearths, and was occupied by Timothy Gawkroger (so it was probably Cook Gate) and the second was the house of John Ramsden, with five – almost certainly Emmott Old Hall.[16] As with many sources from this period, the hearth tax is prone to error and misinterpretation, not least because there was widespread evasion and avoidance by the early 1670s: Robert Heaton admitted to four hearths at Ponden in 1666 but only two in 1672! A recent examination of Ponden revealed two seventeenth-century fireplaces attached to the parlour stack. There was certainly a third in the housebody and probably a fourth in the shop chamber.[17] A comparison with the 1672 returns for Keighley, not a conspicuously prosperous place, is revealing. Of its 243 houses, 154 (63 per cent) had one hearth and 63 (26 per cent) two hearths, with 35 (11 per cent) three or more. Keighley therefore had a significantly larger proportion of medium-sized properties, and proportionately fewer with one.

This suggests that Haworth was a relatively poor community of small houses, and the inventories reveal a lifestyle which matches the modesty of the housing stock. All of the inventories relate to people who were in comparatively comfortable circumstances, since the really poor neither left wills nor had inventories made of their few possessions. The way in which people described themselves can also be misleading: for example, Robert Heaton of Ponden and William Ogden of Sawood both described themselves as yeomen but Heaton had household goods worth £58, the largest in any of the inventories, while Ogden's only totalled £5 17s.[18]

The life of most households was centred on the main living room, often called simply 'the house'. This room contained the main fireplace, with its open grate and a chimney jack or *reckon* (an adjustable bar from which pots could be hung over the fire). Typical equipment included a pair of tongs, a spit for cooking meat, and a pair of fire irons to support it, with iron runners to retain the fire in place. Most inventories list beef and bacon or simply 'hang flesh'. Meat does not keep – only one inventory includes a spice cupboard, but every house of a decent size had its salting vat. Oatcake was usually made at the fire, cooked on a bakestone. The best of those were made of a special sandstone, found at Delf, but some people had to make do with shale or mudstone. During the eighteenth century iron bakestones began to replace the earlier types. Every household had its box or 'ark' in which oatmeal was stored. Some inventories itemise baking spittles, knead kitts in which the oats were mixed, and bread fleaks on which the oatcake was dried. Oats, in various forms, were the staple foodstuff – potatoes are first noted in the Keighley area in 1704 at Brownhill in Morton and none of the Haworth inventories mentions them. The larger houses had churns in which butter was made, cheese was also eaten but only two inventories mention cheese presses. Fowls were so commonplace that they were not even mentioned, but eggs would certainly have been available. The reference to a hive of bees suggests that honey was used as a sweetener. Other foods were seasonal and, since inventories do not record perishables, we can only assume that they were eaten – fish from the streams; apples and pears from orchards; berry fruits and nuts from the hedges in the autumn. Spring was the worst time, since fresh food was almost absent and stores ran low, so for most people that meant salt meat and oatcake until fresh crops were available.

Meals were usually taken at a board which rested on trestles, people sitting sometimes on chairs, sometimes on forms. Meat was generally served on wooden plates known as trenchers, and each person would cut the meat with their own personal knife. In better-off households there would be a basin of water and a napkin with which to wipe off the grease. Some inventories in the Keighley area list these napkins under 'linen' but none of the Haworth ones do. Some households had pewter plates and a court cupboard on which they were placed, or a glass-case or perhaps a large oak dresser like the one described in the opening pages of *Wuthering Heights*.[19] Some inventories mention chafing-dishes which kept the food warm until it was eaten. Liquid refreshment rarely figures in the inventories. Milk was always available and indirect evidence shows that the consumption of locally brewed ale was almost universal. The larger households brewed their own – there are references to malt and to 'dust' which is its leavings – but otherwise it could be obtained from inns, such as the *Black Bull* which was the principal one in Haworth. Alternatively, there were small alehouses such as that run by Robert Pighells at Moorside in Oxenhope, whose inventory records 'brewing vessel and licker'.[20]

This dresser came from Ponden Hall and is reputed to be the one Emily Brontë had in mind in the first chapter of *Wuthering Heights*. It is typical of its period, but the description of the large housebody with a small room off the back in the book also fits Ponden Hall, which provides some backing for the story.
AUTHOR COLLECTION

The inventories mention a variety of furniture. Oval, round or square tables feature and a few have long settles, while larger houses had desks, safes or coffers for business papers. Shelves are mentioned in a number of inventories but they were usually in the milkhouse or kitchen and used for crockery or for cheese-making. Other items were stored in the ubiquitous 'chists'. Practically every inventory has an entry for 'beds' and 'bedding' but few provide details. Some mention pairs of bedstocks, a bedframe that could be dismantled to economise on space, while others refer to half-headed beds of the modern type and a couple list curtains showing that the bed was a four poster. Soft furnishings were unusual, the commonest type being the cushions used on hard wooden chairs. There are no references to window curtains. Bedclothes are usually undifferentiated, though John Smith, the Stanbury blacksmith, and George Taylor had linen sheets and some others mention linen. Sara Smith at Coldknowle had three bolsters and a 'caddow', a sort of quilt to give extra warmth.[21] Floor coverings are also absent, implying bare stone like the one Emily Brontë described at *Wuthering Heights*, perhaps spread with rushes.[22]

Eleven inventories list clocks – the term 'clock and case' indicated what is now called a grandfather clock, but two include brass mantle clocks, one has a watch and another an hour glass. Strict time had relatively little meaning for most seventeenth-century people, who got up and went to bed with the sun. Sundials were used extensively – there is one cut into the windowsill of the Parsonage Museum and another, originally the property of Richard Pollard, used to be in front of the Yorkshire Penny Bank building where it was wrongly reset to summertime, not 'sun time'.[23] In Haworth inventories candlesticks were separately entered, but most householders made do with dim and smoky rushlights. Only seven inventories refer to books, three of them identified as the bible. Richard Pollard also had an exposition of the New Testament and some 'sermon books'. Three mention 'mirrors' (those of John Heaton the younger of Oldsnap, Richard Pollard of Hob Hill, and Joseph Midgley of Haworth). Occasionally, other personal goods are listed. Christopher Holmes of Old Oxenhope had a side saddle for his wife and Jane Sutcliffe one for herself, while John Heaton and George Taylor had guns and Heaton also had a sword. Robert Heaton had a musket in 1679 but it was not there when he died in 1714.[24] Christopher Holmes preferred to lend most of his money out rather than indulge in conspicuous consumption. The £301 in money owing to him at his death in May 1693 must have been what his son John used to buy the estate at Yeadon.[25]

In general status was indicated not so much by the possession of exotic items as by the style and quality of more everyday furnishings. Were your pots of brass or iron? Did you eat from a board or a table? Did you sit on chairs or forms? Did you eat off wood, pewter, earthenware or white ware? Were your chairs the ordinary high-backed wooden ones, or were they 'joyned', 'railed' or 'seild'? Did you sleep in a four poster with curtains and a feather bed, or on a flock mattress, or on bedstocks with a sack filled with chaff?

Another measure of status was the extent to which your house was separated into different rooms for particular purposes. The simplest houses had just one room, a housestead with a laithe (or barn) attached, so eating, sleeping and working were done in the same place. A three-bay house could be divided into a housestead and a parlour, with the sleeping quarters moved into the parlour (which might also be used as storage space). Many houses were single-storey, although by the mid-sixteenth century upper floors were becoming more common. At the same time, slate was increasingly substituted for thatch as a roofing material — at Ponden, for example, the changeover took place in about 1634.

As domestic properties were adapted for textile production lack of free space became a problem. During the seventeenth century weaving might be done in a downstairs room, but the change to worsted weaving led to a demand for better lighting so during the eighteenth century upper rooms were adapted, or attics and roofspaces converted, to provide loomshops. This coincided with the reroofing in slate or stone, so John Heaton's slate-dealing, noted earlier, may have been prompted by this demand. Among the inventories which mention both rooms and textile equipment, eighteen had looms upstairs and twelve downstairs. Bedrooms, too, were increasingly likely to be upstairs, although 54 inventories have the principal bedroom downstairs and 16 upstairs. Cooking arrangements were more inflexible because the overwhelming majority of houses had only one hearth. The kitchen was often used only for food preparation and storage, including salting meat, with a separate milkhouse in larger houses for the production of butter and cheese.

In the 1666 and 1672 hearth tax returns Timothy Gawkroger is recorded as occupying a house with six hearths, so it was certainly arranged with different rooms for different purposes. His son's inventory shows no cooking implements in the principal room, which it describes as a 'hall', and all food preparation was done in the kitchen. His parlour had no beds (so sleeping was separated from other uses) and his downstairs rooms were completed by a study in which he had his books. He slept upstairs in a bed with curtains, and all four chambers contained beds and bedding. Elsewhere, Richard Pollard slept upstairs but his cooking was done in the 'house' and that appears to have been the situation at Townend as well. There were chambers for sleeping but the kitchen seems to have been simple.[26] The inventory of Jane Sutcliffe, widow of Simeon, a Haworth butcher and blacksmith, has a remarkable array of pewter and earthenware flagons, porringers and chargers but like practically everyone else she cooked in the housestead and slept in the parlour. So did Joseph Midgley, the lord of the manor. Robert Heaton's £58 of personal property reflected a large household rather than a high degree of sophistication. He had seven beds, for example. At Ponden there was probably a kitchen and milkhouse at the rear, and the present two-storey did not replace it until the nineteenth century.[27]

The other side of the coin

The Haworth chapelry registers do not begin until 1645 and even then what survives is so fragmentary that it is impossible to calculate the size of the population before the early eighteenth century. Other sources have their problems but they do give us a rough idea of the chapelry's evolution. Most taxation returns affected only the richest in the community but the 1545 subsidy cast its net so widely that most householders were caught – 73 are listed in the township of Haworth, which at 4.5 people per family suggests a population of at least 300, almost twice the figure for 1379. In 1643, 139 individuals contributed to the so-called 'Fairfax' ley, raised to pay the parliamentary forces, which would imply a total of about 650. Most people had to pay, so the listing is probably relatively comprehensive. In Stanbury, 40 inhabitants were recorded in a 1640 tax list, which is almost identical to the 38 of the Fairfax ley. In 1662, 490 Haworth inhabitants paid the poll tax, which in principle meant everyone over 16, and Horsfall Turner reckoned this to give a total population of around 700, which accords well with the 158 houses in the 1666 hearth tax (at 4.5 people per family, almost exactly the same figure). In 1689 the assistant overseer of the poor collected money from 166 householders, and in 1704 from 145.[28] The pattern which these figures reveal is common to the whole of northern England. A rapid growth in population during the late sixteenth century petered out in the 1630s, and was followed by slow decline or no growth for the rest of the century.

Population did not increase steadily, for although the number of baptisms generally exceeded burials, and often by a considerable margin, infant mortality was high and there were crisis years when the number of burials rose dramatically. The lack of reliable figures from the chapelry registers make it difficult to identify these years in Haworth but a number of them can be inferred from the experience of neighbouring parishes.

For example, 1596 was a very bad year across the entire country – a combination of a very bad harvest with influenza or fever was responsible. The registers of Kildwick and Keighley both show a large increase in burials, and there are six wills for the township of Haworth, more than for any other year in the sixteenth century. Another bad year both locally and nationally was 1603, and plague was recorded at Heptonstall and Halifax in 1631.[29] The last widespread outbreak outside London was in 1644–45. Keighley burial registers show sharp increases in these years and plague affected both sides during the siege of Skipton in 1645. This, coming so soon after the burning of the village, made the closing months of the first Civil War a miserable experience for the people of Haworth.

Although plague disappeared in the mid-seventeenth century, other epidemic diseases remained. Smallpox was endemic, with visitations roughly every seven years, and typhus was another widespread killer which could carry off whole families. Anecdotal evidence suggests that the burial peak in Keighley between 1675 and 1678 was caused by typhus.[30] Yet, though smallpox and typhus were prominent, many more people died of tuberculosis (popularly known as 'consumption'). Another cause of crisis was famine – the harvest failures in 1586 and 1587 show up as high burial totals in the Keighley and Kildwick registers. Across northern England as a whole, by far the worst crisis was in 1623–24, when there was a dramatic increase in the number of deaths across Lancashire and Cheshire and into Cumbria, the West Riding and the Peak District. The cause is still debated, but a combination of famine and disease is likely. Keighley, Kildwick and Colne were all affected, though not among the worst afflicted,[31] and a concentration of twelve Haworth wills in 1623–24 suggests that the chapelry did not escape. By the time of the notorious 'seven lean years' of 1692–99 (conditions in 1698 were particularly bad) many of the inhabitants of Haworth were making cloth and could use cash to buy what they needed, instead of relying on subsistence, but bad harvests could still send up prices to levels which the poor could not afford.

The problems of bad harvests are associated with the steady deterioration in the climate from the early fourteenth century onwards. Average winter temperatures reaching their lowest in the mid-seventeenth century, exacerbating the disruptions of the Civil Wars. In Haworth the spring of 1649 was particularly bad: 'A great Snow fell about ffastens Even, [Shrove Tuesday] the Week following being the 2nd week of the year which continued till the last week of the same winter'. Yorkshire experienced protracted frosts in 1638, 1661, 1684, 1708, 1716 and 1739, but the coldest winter on record was that of 1684–85. The Thames froze solid for six weeks, so imagine what Haworth was like! The rights of turbary, which allowed households to cut peat on the moors, were vital for their survival, but unless peat was in store for the winter it was impossible to dig. Winters could be endured stoically so long as the harvests were good and foodstuffs had been put by, but the notoriously wet summers of 1644 and 1648 must have caused acute hardship to many families. Comments in the parish registers suggest an improvement thereafter, though there were droughts in 1652 and 1657 and the summer of 1658 was very wet.[32]

The seventeenth century saw a catastrophic fall in living standards for a large part of the population. The real wage index in Schofield and Wrigley's *Population History of England, 1540–1840*, calculated on a scale starting at 1,000 in 1500, fell from a peak of 1087 in 1506–07 to 292 in 1596–97 – in other words, a 70 per cent fall in real incomes over the sixteenth century. Real wages remained very low in the first half of the seventeenth century and then began a gradual recovery, to 706 for 1760–61, but the standard of the first decade of the sixteenth century was not achieved again until 1878.[33] The real wage index has its limitations, because evidence was drawn exclusively from southern England. The situation in the north seems to have been even worse in the early seventeenth century but significantly better a century later. Another way of looking at general wellbeing is to consider the longevity of the population. A rough index can be compiled from Haworth wills by counting those which mention grandchildren, indicating that the testator or testatrix lived long enough to see them. The result is a pattern similar to that of the real wage index.

period	total wills	with grandchildren	percentage
1521–1560	21	6	29
1561–1580	17	3	18
1581–1600	29	4	14
1601–1620	46	9	20
1621–1640	34	9	22
1641–1660	23	4	17
1661–1680	36	7	17
1681–1700	29	9	31
1701–1720	31	11	32
1721–1740	42	13	31

The real wages index is based largely on the building trades and does not take into account the experience of other social strata. Sometime between 1710 and 1720 the rector of Keighley, Miles Gale, wrote an account of his parish which provides evidence for a basic population analysis that provides and allows possible comparisons with Haworth.[34] He computed the total population at 1,704, of whom 112 were freeholders. If the usual multiplier of 4.5 per family is used, the freeholder community numbered 509. In his description of the church Gale lists 54 pews and 195 people who rented space in them. The 83 extra families were probably the chief tenants of the manor. They account for another 373 people. The records of the Thanet charity for 1686 show that 20 per cent of the population of Keighley qualified for assistance, while between 1781 and 1792 20 per cent of those buried at Keighley were given free burials because they were poor.[35] This suggests a constant 20 per cent who were in some way and to some extent paupers. This implies about 381 out of the 1,704, leaving us with 451 people, or about 100 families, who were not destitute but not rich enough to rent pew-space. These were the servants, artisans of one sort or another, and labourers. They are the ones the real wage index is measuring. Thus, in the early eighteenth century roughly 50 per cent of the population prospered, 30 per cent were exposed to the vagaries of the economy, and 20 per cent were destitute.

Haworth had no Miles Gale to count the population, but from 1702 onwards the chapel register gives us sufficient baptism data to suggest that the total population was about 800, a good deal more than the taxable population referred to earlier in this chapter. Other evidence confirms that calculations based on tax returns underestimate the population. Bradford church was repewed between 1703 and 1705, and seats or shares of seats were allotted to 92 properties in the township of Haworth. This represented a notional 414 people or just over 50 per cent of the population. In 1704 there were 145 taxpayers, which at 4.5 per family gives a total of 653 people or 82 per cent of the probable population, implying that some 18 per cent were too poor to pay.[36] Of course these are only approximations, but the broad agreement between the figures for Haworth and for Keighley, where we do have a population count and reliable figures, is no coincidence.

Where did the 'extra' people live? Only eight houses were exempt in the 1672 hearth tax, and it is unlikely that there was a large number without hearths. It is possible that they lived at their place of work. The eighteenth-century textile industry required on average ten spinners to supply the yarn for one full-time weaver. In Airedale, William Law, the Keighley innkeeper, organised a pack train which distributed wool to spinners between Keighley and Kendal on the outward trip, collected the yarn on the way back, and then transported it to London. In contrast, at Haworth the larger clothiers apparently employed spinners at a central location. The size and lack of sophistication of Robert Heaton's 1714 inventory suggests that as well as his own family he had servants, spinners and weavers at Ponden, living and working on the premises. When worsted replaced kerseys, clothiers employed combers on the premises, as evidenced by the combing equipment in Adam Wright's inventory. Many of the lesser weavers also employed spinners and carders, making their households larger than the notional 4.5 people.[37]

These extra hands were the people to whom the real wage index applied. In Elizabethan and early Stuart times they suffered acute financial distress and their standard of living only recovered slowly. For Daniel Defoe the area, with its thriving dual economy, was an example to the rest of the country but it was all a matter of comparison.[38] The yeomen freeholders became the clothiers. They were the 'haves', the ones who could afford to buy their land when the manorial lords sold out. The people they employed were the 'have nots', who became landless. And then there were the poor, a steady one-fifth of the population and more in the really bad times. The bequest of David Midgley in 1723, leaving money for the clothing of ten poor children in 'good blue clothes', and the 50s. which Richard Pollard bequeathed in 1735 to be distributed among the poor at Christmas each year, testified to a sense of charity among some more prosperous local people, but this did little to lessen the burden of the poor relief which the community as a whole had to pay.[39] The absence of a gentry class meant that gross examples of conspicuous consumption were less evident here than in the lowlands, but eighteenth-century Haworth society was not as egalitarian as might first appear.

7 The evangelical revival

Decline

On 21 November 1689 Oliver Heywood wrote in his diary that 'Old J. Gawkroger (father to Mr Gawkroger, vicar of Haworth) buryed at Bradford aged 80',[1] thus confirming that Richard Gawkroger was already perpetual curate. Nothing of note happened during his incumbency, and his successor, Timothy Ellison, who followed him in 1702, lasted less than a year. Soon after the induction of *his* successor, William Clifford, disputes flared up with Bradford. Haworth continued to object to paying church rates to Bradford and had made much of the absence of any specific pews, assigned to the chapelry, in the parish church. In 1703 Bradford deciding to repew the whole church, which was not what Haworth wanted at all. Church rates of £24 in 1703, £36 in 1704, and £24 in 1705, were imposed on Haworth as its share of the cost. Those who owned the pews could recoup part of the expense by renting them out, but for the majority of both Anglicans and Dissenters the repewing was an unwelcome expense.[2]

There is no record of any protest by Haworth over the decision to recast and rehang the peal of six bells at Bradford, which led a levy of £48 on the chapelry in 1715, but ten years later there was another row. Until then the parish church had been open to the roof timbers but the vicar, Benjamin Kennet, now proposed to put in a plaster ceiling. This involved considerable costs, because the walls had to be reinforced to take the additional weight. Anticipating opposition, Kennet only advertised the annual meeting as one for auditing the churchwardens' accounts (about which information was not usually circulated to the chapelries) so the decision to proceed was a *fait accompli* before Thornton, Wibsey and Haworth knew what was happening. Legal action followed, and when the case was heard at York, Kennet claimed that he was not obliged to inform the chapelries about his intentions. He was supported by his clerk, Samuel Ward. The strict legal position is unclear but successive witnesses testified that it was the established custom to advertise a parish meeting in all the chapelries whenever any expenditure above the usual rate was intended. This had been done over the repewing and the recasting of the bells, and in the former case the chapelries fought the repewing through five meetings before being outvoted. The cause papers do not tell us what happened, but the rate for 1725 was little different from that in neighbouring years so the chapelries may well have won their case.[3]

William Clifford appears to have been an absentee, leaving the chapelry to be administered by Jeremiah Jackson, one of the Bradford curates. In 1715 Clifford was living at Shelf and had the oath of allegiance tendered to him, indicating that he might have had Jacobite sympathies.[4] His presence would have made little difference to the disputes with Bradford, but he could have exercised a restraining influence over the master and trustees of the grammar school. In 1714 there was an unseemly affair in which the trustees accused the schoolmaster, Timothy Gawkroger, of raping Mrs Martha Appleyard. The depositions are contradictory and they exposed factions among the trustees, but in the absence of the ecclesiastical court's decree the outcome is difficult to determine.[5]

Clifford resigned in 1726 and was replaced as perpetual curate by Isaac Smith, the younger son of Matthew Smith who was the dissenting minister of first Kipping and then Mixenden chapels. Isaac's elder brother John succeeded his father at Mixenden but he himself conformed to the Established Church.[6] At Haworth he made a number of improvements, spending £20 on rebuilding the church barn and providing the church clock (at a cost of £8) but he was chiefly remembered for the strictness with which he held the inhabitants to their financial obligations, collecting his rents with 'vi et armis'.[7] Gawkroger and Clifford both had money of their own but Smith did not, so he may have found difficulty in making ends meet. The income from church lands was £21 a year and the rent charge from Christopher Scott's money another £10,[8] but £31 was insufficient, especially as the perpetual curate had to find his own accommodation. Smith appears to have been the first to live at Sowdens and went through an elaborate though futile procedure to try to establish it as the parsonage.[9]

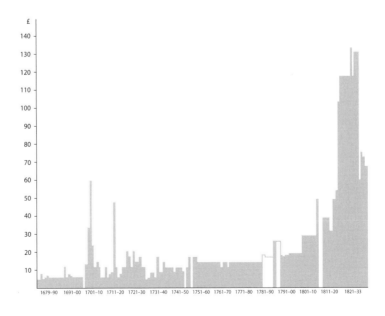

Graph showing the church rate paid by Haworth to Bradford from 1679 to 1833. No figures are available for the years 1701, 1748, 1751, 1811 and 1812. Haworth made no payments during the years 1785–89 and 1791–92.

Shortage of money may well have been why he involved himself in the clandestine marriage market. In his period the Haworth registers include sixteen marriages of couples from outside the chapelry, seven of which are described as 'clog and shoe'. Canon Dixon wrote that 'the fashion of a clog and shoe marriage was that the bride would take off her shoe and the bridegroom his clog. The bride would put her foot in the clog and her partner his foot in the shoe and it was considered a legal marriage if this Lancashire ceremony was performed in the presence of witnesses.'[10] Civil marriages had become common, especially when the Church of England was abolished between 1649 and 1660, and during the persecution of dissenting sects down to 1689. All subsequent efforts to eradicate them failed. The aim of the Haworth couples was probably to avoid the expense of a church wedding but there was one major drawback. Children born of such a marriage were legitimate under ecclesiastical law if the couple subsequently married in church but were always regarded as illegitimate at common law. When a woman who had married by 'clog and shoe' found herself pregnant there was a rush to find a clergyman to grant a license before the child was born.[11] Ironically, though, it was not these marriages which got Smith into trouble but the other nine, registered as being married at Bradford. By issuing cheaper licenses for them Smith was making money at the expense of his vicar. He was suspended from office for the statutory three years on 17 March 1738, services being taken in his absence by John Kighley, one of Bradford's curates. Smith was readmitted on Whitsunday 1741 but died the following December.[12]

Could the Quakers take advantage of the disarray into which the Established Church had fallen? The granting of toleration in 1689 inaugurated their most prosperous period, and they registered James Smith's house in Stanbury as their meeting place. In 1696 the houses of Jonas Smith and William Clayton were also registered. The Laycock group, which included the Stanbury Quakers, became part of the peripatetic Keighley meeting. In 1701 it was resolved that on the middle first day of each three weeks they should meet at Thomas Brigg's house on Calversyke Hill in Keighley. On the first day of the first week they would meet either at Timothy Maud's (Gawthrop Hall) or Richard Shackleton's (Harden), and on the first day of the third week either at John Wade's (Whitley Head, Steeton) or John Smith's (Laycock). On the first day of each three months the quarterly meeting would be at Henry Wood's.[13] Administration of the Keighley and Stanbury burial grounds was centralised. Richard Shackleton of Harden, John Smith of Stanbury and William Davie of Whitley Head held the deeds in turn.[14] The Keighley meeting also contributed to the building of a meeting house at Askwith, where Quakers assembled every quarter,[15] and this in turn was responsible to the main Quaker assembly which met at York.

Quaker influence reached its peak between 1710 and 1730 when the Keighley meeting had around 80 members. In 1723 the Laycock group moved to Stanbury where it met in an upper room at Horton Croft which, in 1905, was occupied by the local schoolmaster, Jonas Bradley.[16] After 1730 there was a sharp contraction. The deaths within a year of Thomas Brigg the younger and Timothy Maud were heavy blows at a time when the strictness of their beliefs was causing dissent within the group. Quakers were already pacifist, but more troublesome was the notion that all people were equal in the sight of God and the insistence that Quakers should only marry among themselves.[17] A small group was meeting in Stanbury as late as 1802 but the majority of those who did not like the Church of England had turned to other creeds for sustenance many years before.

In Haworth the main dissenting group was the Particular Baptists. Baptists objected to the practice of infant baptism on the grounds that it was unscriptural. In an age of high infant mortality, and when most Christians believed that the unbaptised went to Hell, this was regarded as condemning a large part of the population to perdition unheard. Baptist views date back to the early days of the Reformation but there is no evidence for them in Haworth before the late seventeenth century. The seed was planted by William Mitchell of Hebden Bridge, a handloom weaver, and his cousin, David Crosley, an itinerant stone mason. They underwent a conversion experience in 1685 but at the time of Mitchell's visit to Stanbury in 1687 their early preaching resembled that of the 'free grace' movement.[18] In 1692, while on his travels, Crosley was converted to the Particular Baptist faith by the Reverend John Eckells of Bromsgrove in Worcestershire and when he returned to the chapel they had set up at Bacup, Crosley converted Mitchell.[19]

By this time they had a circuit of preaching places in the Pennines, including Haworth. After the 1689 Revolution two nonconformist meetings were established in Haworth. One, at the house of John Rhodes, appears to have been Presbyterian because Oliver Heywood preached there in 1692 but he was no more successful than he had been earlier and it soon disappeared. The other was at North Ives, licensed in 1693 to nine men including Thomas Feather, Michael Pighills, Christopher Holmes and John Moore. The denomination was not stated but it was almost certainly Baptist. The most striking of the nine was John Moore, who was born at Oakworth Hall and had Quakers among his family. He was converted by Mitchell and between 1689 and 1698 was based at Rawdon, where he was described as 'not only a well taught divine and sound doctrinalist, but also an amazing textarian, one "mighty in the Scriptures"'.[20]

Mitchell died in 1707, two years after the Bacup church moved to Cloughfold, and his successor there, Richard Ashworth, set up the Lancashire and Yorkshire Baptist Association. The founding societies were at Liverpool, Cloughfold and Tottlebank-in-Furness in Lancashire, and Barnoldswick, Sutton-in-Craven, Rawdon and Heptonstall Slack in Yorkshire. The Association flourished for a time but the minute book records no more meetings after 1732.[21] Haworth was never registered and the cause seems to have languished after the original foundation. Archbishop Herring's visitation of 1743 records only three dissenting families in Haworth and they were probably Quakers.[22] By 1740, therefore, an uneasy calm prevailed and religious enthusiasm was almost entirely dormant.

Revival

Isaac Smith's successor as perpetual curate was William Grimshaw, born in 1708 at Brindle near Preston and a graduate of Christ's College, Cambridge. He was ordained

William Grimshaw, perpetual curate of Haworth, 1740–63, was a renowned Anglican Evangelical. John Wesley named him as his successor as the leader of the Methodist Movement within the Church of England, but Grimshaw predeceased him. Grimshaw is popularly believed to have put a stop to Haworth races by his prayers.
AUTHOR COLLECTION

in 1730 and preferred to the perpetual curacy of Littleborough in Lancashire. An inability to bring spiritual comfort to parishioners who had lost an only child bred doubts about his beliefs and he experienced deepening depression, at its worst after he moved from Littleborough to nearby Todmorden and exacerbated by the death of his first wife, Sarah, in 1739. When he was inducted at Haworth the worst was over. He had remarried, to Elizabeth Cockcroft, and he was becoming known for the evangelical preaching which was to be his hallmark. The vicar of Bradford, Benjamin Kennet, disliked it and tried to prevent the trustees from selecting Grimshaw, but when he took his case to the ecclesiastical court he lost. The deeds allowed the trustees to reject his candidates and so, reluctantly, Kennet was forced to accept Grimshaw, who was inducted on 16 May 1742.[23] Grimshaw soon justified his selection. His fervent preaching was much to the taste of his new congregation, while his willingness to waive most of the usual dues was a welcome change from Isaac Smith. He was also a conscientious priest, holding services regularly and visiting the whole chapelry. But crisis came one September day in 1744. Grimshaw felt so dizzy when preaching that he had to be helped from the church and was carried to the nearby Black Bull, of which the parish clerk, Jonathan Whitehead, was the proprietor. Grimshaw was laid on a couch in the parlour, his arms and legs so cold that frantic attempts to massage them with hot towels had little effect. Then, quite suddenly, the blood flowed into them and he recovered so completely that he could preach again that afternoon without any ill effects. During his loss of consciousness, though, he had an extraordinary vision in which he saw 'a dark, foul passage into which he must go; and being entered, saw on the right hand a great high wall, on the other side of which was Heaven, and another on the left which was Hell'. He overheard a conversation between God and Christ in which they debated what should happen to him. God was for condemning him to Hell but Jesus pleaded for him, reached down, and drew him up into Heaven. Grimshaw recalled how vivid were the nail holes in his hands and the wound in his side.[24] His vision convinced Grimshaw that a person could be forgiven his sins and that this could happen before his death. Soon he was proclaiming what was to become one of the characteristic doctrines of Methodism with such conviction that in the next 18 months he made 120 conversions.

Before long Grimshaw acquired an ally. William Darney was an itinerant pedlar who roamed the Pennines and was known to everyone as 'Scotch Will'. He may have been the product of an earlier revival in Scotland, led by James Robe, the minister of Kilsyth from 1733 to 1740. Darney founded a series of religious societies, mainly in Rossendale,[25] but at first Grimshaw was reluctant to be seen openly consorting with a pedlar. He arranged some secret meetings, reputedly in a stone quarry just outside Haworth, and soon the two men were working openly together. Darney addressed meetings in Haworth and Grimshaw preached to Darney's societies in Rossendale. As the locals put it, 'Mad Grimshaw has turned Scotch Will's clerk'. One of Darney's peculiarities was that among the wares he offered for sale were hymns written by himself. Many of them glorified his own witness and one had 104 verses in which he reviewed the religious state of every Pennine township in turn. Five are devoted to Haworth.

43. Haworth's a place that God doth own, with many a sweet smile;
    With Power the Gospel's preached therein, which many a one doth feel.
44. Both far and near they hither come, their hungry souls to feed;
    And God from Heaven sendeth down, to them the living Bread.
45. There's many go rejoicing home, in praising of their GOD;
    And want their neighbour's for to come, and taste the heavenly Food.
46. But while the strangers do receive, the Blessing from above,
    There's many near the Church that starve for want of JESUS Love.
47. They do content themselves like Swine to feed on husks and Dirt;
    For all their pleasure is to Sin, and live in Carnal Sport.

It was at this point that the Keighley draper and early Methodist, Thomas Colbeck, first visited Haworth. A firm friendship soon grew up between Grimshaw and Colbeck, the former becoming aware of the small Keighley Methodist society, of the pioneering work of Benjamin Ingham and John Nelson, and of the Wesley brothers. In February 1746 John Wesley visited Keighley for the first time *en route* for Newcastle.[26] He could not spare the extra day necessary to visit Haworth but Colbeck's commendation of Grimshaw was not forgotten. When Charles Wesley visited Keighley in October, Haworth was included in his itinerary. Grimshaw was initially cautious: Wesley was welcomed warmly and addressed an enthusiastic meeting at Sowdens, but was not invited to preach in the church. He soon dispelled Grimshaw's doubts and John Wesley made his first appearance in Haworth church on 1 May 1747, preaching to a large and enthusiastic congregation. Grimshaw persuaded Darney to throw in his lot with the Methodists and the result was an enormous upsurge at Haworth. Grimshaw wrote to John Wesley in November 1747, 'You desire a particular account of the Lord's work here. Indeed, I have the pleasure of assuring you that it never went better, from its first appearance among us as it has done these last two months.'[27] Every Sunday Grimshaw attracted enormous congregations, many people walking across 20 or 30 miles of wild moorland to sit at his feet.

Grimshaw had little difficulty in convincing successive archbishops of York of the validity of his approach. The first he dealt with was William Herring. He wanted a resident clergyman who attended conscientiously to his parochial duties. Grimshaw was a model incumbent. During 1745 Jacobite rebellion Grimshaw showed himself to be a stout supporter of the Hanoverians, which further endeared him to the archbishop (who had raised a regiment to fight the Scots, earning himself the nickname of 'Red Herring').[28] Herring's successor was Matthew Hutton. In 1748 Grimshaw was called before him at Wakefield. 'How many communicants had you at your quarterly sacraments, when you first came to Haworth?' the archbishop inquired. 'Twelve, my Lord,' replied Grimshaw. 'How many communicants have you now at such solemnities'? Grimshaw answered. 'In winter four to five hundred, and sometimes in summer near twelve hundred.' After that revelation Hutton would never again listen to any who tried to traduce the curate of Haworth. Nor were Grimshaw's enemies any more successful under Hutton's successor,

This communion table in the parish church is particularly associated with Reverend William Grimshaw. It is a typical feature of seventeenth- and early eighteenth-century Anglican churches. Note the simple box frame and turned legs. In the background is a plaque dedicated to the memory of the Brontë family.
PHOTOGRAPH: CARNEGIE, 2009

The font from the old Haworth church, now in the graveyard. It is generally associated with William Grimshaw but it must have been used by his successors as well, including Patrick Brontë.
PHOTOGRAPH: CARNEGIE, 2009

Archbishop Gilbert. After Grimshaw had preached before him for two hours, Gilbert took him by the hand and said, 'I would to God that all the clergy in my diocese were like this good man.'[29]

Grimshaw's determination to get as many as possible of his parishioners into church on Sunday morning caused a great stir. John Newton related how 'It is his frequent and almost constant custom to leave the church while the psalm before the sermon was singing, to see if any were absent from worship, and idling their time in the churchyard, the street or the alehouses; and many of those he so found he would drive into church before him. A friend of mine, passing a public house in Haworth, on the Lord's day morning, saw several persons making their escape from it, some jumping out of the lower windows and some over a low wall: he was at first alarmed, fearing the house was on fire; but upon inquiring what was the cause of the commotion, he was told, that they saw the parson coming. They were more afraid of the parson than of a justice of the peace. His reproofs were so authoritative and yet so mild and friendly, that the stoutest sinners could not stand before him.'[30]

Most churches only held communion services once a quarter and at Easter. The communicants notified the minister beforehand and prepared by prayer and heart searchings, often attending a preliminary meeting on the Saturday evening. This was not sufficient for Grimshaw, who introduced regular monthly communions. For him 'the reading of prayers was not a matter of custom or form, to be hurried over merely as a prelude to preaching; he really prayed; and the solemnity of his tone and gesture induced the people, at least apparently, to pray with him.' Once he interrupted a benediction to rebuke worshippers who were already putting on their hats: 'Let your hats alone, they'll stay if you let them.'[31]

Grimshaw knew that the usual learned disquisitions of Anglican preachers would not attract the mass of the population, so on occasion he could thunder like a hellfire sectary. After one sermon his hearers grumbled that he had preached them to Hell and then left them there, yet his belief in free grace for all who genuinely sought it brought hope as well as fear. A striking aspect of his preaching was his use of dialect expressions and phrases. His version of the ram caught in a thicket was 'a tup which had its head fastened in a bunch of briers'. God's blessings were expressed in everyday terms as 'they who have this God for theirs shall never want a pound of butter for eightpence, or three pints of blue milk for a halfpenny so long as they live'. Commenting on their failure to ask a blessing before meals he fulminated, 'You are worse than the very swine, for the pigs will gruff over their victuals but you will say nothing.' He referred to 'dupes and ninny hammers' and remarked resignedly, 'I may talk to you till my tongue is as small as a sparble. You will all go to hell after all.'[32] A sparble, more properly a sparrowbill, was a small nail used in making clogs.

Like all evangelical clergy Grimshaw tried to enforce what he regarded as proper standards of conduct: 'He endeavoured likewise to suppress the generally prevailing custom in country places, during the summer, of walking in the fields on the Lord's day, between services, or in the evening, in companies. He not only bore testimony against it from the pulpit but reconnoitred the fields in person, to detect and reprove delinquents.'[33] He was particularly worried that this custom led to extramarital sexual behaviour. In his early years he cited many of his parishioners before the church courts for fornication, but soon concluded that the limited penalties which the courts could impose were of little deterrent value without the support – rarely forthcoming – of the local magistrates.

Evangelicals objected particularly to the local festivals which they believed led to immorality, drunkenness and gambling. At the Haworth festival on Penistone Moor, cloth was regularly traded for gin. Men gambled away their money, homes and furniture,

Haworth church reputedly dates from 1137, but nothing is left of it. The oldest portion of the present building are the lower stages of the tower, c.1488. The 1488 church was rebuilt in the early seventeenth century, and most of that was absorbed in the alterations made by William Grimshaw, 1756–68. The clock dates this drawing to after 1870, but it shows the Grimshaw aisle (on the left) end on very clearly.

and even their children into service, as they bet on the pony races. All Grimshaw's efforts to stop the festival failed and in 1759 he had to confine himself to prayers in the church. That year it rained for three days on end. The festival with its associated races were abandoned and according to legend they were never held again – forty years later Haworth folk were still relating how 'old Grimshaw put a stop to the races by his prayers'.[34] It is a pity to spoil a good story, but the races did not disappear. They migrated across the valley to Oakworth where the name 'Racemoor Road' is a reminder of the meetings once held there.

Fallout

While some of the Anglican hierarchy quietly condoned the Methodists, the Church was not prepared to accept the movement openly. Within his own parish the minister was very powerful, for nobody could preach in his church without permission, and preaching outside it was illegal unless it took place within the walls of a licensed meeting house or had the consent of the justices of the peace. Licenses were easy to obtain but Wesley was reluctant to avail himself of them, because he would thereby admit to being a dissenter. He had always claimed that he was an orthodox member of the Church of England attempting to reform her from within.

In the summer of 1748 the perpetual curate of the chapelry of Colne was George White, who had been brought up as a Roman Catholic, then apostatised and entered the Church of England. He was a considerable scholar but he had become an alcoholic and was notorious for his long absences. William Grimshaw was well known in the area, for many of his parishioners from Todmorden still journeyed over the bleak moors to Haworth rather than accept the ministrations of his successor, Robert Hargreaves, and he still held house meetings within his old parish. A similar relationship developed with Colne, which had a short common boundary with Haworth. White would neither invite Grimshaw into his pulpit nor minister to his flock, so Grimshaw came and ministered to gatherings in barns and houses unbidden.[35] On 23 August 1748 John Wesley preached to an overflowing church at Haworth and the next morning set off for Roughlee, near Pendle in the chapelry of Colne, accompanied by Colbeck and Grimshaw. The meeting, which was to be addressed by Wesley and Ingham, was broken up by a drunken mob. They were assaulted and Colbeck and Grimshaw were knocked down. Wesley, Colbeck and Grimshaw were hauled before the constable of Barrowford, Robert Hargrave. White attempted to force Ingham and Grimshaw to sign a document promising not to preach within the chapelry of Colne for the space of a year, under a penalty of £50. They refused and were confined in the *Swan Inn*. Fortunately the local justices of the peace refused to support White and Hargrave and the embattled Methodists were released.[36]

At Haworth events took a different course. A 1716 description shows that the church was small – just 51 feet long and 32 feet in width, with 'only two aisles, a row of columns up the middle and three windows at the east end, one opposite to the columns'.[37] A building of this size was completely inadequate for the congregations which Grimshaw was now attracting but the township, burdened with the need to pay church rate to Bradford, insisted that any extensions be paid for out of voluntary contributions. In 1753 the quarter sessions agreed to allow Grimshaw to advertise nationally but it was not until 1756, when he had been incumbent for fourteen years, that enough was raised to add the necessary extra aisle and the galleries on the west and north sides.[38] Most of the money was raised by selling the pew-rights. A list of the occupants for the year in which the alterations were completed reveals that prices depended on which gallery the seats were in and how far back they were. The cheapest were a guinea and the highest price was £15, paid by Thomas Pighells to William Roberts and Joseph Ogden for three seats 'in the Front Pew No.16 in the North Gallery.'[39] The rents did not cover all the cost so economies were made to save money, with important long term consequences. Nevertheless, Grimshaw still had to pay for the shortfall out of his own pocket.

Grimshaw threw himself into the Methodist movement with great enthusiasm. Two days each week were spent within his own chapelry but he was available during the rest for preaching elsewhere.[40] Most of his work was within the Methodist circuit known as the Great Haworth Round, of which he was the treasurer and which stretched from

Methodist Chapel, West Lane. The original chapel was built in 1758, where the chapel car park is now, as a reinsurance against an unpopular perpetual curate. The building was extended and enlarged a number of times, but in 1950 it was found to have dry rot and was demolished. The present building is the old Sunday school.
PHOTOGRAPH: CARNEGIE, 2009

The datestone from the original 1758 Methodist chapel building was subsequently built into the later structure and is now above the porch at the rear. A close inspection of the inscription reveals that it has been altered, and where it would once have read 'This Chapel', it now reads 'The 1st Chapel.'
PHOTOGRAPH: CARNEGIE, 2009

The Caretaker's House. This building may have been attached to the original chapel, as evidenced by the orientation of the stone quoins on the side of the house, which aim towards the now empty land to the left but are curiously truncated.
PHOTOGRAPH: CARNEGIE, 2009

Haworth to Whitehaven in Cumberland. So great was the influence he came to wield that the Wesleys named him as their successor, but he died before them, in 1763, of typhus and a constitution worn out by the double labour of running a parish and incessant circuit preaching.

Grimshaw's dominance forced the Methodists within Haworth to live in his shadow. Even before he met the Wesleys he had been persuaded by William Darney to use lay assistance in running societies, and this produced a crop of excellent class leaders and preachers. There were limits beyond which he would not go – in 1755 news that lay preachers were administering holy communion in other circuits led Grimshaw to make a special trip to Norwich to get the practice stopped, though two of his principal opponents were his own disciples, Jonathan Maskew and Paul Greenwood.[41] In 1758 a Methodist chapel was constructed in West Lane, Haworth, financed by a bequest from an elderly woman. The funds were insufficient, so Grimshaw bought tickets in the national lottery and won one of the prizes. The money was enough to complete the building but the local society was burdened with the debt for some time,[42] and the chapel was hardly used because early Methodists attended Haworth church while there was a sympathetic incumbent.

The graveyard of the West Lane Methodist chapel is built on the old townfield, and looks out over the Worth Valley. Scholes Farm near Oakworth can be seen to the right of the obelisk.

PHOTOGRAPH: CARNEGIE, 2009

Like the Wesley brothers, Grimshaw was an Arminian, believing that God's grace was freely available to all who sought it, and like them he favoured a tightly organised church. Many in Haworth were attracted by the Calvinist doctrine of the elect and were no more prepared to accept the dictates of the Methodist Conference than those of the vicar of Bradford. For them the Particular Baptist movement was their spiritual home. In his early days Grimshaw had little time for the Baptists, recording their children in the Todmorden register with the derisory addition of 'dipper'. Later his attitude changed and though he frequently argued with them he came to regard them as fellow workers in a common cause. His fiercest criticism was that they stole his converts when they should have been concentrating on evangelising those who remained in pagan darkness. Even then he was never bitter, remarking in sadness rather than anger on the number of his chickens who had turned into ducks.[43]

The combination of Grimshaw's determination to adhere to Church of England practice and his remarkable and unusually wide tolerance helped both the Baptists and evangelism in general. Charles Wesley and John Newton, who both attended meetings held in the kitchen at Sowdens, commented on the arguments between those who favoured Methodism and those attracted to the Baptist cause. Visits in 1749, 1750 and 1752 by George Whitefield, known for hell-fire preaching, did not encourage unity. In

1748 a division among Grimshaw's supporters in Haworth led directly to the formation of a new Particular Baptist community under the leadership of James Hartley. The inspiration was the Reverend Alvery Jackson of Barnoldswick, who had been chiefly responsible for keeping the Baptist cause alive in the central Pennines in the difficult years after 1732. He influenced two other Baptists who had attended meetings at Sowdens. Richard Smith became the first pastor of the Particular Baptist Church at Wainsgate outside Hebden Bridge, a daughter church of Barnoldswick, and William Crabtree established a Particular Baptist Church at Westgate in Bradford.[44] By 1752 the Haworth Baptists were strong enough to be able to build a chapel in West Lane.

Sometime between 1750 and 1752, Smith came under the influence of John Johnson, a Baptist minister who took a harsher Calvinist line, and persuaded first Hartley and then Crabtree to join him in adopting Johnson's High Calvinism.[45] Johnson's attitude was not shared by the majority of the Lancashire and Yorkshire Baptist Association so in 1757 Liverpool, Haworth, Bradford, Wainsgate and Bacup seceded and joined the High Calvinist Northern Association of Baptist Churches, based on Hexham. This caused dissension within the Haworth Baptist community and led to the links with Johnson being severed. By 1764 Haworth had rejoined the Lancashire and Yorkshire

Haworth Parsonage, originally built by Rev. John Richardson in 1778. His two predecessors Isaac Smith and William Grimshaw had used the farmhouse at Sowdens. James Charnock, perpetual curate from 1791 to 1819, lived here as did Patrick Brontë, perpetual curate from 1820 to 1861. In 1820 Patrick and Maria Brontë and their six children moved in. After Patrick Brontë's death in 1861 his successor Reverend John Wade added the wing on the right-hand side.

PHOTOGRAPH: CARNEGIE, 2009

Association and during the remainder of Hartley's pastorate it prospered. He was widely respected for his personal qualities, and was an excellent speaker. In 1764 there were 40 individual Baptists in Haworth, but Charles Knowlton, rector of Keighley, admitted that there were some sixty Baptist families in his parish. There was no Baptist chapel in Keighley at this date, so they probably lived in the Oakworth area and attended Haworth chapel. In 1775 the chapel was enlarged, the money being put up by the Greenwoods, a prominent family of clothiers, who had also been among the trustees of the original chapel.[46] In 1760 Grimshaw told John Newton. 'When I first came into this country, if I had gone half a day's journey on horseback towards the east, west, north and south, I could not meet with or hear of, one truly serious person -and now, through the blessing of God on the poor services of the most unworthy of his ministers, besides a considerable number whom I have seen and known to have departed this life, like Simeon, rejoicing in the Lord's salvation; and besides five Dissenting churches or congregations of which the ministers, and nearly every one of the members were first awakened under my ministry; I still have at my sacraments, according to the weather, from three to five hundred communicants ...'[47]

Grimshaw was succeeded by John Richardson, born at Mossgill House, Crosby Garrett, Westmorland.[48] Like Isaac Smith, Richardson came of dissenting parents and though he conformed his niece, Nancy, married George Greenwood of Hull, a member of the most prominent Baptist family in Haworth. Richardson graduated in 1761 and was ordained the following year, beginning his career as curate to Henry Venn, vicar of Huddersfield and the leading Anglican Evangelical in the north. In 1766 Richardson was preferred to the perpetual curacy of Baildon but never resided there. Indeed, he may not have taken up residence at Haworth until after Venn's resignation from Huddersfield in 1771.[49] This would account for Wesley's disappointed comments about the turnout on his visits in 1766 and 1770, which contrast sharply with his note for Sunday 5 July 1772: 'Not half the congregation at Haworth could get into the Church in the morning, nor a third part in the afternoon; so I stood on a kind of pulpit, near the side of the Church. Such a congregation was never seen there before; and I believe all heard distinctly.'[50]

Once he was resident Richardson proved a popular choice. His obituary described him as 'a man of polished manners, of the most unaffected piety and of a mild and amiable disposition.' One of his servants later remembered him 'as a very handsome gentleman, and strong in appearance; generally dressed very neat, and wore a powdered wig, which was fashionable for clergymen at that time and he mostly wore a clerical three-cornered hat, and wore his bands regularly on week days, when visiting his parishioners. He was never married, except to his Church and his people. In his time there was a favourite spot, named Folly Spring, in the valley, adjoining Bridge house, which had one of the strongest springs in the locality, and where a convenient place once stood, as a place to undress in for bathing purposes. In summer time he often bathed in that crystal spring of water.' He did not care for Sowdens and lived initially at Cook Gate, but in 1778 he was responsible for the construction of a new parsonage, the building which now houses the Brontë Museum.

<h1>The pace quickens   8</h1>

Coal and limestone

The previous chapters have considered the changing economic structure of the Haworth area in the seventeenth and eighteenth centuries, and have focused particularly on the development of the textile trades. Although cloth production was undoubtedly the most important, other industries were emerging, and the economic activity had a direct impact upon the infrastructure of transport within Haworth and in its links with the wider world. An increasing burden was placed on the local roads and therein lay major problems. Responsibility for maintaining roads lay with the township, which appointed the highway surveyor and whose inhabitants were obliged to undertake statute labour on the roads each year. The idea of contracting out these irksome obligations was attractive, and in 1738 the principal ratepayers of Haworth made an agreement with Joseph Wood of Hobcoat for the repair of the roads within the chapelry, to be paid for by a rate of 2½d. in the £ for a period of twenty-one years. The scheme was not a success,[1] partly because a major problem related to roads which crossed township boundaries – it only needed one township to be negligent for the work of the others to be negated.

For more important roads the solution was to establish turnpike trusts which undertook to repair and maintain substantial lengths of road. They were entitled to demand work from the inhabitants but, more significantly, could levy tolls on those using the road – the principle of 'user pays' thus superseded 'community pays' on the roads affected. In 1755 a turnpike trust was set up for the road from Bradford through Haworth to Colne. The early impetus came from a group of enterprising Bradford businessmen, interested in trading local coal for the limestone of the upper dales. One of them, Samuel Lister, chaired all the early meetings (the first was at the King's Arms in Haworth) and became clerk and treasurer.[2] It was a difficult scheme, for the road had three major hills on its route, none of which could be easily circumvented. The Bradford interest rapidly evaporated and its entrepreneurs turned to more vehicle-friendly routes up Airedale. Lister became clerk and treasurer of the Keighley–Bradford and Keighley–Halifax trusts, and was replaced in those roles on the Bradford–Colne trust by Rowland Watson, a Keighley lawyer. He and his son, another Rowland Watson, who succeeded

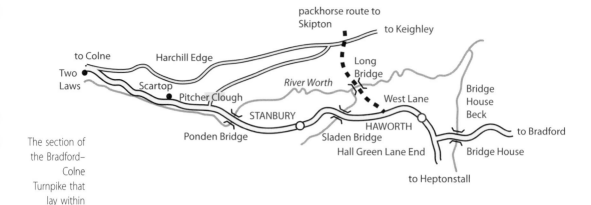

packhorse route to
Skipton

to Keighley

to Colne

Harchill Edge

Long
Bridge

Two
Laws

Scartop

River Worth

Bridge
House
Beck

Pitcher Clough

West Lane

STANBURY

to Bradford

HAWORTH

Ponden Bridge

Sladen Bridge

to Heptonstall

Hall Green Lane End

Bridge House

him in 1776, were to be the trust's key administrators. The usual method of financing repairs was to persuade a number of wealthy men to advance money on the security of the future tolls. In this way £1,000 was raised to start work on the Bradford–Colne trust; of this, £450 came from a Leeds businessman, William Baynes, but the rest was raised in Haworth. Joseph Midgley, the lord of the manor, contributed £325 – he had land in Haworth and Oldfield which bordered on the road. John Greenwood, a textile manufacturer whose premises were alongside the road at Bridgehouse in Haworth, gave £125, and £100 was contributed by William Grimshaw, the curate.[3]

Packhorse bridge over the river Worth, known locally as 'Long' Bridge. Note the typical 'hump back' necessary to support the central keystone. This bridge was used by packhorse trains from Calderdale to reach Airedale without using the Bradford–Colne turnpike.

© KEIGHLEY LIBRARY

Contracts were placed for the tollhouses and repairs were put in hand. A shop in Stanbury, owned by Joseph Midgley, obstructed the road and was demolished, and three stretches of road were identified as being in particular need of repair: from Bridgehouse in Haworth to Stump Cross; from Scartop to Two Laws; and from Chellow Height to the low corner of Cullingworth Field. By the time these had been brought up to a proper standard credit was already exhausted: the minutes for 30 July 1755 record that £1,399 9s. 4½d. had been spent. Toll revenues were never large and henceforth the trust only responded to criticism when complaints were made to the quarter sessions. Stanbury Lane was repaired in 1771 and the road around Ponden in 1775. In 1767 orders were given for the widening of the road between Stanbury and Haworth and the reconstruction of Sladen bridge, but Bridgehouse bridge was the responsibility of the West Riding magistrates and a complaint about its narrowness led to its complete rebuilding in 1771.[4]

Enforcing payment of the tolls was a continual headache, with problems at every gate. The position of that at Two Laws, west of Stanbury, caused endless debate. The main route from Keighley to Colne ran through Oakworth and along Harehill Edge to join the Bradford-Colne turnpike at Two Laws. If the gate were positioned on the Stanbury side, traffic from Keighley to Colne could evade payment, but if it were on the Colne side, traffic from Haworth and Stanbury to Keighley could avoid tolls. In any case, traffic from Keighley to Haworth could readily evade payment by using the track through Pitcher Clough and Oldfield, rejoining the Harehill road at Pickles Hill. The trustees tried to solve this problem by setting up an additional gate in Stanbury, which brought protests from the inhabitants, who accused them of charging for the use of the village street and for driving cattle into the surrounding fields. Haworth presented similar problems. In 1759 a toll gate was erected in West Lane but an entry in the minute book for 1763 shows that it had been moved to opposite the *Black Bull* in Main Street. On 7 December 1763 it was resolved that it should be moved again, to 'some convenient place between that place and Hall Green End'. Later in the century the gate was moved back to West Lane and in 1777 the trust was forced to refund 14s. to the collector, William Rushworth, for 'Loss sustained by him for want of a Barr leading to Heptonstall.'[5]

A main source of income was traffic in lime, carried on packhorses from Lothersdale through Cowling and Slippery Ford, across the Worth at Long Bridge and then along the turnpike at West Lane. The hollow way and parts of the stone packhorse causeway can still be traced at Oldfield Gate and Lumbfoot near Long Bridge. Instead of going along the turnpike into Haworth the packhorses continued through Upper Marsh and Old Oxenhope and then turned up the old road to the Calder valley, thus avoiding tolls altogether. Cattle drovers took similar avoiding action. As late as the mid-nineteenth century George Sowden reported seeing herds being driven across the moors from Airedale into Calderdale.[6] Another important source of revenue was coal from the pits at Denholme. The most important gate for tapping the coal trade was at Hewenden Brow, east of Cullingworth, and there were continual problems around Wilsden. In Haworth

Bodkin Lane. This was one of the old roads over to Calderdale before the construction of the Lees to Hebden Bridge turnpike in 1813. Bodkin Farm can be seen to the right. Note the narrowness of the road. They were known as 'causeys', or causeways, and they were not designed for wheeled traffic – you either walked or rode! The local clothiers used to walk beside their Galloway horses which were loaded with their cloth pieces. The route was a favourite one of cattle drovers, too, as well as those taking lime from Lothersdale.

PHOTOGRAPH: CARNEGIE, 2009

it made no sense to use the packhorse trail from Cullingworth, crossing Bridgehouse Beck at 'Donkey' bridge and joining the Lothersdale trail near North Ives. Little coal would have gone that way to the Calder valley. The extent to which the turnpike was used for the carriage of coal and lime is indicated by the number of people who paid an annual lump sum charge of £8 instead of individual tolls.

Complicated arrangements were made to ensure that nobody paid twice. In 1772 the trust proposed that half-tolls should be paid at two successive gates in three combinations: (1) Ling Bob at Wilsden, and Haworth; (2) Two Laws, and Haworth; or (3) Hewenden, and Ling Bob. The plan failed and instead a ticket system was substituted, to pacify objectors (particularly those from Stanbury). There was still abuse: an entry in the minute book for 14 May 1803 instructs toll bar keepers that 'full tolls for carts, carriages and horses going to or returning from Denholme Coal Pits with Coals, shall be paid at the first bar they shall pass'. Little repair work could be done because the income from the tolls, never very great, soon stagnated. Toll farmers did not stay long and court proceedings often had to be taken to recover the money from them. Thomas Howgate was committed to York Castle in 1773 and in 1781 the clerk took action against John Butterfield and Jeremiah Smith. Legal action was threatened against Thomas Sugden in 1806.[7] In 1776 the turnpike had outstanding loans totalling £2,205 2s. 6d. on which the accumulated interest was £477 7s. 4¼d., and many creditors had been paid nothing for five years or more. Bradford interest had disappeared altogether, because by 1777 the Leeds and Liverpool Canal was open as far as Skipton and it was easier to trade coal for limestone from Skipton.

Neither had there ever been much involvement at Colne. The only landowner there

Lords of the Manor of Oxenhope 1587–1999. In 1587 the Lord of the Manor of Oxenhope was Edmund Eltoft. He was succeeded by his son Thomas who was lord until at least 1614. By 1629 the manor had been sold to Edward Slater. He in his turn sold it to William Batt in 1665. The later history of the manor is tangled. It appears to be as follows:

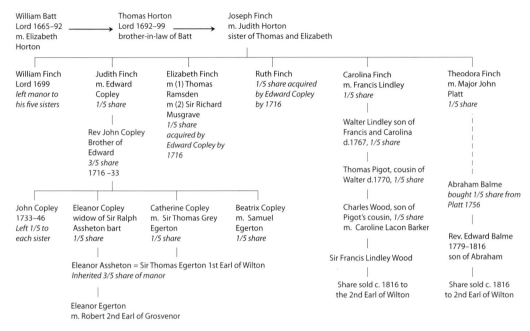

William Batt
Lord 1665–92
m. Elizabeth
Horton

Thomas Horton
Lord 1692–99
brother-in-law of Batt

Joseph Finch
m. Judith Horton
sister of Thomas and Elizabeth

William Finch
Lord 1699
left manor to
his five sisters

Judith Finch
m. Edward
Copley
1/5 share

Rev John Copley
Brother of
Edward
3/5 share
1716–33

Elizabeth Finch
m (1) Thomas
Ramsden
m (2) Sir Richard
Musgrave
1/5 share
acquired by
Edward Copley by
1716

Ruth Finch
1/5 share acquired
by Edward Copley
by 1716

Carolina Finch
m. Francis Lindley
1/5 share

Walter Lindley son of
Francis and Carolina
d.1767, *1/5 share*

Thomas Pigot, cousin of
Walter d.1770, *1/5 share*

Charles Wood, son of
Pigot's cousin, *1/5 share*
m. Caroline Lacon Barker

Sir Francis Lindley Wood

Share sold c. 1816 to
the 2nd Earl of Wilton

Theodora Finch
m. Major John
Platt
1/5 share

Abraham Balme
bought 1/5 share from
Platt 1756

Rev. Edward Balme
1779–1816
son of Abraham

Share sold c. 1816
to 2nd Earl of Wilton

John Copley
1733–46
Left 1/5 to
each sister

Eleanor Copley
widow of Sir Ralph
Assheton bart
1/5 share

Catherine Copley
m. Sir Thomas Grey
Egerton
1/5 share

Beatrix Copley
m. Samuel
Egerton
1/5 share

Eleanor Assheton = Sir Thomas Egerton 1st Earl of Wilton
Inherited 3/5 share of manor

Eleanor Egerton
m. Robert 2nd Earl of Grosvenor

c.1816, the entire Manor of Oxenhope in trust for her son 2nd Earl of Wilton

The manor was bought by Joseph Greenwood from the Earl of Wilton in 1833. As a result of Greenwood's bankruptcy in 1853 it was sold to one Captain J.P. Edwards of Fixby, who also acquired the adjoining property at Castle Carr in Warley. In 1877 the manor and Castle Carr passed into the hands of Joseph Laycock of Low Gosforth, Northumberland, and from him to John Murgatroyd in 1901. In 1999 the manor was in the hands of a Mr Frank Scholefield.

to take an interest was Richard Emmott, and he had another estate in Haworth. The Ramsdens had married into the Hawksworth and Fawkes families, inheriting large estates on condition that they adopted the name of the family into which they married. In 1750 they sold their property in Haworth to the Emmotts. Included in the sale was the hall, which became known as Emmott Old Hall although the Emmotts never lived there. Richard Emmott loaned the turnpike trust around £100 but probably wished he had not, because in 1779 he was owed nine years' interest. Although parliament renewed the trust in 1781 for another 22 years, there was even less local involvement. The quorum was reduced from nine to seven but Watson found the greatest difficulty in getting anyone to attend meetings.[8]

In 1771 proposals were put forward for enclosing what remained of the moors and wastes of Oxenhope. Reaching agreement took a long time and the final award was not made until eight years later, in 1779. The main reason for the enclosure, and the cause of delay, was continual encroachment on the wastes. For example, an agreement was concluded between the freeholders of Near Oxenhope in 1730 not to exercise their rights of turbary on the Marsh, but in 1760 it was challenged by James Ogden. When he proceeded to encroach by building a cottage, the agreement could only be maintained by George Greenwood of Moorhouse undertaking to buy the cottage from him.[9] In 1773 the enclosure commissioners ruled that encroachments made within the last thirty years were part of the wastes, so the contemporary maps show the extent of the moors in the 1740s rather than after the 1770s.[10] At enclosure one-sixteenth of the moors and wastes were allotted to the lords of the manor, in lieu of mineral rights and corn mill rents. The rest was divided among the freeholders in proportion to the valuation of their holdings, provided that they had deeds entitling them to rights of turbary and digging stone for their own use.

The Oxenhope enclosure was one of a series of moorland enclosures which took place around Bradford, allegedly the result of the need to feed the town's fast-growing population. In the case of the Oxenhope award such a purpose seems unlikely. Stanbury's moors had been in the hands of its freeholders since the early seventeenth century and there is no evidence of an increasing trade in foodstuffs there.[11] Parts of Black Moor in Far Oxenhope provided good pasture, as did some of the area enclosed in Near Oxenhope, but the Great Moor was of poor quality. James Charnock, Haworth's perpetual curate in 1801, considered that the old enclosures 'are very capable of producing abundant crops', but that the tenants were not interested. He concluded that it was 'lamentable that the general methods of cultivation are not resorted to here'.[12]

The most likely motive was the search for coal, as deposits had been found in areas near Denholme and in South Dean.[13] In 1665 the manor of Oxenhope was bought by William Batt from Edmund Slater for £500. After Batt's death it was sold to Thomas Horton of Barkisland, whose son William passed his interest to Joseph Finch of Westenhanger in Kent. Finch's son William had five daughters, each of whom inherited a fifth of the manor. At the time of his death in 1716 Edward Copley had acquired three-fifths of the manor, which he willed to his brother John and then to his nephew and his nephew's heirs. By 1746 both the brother and the nephew were dead and at the time of the enclosure this three-fifths share had descended to Lady Eleanor Assheton, and to Sir Thomas Egerton and Samuel Egerton, her brothers-in-law. Another fifth had descended via Sir Francis Lindley to Charles Wood, and the last fifth was bought from the remaining heir by Abraham Balme.[14] Sir Thomas Egerton owned an estate in Heaton near Manchester, which had collieries, while Charles Wood was the owner of Bolling Hall. He was a naval captain and away from home for long periods, so the estate was managed by his wife, Caroline. Bolling also had coal pits. Abraham Balme had been agent at Bolling during the time of Wood's predecessor, Thomas Pigot. He owned property in Denholme and was one of the same business group as Leach and Lister. Although coal was sought by these owners, and some thin seams were found, there was nothing worth exploiting. Most of the moorland, apart from the stone quarries, soon became game preserves.

Worsted

By 1740 the manufacture of worsted cloth had become general and every group of houses had its family of clothiers. The most important were the Greenwoods, who settled in the township in about 1692 when John Greenwood bought the property at Bridgehouse which was to be the family centre until 1848. His cloth making business prospered and in 1716 he bought three closes on the north side of Mill Hill and the following year a messuage called Stubbin, both near to Bridgehouse.[15] John had three sons who survived to maturity. The eldest, John II, was born in 1696. He married Elizabeth, daughter of George and Susanna Taylor of Stanbury, who were already active in the worsted business. John I continued to accumulate property and in 1727 bought two cottages on Haworth Common from James Moon, grocer, and Isaac Mitchell. In 1729 he granted Stubbin and another messuage, Hawkcliff Scarr, to his second son, William. The youngest son, James, was living on land owned by his father at Braithwaite near Keighley. He was also left property at High Binns in Far Oxenhope.[16]

By the time John I died in 1738 his eldest son already had four sons of his own and was probably running the cloth business with him. John II prospered greatly. In 1746 Bridgehouse was described as 'a capital messuage newly erected.', though the new house, a handsome two storey building, was grafted onto an earlier structure and its Georgian front may have been added later. In 1753 John II's in-laws upgraded their property, building what is misleadingly called the Manor House in Stanbury. Two years later John II invested £125 in the turnpike, he had interests in lead mines at Grassington,[17] and he extended the family's land-holdings. In 1705 the elder John Holmes moved to Yeadon but he still held five messuages in Oxenhope. His son, no more enamoured with the place than his father, was described as John of Eldwick. In 1738 the family finally sold its holdings, three of the five messuages being purchased by John Greenwood II and then passed on to his third son, William. John also bought an estate at Moorhouse, eventually inherited by his fourth son, George, and also property at Lowertown. John II, John III, William and George were all involved in the textile trade.

We know most about William Greenwood of Old Oxenhope because a ledger covering the years 1762–79 has survived, together with a detailed inventory.[18] He was a master worsted spinner and began with wool provided by his father. He worked with his brothers John III and George, all three attending markets themselves and sometimes dividing the labour among them. Once the wool had been bought it was washed and cleaned. Between November 1761 and October 1762 Greenwood used 540 lbs of British soap in scouring 5,400 lbs of sheep and lambs wool. The merchant who supplied most of the soap and oil was Thomas Hardcastle of Bradford. The wool was then combed – Greenwood's inventory lists 12 pairs of combs and eight combing stocks in his combing shop – and then put out to be spun.

The ledger does not allow us to calculate the number of spinners but at one point Greenwood had 1282 lbs of tops out. Some spinners might have been local, but Greenwood, like other master spinners, had to spread his net widely. He was also

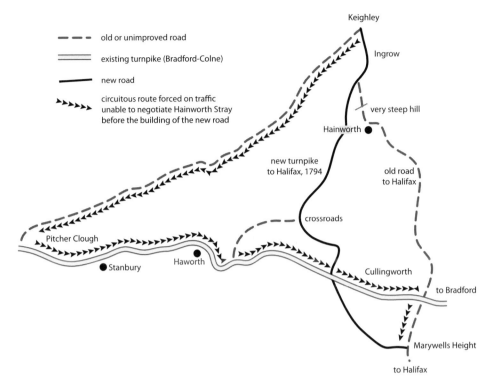

responsible for dyeing the wool, which could be either at the same time as the washing or when the yarn was returned from the spinners. His dyewares included logwood, pearchwood, cochineal, orchel and indigo. When he died Greenwood had a winding shop full of 'soap, allum, noils, wheels and swift stocks', an 'outwarehouse' containing 'soap and seville oil', a dyers' warehouse with dyeing stuff and a millhouse with 'dyeing ingredients'. Unfortunately the ledger does not list sales of worsted yarn so building up a complete picture of his business is difficult.

William was also a farmer. The estimated value of his animals, crops and equipment was £81 17s. 6d., but this was dwarfed by the total of his assets, which was no less than £4,333 5s. 4d., an exceptionally large sum. Even when liabilities are taken into account, farm goods were less than 5 per cent of the net worth of the estate. Sigsworth comments, correctly, on the frugality of Greenwood's way of life, his personal possessions being valued at less than his farm goods, but he had a better lifestyle than practically anyone two generations earlier. No inventory before 1750 lists any pictures, but Greenwood had two in his housebody, together with two maps, five pictures in the parlour and seven in his 'Sun chamber'. He was deeply religious and possessed a very valuable bible worth £1 10s. and other books worth 5s. In 1748 the Greenwoods were among those who supported James Hartley rather than William Grimshaw, and when the chapel was built in West Lane in 1752 they were prominent subscribers. John, James and William Greenwood were among the first trustees.[19]

There is much less information about John II and John III at Bridgehouse. They certainly did their own dyeing, as John II's inventory of 1770 lists a mill specially constructed to grind indigo.[20] In 1763 John II had called himself a 'shalloon maker' but John III's 1790 inventory shows that he too had become a specialist worsted spinner.[21] The family was more interested in the wool-stapling end of the business than in cloth sales. At first William Greenwood of Stubbin was the family's woolstapler, but after his death in 1762,[22] they probably employed the Haworth grocer and woolstapler, William Helliwell, who died in 1768.[23] In 1773 Ann Greenwood, daughter of John III, married William Hardcastle, a Bradford woolstapler,[24] and the next year her sister Elizabeth married William, son of William Blakey, a wealthy Keighley woolstapler. Unfortunately Blakey and his father died within a year of each other in 1776–77, while Hardcastle was a partner in the first Bradford Bank, which collapsed in 1781. Another of John III's daughters, Rebecca, married William North, who dealt mainly in soap and oil but whose 1791 obituary also described him as a woolstapler.[25]

George Greenwood at Moorhouse held an estate which had been occupied by the Tillotson family, who ran their own textile business but had borrowed substantial sums of money from the Greenwoods. In 1740, when they were unable to pay it back, John Greenwood distrained on their goods.[26] They traded across country through York, and the Greenwoods may have acquired their contacts and goodwill because they attended wool markets there and at Bradford and Halifax. The Greenwood family's interests also reached out across the North Sea. William's fourth son, George, became a merchant in Hull and one of his daughters, Sarah, married another Hull merchant, John Carlile. Her brother and her husband traded together with Russia – on 3 March 1804 the *Halifax Journal* advertised the fast sailing ship *Oxenhope* which regularly made voyages to Elsinore and St Petersburg.[27]

The Heatons were another important textile family. Robert Heaton IV died in 1714, leaving the business to his son, Michael. Subsequently, Michael's eldest son, Robert V, was apprenticed as a comber, while Michael himself was sufficiently wealthy to raise £1,200 for a dowry when his daughter Ann married John Greenwood III of Bridgehouse.[28] When Michael died in 1746 young Robert was only 20, and for a time lived with his sister at Bridgehouse.[29] In September 1756 Robert V married Elizabeth, daughter of Henry Greenwood of Robertshaw in Heptonstall. She died early in the following year but Robert quickly remarried, to Mary, daughter of Joshua Shackleton of South Dean, Stanbury.[30] Arrangements had already been made to terminate the tenancy of Ponden's occupant, Thomas Simpson, before the death of Heaton's first wife, and Robert returned to Haworth, where his son, Robert VI, was born on 3 October 1758.[31]

Heaton's ledgers are more complete than those of William Greenwood. The first begins in 1749 when he was 23 and just out of his indentures. It shows him already operating as a master worsted spinner. Most of his wool and oil was bought in Bradford but he dealt with a variety of woolstaplers. From 1770 onwards he bought regularly from Abraham Bowers & Co., and was also a good customer of William Hardcastle until the latter's bankruptcy, when he switched to Hustler and Peckover.[32] Heaton was a comber himself and he employed combers at Ponden. His yarn was put out to be spun and in the 1760s his agent, John Ivens, was dealing with some forty spinners at Sawley, Rimington, Chatburn and Downham beyond Pendle. Later ledgers show his agent delivering wool and collecting yarn at Long Preston, Giggleswick and Rathmell. Many of his tenants paid off part of their rents by spinning for him. Unlike Greenwood, Heaton was also a manufacturer and put the yarn out to be woven into cloth, mainly to weavers around Trawden and Colne.[33] Most of the cloth was sold through Halifax but Heaton used other markets including Leeds and Bradford, and in the 1760s there are references to sales to 'bro. John Greenwood'.[34] Heaton usually did his own dyeing and we learn of 'fine red edged' shalloons selling at 42s. each in 1764 and 'blew lists'. Some merchants preferred to dye the cloth themselves. Between 1777 and 1783 a London firm, Messrs. Jones, Havard and Jones, ordered fine shalloons from Heaton in batches of thirty pieces which were 'delivered … for their use to Ab[raha]m. Meller, the dyer, in Halifax'.[35] After 1783 shalloons disappear to be replaced by russells, dinims, twilled lastings, plainbacks, drawboys, derroons and a myriad others. Analysis of the ledgers shows an upward trend in business from 1761 to 1791, with 1785 the peak year.[36]

Cotton

Improvements in spinning and weaving in the cotton industry were faster than those in woollens and worsteds. John Kay's flying shuttle of 1733 and James Hargreaves's spinning jenny of 1764, both of which were useable in domestic production, were followed by Richard Arkwright's water-frame for spinning, which was only suitable for water-powered factories. Arkwright's first successful spinning mill was at Cromford in Derbyshire (1774) and within a decade factory entrepreneurs were active in the West Riding. In 1780 Low Mill in Keighley, built as a speculation by Thomas Ramsden of Halifax, was quickly occupied by Clayton and Walshman, who began spinning cotton on water frames there under license from Arkwright.[37]

The Greenwoods waited until Arkwright's patents were broken before starting cotton-spinning at Bridgehouse. The mill there was spinning cotton by 1785 because in that year Brookes Priestley, John III's son-in-law, insured his stock for £300.[38] John III died in 1790 and in 1793 his son James insured Bridgehouse and its contents as a cotton mill for £600, but he took little direct interest in cotton spinning, contenting himself with letting space on a 'room and power' basis. In 1803 William Ellis had 25 operatives there spinning cotton. The Heatons were slower off the mark but ended by committing themselves to cotton more fully than the Greenwoods. John Heaton of Birks was building a cotton-spinning mill at Springhead in 1786, when he bought iron rods for it from Kirkstall forge. He also built a house and cottages, employed handloom weavers, and was a regular visitor to Manchester where he sold cotton pieces and bought his raw cotton.[39] In 1801 he insured the mill and contents for £600 and the 1803 returns show that he had 40 employees. He died in 1804 and the firm continued as Dinah Heaton and Sons, cotton twist spinners, dealers and chapmen.

During the 1770s the Ponden branch of the family focused on manufacturing worsted pieces but they carefully monitored what was happening. Between 1777 and 1783 they were selling pieces to Jones, Havard and Jones of London, who paid them with bills drawn on Ann Illingworth & Co.[40] The Illingworths were drapers, grocers and provision merchants in Keighley and were also involved in the Castle, West Greengate and Grove cotton mills. In 1781 Robert Heaton VI married Elizabeth, daughter of John and Sarah Murgatroyd of Roydhouse, and all his older children were born there.[41] The Murgatroyds were also worsted manufacturers, but in 1791 Robert and his father-in-law joined the rush to produce cotton, building a mill at Roydhouse. At the same time Robert's father was erecting a cotton mill at Ponden. The two branches of the family were clearly working together, both using John Brigg of Keighley to cut their brasswork. They also encountered much the same initial difficulties. The outbreak of war with France in 1792 caused a trade depression. Work at Roydhouse slowed down – the mill was still being fitted with machinery as late as 1795 – and although Ponden had enough space for sixteen water frames it appears that only six were in operation. When the elder Robert Heaton died in 1794, Robert VI inherited Ponden Mill as well. In 1795 the mill

The first mill on this site was built by Robert Heaton VI for cotton spinning and it was run by the family until 1813. Cotton spinning continued until 1840, when the mill was converted to worsted. Ponden then had a variety of owners until it closed down in 1973. Since then it has been revived by Barry Brookfield as a mill shop, and 'Ponden Mill' fabrics have become widely known. The photograph dates from 1968 and shows the mill from a vantage point near Two Laws.

burned down but Robert and his younger stepbrother William quickly rebuilt it with the aid of the insurance money. In 1799 William left the business to become a cotton broker in Liverpool. The new mill and its contents were insured for £1,450 and by 1811 all 16 frames had been installed.[42]

The change from worsted to cotton spinning may also have inspired the alterations to Ponden Hall, which are very visible from the outside. During the eighteenth century the low end was used for textile production, the ground floor being occupied by a comb shop and a storage area and the first floor serving as a loom shop. Robert Heaton V only made cosmetic changes affecting the fenestration of the housebody, but once the mill was fully operational it was no longer necessary for the house to be used for cloth production. In 1801 Robert VI had the whole of the low end refaced and a grand pedimented porch was built in front of the cross passage. The other end was blocked to prevent draughts, an alternative rear exit being provided through the back room of the low end. The Hall was extended by an extra bay which apparently housed a stable and a hay loft after.[43]

The remaining suitable mill sites on the Worth were soon occupied. In 1791, the year that Roydhouse and Ponden were completed, another cotton mill began operation at Mytholmes near the confluence of the Worth and Bridgehouse Beck. The Kirkstall Forge records show that it was occupied for a number of years by the partnership of John

James Greenwood Senior and his wife, Martha Clapham. During his time as head of the Bridgehouse textile dynasty, Greenwood converted the business from cotton spinning to worsted manufacturing, building both the Upper and Lower Mill there (since demolished). Martha was a member of the Keighley Clapham family which owned Aireworth mill.

and Lupton Wright, William Newsholme and Robert Sugden. In 1803 the mill had 45 employees. Griffe Mill, on the Worth below Ponden, where it passes between Stanbury and Oldfield, was begun in 1791 by the firm of Hollings and Ross. There is confusion over the early history of Hollings Mill, some giving Michael Cousin, the original owner of the land, as its builder, others James Robinson to whom it was mortgaged in 1793 and yet others to William Hollings. By 1815 its tenant was Thomas Lister.[44] In 1797 the last suitable site at Lumbfoot was used for a mill owned by Joseph Wignall of Keighley and tenanted by Jonas Turner and John Rishworth.

It is easy to forget that until the 1830s most of the textile processes took place outside the new mills. The career of John Kitson illustrates the relationship between cotton-spinning and the worsted trade, which remained the most important source of employment. He was born on 1 September 1781, but his father enlisted as a soldier and never returned, so the family was destitute. In 1786, aged only five, John began spinning (probably worsted) at home. More money could be earned in the new mills and two years later he went to work for Blakeys at Bridgehouse, spinning cotton. In about 1791 he moved to Mytholmes, where Wrights, Sugden and Newsholme worked their machinery 24 hours a day, using their children in two shifts. Kitson worked for three years on the night shift and then spent two more making up twist. However, he was a capable young man and in 1797, aged sixteen, he left the mill to learn the trade of a weaver. For the next five years he worked for James Greenwood of Bridgehouse as a handloom weaver, producing worsted cloth. In 1802 he persuaded Greenwood to allow him to change to combing and he spent the rest of his working life employed at Bridgehouse as a woolcomber.[45]

The building of cotton mills in the Worth valley stimulated a demand for better roads, which could be used by wagons and coaches. The climb of the Keighley-Halifax turnpike up Hainworth Shaw was fearsome, so most vehicles took the longer route along Harehill Edge and the Bradford–Colne turnpike. The owners of the new mills along the river sponsored a further turnpike, through Ingrow and up past Barcroft end, rejoining the old line of the Keighley–Halifax road at Manywells Height. The first meeting to consider the new road was held on 15 December 1789 and the route was opened to traffic on 30 January 1794.[46]

The road through Colne was very suitable for cotton twist manufacturers when they were selling their yarn to the handloom weavers of north-east Lancashire, but was indirect when they wanted to go to Manchester to purchase raw cotton. There was considerable local support for a more direct link through Haworth and Oxenhope to Hebden Bridge. Since the opening of the road from Ingrow, traffic through Haworth avoided Haworth Brow by going through Lees and joining the Keighley–Halifax road at Crossroads. The inevitable result was that the volume of traffic damaged Sykes Lane and made it almost impassable.[47]

The existing road to Hebden Bridge ran from the Bradford and Colne turnpike at Hall Green through Near Oxenhope and over Stairs into Crimsworth Dean. The road, now known as 'the Old Road', then crossed the valley above Kitling Clough, climbed

The New Road to Hebden Bridge, 1814.

Bradford–Colne turnpike

Lees

Haworth

Stanbury

Moor House Lane

The old road from Haworth
to Hebden Bridge
via Stairs

Oxenhope

Brooks meeting

Bodkin Lane

Top of Stairs

Leeds–Hebden Bridge
turnpike

Pecket Well

Old Town

Hebden Bridge

through Pecket Well and reached Hebden Bridge by way of Old Town. There seems to have been a proposal to turnpike this route: on 5 February 1765 the Wadsworth township surveyor recorded in his accounts that he 'Paid for 5 days making turnpike road at Top of Stairs 1s.–6d. = 7s.–6d'. However, the idea was not followed up and in 1771 the freeholders at the Haworth end made an agreement with the highway surveyor for the repair of the road in Near Oxenhope, from the Haworth boundary at Stubbing to Brooks Meeting gate, though this was not the most heavily trafficked section. In 1799 Haworth was presented at quarter sessions for failure to repair 300 yards of the Keighley–Heptonstall road from Mill Bridge to Sykes Lane.[48]

A new turnpike was planned in 1813, disregarding most of the old road because it was largely causeway, which would have to be widened, and had unacceptable gradients where it crossed Crimsworth Dean. The alternative road began on the Bradford–Colne turnpike at the edge of Haworth hamlet and then ran along the opposite side of Oxenhope Beck. From Lowertown it climbed onto the moor and then stayed on high land as far as Pecket Well, where it crossed the old road and descended directly, with easier gradients, into Hebden Bridge. The turnpike, which was designed by Hiram Craven of Dockroyd, was a considerable engineering achievement and it is unfortunate that few details have survived of its construction and operation. A new coach, the 'Enterprise', began the first direct service between Manchester and Keighley, via Rochdale, Todmorden and Hebden Bridge, the daily journey taking five hours.[49] Previously travellers had to change at Halifax. The road improved communications between Keighley, Haworth and Calderdale and helped to create the industrial villages of Oxenhope and Pecket Well.[50] After the Bradford–Colne trust was renewed for a second time in 1803 it was allowed to raise its tolls, and revenue reached a peak of £269 in 1805. It then fell steadily, to only £190 in 1819. In contrast, the tolls of the Hebden Bridge road were let in 1818 for £298.[51]

The textile revolution in Haworth 9

Factory spinning

Even at the height of the cotton boom the amount spun in the new mills was small compared with the domestic production of worsted yarn, not least because the distance from Manchester put all the firms in the West Riding at a disadvantage. The quest to apply water power to the spinning of worsted yarn began – the earliest documented worsted mill being at Dolphinholme near Lancaster in 1784. A draft agreement of 1781, between John Greenwood III of Bridgehouse, his son-in-law Brookes Priestley of Bridgehouse, and Thomas Lawson, clockmaker, refers to an engine to spin worsted by water power which was said to be 'far advanced',[1] but it was apparently unsuccessful and although John Greenwood III may have been spinning worsted at Bridgehouse when Blakey and Lomax were spinning cotton there, the first purpose built worsted mill in the district did not begin production until 1788. It was at Midgeholme and was operated by Michael Pighills.[2]

The yarn spun in all these mills was of poor quality and the crucial breakthrough did not come until 1800, when Michael Greenwood of Halifax invented the false reed or slay.[3] The new device prompted a major increase in the number of worsted mills. Most of the suitable sites on the upper Worth were already occupied, so attention turned to Oxenhope and Bridgehouse Becks. A mill was built at Dunkirk in 1798 and was soon occupied by Bernard and James Hartley,[4] while in 1801 Oxenhope cornmill was adapted for worsted spinning by James Ackroyd, who described himself as corn miller and worsted spinner.[5] Fisher's Lodge, often known as Rushworth Mill, was built for spinning in about 1808: its datestone is inscribed with the text 'Repent no grievances, but Study to be quiet, and mind your own business'.[6] A small mill at Bodkin Bottom is marked on an 1818 map of Oxenhope. William Greenwood's mill at Old Oxenhope was not on the beck but had a water wheel supplied from springs on Haworth Moor. The date given for the mill is around 1800 but it could have been built earlier.[7]

Leeming Water also attracted attention. In the early nineteenth century Midgeholme Mill was joined by three more, sited close to one another. One was built at Wadsworth House by the owner of the property, Isaac Denby. He was also involved in the nearby

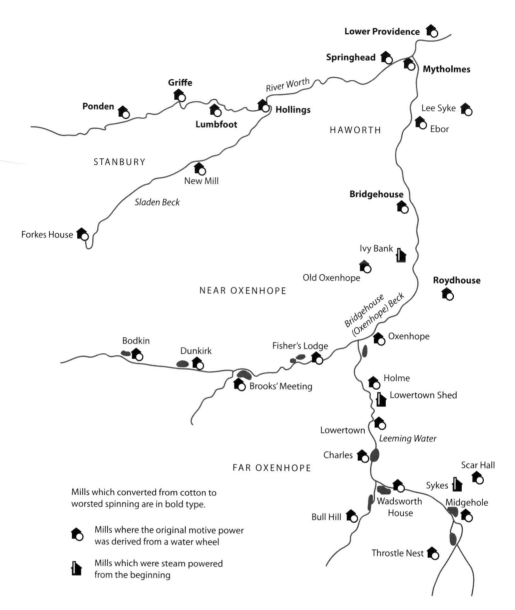

Worsted
textile mills
in Haworth,
Oxenhope
and
Stanbury.

Lower Providence

Springhead

Mytholmes

Griffe

River Worth

Ponden

Hollings

Lee Syke

Lumbfoot

Ebor

HAWORTH

STANBURY

New Mill

Bridgehouse

Sladen Beck

Forkes House

Ivy Bank

Old Oxenhope

Roydhouse

NEAR OXENHOPE

Bridgehouse
(Oxenhope) Beck

Bodkin

Oxenhope

Dunkirk

Fisher's Lodge

Holme

Brooks' Meeting

Lowertown Shed

Lowertown

Leeming Water

Charles

Scar Hall

FAR OXENHOPE

Sykes

**Mills which converted from cotton to
worsted spinning are in bold type.**

Wadsworth
House

Midgehole

Bull Hill

Mills where the original motive power
was derived from a water wheel

Throstle Nest

Mills which were steam powered
from the beginning

Charles Mill, whose goit crossed his land, and which was named after the active partner,
Charles Ogden. A third, at Bull Hill, was occupied by John Denby and appears to have
been owned by Nathan Ogden. Whether John and Nathan were related to Isaac and
Charles is not clear but information about all three mills relates to their sale after the
death of Isaac Denby in 1808 and the bankruptcy of Charles Ogden in 1810.[8] There
was even a small mill, known as the 'New Mill', built on Sladen Beck in 1806.[9]

The economic upheavals of the early nineteenth century, including war with the
United States in 1812 to 1814, had a damaging impact on the Yorkshire cotton industry,
where operations were always of marginal viability. The mill at Lumbfoot seems to have
abandoned cotton as early as 1806, while at Roydhouse the burning of the mill in 1808

was the excuse for changing to worsted two years later. By 1810 all cotton spinning had ceased at Bridgehouse, and James Greenwood's new Upper Mill was devoted entirely to worsted. Dinah Heaton and Sons at Springhead were declared bankrupt in 1808 and the mill was bought by James Greenwood of Bridgehouse. His son Joseph finally abandoned cotton in 1822. Nevertheless, some cotton spinning did survive into the Brontë era. Mytholmes was in difficulties in 1813 but the business was reconstituted and the firm of William Newsholme & Sons continued to use part of the mill for cotton spinning. Thomas Lister spun cotton at Griffe and Hollings. Robert Heaton VI at Ponden was badly hit on the death of John Murgatroyd Heaton in 1807 by the revelation that the deceased had embezzled £500, and the war with the United States finished him off. He went bankrupt in 1813 and ceased trading but Ponden mill was let for cotton spinning for thirty more years.[10]

The end of the Napoleonic Wars in 1815 encouraged business recovery and there was something of a boom between 1819 and 1825 as the Yorkshire textile industry exploited new markets in South America. Two more worsted mills were opened in Oxenhope. Lowertown Mill, also known also as Goose Green or Bridge Mill, was working by 1818 and nearby Holme Mill appears to date from the early 1820s. In about 1819 Hiram Craven of Dockroyd, the noted builder and engineer, bought and rebuilt Mytholmes Mill and Higher Providence Mill in Oakworth. The rebuilding at Mytholmes probably took place in 1822 after which the Cravens themselves ran it as a worsted mill, while as part of the 1825 reconstruction of Higher Providence, Craven made a large reservoir, the entrance to which was framed by two rib-bones of a whale. He also constructed a new mill at Ebor, which was occupied by George Townend & Co and appears always to have produced worsted.[11] Short-term economic problems in the mid-1820s led to the bankruptcy in 1828 of Michael Heaton of Roydhouse, though he survived and was listed as the owner of Roydhouse Mill as late as 1854. New mills were still being built,

ABOVE

Griffe Mill at Stanbury was built by Hollings and Ross in 1791 and was used for cotton spinning until Thomas Lister hanged himself in 1842. Merralls had it for a short time before moving to Lee Syke. It was operated successively by the Williamson Brothers and Townend Co. during the late nineteenth century. The weaving shed is in the foreground with the chimney of the engine room visible above the spinning mill.

© KEIGHLEY LIBRARY, THE JONAS BRADLEY COLLECTION

LEFT

Griffe Mill is in the Worth valley, north of Stanbury village. An early water-powered mill, it also incorporated some cottages, evidence of which can be seen in the remains of a domestic fireplace visible in the wall on the left of the picture. Stephen Merrall, a member of the family which owned the mill, is recorded in the 1841 census as living here with his wife and five children, although strangely he is listed as a lowly worsted spinner.

BY COURTESY OF IAN PALMER

with Brooks Meeting Mill at the junction of Rag and Dunkirk (Leeshaw) Becks first mentioned in 1827 and Throstle's Nest on Leeming Water in 1828.[12] By that time there may also have been another small mill at Forks House on Sladen Beck, although it is possible that it was a stamp mill, not a textile mill.[13]

Each change in technology created acute social problems as well as opportunities. In the cotton trade one attraction of factory spinning was that it created jobs for children.

Many of those employed in the late eighteenth century were officially apprentices but little control was exercised over their terms of employment and they were often abused. John Kitson's career demonstrates that employers often worked their machinery through the night. He did not complain about night work – wages were better than during the day – and he was free to leave if he did not like it, but his employers could discharge him when trade was bad. Their responsibilities to apprentices remained, though some ill-treated them or tried to economise by reducing their diet to starvation levels. In 1802 Sir Robert Peel senior secured an Act to regulate the conditions of their employment, and on 12 February 1803 a meeting of cotton spinners in Keighley resolved that the Act's effects would 'be highly injurious to the Spinners of Cotton and Proprietors of Mills'. A committee of fifteen was appointed 'to obtain a Repeal or Modification of the said Act'. Among its members were Messrs. William Ellis, William Hollings, James Ross, Robert Heaton and Thomas Leach, all active cotton spinners in Haworth. Nothing came of the committee, because only a fraction of the workforce were apprentices.[14]

During the 1820s a group of Tory Anglican Evangelicals, led by Richard Oastler, protested loudly against the ill-treatment of children in Yorkshire mills. In 1830 a parliamentary committee recommended a maximum ten-hour day for all workers in the textile industry and Lord Grey's Whig government established a royal commission on the subject. The answers given by Haworth manufacturers to its questionnaire were typical. The standard working week was 69 hours (twelve hours, Monday to Friday, and nine on Saturday). Hartley Merrall, who had leased part of Springhead Mill in 1829, did not think the hours were excessive for young children and agreed with a Bingley surgeon that they did not need any recreation. William Greenwood junior kindly let them finish earlier on Saturday – provided they made up the time on other days. Unpaid holidays varied from four to eight days a year but if the employees wanted pay they had to make up the time. All delays, whatever the cause, led to extra hours or a cut in wages.

None of the Haworth respondents answered the questions about how many hours the children had actually worked in 1831 and 1832. They were two very good years and some spinners, honest enough to provide figures, showed that the actual working day could be as long as sixteen hours. Every employer thought the work given to young children was easy. The most common was 'doffing', changing the bobbins on the frames, or piecing, repairing broken threads. Both required continuous concentration as failure to act quickly delayed production. Children often fell asleep and were beaten – no employer admitted using corporal punishment, and they usually blamed the overlookers if any was detected. Doffing required the children to stand continuously, which led to distorted limbs in later life. Half the Keighley respondents said that they would be prepared to support a bill provided that it was compulsory on everybody. Neither James Greenwood nor William Greenwood answered the question. Jonas Hird objected to regulation by act of parliament, and Hartley Merrall said bluntly that if the bill was passed 'we shall be obliged to curtail both in the number of hands and wage'.[15]

The resulting legislation was a messy compromise. The employment of children under nine was forbidden; those aged 9 to 13 were restricted to eight hours, with two in school;

and young persons under 18 could work no more than ten hours. This satisfied nobody. The employers realised that the Act effectively limited the hours of adults, because the factories could not work without children, so they tried every means of evading it. Before 1837 there was no official record of births, so until 1846 the inspectors who had to enforce the act, and the magistrates who adjudicated on disputes, had to guess ages. Many magistrates sympathised with the employers and imposed only nominal fines for infringement, and campaigns for a ten-hour day for all continued through 'short time' committees.

Haworth played its part in the campaigns before and after the 1833 Factory Act. A prominent leader of the reform movement in Keighley was Abraham Wildman from Haworth, while Patrick Brontë, Haworth's perpetual curate, was an advocate of factory reform and agitated successfully for the selection of Joseph Greenwood as a magistrate. Greenwood, he claimed, was a major landowner warmly attached to the country's institutions, of sound principles and a regular church attender. What Brontë did not say was that he could be relied on to prosecute employers who broke the Factory Act. Jonas Hird at Roydhouse was prosecuted in 1835 and James Mitchell of Mytholmes in 1845.[16]

Brontë was also a strong supporter of the Reverend George Bull of Bierley, the famous 'short time' parson. But other Haworth clergy did not share his enthusiasm: in 1834 a correspondent of the *Bradford Observer* attacked Bull as a 'Tory Demagogue, under the mask of pleading for the poor Factory children',[17] The comments were traced to John Winterbotham, pastor of the West Lane Baptist chapel in Haworth. Brontë offered the church schoolroom for a debate on the subject but when Bull appeared Winterbotham was nowhere to be found. As the next chapter shows, Winterbotham had good cause to be annoyed with the Church of England but it is unfortunate that religious divisions affected issues such as factory legislation. 'Ten hours for everyone' was not conceded until 1847 and by that time other problems occupied the minds of Haworth workers.

Powerlooms

Powerlooms were well established in Bradford by 1830 but when they appeared in the Haworth area is unclear. The 1841 census lists 25 powerloom weavers in Stanbury, probably employed at Lumbfoot, where the mill had been bought by the Butterfield Brothers in 1828. Their main mill was Prospect at Ingrow, and the firm was on friendly terms with William Lund, the worsted manufacturer who introduced powerlooms to Keighley in 1833. There were three powerloom weavers at Old Oxenhope and one at Hanging Gate, and 46 more in an arc from Westfield through Marsh and North Ives to Hall Green, Main Street and Gauger's Croft. This suggests that the innovator was William Greenwood junior at Old Oxenhope, though documentation is lacking.

During the trade depression of 1837–42 the employers of handloom weavers faced a major crisis. The worst affected were those who worked in the old way, buying the wool themselves, putting it out to be spun and woven, and then taking the pieces to market to be sold. In 1830 *Parsons and White's* directory lists ten of them in Haworth – Tobias Lambert, Robert Newsome, Holmes Pickles, William Stancliffe, Thomas Starkey, John Sutcliffe, John Thomas, Abraham Whitham, John Wood and James Wright. Only Lambert, Pickles, Whitham and Wright survived to 1842; in 1848 just two remained; and in 1853 there was none. In 1830 there were four such manufacturers in Oxenhope but by 1854 Abraham Beaver was the only survivor. Most were small men who had other businesses – the Lamberts, for example, were grocers, while Isaac Overend at Oxenhope was listed in 1838 as a worsted manufacturer but by 1857 was simply a tailor.

The remaining cotton spinners were also badly hit. Thomas Lister had ceased spinning at Griffe by 1834, retaining Hollings until 1841 when he went bankrupt, and hanged himself in his hayloft in May 1842.[18] The last cotton spinner at Ponden was John R. Wright in 1840. Cotton warps continued to be used extensively in the manufacture of pieces for the 'fancy' trade but the yarn was mostly imported from Lancashire. Neither did the worsted spinners escape, the small mills being particularly seriously affected. Bodkin Mill is listed in the 1841 census but never mentioned again. New Mill had prospered in a small way after it was taken by George and William Robinson in 1823. In 1830 the mill was converted to weaving and people remembered the brothers taking their pieces to Halifax market. George died in 1833 and William sold out to George Taylor in 1839. For a time the mill was occupied by James Feather but there is no more information after 1842 and the site is now under Lower Laith Reservoir. Townend & Co., who had occupied Ebor since 1819, left sometime after 1838, forcing the Cravens to run it themselves. Robert Ogden, who had occupied Lowertown for a number of years, left in 1841. Jonas Hird departed from Roydhouse to be replaced first by Richard Knowles and then by Benjamin and John Greenwood. Roydhouse's prosperity was never to return.[19]

The worst affected were the handloom weavers themselves. In their efforts to compete with cloth produced on powerlooms, manufacturers progressively reduced wages until the weavers were unable to live off them. By 1840 it was reckoned that 150 families in Haworth had weekly earnings amounting to less than 2s. a head. In March of that year £100 was collected for aid to the distressed poor in Haworth. To make matters worse a poor summer led to high corn prices and the peat for winter fuel was very scarce.[20] In November 1842 even more people were being thrown out of work and the burden of the poor rates on those who still had employment was very heavy.[21] Powerlooms brought about a revolution in the labour market. Analysis of the Book One 1841 Haworth census shows three male powerloom overlookers and one male powerloom weaver. All the rest were women, mostly aged between 15 and 25. There were 34 male handloom weavers and 38 female, but there would be few jobs in the new weaving sheds for the men, or for other male handloom weavers in other parts of the township.

It is not surprising, given the circumstances, that there were disturbances. Working people had been disappointed by the 1832 Reform Act and in 1836 a charter was drawn up in which the principal demand was for universal suffrage. At first the 'Chartist' movement was peaceful but when it gained the support of only a handful of MPs many of its advocates turned to more direct action to secure its implementation. The first large demonstrations were in 1839–40, but though Chartists unsuccessfully contested the election of the churchwardens in Keighley there were no reports of activity at Haworth.[22] In 1842, though, mobs of workers went from town to town, stopping the mills by forcing the employers to remove the plugs from their steam engines. In August 1842 a mob surged up the road from Bradford to Bingley and Keighley, stopping mills with the help of local supporters. Groups went on to Morton and Haworth,[23] and at Haworth they were met by plug-drawers from Lancashire.[24] Employers who voluntarily stopped work were not further molested but those who resisted had their mills invaded and machines smashed. Few millowners were actively supported by their workforce. The plug-drawers levied food contributions as they passed and plundered those who refused their help. Dick Brook, an Oxenhope farmer and shepherd, regaled his listeners with stories of the 'dreadful invasion' for years afterwards.[25] Mrs Greenwood of Lees, who was five at the time, remembered the 'hungry and lawless crowd of plug drawers and machine smashers who marched through Crossroads from Lancashire'.[26] Jacob Earnshaw of Ovenden was later committed to the House of Correction 'for that he with others joined a riotous mob in the parish of Haworth, going from house to house and asking for meat etc. of the peaceable inhabitants'. The insurrection was finally ended by the arrival of a troop of the 17th Lancers from Leeds, supported by a company of the 73rd regiment of foot.[27]

As a consequence of the disturbances the magistrates sent a precept to every vestry instructing them to raise a body of special constables. Haworth's quota was 25 men. The *Bradford Observer* of 25 September 1842 reported that a meeting had taken place the previous Friday with Mr R. Pickles in the chair. Two or three lists of competent persons were presented but the chairman rejected all those who did not meet the £4 annual income qualification. This so much reduced the number available that 'he showed little or no reluctance in putting in a man with a cork leg, notwithstanding the act specifies that the constables are to be able bodied'. The meeting also refused to pay them anything so it cannot have been much of a surprise that the 'anti-Plug Dragoons' only captured a fisherman, an idiot, and a party of children engaged in hunting for a wasps' nest. These inadequate defensive measures were still worrying Patrick Brontë the following spring. He was called as a witness in a legal case at York and had to leave Emily alone in the parsonage. He had a pair of pistols, acquired when he was a member of a Yeomanry Corps in his undergraduate days at Cambridge, so he taught her how to fire them.[28]

The depression of 1840–42 did not affect every firm, and when business confidence began to return in the middle of 1843 those who had weathered the crisis were able to expand. One such family were the Merralls. Hartley Merrall, after periods at Acres and Low Bridge Mills in Keighley, had taken part of Springhead Mill in 1828. He spun worsted and manufactured stuff pieces, while his four sons, Edwin, Stephen, Michael and Hartley junior, jointly operated Griffe Mill in the years around 1834. They were so successful that ten years later they vacated Griffe for a new mill and warehouse at

Lee Syke. This has now disappeared, but it was on the south side of Sykes Lane and was of 16 bays and 4 storeys high. The existence of a reservoir suggests that it was originally powered by a water wheel from a stream fed by Sugden swamp.[29] By 1851 the Merralls were employing 83 boys, 93 girls and 222 women. The only adult men were the four brothers. At Mytholmes, where two-thirds of the mill was occupied by Jonas Sugden & Son and one-third by James Mitchell, the valuation rose from £83 in 1844 to £170 in 1847. Another firm to profit was Abel Kershaw and Brothers, who were first mentioned in 1836 at Wadsworth House and in 1847 moved to a new purpose-built spinning mill at Sykes.[30]

A further trade depression, which began in 1847, was aggravated by intense railway speculation that led to a stock market crash, and by a third, though less dramatic, bout of Chartist agitation. These events shook the worsted industry in Haworth to its foundations. One of the constants throughout its rise had been the Greenwood family of Bridgehouse. When John III died in 1790 he had been succeeded by his son James. Under him the business prospered and he made the transition from cotton back to worsted so successfully that he was able to add Springhead to the portfolio of Greenwood mills in 1808. He also built a second spinning mill at Bridgehouse, known as Upper Mill, and a new goit. After James's death in 1824 the business was run by his first and third sons, John and James. At the time of John's death in 1833 the future seemed rosy. Bridgehouse Mill had a valuation of £195, the biggest by far in the township, and James built himself a fine new house at Woodlands in 1832. Unfortunately the finances were not healthy. The elder James had made bequests to his children and relatives which absorbed all the capital of the business. A family meeting agreed to postpone the payment of the capital sums, but the interest which the younger James had to pay on them crippled him financially. The firm was already in difficulties during the 1840–42 crisis, the valuation falling to £110, and the 1848 crisis finished it off.[31]

James Greenwood junior, the last of the Bridgehouse textile dynasty. His bankruptcy in 1848 was apparently due to lack of liquid capital because his father's will had distributed most of the company's assets equally between his three children.

Greenwood was far from the only victim. No tenant could be found for Hollings after Lister's suicide, or for Griffe after the Merralls moved, and Ponden was unoccupied. At Oxenhope there were no takers for Roydhouse or Wadsworth House. The Cravens at Ebor had taken John Sugden as a partner but that did not save them and the mill was empty by 1849. George Feather disappeared from both Brooks Meeting and Charles Mills, and Henry Binns moved from Fishers' Lodge in 1844, leaving it empty. He went to Lowertown but is not listed there after 1848. Robert Feather at Bull Hill was not mentioned after 1847 nor Robert Pickles at Oxenhope after 1848. George Greenwood, the owner of Oxenhope, tried unsuccessfully to resume work there in 1851, and then experimented with

Bridgehouse Mill buildings. A large part of the both the upper and lower Greenwood mills were taken down when Butterfield bought the property, and the rest has disappeared, so that only the façade of the house is left. This block, built by R.S. Butterfield in 1849–52, is now the earliest part still surviving.

© BRADFORD LIBRARY

a silk spinning machine invented by John Clayton, who was living in the old mill at Bodkin Bottom. That venture also failed.[32]

After 1849 the worsted industry staged a rapid recovery, 1850 and 1851 being particularly good years, and a new generation of employers took over. Bridgehouse was bought by Richard Butterfield, who gave it a face lift: in 1849 its rateable value was £135 but by the end of 1852 it had increased to £220, the description indicating that a weaving shed to house powerlooms had been erected. Butterfield's example was imitated by the Merralls, who first rented Ebor in 1851 and bought it in 1853. They lost no time in installing more powerlooms there, and also a steam engine at Lee Syke which served both mills. John Feather, the occupant of Holme Mill, raised capital for considerable extensions by forming the company of Feather and Speak. The valuation of the mill rose from £35 in 1847 to £150 in 1851. At first the firm confined itself to worsted spinning but by 1854 it had acquired Lowertown Shed whose occupant, Joseph Whitaker, was manufacturing worsted pieces on powerlooms. In 1849 Charles Mill had been taken by the spinner John Bancroft, a nephew of George Feather, and in 1851 he was employing 22 hands – 13 boys and 22 girls. Another newcomer was John Williamson who took both Griffe and

Ponden. He died in 1851 but his sons continued the business as Williamson Brothers. In the 1851 census for Haworth powerloom weavers outnumbered handloom weavers by 622 to 366, but continued expansion meant that in 1861 there were 129 handloom weavers, 719 powerloom weavers and 95 who were unclassified.[33]

Machine-combing

As early as 1827 a combing machine had been introduced into Bradford, but trials proved unsatisfactory. By the 1840s more sophisticated machines, constructed by Samuel Cunliffe Lister and Isaac Holden, were available. Employers could adopt tactics similar to those employed in powerloom weaving: some installed the new machines but most used the threat to beat down the wages of the handcombers. In 1846 there was a protracted struggle in Keighley, ending in stalemate, but during the 1847–48 crisis lay-offs in Bradford were so extensive that serious consideration was given to subsidising those who wished to emigrate to Canada. By 1850 much depended on whether Lister could maintain his patent rights to the combing machines. After G.H. Leather had successfully brought a court case against him in 1852 there was a rush to install them.[34] The result was a social disaster. In 1841 there were 732 combers in the township of Haworth, but as ever more powerlooms were brought into use many male handloom weavers had switched to wool-combing so that by 1851 there were 1200. Then came the machines, and a catastrophic fall made even worse by the introduction of James Noble's more advanced version in 1853. By 1861 the number of handcombers had dwindled to 302.

What happened to the other 900? Many tried to get jobs as powerloom weavers. The census returns for enumeration district 1, which covered much the same area as the 1841 returns quoted earlier, show that although the 104 women were still in the majority, 44 men were now also powerloom weavers. The relationship between combing and weaving has been demonstrated elegantly from the Haworth marriage registers by Lewis Burton. The job descriptions of the grooms from the mid-1840s reveal that as the number of handloom weavers declined the number of handcombers soared, but from 1848 to 1852 there was a dramatic fall in the number of combers. There were other jobs – all wool sorters were male, as were warehousemen – but the opportunities were relatively few and employers found themselves in the happy position of having a pool of unemployed men to use as a level over their workforces.

Richard Butterfield was the leader of this movement. The 1851 valuation showed that the comb shop at Bridgehouse was empty, so he must either have adopted the new machines already or was buying in machine-combed wool. He now tried to bring pressure to bear on his powerloom weavers. The usual practice was to set up the warp and then weave up to fifteen pieces from it. Butterfield tried to force his weavers to superintend a second loom while the pieces were weaving on the first one. This led to a strike in May 1852. After an increasingly bitter confrontation he took eight weavers to court for failing to complete their warps, which he claimed was illegal under the worsted acts. The evidence showed that after the completion of the first couple of pieces he had arbitrarily reduced the amount he paid on the remainder to those who would not take on a second loom. The magistrates found for the weavers because they regarded Butterfield's behaviour as breach of contract. The strike continued into August, when Butterfield seems to have been forced to retreat. A downturn in trade during 1853 led Merralls to reduce weavers' wages and there was another strike. They, too, were forced to make concessions but the weavers' grievances were soon swallowed up in a wider crisis.[35]

The outbreak of the Crimean War led to a steep fall in the output of worsted cloth, which affected all branches of the trade. There were extensive lay-offs and Butterfield, hard nosed as ever, took the opportunity to close Lumbfoot down. The mill was entirely rebuilt but did not open again until 1858, during which time the entire workforce was unemployed.[36] The records of the Keighley Poor Law Union for the period are too fragile to use, but fortunately some statistics concerning the number of people relieved were recorded by two ephemeral newspapers. Even during the good times in the late 1860s and early 1870s, the number of paupers relieved each week in Haworth township was between 100 and 150, but according to the *Keighley Visitor* the number relieved at the beginning of October 1854 was already 496, while the *Keighley and Haworth Argus* of 1 March 1855 reported a record 632 for the week ending 21 February.

LUMBFOOT MILLS. FROM NORTH-WEST.

Lumbfoot Mills. The first mill on the site was built in 1797, but it was demolished by R.S. Butterfield and replaced by a new mill between 1854 and 1858. Despite being flooded in 1864, it was still much the same in 1914 when this photograph was taken. This view from the north-west shows the spinning mill on the left and the single-storey weaving shed on the right. The engine room and its chimney can be seen beyond the spinning mill.

© KEIGHLEY LIBRARY

The implications of these figures are difficult for us to appreciate today. Many people, especially the combers, gave up and left the area. Dick Brook remembered the Crimean War as a period of desperate poverty and hardship. John Snowden reckoned that the wages of handcombers fell by 40 per cent between November 1850 and December 1853 and accused the manufacturers of treating them worse than felons. In 1908 Joseph Normington reminisced that breakfast in the 1850s was 'Old Bob', a bowl of water porridge with skimmed milk bought at ½d. a pint, together some oatcake. For thirteen weeks no wheaten bread was seen in the house at all. There was no money to buy butcher's meat, except perhaps a scrap on Sunday, and the family made do with a bit of suet fried or roasted with potatoes. Any vegetables came from their own gardens. If a working man was able to keep a pig, like *Mrs* Greenwood's father, his fellows regarded him as really affluent.[37] When the war ended in 1856 trade improved but prosperity did not begin to return until 1859. The whole textile district suffered but Haworth was among the worst-affected places. There was another significant bankruptcy, that of James Mitchell. His Oakworth mill, Lane Ends, was sold in 1856 and he gave up his share of Mytholmes. Jonas Sugden had already moved to Vale Mill so Mytholmes remained empty until taken by Hattersleys in 1863.[38] Of the old Craven family mills on the Oakworth side, only Springhead remained in operation. Hartley Merrall junior took over the mill in 1855 and ran it as a business quite separate from that of his brothers at Lee Syke and Ebor. Lewis Burton's figures again confirm what was happening. The number of comber bridegrooms remained low but those claiming to be weavers showed two peaks, one after the Butterfield and Merrall strikes and the other at the end of the Crimean War. Neither was sustained. Between 1851 and 1861 the population of Keighley grew from 18,259 to 18,819, the smallest increase in the century. In Haworth the population actually fell from 6,848 to 5,896.

Railway plans

When he was asked to account for what had happened one of the 1861 enumerators, John Greenwood the stationer, gave three reasons. He blamed first the trade depression and then the high rates, but his third reason was the want of a railway. The latter was not for lack of schemes, for during the Railway Mania of 1844–45 several different projects had been proposed. In 1844 a company had been formed to build a railway between Leeds and Bradford, and the directors considered that there would be considerable profit in extending it up Airedale to Keighley and then building a connecting link to Colne. Haworth manufacturers tried to persuade the company to follow a route up the Worth valley. On 25 July 1844 the *Bradford Observer* reported a meeting about a line from Keighley via Stanbury to Colne, but the scheme was abortive because the surveyor reported that the gradient beyond Stanbury would be 1 in 80.[39] The railway was eventually constructed on the more circuitous route through Skipton which involved fewer engineering difficulties.

Undeterred, the Haworth interest persuaded the August 1844 meeting of the Leeds

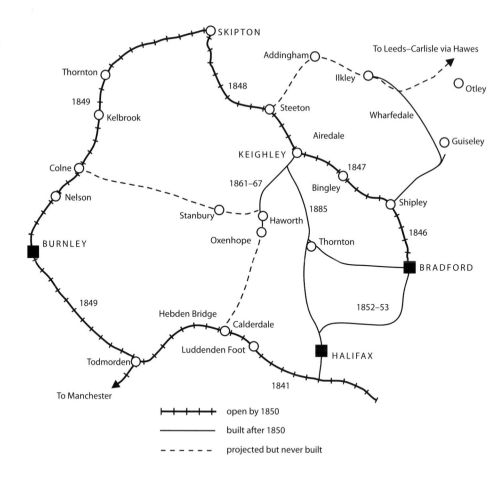

SKIPTON

Addingham

To Leeds–Carlisle via Hawes

Thornton

Ilkley

Otley

1848

1849

Steeton

Wharfedale

Kelbrook

Airedale

Guiseley

KEIGHLEY

Colne

1847

1861–67

Bingley

Nelson

Shipley

Stanbury

1885

Haworth

1846

Oxenhope

Thornton

BURNLEY

BRADFORD

1849

1852–53

Hebden Bridge

Calderdale

Luddenden Foot

HALIFAX

Todmorden

To Manchester

1841

├──┼──┼──┤   open by 1850

──────────   built after 1850

─ ─ ─ ─ ─   projected but never built

and Bradford Extension Railway to promote a four-mile line along the valley at an estimated cost of £10,000. A survey anticipated no significant difficulties and identified valuable beds of stone near the terminus. The draft bill therefore contained provision for a branch line to Haworth but there was no support from Keighley and its inclusion was due more to local pressure than enthusiasm on the part of the directors. It was dropped before the Act received the royal assent on 30 June 1845.[40]

In the meantime the directors of the Manchester and Leeds Railway, which ran along Calderdale, concocted a scheme for a line from Manchester to Scotland, routed from Hebden Bridge through Oxenhope and Haworth to Keighley. From there it would proceed along the Leeds and Bradford Extension Railway to Steeton before tunnelling through to Addingham, where it would join the Wharfedale Railway, a subsidiary of the Leeds and Carlisle Company. The plan was received with great enthusiasm in Haworth, Oxenhope and Oakworth. Three of the provisional directors were the textile manufacturers James Greenwood of Woodlands, Jonas Sugden of Oakworth House, and James Mitchell of Lane Ends, and several other local people, including Patrick Brontë, were among the subscribers.[41] In reality, though, the proposed railway was a chimera. There was little chance that the traffic generated would recoup the enormous engineering costs. The Leeds and Bradford line opened in 1846, extending to Keighley in March 1847,[42] Skipton in 1848, and Colne in 1849, but Haworth was as yet unconnected to the railway network.

The failure of Haworth to acquire a rail link until 1867 was a real problem. The suggestion has been made that its situation, between the cotton of Lancashire and the worsted of Yorkshire, placed the township at the centre of the textile industry.[43] Nothing could be further from the truth. It lay on the extreme edge of the coal measures. Although some coal was mined on Penistone Hill, the pits at Sawood and Cobling fed Denholme mills so that Haworth employers had to import coal for their steam engines. They had to move their goods and fuel supplies along inadequate roads on which tolls were being charged as late as 1860, while rivals in Keighley had the choice of the railway or the canal. Haworth's only attraction, as one mill sale notice brutally put it, was 'an abundance of cheap labour'. This chapter has shown how insensitive many of the manufacturers were to the interests of their workforce but they had genuine difficulties, as they could only compete if they paid lower wages and cut their costs whenever possible. Low wages reduced the number of potential ratepayers, thus increasing the average rates employers had to pay in bad times, and that made trade depressions longer and deeper in Haworth than elsewhere.

The importance of communications is highlighted by the one township in the immediate area which fared even worse than Haworth. Heptonstall lost 17 per cent of its population in the mid-nineteenth century.[44] Anyone who has visited the lovely Wesleyan chapel there will have experienced the steep and winding road, which even today is difficult to negotiate. No railway would ever climb the hill from Hebden Bridge to a place which had been at the leading edge of the textile industry in the sixteenth century. Heptonstall withered away.

This modern photograph shows the interior of St Michael and All Angels, the Haworth Parish Church. Note the octagonal piers supporting the pointed-arch arcade and the marble pulpit beyond the pews on the left.

PHOTOGRAPH: CARNEGIE, 2009

The Church of England in danger 10

The Methodist challenge

To most appearances the Methodist cause was in disarray in Haworth in the third quarter of the eighteenth century. J.W. Laycock records that 'On April 16th 1773, the preaching house was let to William Riddihah, of Bingley, with liberty to teach a school in the chapel. Shortly afterwards the Haworth Methodist society diminished in numbers and the chapel fell into such a dilapidated state that it was propped with timbers and grass grew between the flags. The schoolmaster was obliged to teach in the dwelling house and the religious services were conducted in the house of Mr Abraham Sharp.' A Methodist class had been founded at Sawood before 1787 and though its leader, John Hey, sought to revive interest at Haworth, membership dwindled to five and in 1788 it was omitted from the circuit plan.[1]

Laycock, looking back from 1909, saw everything in terms of an organised noncon-formist church, but people at the time did not. As Laycock himself admits, William Grimshaw built the chapel and house 'lest he be succeeded by a carnal minister and his flock scattered'.[2] The church trustees controlled the income of the living and could ensure that whoever was appointed shared their views – many held Methodist beliefs, some were even Baptists. John Richardson, Grimshaw's successor, was more than acceptable to those with Methodist inclinations and Wesley preached in the church as late as 1788.[3] Every landowner within the chapelry had a proprietary interest in the church because they had paid for its extension by buying sittings. John Greenwood the younger, a Baptist, was one of those who undertook the apportioning of the pews.[4] They could rent them out or even sell them – there is a list of such sales in the Haworth registers – but their owners were conscious of the social cachet involved in being seen in church. This lay behind a dispute in 1779, when Joseph Midgley wanted a separate small loft in the south-east corner so that he would not have to push past people of inferior status to get to his seats. In return for a share of the loft, he managed to persuade John and George Greenwood to support his application for a faculty, but they quarrelled when Midgley, as lord of the manor, demanded the front row. The Greenwoods both had incomes more than double that of Midgeley, and they demurred, so Midgeley rather belatedly

INTERIOR OF HAWORTH CHURCH.—P. 191.

The interior of the old Haworth Church. This engraving is undated, but the dress suggests the Brontës' time. The end of the east gallery which accommodated the organ and the choir can just be seen on the left. The nave is full of box pews. The minister's seat is middle right with the pulpit above it. Note the loft at the back on the right which caused so much argument between Midgley and the Greenwoods.

remembered that they were 'anabaptists' and rarely attended church.[5] Dissent was still around, and would quickly revive if a 'carnal' minister were to appear.

The Methodist recovery began with an initiative from Keighley. The practice there was to attend service at the parish church at 2 p.m. and then go to the Methodist class at around 4 p.m. After John Richardson died in 1791 a similar system was introduced under his successor, James Charnock, at Haworth with considerable success by Jonathon Maskew. By 1799 the Haworth society had 64 members and Sawood 25, and by 1811 the figures had risen to 128 and 86 respectively. Most Haworth members still attended church, but at Sawood this was difficult so a Methodist chapel was built at Lowertown, to which they moved in 1806 and remained until a chapel was built at Sawood in 1836.[6]

This was symptomatic of the growing confidence of the Methodist movement and its increasing exasperation with the Church of England. In 1812 the Halifax and Bradford Methodist circuit finally decided to organise services in direct competition with the Church of England. A year later, Lowertown had gained only four new members, but numbers at Haworth had increased to 182, suggesting that when forced to choose many who were not class members had deserted the parish church. With 272 members between them the two societies probably already outnumbered the Anglican congregation. In 1817 James Charnock fell seriously ill and until his death in 1819 the church was left almost rudderless, its services being taken by other clergy and with little pastoral care being undertaken. The Methodist societies profited from the hiatus, with numbers at Haworth increasing to 240 by 1819, though they fell back to 199 once a new perpetual curate was in place. At Lowertown the figure was 90 until 1820, but it then rose to 130, suggesting that the disturbances described later had a more lasting impact on Oxenhope.[7]

By the time Patrick Brontë was inducted in 1820 the damage had already been done and he was not the man to pick holes in the Methodist position. Brontë was born in Northern Ireland in 1777. He worked as a tutor for the family of Thomas Tighe, rector of Drumballyroney, who was an enthusiast for Wesley. Brontë imbibed from him the typical Wesleyan doctrine of the availability of free grace. He arrived at Cambridge almost penniless and was recommended to the Elland Society for a grant by the Cornish Wesleyan missionary Henry Martyn. After ordination Brontë spent a short time at Wethersfield and then went as curate to Wellington in Shropshire, a notable centre of Methodist influence. There he formed a firm friendship with John Fennell, head of the local boarding school and a Wesleyan preacher. His next move was to a curacy at

Wesleyan Methodist Chapel and Sunday School. This photograph, which dates from c.1910, shows the Sunday school on the left, built in 1853, and the chapel of 1845 (which replaced an earlier building of 1790) on the right. The discovery of dry rot in the chapel led to its demolition in 1951. Services are now conducted in what was originally the Sunday school, which also has incorporated into its walls the few remaining fragments of Grimshaw's 1758 building.

Patrick Brontë, perpetual curate of Haworth, 1820–61. Patrick was not quite the reactionary he has sometimes been painted, but was, rather, a Peelite conservative. He supported Sir Robert Peel's penal reforms and the cause of Catholic Emancipation, and also shared Peel's attitude to the Great Reform Bill of 1832. Brontë was also opposed to the employment of young children in textile mills, and opposed the Poor Law Amendment Act of 1834. He also initiated the process that led to the establishment of the Haworth Local Board of Health in 1851.

Dewsbury, where he was noted for his encouragement of cottage meetings like those of the early Methodists. In 1811 he became perpetual curate of Hartshead cum Clifton and in 1815 moved again to Thornton in Bradford.

Meanwhile Fennell had been appointed headmaster of Woodhouse Grove School at Apperley Bridge, in the parish of Bradford. There Brontë met and married Fennell's niece, Maria Branwell, in the fateful year 1812. Woodhouse Grove was a Methodist foundation and the decision to form an organisation independent of the Church of England forced Fennell to make a choice between the two. He resigned and became one of the curates at Bradford, before taking up the position of perpetual curate of Crosstone. Fennell's predicament caused Brontë much heart-searching. He never entirely forgave Jabez Bunting, moderator of the Halifax and Bradford circuit, whom he blamed for the split which he lamented for the rest of his life. It is thought that Emily Brontë based the figure of Jabez Branderham, the preacher of the sermon divided into 490 parts who figures in Lockwood's nightmare in *Wuthering Heights*, on what her father told her about Bunting.

For Brontë, as for Grimshaw before him, Anglicans, Methodists and even Baptists were fighting the same foe – the immorality, ignorance and superstition of a large part of the population. What they were up against was summed up in the career of 'auld Jack Kay' which showed that systems of thought generally associated with the seventeenth century still flourished in the countryside. Kay was born in 1766 and in the course of a long life gained such a reputation as a 'cunning man' and a 'soothsayer' that clients came to consult him from all over the central Pennines. His methods ranged from the use of herbal remedies, through foretelling the future by means of astrology, the crystal ball or a saucer of water, to the use of charms against ill-luck and the exposing of supposed witches. There is the possibly apocryphal story that two young ladies, strangers to Haworth, who enquired the way to the house of the 'wise man' were directed to the parsonage in mistake and received a lecture from Brontë on their foolishness and wickedness.[8]

Brontë was in broad theological agreement with the Wesleyans and he preached in the same extempore manner, yet he accepted the limitations on the use of the laity placed on him by the Church of England. In 1847 he gave a conditional welcome to the appointment of sub-deacons, as long as they did not administer the holy sacrament and were not given examinations in Greek and Latin 'so they become clergy circumventing a university education'. He always spoke in respectful terms of Methodist circuit ministers but his criticisms of the local preachers are clearly reflected in Charlotte's comment that Cardinal Wiseman 'spoke in a smooth, whining manner just like a canting Methodist preacher'.[9] Brontë held cottage meetings in Oxenhope but was unable to compete with the lay activity of the Methodists, whose position steadily strengthened. Another class had begun at Stanbury as early as 1812, perhaps that later referred to as on Henfieldside, and a chapel was built there in 1831. Dissension led to the collapse of the Stanbury class in 1832 but it was revived three years later by Joseph Craven and prospered under his leadership. By 1842, with 598 members, the Wesleyan Methodists dominated the chapelry.[10] The increasingly conservative political outlook of the Wesleyans led to breakaway movements, among them the politically radical Primitive Methodists who sought to organise mass outdoor meetings in imitation of events such as the feeding of the five thousand. Locally, the first Primitive Methodist services were held around

Stanbury Wesleyan chapel. The original building of 1832 had only one storey; the second was added in 1845, and the building was further enlarged in 1860. The caretaker's house on the right was built some time after 1860.

St Gabriel's church, Stanbury. Stanbury's first curate was John Stuart Cranmer, but the church is most closely associated with his successor, Arthur Bell Nicholls, the husband of Charlotte Brontë, who was responsible for raising money to get it built. It houses the top section of William Grimshaw's pulpit that used to be in Haworth church.

PHOTOGRAPH: CARNEGIE, 2009

1820 in a cottage at Mill Hill known as the 'Old White House', overlooking the present railway station. In 1833 another society was started at Sawood and in 1836 the circuit allowed Haworth to build a proper chapel in Mill Hey.[11]

The pattern of Sunday school development was symptomatic of the relations between the denominations. John Richardson started a Sunday school at Haworth in 1785 but after the first enthusiasm had passed it closed because there was no money to pay the teachers.[12] In 1802 the school was revived by the Methodists, meeting in the West Lane chapel and taught by 'voluntary' teachers who gave their services free. The school was a great success and, like its Anglican predecessor, interdenominational, but by the time

Marsh Wesleyan Sunday school. There was a Methodist class at Marsh as early as 1753, but the Sunday school was not opened until 1836. Reputedly over 1,000 people attended the opening, over 20 per cent of the population of the township at the time. This photograph from 1979 shows the enlarged building of 1874.

© BRADFORD LIBRARY

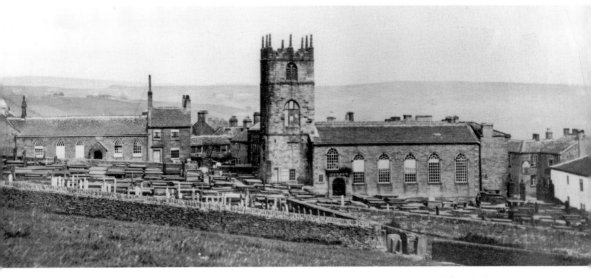

Haworth old church. This early photograph dated 1860 shows the Kirkgate Sunday school of 1832 on the left, with the sexton's house to its right. There is no clock on the church tower because the present one was not put in place until 1870. Its predecessor only had a dial on the Main Street side.

Brontë arrived in Haworth attitudes inside the Methodist Movement had hardened. The religious function of such schools took precedence over simple instruction in reading, writing and arithmetic, and in 1826 the Methodist Conference decreed that all their Sunday schools should have religious teaching according to the movement's formularies. Brontë regretted this abandonment of ecumenicalism but he had no quarrel with Methodist doctrine. In Haworth the denominations finally parted company in 1831 because of objections from the new Baptist pastor, John Winterbotham, not from Brontë.

The split dramatically underlined the weakness of the Established Church. The Wesleyan Methodists organised their own separate Sunday schools at West Lane and Lowertown and took effective control of the joint school which had been established at Scartop in 1818. By 1840 they had three more, at Stanbury, Sawood and Marsh. Even the Primitive Methodists had a school. Brontë's only answer was a school in a building erected for the purpose in Kirk Gate in 1832. Nancy Drake recalled her baptism by Brontë, but what she really treasured was the bible won at Leeming Methodist Sunday School.[13]

The Baptist offensive

For the first decade of his incumbency Brontë had little trouble with the Baptists and maintained good relations with the Greenwood textile dynasty, which provided much of the funding for the denomination in Haworth. James Hartley died in 1780 and was succeeded by Isaac Slee, whose short ministry was ended by illness brought on preaching

Hall Green Baptist chapel, erected to accommodate the Baptists who broke away from West Lane in 1821. Tradition has it that music caused the division, but it is more probable that it was the refusal of the West Lane pastor, Rev. Miles Oddy, to rejoin the Lancashire and Yorkshire Baptist Association. They met in Bridgehouse barn, which was near the mill goit, until the Greenwood family donated enough money for a new chapel. Later in 1862 the chapel adopted Strict Baptist tenets and charted a course different from the other Baptist chapels in the township. Opened in 1826, its exterior had hardly changed when this photograph was taken in 1974.

at a funeral in bleak winter weather. His successor, Mr Thomas, took his place and also married his widow, but on her death from fever after less than a year of marriage, he retired to the milder climate of Devonshire. In 1785 the reins passed to an altogether tougher character, the Rev. Miles Oddy, who served as Baptist pastor for 45 years. Work on the chapel included a new gallery in 1786, financed by money left by Israel Sutcliffe.[14] In 1805 a further bequest enabled the Baptists to start a free school at Stanbury, the master being paid from interest on shares in the Leeds and Liverpool Canal. In 1808 John Town, a Haworth member, founded a Baptist church in Keighley.[15]

Oddy had a stubborn streak which may explain the disputes marring the later years of his pastorate.[16] Around 1820 a group of Baptists seceded from the West Lane Chapel and began meeting in a private house. In 1821 they started separate services in a high-windowed building which formed the part of Bridgehouse barn close to Goit Edge. By 1824 they were strong enough to be able to invite Moses Saunders to be their pastor,[17] and in 1825 a new chapel was built at Hall Green on land bought from Edward Ferrand, the lord of the manor, at a cost of £1,700. The brothers John, Joseph and James Greenwood of the Bridgehouse family figured prominently among the trustees as did their cousins John of East Morton, William of Old Oxenhope and George of Moorhouse and Ilkley.[18]

As both chapels maintained the doctrines of 'Particular Personal and Eternal Election, the Saints final perseverance, and other Doctrines consonant thereto and now commonly called Calvinistic' and both practised closed baptism and communion the reasons for the split have caused considerable debate. John Kitson the woolcomber, a Hall Green trustee, wrote that they quarrelled about music but gave no details.[19] The accompaniment during services at West Lane was provided by the Pogmore band until at least 1832 but there was widespread dissatisfaction with the quality and reliability of such bands, and among Baptists music often became entangled with doctrine. The behaviour of the Hall Green Baptists suggests that music was not the only issue. By 1780 the Lancashire and Yorkshire Baptist Association had run into difficulties and many chapels, including West Lane, let their membership lapse. In 1787 the Association was reconstituted and reinvigorated by John Fawcett, pastor of Hebden Bridge. He had originally been appointed in 1765, at the instigation of James Hartley, so he must have been frustrated by the refusal of West Lane to rejoin. West Lane's long absence from associational life may have been due to Oddy's determination to remain independent, for Hall Green had already joined by the time Moses Saunders arrived.[20] In 1831 Oddy retired aged 75, and was succeeded at West Lane by John Winterbotham, his assistant since 1829.

In 1831, when the first bill to reform parliament was defeated, that uncompromising Tory Charlotte Brontë recorded 'the extreme pleasure I felt at the news of the Reform Bill's being thrown out by the House of Lords and of the expulsion or resignation of earl Grey.' Her father disagreed. Writing to Mrs Franks at Huddersfield he avowed that 'a truer friend to church and state does not breathe the vital air' but he believed that 'unless the *real* friends of our excellent institutions come forward and advocate the cause of temperate reform' the result would be revolution.[21] The bill was reintroduced, amid extensive disturbances across the country, which were only calmed by the agreement of William IV to create as many peers as was necessary to swamp the large Tory majority in the Lords to ensure that it passed. The victory of 'temperate reform' did not please militant Baptists such as John Winterbotham. He publicly advocated disestablishment of the Church of England, the removal of the bishops from the House of Lords, and breaking the Anglican monopoly over higher education. Only Anglicans could attend or teach at the two English universities, all others had to study at a Scottish university. Brontë defended the Anglican monopoly, for like all who had succeeded against the odds he was jealous of the sanctity of his degree. In an exchange of letters with Winterbotham, published in the *Leeds Mercury*, he attributed the Baptist pastor's 'erroneous' views on baptism, and his lack of a university education, to an inability to master Greek and Latin. To Brontë, only a classical education could fit a man for the cloth, a claim Winterbotham denied and Brontë's failure to answer his second letter suggests that the pastor got the better of the argument.[22] Oxford and Cambridge remained Anglican preserves until 1870, but the non-denominational University College in London opened its doors in 1828.

Another monopoly was the right to marry people, since the only legal marriages – except for those in Quaker and Jewish places of worship – were those performed by an Anglican clergyman according to the rites of the Established Church. After 1837, however, not only were all births, deaths and marriages recorded by a secular registrar, but any church or chapel could apply for registration for the celebration of marriage. The first ceremony at Hall Green was witnessed by a large crowd, but William Hodgson, Brontë's curate, commented sourly that 'conscientious Dissenters' and 'old Infidels' could now be relieved of the services of the 'Font and Altar of the Established Church'. Even Brontë, though aware of the practical advantages of the measure, declined initially to perform the burial service over those who avoided attendance at any place of worship.[23] He cannot have maintained his ban for long, because in 1847 he consented to take the burial service of that old reprobate Jack Kay.

Brontë was convinced that an Established Church supported by the secular state was essential, but he also believed in toleration for Dissenters, provided that they accepted the broad lines of the political and religious settlement. By the 1820s, however, questions were being asked about how the Established Church should be financed. Like many Northern Ireland Protestants, Brontë was hostile to Roman Catholic demands for emancipation, and in December 1812 had signed a petition opposing this idea. By 1828 he had moved towards the moderate Tory view, which accepted emancipation subject to safeguards against 'papal pretensions'.[24] Emancipation in Ireland raised the question of whether Roman Catholics should have to support the minority Church of Ireland through tithes and church rates. The debate spread to England, with Dissenters arguing that they should not be required to pay towards a Church of which they were not members.

In Haworth most of the great tithes had been bought out in the seventeenth century. What was left financed the vicar of Bradford, not the perpetual curate of Haworth, so Brontë supported the Tithe Commutation Acts of 1836 and 1845 which, upon completion of the apportionment in 1853, substituted money payments for those that remained.[25] As far as church rates were concerned, the money went to Bradford parish church – as we have seen, and was a frequent cause of conflict – but from 1835 the Haworth vestry, led by James Greenwood of the Hall Green Baptists, refused to levy a rate for local purposes and Brontë knew there was little he could do about it.[26] Except for 1840, when his curates pushed him into a futile confrontation, Brontë preferred to be conciliatory, an attitude which paid handsome dividends. In normal years he could raise money from his own congregation. When extraordinary expenditure was needed the vestry would vote for a 'voluntary subscription' if Brontë made a good case for it.

Relationships with Bradford were often sour, with disputes every time a perpetual curate was appointed. In 1791 the vicar nominated Thomas Atkinson, master of the free grammar school at Keighley, and the trustees had to threaten legal action before they could appoint their own nominee, James Charnock.[27] When Charnock died. Henry Heap, who had succeeded as vicar in 1815, nominated Patrick Brontë, who was rejected by the trustees and withdrew. Heap then nominated Samuel Redhead, curate of Great Horton, who was duly appointed, but he had offended the trustees and was boycotted. A visit by Heap, supported by the local gentry, had an 'uproarious reception', and after three weeks Redhead prevailed on a reluctant archbishop of York to allow him to resign. Brontë then applied to the trustees for nomination, was promptly accepted, and Heap happily gave his approval. Perhaps financial interest was involved, for during the Interregnum there was no money from marriages, funerals, baptisms and churchings, half of which went to Heap![28] Responsibility for good order in the church lay with the churchwardens, but the only active warden was George Greenwood, a Baptist, and on 2 October 1820 he was cited before the archdeacon's court for not discharging his office at the late visitation and for not making a return of the churchwardens for that year.[29]

The Baptists gleefully exploited the differences in the Anglican community over the Bradford church rate. Between 1785 and 1789 Haworth was cited before the ecclesiastical court at York for refusing to pay its proportion of the costs of new galleries in Bradford parish church and the installation of an organ, and in 1791–92 for objecting to extensions to the building. There were further disputes in 1811–12 and again in 1817 when Bradford parish church obtained a private bill for extending its graveyard. From 1800 to 1817 payments to Bradford from Haworth averaged £40 *per annum*, but between

Hawksbridge old chapel and Sunday school. Originally built in 1832, it did not have a baptistry, so most baptisms took place at West Lane. There is a story, however, that in 1839 some hardy souls had the traditional baptism, by immersion, in the mill dam close by.

1817 and 1825 they soared to £118. In 1834 John Winterbotham estimated that Haworth had paid over £2,000 to Bradford during the previous two decades.[30]

In 1837 the Haworth Baptists, led by Saunders and Winterbotham, raised a petition against church rates, which was enthusiastically supported by a packed meeting in Hall Green chapel. Brontë, his son Branwell, and his curate William Hodgson, attended but other Haworth Anglicans pointedly stayed away and attempts to raise support for the church rate failed.[31] In 1836 Brontë wrote to the *Leeds Intelligencer* supporting the principle of a church rate, but by 1840 he advocated one only for the church in the ratepayers' own district and in 1842 he flatly refused to endorse any rate not supported by a majority of the ratepayers. This ended payments to Bradford, as the Bradford vestry regularly voted church rates, allowing Haworth Anglicans to support their own church and eliminate the encumbrance of paying church rates to Bradford.

The role played by the Baptists in these disputes improved their standing in the township, and the collaboration between Saunders and Winterbotham healed the rift between the two chapels. Membership of West Lane chapel had fallen sharply but under Winterbotham's leadership it recovered and sometime between 1836 and 1842 the chapel joined the West Riding Baptist Association. Each chapel started its own Sunday school and in 1832 the Baptists began evangelising Oxenhope, the two chapels jointly sponsoring a Sunday school at Hawksbridge in Near Oxenhope. A service there in 1836 attracted a congregation of 1,500.[32] Most baptisms took place at West Lane because there was no baptistry at Hawksbridge until 1915, but on one occasion nine hardy spirits were

Baptist chapel, West Lane, Haworth. The original chapel was built in 1752 and extended in 1775. It was replaced by a second chapel in 1819, which then made way for an even grander one in 1845. The 1819 chapel had a Sunday school attached to it, and a primary school was added later. In 1997 all the former primary school and most of the Sunday school were demolished and the land sold for housing. The money was used to create a revamped chapel upstairs and function room downstairs. Today the frontage remains as it was, but the interior has changed dramatically. The Gilbert and Sullivan Society, which used to perform in the Sunday school, now gives its shows in the chapel itself.

© KEIGHLEY LIBRARY

immersed in the Brooks Meeting mill dam! In 1837 Hall Green opened a new chapel, seating 400, and a Sunday school at Horkinstone.[33] With the Dissenters running ten Sunday schools to his one, Brontë must have felt beleaguered.

Divided counsels

The Church of England realised, somewhat belatedly, that it needed many more clergy if it were to meet the challenge of the Dissenters. From 1835 a grant of £100 from the Pastoral Aid Society enabled Brontë to employ a curate. The first was William Hodgson, who was followed by Willie Weightman and, from after his death in 1842, James Smith. By 1844 Brontë had two curates – Smith, and Joseph Brett Grant. One helped Brontë with his duties at Haworth, the other at Stanbury. When Smith left in 1845 he was replaced by Arthur Bell Nicholls, who was heavily involved with the foundation of the National School. When Grant became vicar of Oxenhope, Brontë filled the vacancy at Stanbury with James Stuart Cranmer, who remained until 1847 when he was replaced by Nicholls. Brontë had raised a subscription for a mission church and there Nicholls had responsibility for superintending its construction.[34] In 1836 Bradford and Haworth were included in the new diocese of Ripon, carved out of the archdiocese of York. Stimulated by the first bishop, Charles Longley, a church building society was founded. A plan to divide Haworth chapelry was put forward in 1839, and under the 1843 District Churches Act it became possible to split parishes without encroaching on the emoluments of the existing incumbent. In 1847 Oxenhope was detached from Haworth (and Bradford) and made into a separate parish with its own vicar, Joseph Brett Grant, Brontë's former curate.[35]

These changes strengthened the position of the Church of England, so it was well placed to meet further social challenges, including the demand for better educational provision for working children. In 1844, encouraged by William Scoresby, who succeeded Heap as vicar of Bradford in 1839, Patrick Brontë established a National Society day school in the premises of the Sunday school. Under its first master, Ebenezer Rand, the school flourished. A second church school was opened at Stanbury and Grant was planning a third even before he was inducted at Oxenhope. The Dissenters were not slow to respond. In 1845 the Wesleyans opened a rival British and Foreign Society school in Haworth – from 1850 to 1865 its master was John Beaumont Smith, the organist at West Lane chapel – and another school was soon opened at Lowertown.[36] The Baptists were already running a free school in Stanbury and in 1854 Horkinstone, which became an independent chapel in 1849, also had a school, supported by the firm of Kershaw Brothers, worsted spinners.[37]

The Church of England fought hard, but the position of the Dissenters was also strengthening and during the 1840s and 1850s the signs of building and expansion were everywhere. By 1840 Hall Green had 160 members and 300 Sunday school scholars: in that twelve months a gallery and a vestry were added to the chapel and an organ installed.[38] John Winterbotham emigrated to Canada during the 1842 industrial depression, but his successor, Abraham Berry, could build on solid foundations. Between 1840 and 1846 there were about a hundred new members, and a new chapel, twice as large, was built. The Wesleyans rebuilt West Lane Chapel, the design, reported the *Leeds Mercury*, 'after a chaste and appropriate style by Mr Simpson of this town'. The stonework of Grimshaw's original chapel was incorporated into the vestry. The chapel was enlarged in 1853. At Lowertown and West Lane new organs were installed in 1845 and 1857. In 1845, at the Marsh Sunday School anniversary, the congregation was of a size not seen 'since the days of Whitefield and Wesley'. At Stanbury the Methodist chapel had also become too small so the roof was raised and a gallery inserted.[39]

The 1851 religious census invited clergy to count the attendance at each service on 30 March, carefully distinguishing between adults and Sunday school scholars. They were also asked to note what they believed were the average attendances at the same services over the previous year. Although the results are often ambiguous. The statistics in Haworth must have made dismal reading for supporters of the Church of England. The Anglicans mustered an adult congregation of around 500, whereas the Baptists had 689, the Wesleyan Methodists 520 and the Primitive Methodists 62.[40] Many Church of England incumbents treated the census with lordly indifference. Nicholls did not bother to count the congregation on 30 March but did make an estimate for attendances at each service over the previous year. Grant did neither and the estimate for Oxenhope was supplied by the registrar, James Ogden. The Wesleyan Methodists counted their congregations conscientiously, but by chance many of their members had that day attended a special service outside the chapelry – their 'real' numbers were probably around 700, as shown by the general attendance figures which correspond almost exactly to the society membership. The Baptists, on the other hand, shamelessly used the occasion for propaganda purposes. Hall Green claimed an attendance of 350, which was three times its 1849 membership figure and no less than six times that of 1852.[41] Yet even when all the caveats have been entered, it is clear that the Church of England only commanded the loyalty of about 30 per cent of those in Haworth who regularly attended divine service.

Sectarianism was a growing problem for Brontë and those of like mind. Joint ventures, once quite common, were now rare. In the 1820s Brontë had supported an interdenominational Auxiliary Bible Society, until the increasingly bitter attacks on the Church of England by Winterbotham led him to withdraw.[42] In November 1834 an interdenominational Temperance Society was founded and the Preston temperance pioneer, Joseph Livesey, came to Haworth give his famous 'malt liquor' lecture.[43] John Brown, Brontë's sexton, was addicted to the bottle and drinking with him was one of the causes of Branwell Brontë's descent into alcoholism. The Primitive Methodists soon began advocating strict temperance (including abstinence from beer), which split the movement. All Haworth churches and chapels encouraged voluntary temperance and excessive drinking does not seem to have been a serious local problem, but there was little formal cooperation between the denominations.

The divisions were accentuated by the determination of Brontë's curates, incited by

William Scoresby, the vicar of Bradford, to turn any disagreement into an opportunity for sectarian point-scoring. Thus, they capitalised on the bickering over the church rate, in an attempt to deflect Brontë from his moderate stance. Charlotte Brontë reported to Ellen Nussey how at the 1840 vestry meeting her father had his work cut out to keep Weightman and John Collins, the Keighley curate, quiet – only to be obliged to sit through a tirade from each of them the following Sunday, when they gave the Dissenters 'their kail through the reek'. Collins's sermon 'lasted an hour yet I was sorry when it was done' she concluded, showing where *her* sympathies lay.[44] Even more ill-advised was Scoresby's attitude to Haworth Free Grammar School. In January 1844 he wrote to Brontë, pointing out the failure of the trustees to fulfil the terms of Christopher Scott's will, which required the master to be a graduate of Oxford or Cambridge and to prepare the boys under his charge for university entrance by teaching Latin and Greek. The current master, William Ramsbottom, was not a graduate, but he was a Methodist lay preacher and taught reading, writing and simple arithmetic. Under the scarcely veiled threat of legal action, the trustees replaced Ramsbottom with Joseph Brett Grant, Brontë's curate.[45] The move was very unpopular and educationally counter-productive. Grant was an able scholar and attracted pupils, but when he became vicar of Oxenhope he took them with him and taught them privately, depriving the free school of valuable support and rendering it moribund.

Grant was also at the centre of the 'foundation stone farce'. Having raised the £125 necessary to trigger a matching grant of £308 from the National Society for building a day school at Oxenhope, he was eager to complete the project as soon as possible and decided to dispense with the ceremonial laying of a foundation stone. However, while Grant was absent on business Thomas Crowther, incumbent of St John in the Wilderness, persuaded the school trustees to organise an elaborate ceremony. In 1841 Crowther and Brontë had tried

Joseph Brett Grant. Curate to Patrick Brontë, 1844–45 and master of the free grammar school 1845–49, Grant was the first vicar of Oxenhope, for thirty years from 1849 to 1879. He organised the raising of the money for the building of the parish church, the vicarage and the national school within the space of five years. He is reputed to have worn out no fewer than 14 pairs of shoes in going around asking for subscriptions, and even to have received a contribution from Queen Victoria. Charlotte Brontë did not like Grant, and portrayed him as Mr Donne, one of the three idle curates in her novel, *Shirley*. There is an acerbic description of his money-raising methods in Chapter 15.

Now a much-modernised private dwelling, this building used to be Oxenhope National School, which opened in 1846 and was a school which Patrick Brontë had been prominent in pushing for since 1841. The original entrance porch for 'Girls and Infants' can be seen attached to the left of the taller of the two sections of the building.
PHOTOGRAPH: CARNEGIE, 2009

unsuccessfully to establish a school at Oxenhope, and Grant interpreted the stone-laying scheme as an attempt by Crowther to claim the major part of the credit for himself. The involvement of Thomas Parker complicated matters. He was Haworth's most celebrated singer, a tenor of national renown, and had returned to his birth place for a testimonial concert when he was invited to lead the singing at the stone-laying. He was, however, a Baptist – his presence turned an Anglican triumph into an interdenominational celebration. The concert in Haworth church a few days later was packed, and Brontë and Crowther were prominent among the listeners. Grant and Nicholls stayed away.[46]

Nonetheless, Grant rapidly proved to be the most successful Anglican clergyman to grace the chapelry since Grimshaw. In the seven years between 1846 and 1853 he raised enough money to build a school, church and parsonage. Oxenhope church was completed in 1849 in just eight months. Perhaps there was too much haste, for in February 1855 a gale blew down the chimneys of the new parsonage and considerably damaged the roof. Grant's abilities became legendary. He was reputed to have worn out fourteen pairs of shoes while fundraising, and even to have extracted money from Queen Victoria! His energy, genuine piety and innate kindliness made him loved throughout his parish and gained him the respect of the Dissenting community. His missionary work among the Halifax reservoir labourers at Fly Flat was long remembered.[47]

Seeing what Grant was doing, and contrasting it with what was happening in Haworth, the curates believed that the obstacle in the way of a comparable renaissance at Haworth was the Brontë family. When Brontë first applied for a grant to pay a curate he made it clear that he did not want one 'who would deem it his duty to preach the appalling doctrines of personal Election and Reprobation'. He wanted one 'not fond of innovation, but desirous of proceeding *on the good, old plan*'.[48] The two stipulations were incompatible, for most of the latter were those who held the 'appalling doctrines' he detested. He was therefore forced to accept curates influenced by the Oxford Movement which sought to move the Anglicans away from evangelicalism towards a High Church emphasis on ritual. Brontë could come to terms with the milder version, represented by Willie Weightman ('Celia Amelia', as the girls nicknamed him), and he supported changes such as the replacement of the orchestra by an organ in 1834. He also shared the Victorian passion for bell-ringing, supporting the subscription in 1845 which increased the peal from three to six. There were memorable events such as the 5,040 changes rung in 1849 and 1853, an achievement still unequalled a century later.[49]

Yet Brontë was seriously uncomfortable with the 'muscular Christianity' of Nicholls and Grant, and looked with disfavour on the enthusiastic discussions among the curates about the ritual rubrics in the Book of Common Prayer. Charlotte told Ellen Nussey in 1847 that Nicholls was on holiday in Ireland and 'that many of the parishioners express a desire that he should not trouble himself to recross the channel'. In 1871 the sexton, John Wood, recalled that 'it took sometime for the inhabitants to understand him [Nicholls] thoroughly', as he introduced changes 'which were considered at first merely as innovations' in both church and school.[50] Brontë was now in his late sixties and he confined himself to preaching, leaving Nicholls to run the services as he wished. People remembered the old man, leaning on Charlotte's arm and stumping off to events at the Methodist chapel, giving the impression that he was more at home there than in his own church.

Arthur Bell Nicholls, curate to Patrick Brontë, 1844–61. Like his fellow curate, Joseph Brett Grant, he was one of the new breed of High Churchmen whom Brontë regarded with suspicion. Nicholls played an important role in the development of both the mission church at Stanbury and Haworth National School. He married Patrick Brontë's daughter, Charlotte, in 1854 and looked after him until his death in 1861.

The National Sunday School where Charlotte Brontë taught. The main part of the building was erected in 1832 but from 1844 it was also used for the day school, which necessitated the addition of extensions. The first gable towards the left of the picture was built around 1853 and the far one in 1870.

PHOTOGRAPH: CARNEGIE, 2009

Patrick was not the only problem. The publication of *Jane Eyre* had made Charlotte a national celebrity. In 1850 she published her second novel, *Shirley*, the first chapter of which describes a meal shared by three young curates. The story is set in 1811, long before the Oxford Movement, but the young men are anachronistically linked to it. They were so closely based on Grant, Smith and James Chesterton Bradley, curate of Oakworth, as to be instantly recognisable. They behave with unbecoming levity. Malone (Smith) is represented as being too fond of the bottle and Donne (Grant) as being mean. The character of Macartney (Nicholls) was handled with greater diplomacy, which is not surprising as Charlotte eventually married the original. Nicholls' friend George Sowden later recalled how Charlotte 'very amusingly if not quite justly' described the meetings, but others were less amused. Charlotte was sharply criticised by the clergy who came with Bishop Longley to a confirmation service at Haworth in 1853.[51]

What the Church considered as Charlotte's malign influence continued after her death in 1855. In 1857 there was uproar when Elizabeth Gaskell revealed that the unpleasant Reverend Mr Brocklehurst in *Jane Eyre* was a portrait of William Carus-Wilson, founder of the school at Cowan Bridge which Charlotte had attended with her elder sisters Maria and Elizabeth. The deaths of Maria (the original of Helen Burns) and Elizabeth at the school were painful memories when the book was written. Having offended the High Church Anglicans in her lifetime Charlotte compounded her sin by alienating the Evangelicals posthumously.[52] Emily did not improve matters, as persistent rumours claimed that the plot of *Wuthering Heights* was based on legends relating to the Heaton family which they would rather have kept quiet. Even Anne, who stayed clear of these polemics, shocked respectable society by introducing violent characters in *The Tenant of Wildfell Hall*. Sir Thomas Wemyss Reid reported as late as 1879 that in the West Riding there was a distinct antipathy to the Brontës. A lady travelling companion told him that the sisters, 'embittered by the fact that they were not admitted to the good society of their neighbourhood deliberately revenged themselves by writing scurrilous libels and caricatures in order to bring Yorkshire men and women into contempt.'[53]

Plaque in the parish church, in memory of Emily and Charlotte Brontë.

PHOTOGRAPH: CARNEGIE, 2009

When Patrick died in 1861 there some relief among the local Anglican community. During his last years he was a sad figure. Not only had he buried his wife (1821), son Branwell (1848), and five daughters Maria (1825), Elizabeth (1825), Emily (1848), Anne (1849) and Charlotte (1855), but he had outlived his own time. His curate, Arthur Bell Nicholls, had married Charlotte in 1854 and had looked after him since her death. Nicholls hoped to be chosen as the next perpetual curate, but found himself in a dilemma. He was proud of his wife's reputation as a novelist and was quick to defend her version of the Cowan Bridge affair, but was well aware that her books prejudiced his chances. John Wood, the sexton, said that the innovations Nicholls had introduced were in due course accepted as 'improvements', and he became 'quite liked', but was as capable as his late wife of causing offence. In 1854 he refused to baptise a child with the name Brontë Greenwood, because of a quarrel with the family, and Patrick had to take the ceremony. He was also believed, probably incorrectly, to have tried to prevent Michael Heaton from being interred in the family grave, using the closure of the burial ground as an excuse. It only needed the rumour that he had the support of the vicar of Bradford, John Burnett, to damn him in the eyes of many of the trustees.[54] Perhaps it was a good thing both for himself, and for Haworth, that he was not chosen. Both would have lived in Charlotte's long shadow had he stayed.

11 New bottles for new wine

Poor law and criminal law

From the late sixteenth to the early nineteenth centuries effective administrative control lay with the township authorities, whose actions were loosely supervised by the magistrates through the quarter sessions system. Under a sequence of legislation from the mid-sixteenth century onwards, every township had to appoint to four key posts – the churchwardens, overseer of the poor, surveyor of the highways, and constable. These officials bore the burden of implementing the work of local government.

One major responsibility, that of the maintenance of Haworth church and churchyard, disappeared when the substitution of a voluntary subscription for church rate led to the nomination of the people's churchwarden of little interest to those who no longer attended the church. In 1555 an Act of parliament made parishes and townships responsible for repairing most highways within their bounds. In Haworth, except for a small number of bridges maintained by the West Riding magistrates, the township exercised this duty through the annual appointment of a surveyor of the highways. During the eighteenth century responsibility for some major roads passed to the turnpike trusts, and the township no longer had control over them either.

Since 1598 the township had been responsible for the collection of the poor rate and its distribution to those in need. Haworth was part of the parish of Bradford. Every year the chapelry nominated an assistant poor law overseer who attended a meeting there. Nominally this controlled arrangements for the entire parish but in practice the chapelry operated as an independent entity. In 1834 the Poor Law Amendment Act replaced this fragmented structure – there were over 15,000 Poor Law authorities in the country – with a simplified and much more rigorous system. The country was divided into Poor Law Unions, each based on a market town, and every union was required to build a new central workhouse Haworth was included in the Keighley Union. Each union was administered by guardians of the poor, elected by the ratepayers and subject to the overriding authority of the Poor Law Board and its commissioners in London.

There was widespread support for the 1834 Act, because poor rates had allegedly been spiralling out of control and it was generally felt that something had to be done. Expenses and costs were indeed high in some areas – during the strike year of 1826–27 Haworth paid out £2,272 in poor relief, the highest ever sum.[1] However, as the implications of the new Act became apparent, disquiet and opposition grew rapidly. One issue was that local gentlemen saw their authority undermined by 'panjandrums' sitting in offices in Whitehall. Another was that the Act denied assistance to those living in their own homes (a system known as 'out relief') and required instead that only those resident in the workhouse should be helped. This was deliberately designed to act as a disincentive to claiming relief, but guardians in industrial areas recognised that it was impractical, given the numbers of people who would be destitute in times of trade depressions.

Local opposition was headed by William Busfeild Ferrand of Harden Grange, whose mother was lady of the manor of Haworth. His efforts were ably seconded by Patrick Brontë. There was no township workhouse in Haworth and Brontë had opposed the erection of one in 1829. Now it seemed that Haworth's poor would be condemned to be inmates of the proposed new workhouse at Bingley. In an impassioned letter to the *Times* in February 1837, Brontë called the new Act 'a nose-hewing, finger lopping quack, a legal deformity, hunchbacked, and one-handed, though that one hand grasped a trenchant dagger'. He forecast that 'if dear times should come on, starvation deprived of relief, would break into open rebellion'.[2] When the assistant poor law commissioner, Alfred Power, visited Keighley a couple of months later the meeting was so hostile that he had to be smuggled out. Ferrand was elected as MP for Knaresborough in 1841 and continued his campaign against the Act. The new Conservative government refused to repeal it but he found ammunition in a report of the assistant commissioner Charles Mott, which was very critical of conditions at Keighley workhouse. Ferrand's defence of the Keighley Guardians led to a running battle with the Home Secretary, Sir James Graham, which lasted almost as long as the Parliament.[3]

In agricultural areas before 1834 employers, particularly farmers, had raised poor rates to prevent their labourers starving, but this was never the practice in industrial areas. Great play was therefore made with statistics showing a sharp rise in poor relief in such areas. Quarterly expenses in Haworth in 1835–37 averaged £238 but in 1840–42 the figure had risen to £499, because these were years of acute trade depression.[4] However, analysis over a longer period suggests that the real cost in Haworth was relatively little changed between 1819–34 and 1848–59.[5] The Act was not repealed, but 'moderate' guardians, such as those elected at Keighley in 1841, ignored many of its instructions, and continued to pay 'out relief'. The guardians, like their colleagues elsewhere in Yorkshire and Lancashire, refused to improve their workhouse on the grounds that it simply could not accommodate all those wanting relief in a depression. Eventually the Poor Law Commissioners tacitly admitted defeat and Ferrand was able to boast that he prevented the abolition of out relief in the Keighley Union. No new accommodation was built until 1858.[6]

The idea that all able-bodied paupers must work for their relief was also a non-starter. During a trade depression the only work available was on the roads and that was never enough.[7] Perhaps the most obnoxious feature of the new system was 'classi-

William Busfeild Ferrand. Owner of St Ives and Harden Grange in Bingley, MP for Knaresborough 1841–47, Lord of the Manor of Haworth 1854–89. He was a noted opponent of the 1834 Poor Law Amendment Act. His support for the Keighley Poor Law Union (of which Haworth was a part) in its dispute with the assistant Poor Law Commissioner, John Mott. which Benjamin Disraeli satirically called 'the great Mott case', led him into heated arguments with the Home Secretary, Sir James Graham, during which he actually challenged an MP named George Smythe to a duel.

fication', which was used to break up families by separating men from women and children from parents. As early as 1843 Ferrand forced Graham to admit that using classification in this way was an abuse and when the Act was revised in 1847 it was dropped. Ferrand also fulminated over the way elderly paupers had to tramp up to nine miles to claim their relief at the Keighley workhouse, but an investigation in 1855 showed that the assistant poor law overseer for Haworth, John Binns, was administering relief from Haworth church just as his predecessors had done before 1834. He also used his discretion by paying money to the poor in their own homes, a practice specifically banned.[8] The real problem was that the vagaries of the industrial economic cycle produced difficulties which both the old and the new systems were powerless to prevent. The constable, like the churchwardens, the surveyor and the poor law overseer, was an elected township official. In Haworth he was supported by a number of assistants or bye-law men. John Midgley's account for 1725–26 shows that the constable collected the land tax, window tax and county bridge assessment. He was responsible for enforcing the byelaws concerning the quality of the beer, and had to make sure that the orders of his colleagues were carried out.[9] In 1799 the constable presented John Townend who had 'rescued' eight of his sheep from the pinfold where they had been put for unlawfully pasturing in the closes of Abraham Sutcliffe. The same year the constable was himself presented for forcibly removing a pauper from Haworth and dumping him on the highway in Keighley, even though he had been certified sick and too ill to be moved.[10]

Inevitably, most of the constable's duties related to the maintenance of good order in the township. Some minor offences came before the manorial court, which was more active in Haworth than in surrounding districts because of the continued existence of some open field land. Offences such as uprooting or damaging hedges, or allowing animals to graze on the strips of their owners' neighbours, were punished by the imposition of small fines.[11] More serious crimes were committed to the magistrates. The two most common were theft and assault. Between 1740 and 1820 only nine theft cases were brought to court, probably because of the difficulty in obtaining evidence which would secure a conviction. Six of the nine accused were found not guilty, and though Jeremiah Akeroyd, seemingly a hardened criminal, was presented four times in 1746, 1756, 1758 and 1775, he was only convicted on one occasion.[12] Assault charges produced a ratio of six convictions and six dismissals. In 1788 there was a case of riotous assembly, which was clearly a land dispute: Joseph Midgley led a group of men who threw down a wall 126 yards long 'in the peaceable occupation of John Horsfall'.[13] The usual punishments were fines of 3*d*. or 6*d*. and, if the magistrates thought an example should be made, a public whipping on market day. Imprisonment was used sparingly and sentences were short, usually two months.[14] Most of those imprisoned in York Castle were debtors. The only other place of confinement in the West Riding was the Wakefield House of Correction.

May Day at the Ducking Well. Ducking was the customary punishment in early modern England for people (usually women) who had been convicted of offences such as malicious gossip. The well was originally in Sun Street at the foot of Coldshaw but was later moved into the park.

Such a mild system was really only effective in a rural society, and did not work effectively in large towns. The increase in people travelling on improved turnpike roads led to a growth in highway robbery. When William Greenwood of Old Oxenhope travelled to market he always went armed, and his two pistols and sword still survive among the family's heirlooms. James Sutcliffe, who was hanged at York for highway robbery in April 1796, seems to have been a Haworth man – he is buried in the graveyard.[15] Another serious crime was poaching. Michael Heaton advised his brother Robert that if he wanted to shoot partridges at Roydhouse he was to make arrangements quickly as 'the poachers in the Keighley neighbourhood are very active in the same

Most views of Haworth are from Hebden Road, so this one looking across the Worth valley from Oakworth is unusual. Haworth church is visible in the centre. The Baptist and Methodist chapels can also be seen, side by side, to the right.

business'. Edward Ferrand posted notices outside his estate and Joseph Greenwood, lord of the manor of Oxenhope, put advertisements in the papers threatening condign punishment against anyone unlawfully taking game on his land. The usual punishment was transportation if unarmed and hanging if a gun was being carried. In 1852 there was a riot at Keighley when W.B. Ferrand attempted to prosecute some poachers.[16] In 1818 three Haworth men were hanged for burglary but the example had little effect,[17] for during the 1820s Keighley was terrorised by a gang of burglars who resorted to violence when discovered.

Sir Robert Peel, Home Secretary from 1822 to 1829, codified the law and limited the death penalty to murder, attempted murder, treason and forgery. His reforms were resisted by the property owning classes and only gradually implemented. Patrick Brontë wrote to the Leeds papers supporting Peel's reforms, but he was also conscious that the best way to stop criminals was to catch them. On becoming perpetual curate he tried to supplement the constable's efforts by adopting William Wilberforce's idea of setting up an 'Association for the Suppression of Vice'. Its operations were to extend to 'all who shall be guilty of Murder, or of assaulting unoffending Individuals or of robbing and stealing, or committing any depredation etc'. In 1829 William Garnett was paid £1 1s. rent for a house to be used as a prison.[18] Peel established a professional police force in London in 1829 but proposals for a police force in the West Riding were turned down as late as 1855. However, legislation in 1856 made it compulsory for each county to have a force and with the arrival of George Hopkinson, Haworth's first police officer, the last of the four ancient functions of the township disappeared.[19]

Gas, water and sewerage

Every early nineteenth century visitor to Haworth noted the slope down from Crossroads or Flappit Spring, and then the steep pull up Main Street, the dominant feature of its geography even today. Ellen Nussey described it 'as a rough stone-paved road; the horses' feet seemed to catch at boulders as if climbing'. Another visitor remembered 'the heavy tug up its acute slope'. But in other ways Haworth was in the course of rapid change. William Scruton commented with surprise in 1858 that 'We had supposed Haworth to be a scattered and straggling hamlet with a desolate vicarage and a dilapidated church surrounded and shut out from the world by a wilderness of barren heath. Instead of that we found it transformed into a large and flourishing village – a not very enlightened or poetical place certainly but quaint, compact and progressive.' In the same year Walter White noted 'houses on both sides, and shops with plate glass and mahogany mouldings contrasting strongly with the general rustic aspect, and the primitive shop of the Clogger'.[20]

Successive censuses show that the village developed steadily. In 1841 there were 44 tradesmen of various types: fifteen grocers; six innkeepers, spirit merchants or beer sellers; five breadbakers and four butchers. There were also sixty artisans, including twenty shoemakers, ten tailors, six dressmakers and seven blacksmiths, as well as

Rose & Co., Apothecary. During the late nineteenth and early twentieth centuries this building housed a branch of the Haworth Co-operative Society, but before that time it belonged to the Lambert family who were grocers and druggists, and Branwell Brontë might well have purchased his laudanum from here. Note the elegant roof mouldings: it was buildings such as this that helped to convince visitors that Haworth was not quite the rural backwater that Mrs Gaskell had described.

PHOTOGRAPH: CARNEGIE, 2009

two clockmakers, and a barber, Jack Toothill, who regularly shaved Brontë. In other words, the range of service and the number of tradesmen demonstrated that Haworth was far more than a simple rural community, and it possessed some of the characteristics of a small town. By 1851 there were ninety tradesmen and ninety artisans, and in 1843 the village post office had opened close to the church steps. Oxenhope's was opened in 1849, largely due to Grant's persistence.[21] The next decade showed a further rise to 105 tradesmen and 103 artisans, even though the population of the chapelry fell by almost a thousand.

The impressions of visitors depended on the weather. Ellen Nussey cherished memories of delightful summer rambles on the moors with the Brontë sisters, while George Sowden later recalled an ornithological friendship with Branwell and excursions in the company of Nicholls. Winters were severe, though less so than in the eighteenth century, and heavy rainfall, rather than frost or snow, was now the object of comment. Bessie Parkes carried away from her rainy visit impressions of 'a dreary, black looking village' and a parsonage 'without a single tree to shield it from the chill wind'. Elizabeth Gaskell arrived on 'a dull, drizzily, India-inky day' with a leaden sky and gives a dismal picture of a remote and dreary backwater. A thunderstorm in September 1824 triggered a mud slide which carried away a large part of the bog on Crow Hill, thankfully without any casualties – Patrick Brontë thought there had been an earthquake.[22]

If Mrs Gaskell, a resident of middle-class Manchester with its gas-lighting and domestic comforts, had visited a decade earlier she might have had an even worse impression. Haworth did not obtain a public gas supply until the mid-1840s, when a public meeting chaired by Brontë took up an offer by William Thomas to provide the village with the surplus from his son's gasometer at Hollings Mill. Pipes conveyed the gas the half-mile to Main Street and in October 1846 the *Leeds Mercury* reported that the 'village of Haworth was on Wednesday evening last, for the first time lighted with gas'. The church was lit by gas shortly afterwards.[23] When Thomas was forced out of business by the depression of the mid-1850s the supply was taken over by Butterfields at Bridgehouse but in 1856 a public company was formed. Its first year was deeply inauspicious. The Leeds *Intelligencer* of 10 October 1857 reported that the gasholder was not rising properly: 'A little after eleven o'clock a leak was discovered in an elevation in the village in one of the pipes. The person in charge incautiously applied a light to the gas issuing therefrom, which soon traversed the main to the gasholder, and coming into contact with the gas and air there, blew up. The holder was broken to pieces, and one of these lighting on the head of a person in the street injured him severely. We are glad to hear however that some hopes are held out of his recovery.' In 1932 Sir James Roberts recalled his grandfather, a shareholder in the gas company, telling him that the culprit was James Lambert, a Hall Green grocer. When asked what he thought he was doing, Lambert replied 'Ah'm bahn to cap [surprise] t'natives'.[24]

As the village itself grew, and the number of traders increased rapidly, there was increasing demand for water, and traditional sources were clearly inadequate and unsatisfactory. There were two public wells: the quality of the Head Well was by 1840 so bad that even the cattle would not drink it, while the Brigg Well, though better, was tainted. There were also a number of pumps and private wells, while forty houses were supplied with piped water by William Thomas. These, however, were only a small proportion of the 598 households in the hamlet.[25] There were numerous local springs, but those who owned them would not allow public access. Patrick Brontë was well aware of the passing of the Public Health Act in 1848. On 28 August 1849 a letter signed by him, his curate, Arthur Nicholls, and Haworth's two surgeons, Edward South Hall and John B. Wheelhouse was sent to the General Board of Health asking for it to take action over water supplies and public health in Haworth. The Board replied that a petition signed by one tenth of the inhabitants was needed before it could interfere, and one signed by 222 inhabitants was duly sent on 9 October. The Board, overwhelmed by many similar applications, did not act immediately and Brontë had to write another letter before Benjamin Herschel Babbage arrived in April 1850 to make an inspection. After yet more prodding by Brontë in February 1851, the inspector's report was made public.[26]

As Brontë hoped, Babbage recommended that pipes should be laid to connect the Sowden and Hough springs to the village, but he estimated that the supply would be insufficient, so a reservoir would be needed to collect water from the moor. He commented on the complete absence of sanitation, sewers and covered drains in Haworth and advocated the construction of a comprehensive sewerage system, arranged so that the waste could be distributed as manure over neighbouring fields. The new system would allow the removal of the middensteads which disfigured practically every part of the village. Babbage also noted that there were no water closets, and on average one earth privy served four houses, though in some parts the average was one per eight households. He recommended that every house should have an earth privy, and that there should be at least one water closet to every three houses. He also wanted a single public slaughter house, and the closing of all others, while the churchyard was to be closed for burials under the requirements of the 1850 Burials Act. The modest scheme for improving water supplies was turning into a comprehensive reordering of the whole village.[27]

Opposition soon appeared, particularly from the manufacturers – the rateable value of most property was so low that they would inevitably bear the brunt of the expense. Yet the rules were clear – if the death rate was more than 23 per 1,000 the setting up of a Local Board of Health, with rating powers, was mandatory. The current average in Haworth was 25 and draft orders were made. The manufacturers next sought to gain exemption from some of the main provisions of the report. Merralls at Ebor protested that they had a sufficient water supply of their own, as did Richard Robert Thomas of the *White Lion*, Tobias Lambert, and Joseph Hartley. William Thomas, the public-spirited inhabitant who had helped to supply the village with water before Babbage had visited, now considered that he would be financially harmed by the improvement scheme.[28] Richard Butterfield was more astute. He noted that Babbage proposed that the qualification for membership of the Local Board should be property with a £5 rateable value or more, so he engineered a petition in December 1851 suggesting that this was too low. He also queried the boundaries of the proposed area where they included part of Near Oxenhope. In 1852 an inquiry was conducted by William Ranger. Babbage had fixed the qualification at £5 because according to the available statistics only six properties were valued at £10 or more. Revised figures showed that there were actually 43, so Ranger recommended that the usual £10 qualification should be adopted.[29] This enabled the manufacturers to dominate the Local Board. Butterfield became chairman in 1855 and held the position until his death in 1869.

Implementation of the recommendations was very slow and frequently delayed, while attempts were made to shift the cost from the ratepayers to the users. When the principal sewer was constructed in Main Street in 1854 it was routed down one side of the street. Property owners on that side were charged no less than 12s. 6d. in the pound, but others were charged nothing even though their minor sewers flowed into the main one.[30] There were near riots, and some householders tore up the pipes during the night. There were similar absurdities when the main sewer was extended into Stubbing Lane. The Board had no powers of compulsory purchase, which produced wearying battles with property owners reluctant to sell water rights or determined to force the price up. When pipes were laid across private land the Board demanded that the owners should pay for them. Joseph Hartley, the owner of Sowden springs, fought a long delaying action before accepting the £175 for his surplus water, a figure proposed two years before.[31] Eventually, it was discovered that householders could be compelled to take water from the public supply provided that the charge did not exceed 2d. per house per week.[32] By 1860, despite these wranglings, Haworth had a basic sewerage system, clean water was flowing from the two springs, and the small Churchills reservoir had been constructed.

Troubled and dilatory though it was, the work of the Local Board laid the foundations for a considerable improvement in the health of the village. In the short term the effects were limited, because the most pressing problem was poverty rather than sanitation. For the decade 1801–10 the mortality rate for the chapelry was 22.2 per 1,000 and life expectancy at birth was 32.8 years.[33] Babbage's figures for 1838–49 for the *hamlet* of Haworth show a mortality rate of 25.4 and life expectancy of 25.8, which put it on a par with the worst areas of London, such as Whitechapel. The most serious deterioration had been in the health of infants. In the 1840s, 22 per cent of all burials were of infants under six months,[34] whereas in the first decade of the century 13.6 per cent were of infants under one year. Infant mortality had increased with appalling effect. As Babbage was writing his report, the handcombing trade was in its death throes. There was very extensive unemployment, many families were destitute, and even the handcombers in work were earning starvation wages of 4*s.* or 5*s.* a week. They and their families were living in overcrowded and ill-heated accommodation, ill-fed and ill-clothed.[35] Children born in such circumstances were particularly vulnerable – perhaps decent wages were more urgent even than decent sanitation. Twenty-five years later, progress was being made, albeit slowly. Figures for the late 1870s show that mortality had fallen to 21.3 per 1000 and life expectancy had increased to 32.3 – yet those figures were still worse than those for the first decade of the century. By our standards they were totally unacceptable. Haworth had made progress, but there was a very long way to go.

Barbarians and Philistines

In his book *Culture and Anarchy* Matthew Arnold identified two major groups. One he called the 'Barbarians': they looked back to feudalism, chivalry, the 'courtly ideal' of Queen Elizabeth, the Cavaliers, and the Toryism of Queen Anne's time. By the mid-nineteenth century 'Barbarian' modes seemed to pervade the aristocracy, high church Anglicanism, the universities and the public schools. The leading local 'Barbarian' was William Busfeild Ferrand, lord of the manor of Haworth from 1854 to 1889. He built himself a grand new mansion at St Ives in Bingley, to which he moved in 1855. He was passionately fond of fox hunting, rode to hounds as often as he could, was a crack shot, and he occupied much of his time shooting grouse on his own estates and those of his friends. When neither was available he went fishing. He was also a leading light in the Bingley Volunteers, founded in 1859. 'Barbarians' preferred social to intellectual recreations. The young attended assemblies and went racing; their elders played cards and exchanged scandal. If, like Ferrand, one had little taste for either one went to bed early.[36]

Those moneyed families in Haworth who were no longer actively engaged in business, but simply drew the profits, tried to ape such ways. Robert Heaton doubled the size of Ponden in 1801 and James Greenwood built himself a large new house at Woodlands in 1832. Heaton kept a pack of hounds – his huntsman, John Bolton, is buried in Haworth churchyard. Every year the local newspapers carried lists of gamekeepers appointed by the owners of the shooting rights: in 1805 Nathan Midgley was appointed by Joseph Midgley for Haworth; William Kitching by Sir Francis Wood for Oxenhope; and Abraham Sunderland by Benjamin Rawson, lord of the manor of Bradford, for Stanbury. In 1821 Joseph, George and James Greenwood were listed as holding game licenses, as were Jonas Horsfall, Horsfall Heaton and Robert Heaton. Branwell Brontë was interested but the family's limited income effectively confined him to occasional outings. In 1843 the *Bradford Observer* noted sardonically that 'the privileged few who are allowed by law to have a property in the wild birds of the air and the wild beasts of the field, commenced their work of destruction on Saturday week'.[37] Many of those who shot over the local moors had estates or moorland rights within the township but lived elsewhere – one such was the earl of Wilton, lord of the manor of Oxenhope from 1816 to 1833. Others rented the shooting rights.

In the township itself, though, most inhabitants who had money and time to spare were from Matthew Arnold's second group – the Philistines. He considered that their attitudes harked back to the puritan movement, but had been given form by the industrial revolution which created a powerful manufacturing class. Arnold thought these were the ideas of the wealthy manufacturers, the shopkeepers and the clerks, people who were even less intellectual than Barbarians. They kept their children at school for only as long as it took to learn commercial arithmetic. Whether or not Arnold was right in his judgement is another matter. For many of his 'philistines' it was a case of 'needs must', with survival and self-improvement as the essentials. As the combers, weavers, shopkeepers and clerks became slightly more affluent in the late eighteenth century,

The interior of the Three Graces Lodge, photographed in the 1960s. The lodge was founded at Barnoldswick and moved to Haworth in 1806. The original rooms were in Lodge Street. This is the interior of the Mill Hey Lodge to which the society moved in the late nineteenth century. Both Patrick and Branwell Brontë were Freemasons.

they sought to provide for the future
by forming clubs which paid sickness
and funeral benefits or gave pensions to
widows. In 1793 an Act of Parliament
regularised such associations and required
them to adopt formal constitutions. John
Greenwood of Bridgehouse was on the
committee responsible for securing the
1793 Act.

The earliest benefit club in Haworth
was the New Union Society of 1781,[38] and
the returns of 1803–04 show that Bingley
had four societies with 477 members;
Keighley six with 820; and Haworth
five with 960.[39] By the early nineteenth
century most leading societies were
established in the township. In February
1796, for example, the Prince George
Lodge No.308 of the International Order
of Freemasons was consecrated (though
it later moved to Todmorden and in 1806

The Old
Lodge. The
Three Graces
Lodge of the
Freemasons
moved to
this house in
Lodge Street
and finally to
new premises
in Mill Hey in
1907.
PHOTOGRAPH:
CARNEGIE, 2009

was replaced by the Three Graces Lodge No.408, which came from Barnoldswick).[40]
The Woodlands Lodge of the Independent Order of Oddfellows is first mentioned in
1846 but may well have been founded earlier – its name, and George Greenwood's
involvement with the Addingham branch, suggests that his family played a part in its
foundation.[41] The Ancient Order of Foresters is first recorded the same year, celebrating
the anniversary of Court Mount Ararat No.96 on Easter Monday. The Ancient Order
of Rechabites is mentioned in 1859.[42]

As well as providing benefits, many of these societies had other roles. The Freemasons
were in principle a brotherhood of men from all classes but they soon lost those revolu-
tionary credentials and by 1820 had gained the imprimatur of the Established Church.
Patrick and Branwell Brontë were both members.[43] The societies were focal points in
the social life of the township. Each was established at one of the principal inns. The
Freemasons met first at the *Black Bull*, then at the *King's Arms*, and finally at the *White
Lion* before securing their own rooms. The Oddfellows favoured the *New Inn*, Stubbing,
while the Foresters, though they had their own court room, also patronised the *Sun
Inn* and the *Black Bull*. Each society held anniversary celebrations, beginning with a
procession to the church followed by a service and concluding with a dinner at one of
the inns. They also commemorated the deaths of their members in a fitting manner.

The 'Philistines' were not completely unintellectual, because the concept of
'improvement' was allied to that of self help. In his diary for 1794 the eighteen-year-
old William Shackleton, who lived at Whinknowle near Braithwaite, recorded that he

The New Inn, Stubbing. The Independent Order of Oddfellows held their meetings here. George Greenwood was a patron of the Addingham branch and the New Inn is not far from Woodlands built by James Greenwood in 1833, which suggests that he too took an interest in the friendly society.

read three volumes of *Hume's History of England*, a book about the shipwreck of the *Antelope*, one on the *Art of Rhetoric*, and Locke's *Essay on Human Understanding*. He looked at the stars through his friend's perspective glass and read Moore's *Navigation* and Leadbetter's *Astronomy* to make sense of what he saw. He borrowed a book on astrology from his uncle, and read poetry – Milton's *Paradise Lost*, Pope's *Essay on Man* and James Thomson's *The Seasons*. He had heard of David Garrick and quoted from *Hamlet* and *The Merchant of Venice*.[44] There was a thirst for knowledge and circulating libraries already existed to satisfy the demand. Reading poetry led to writing poetry – native Haworth poets included Joseph Hardaker, who started the first druggist shop in the village; John Appleyard Whitaker; Abraham Wildman, assistant poor law overseer in 1840; and the tragic figure of Branwell Brontë.[45]

From the mid-1820s the desire for knowledge lay behind the establishment of mechanics' institutes. That at Keighley (1825) was one of the earliest, though Haworth's was not opened until 1848.[46] The institutes had a reading room, with copies of national newspapers, and a library from which books could be borrowed by members. The Brontës often borrowed books from the Keighley Institute library, and old inhabitants of Lees remembered seeing the girls walking down to Keighley and back again. The institutes also held lectures by visiting speakers, which in many places eventually developed into the provision of adult education. At Haworth the institute was always underfinanced, and after the initial enthusiasm lectures were few and far between.

One cultural activity which did flourish was music. The Haworth Philharmonic Society was founded in about 1780. It initially held a concert every 5 November,[47] but by the 1830s the series was quarterly. In 1844 the audience heard pieces from Handel's *Messiah* and his *Samson*, and Haydn's *The Seasons*.[48] Newspaper reports complimented the choir, which was composed of local singers, though soloists were often recruited from outside and especially from the Halifax Concert Society. The concerts were never complete without a contribution from Haworth's own star, the tenor Thomas Parker. Instrumental music was not forgotten, for the *Bradford Observer* regularly commented

Branwell Brontë's famous oil painting of his three sisters: from left to right, Anne, Emily and Charlotte. The artist appears to have made a crude attempt to erase his self-portrait in the centre, ironically leaving a ghostly apparition in the background that dominates the canvas. The painting was presumed lost until 1914, when it was found by the second wife of Rev. Arthur Bell Nicholls, folded up on top of a cupboard.

favourably on the orchestral accompaniments. Most of the players were local. Typical of them was Joseph Craven of Stanbury, who had no professional training but could play several instruments, his favourite being the violin. By the late eighteenth century nearly all churches and chapels had their own musicians and there was a passion for wind bands. In *Wuthering Heights* Emily Brontë described the Gimmerton Band, fifteen-strong 'comprising a trumpet, a trombone, clarionets, bassoons, French horns and a bass viol' which went the rounds at Christmas with the carol singers. During the 1830s and 1840s they were replaced by organs. By 1852 the Philharmonic Society had moved to Oakworth and it was soon killed off by the trade depression, but the tradition did not die, reappearing in the brass band movement considered in a later chapter.[49]

Thus, Haworth was far from the desolate wilderness that is sometimes imagined. How did the Brontë sisters fit into this world? Apart from being passive auditors, they did not fit in at all. They were not part of Haworth society in any meaningful sense

and, except for a little local colouring, their books owed nothing to it. When Charlotte wrote about the textile industry she chose the Luddites of Hartshead, not the upheavals happening around her. For Emily the worsted trade did not exist. The Earnshaws of Wuthering Heights must have been unique as the only moorland family in the district able to maintain itself without a handloom on which to weave cloth. In 1835 Patrick wrote that 'My happiest days were spent [at Thornton]. In this place I have received civilities, and have, I trust, been civil to all, but I have not tried to make any friends, nor have I met with any whose mind was congenial with my own.'[50] Ten years later Charlotte

The 'Brontë Bridge', which formed part of an old network of farm paths across the moors. It got the name in the late nineteenth century, but there is no hard evidence connecting it with the Brontë sisters in particular, although they probably knew it well. The old Brontë Bridge was destroyed by a flash flood in May 1989, and rebuilt in 1990, when an army helicopter was used to fly in the new stones and the plaque.
BY COURTESY OF IAN PALMER

echoed her father's sentiments: 'Resident in a remote district where education had made little progress, and where consequently there was little inducement to seek social intercourse beyond our own domestic circle, we were wholly dependent on ourselves and each other, on books and study, for enjoyments and occupations of life.'[51] To the locals, Brontë minded his own business and did not interfere with other people. Old ladies, asked to search their memories at the beginning of the twentieth century, could only recall Charlotte's sharp comments on their sewing mistakes during lessons at the Sunday school. Emily was a figure in the distance, with a dog. Anne did not register at all. In February 1850, when the news emerged that Charlotte was 'Currer Bell', who had written *Jane Eyre* and *Shirley*, the Mechanics' Institute hastily ordered copies of the books – until the committee knew of a local connection, it had not considered the books at all.[52] Imaginative fiction played little part in Haworth's intellectual life and in some quarters was regarded with outright hostility.

Arnold himself was an enthusiast, and composed an epitaph for Charlotte on her death,[53] but for most of his followers the Brontë novels did not spread the 'sweetness and light' which they thought should civilise society. Miss Atkinson, headmistress of the Drake and Tonson Girls' Grammar School in Keighley between 1896 and 1925, formed a literary circle to encourage the girls to read suitable fiction.[54] Sir Walter Scott, a favourite of Arnold and the Brontë sisters, was prominent among the selections, but when one girl suggested Dickens the idea was vetoed as 'vulgar'. The Brontë novels were not even considered. They were too dangerous. Parents might not approve. As Sir Charles Grant Robertson observed many years ago, 'It was not Haworth that made the Brontës … it was the Brontë women – particularly Charlotte and Emily – who made Haworth what it has come to be for all of us who care for what English genius has wrought.'[55]

The Worth Valley Railway opened in 1867 and continued operating for almost a century until 1961. The line reopened in 1968, operated by the Worth Valley Light Railway Company and staffed by a volunteer workforce. This photograph shows a typical early Worth Valley Railway tank engine.

PHOTOGRAPH BY COURTESY OF JACK LAYCOCK

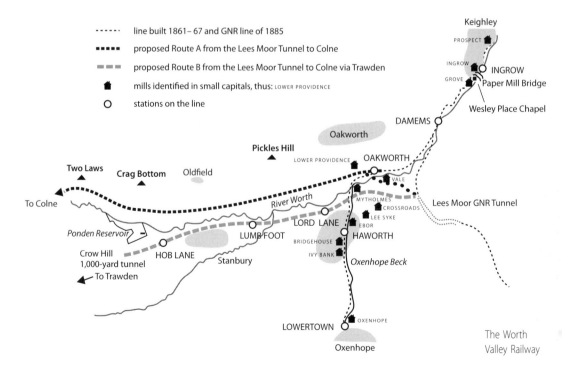

- - - - - line built 1861–67 and GNR line of 1885

▪▪▪▪▪ proposed Route A from the Lees Moor Tunnel to Colne

▬ ▬ ▬ proposed Route B from the Lees Moor Tunnel to Colne via Trawden

🏭 mills identified in small capitals, thus: LOWER PROVIDENCE

O stations on the line

Keighley

PROSPECT

INGROW

GROVE

INGROW

Paper Mill Bridge

Wesley Place Chapel

DAMEMS

Oakworth

Pickles Hill

LOWER PROVIDENCE

OAKWORTH

VALE

Two Laws   Crag Bottom   Oldfield

MYTHOLMES

CROSSROADS

Lees Moor GNR Tunnel

To Colne

River Worth

LEE SYKE

EBOR

Ponden Reservoir

LORD LANE

LUMB FOOT

BRIDGEHOUSE

HAWORTH

Crow Hill
1,000-yard tunnel

HOB LANE

Stanbury

IVY BANK

Oxenhope Beck

To Trawden

OXENHOPE

LOWERTOWN

Oxenhope

The Worth
Valley Railway

The Worth Valley Railway and the late nineteenth-century textile industry 12

Building a railway

Renewed interest in a railway up the Worth valley was reputedly the result of a visit to Haworth in 1861 by John McLandsborough, a civil engineer living at Shipley, who was trying to interest the Midland in a railway extension to Otley and Ilkley. His journey was made 'as a pilgrim at the shrine of Charlotte Brontë'. Traditionally, pilgrims go on foot, staff in hand, but as an engineer McLandsborough knew that the number of worshippers would be greatly increased if they could travel in comfort by railway.[1] At his instance a meeting was held at the *Black Bull*, Haworth on 13 September 1861, which decided to seek the support of the Midland Railway Company. A deputation went to Derby on 1 October and terms were quickly agreed.[2] The local committee was to form a company and raise the money necessary to construct the line, while the Midland would allow the company access to Keighley station, provide the necessary rolling stock, and be responsible for track maintenance. Goods charges and passenger fares would be equivalent to those on the Leeds–Colne line. The Midland would take 50 per cent of the revenue, leaving the other half to be distributed in dividends. The deal appeared to be excellent for both parties: the Midland acquired a branch line without risking any of its own capital, one which would generate a small but useful traffic, and the shareholders would receive a guaranteed half of the receipts.

The initial plan was for a line from Keighley to Haworth, the question of its extension to Oxenhope being dependent on a survey, potential traffic and subscriptions.[3] Shares were to be in units of £5, and manufacturers quickly subscribed substantial amounts: Jonas Sugden & Bros, and Jonathan N. Craven both bought 1,000 shares, while Merrall Bros. and Isaac Holden promised to take 500 each. Pledges totalling £15,420 were received. An extension to Lowertown was agreed at a meeting on 16 October and included in the draft bill, on the announcement that an additional £5,250 had been raised, mainly from Oxenhope. By the time construction began in 1864, another 54 subscribers had been found and the capital of £36,000 was fully paid up.[4]

Vale Mill and the railway viaduct. This fascinating panoramic view shows the Oakworth viaduct. It caused trouble from the start, when the engine used on the opening run was not powerful enough to pull all the carriages up the track and the train had to be divided. There were worries later about the safety of the viaduct, and in 1893 it was dismantled and replaced by the Mytholmes Tunnel. Vale Mill in the background was originally built by the Keighley Greenwoods in 1807. Though just outside Haworth township, a large part of the population of Lees and Crossroads was employed there in the late nineteenth century.

The Act received the royal assent in June 1862 but the first sod was not cut until Shrove Tuesday 1864. Rev. John Wade commented at the ceremony on the scepticism expressed, at the time he succeeded Brontë as perpetual curate, about whether a railway up the Worth valley would ever be constructed. He recalled how when he took 'the only honourable conveyance' in Haworth for his journey down to Keighley, a little lad ran after it calling out 'there's the Haworth train', much to his disgust. Now everything had changed and he remarked amid laughter that 'they knew how all the oven doors in the place had been thrown off their hinges by being slammed in imitation of the slamming of the doors of railway carriages'. Handing the silver spade to Isaac Holden, who was to perform the ceremony, Wade expressed the hope that the line would be open by the next Shrove Tuesday.[5] He was being wildly optimistic. It took three more years before the sceptics were confounded. A number of reasons for the delays were put forward. One wag suggested that the plans had been eaten by a cow when the engineer dropped them during a route inspection.[6]

Some of the delays were because of engineering difficulties at Ingrow. When the tunnel under the Halifax road was being built, the contractors found that the only way to create a stable structure in the wet, sandy soil was to drive piles until bedrock was reached. Unfortunately the removal of large amounts of material, and the vibration caused by the pile-driving, affected the nearby Methodist chapel, opened by Isaac Holden in March 1863. The building was so seriously damaged that it had to be taken down and rebuilt further back.[7] To the railway company this was a clear case of what happens when people build on sand, not on rock. The chapel trustees naturally did not agree and sued the company, obtaining £1,950 in damages. The Worth Valley directors must have got thoroughly fed up with deliberations about ''th bog hoil wot's called 't Paper Miln Brig'.[8]

The track was complete by the autumn of 1866 but the trial run on 1 November was far from impressive. The start was delayed and the train took almost an hour to reach Damems. There were further delays at Haworth while workmen cleared the metals of debris, and the passengers arrived at Oxenhope, rather the worse for wear, at 1.30 p.m. The turntable was not finished and everyone had to help push the train round for the return journey. This was completed in 13 minutes flat, the driver omitting to stop at any of the intermediary stations, much to the annoyance of those who had got on at Haworth and had to pay for transport to take them back.[9] A fortnight later Yorkshire was struck by a series of freak storms, which swept away 40 yards of the embankment near Damems. Reconstruction work delayed the formal opening until the following spring. A quatrain in the *Keighley News* summed up the general frustration.

> Tunnels sink, and navvies drink
> And chapels are upsetting,
> For railway shares, nobody cares,
> And everybody's fretting.'[10]

Haworth station was built for the opening of the Worth Valley Railway in 1867, and the current entrance and main building date from that time. The gable in the right of the picture was added later in the nineteenth century.
PHOTOGRAPH: CARNEGIE, 2009

Stephen Merrall (1809–74) and Aleithia his wife. Stephen was one of the three brothers who built and ran Lee Syke Mill. He retired from business in 1860 to become a Methodist minister.

A mishap even affected the opening ceremony on 13 April 1867. The engine could not raise enough steam to get all the fully loaded carriages up the incline onto the viaduct beyond Oakworth station and the train had to be divided, much to the annoyance of those relegated to the second section.[11] But though technical problems certainly contributed to the delay in building the line, they were not the chief cause. There was a complete lack of interest among Keighley manufacturers in a line which would improve the position of their competitors up the valley, and landowners were also obstructive. Richard Butterfield, who owned Bridgehouse and Lumbfoot Mills, was keen to get the railway built but the focus of his interest was Prospect Mill at Ingrow, on land through which the line had to pass. He attended the early meetings and supported the proposals but tried to avoid committing himself to buying shares. Eventually he was told that the project would not go beyond Springhead until he did. His fellow manufacturers were determined to ensure that he would receive no compensation for his Ingrow land and a railway for his Haworth mills without bearing some part of the risk. He bought the shares, but charged the company with the costs of building a carriage road and bridge from his Woodlands mansion across the line to Sun Street.

Other textile manufacturers joined in the arm-twisting. John Clough of Ingrow Mill

Michael Merrall, 1811–81, the most important of the Merrall brothers, who founded Lee Syke. After the retirement of Stephen and the death of Edwin he ran the firm alone. He also financed the building of the present Haworth church. He was succeeded in the business by his three sons, George, Edwin and Alfred.

claimed that he too needed a new road across the line to link his mill with his house. Robert Clough posed even greater problems, arguing that the railway would so interfere with operations at his Grove Mill that an entirely new factory had to be built on the opposite side of the line. He claimed £5,562 1s. 6d. compensation for land depreciation, line construction, inconvenience to his business, and extra wages. In 1868, after much wrangling, he was awarded £2,553 6s. 6d. by a jury. Even after the first sod had been cut, delays were experienced because landowners refused to allow the contractor onto their properties.[12]

Butterfield's ambivalent attitude to the railway may have been because expansion of the plant at Bridgehouse had been planned before the company was formed,[13] so that the line was not essential to the firm's wellbeing. For the others the position was quite different. The most consistent supporter of the railway was Michael Merrall. In 1860 Stephen Merrall decided to leave the business and become a Methodist minister. Edwin Merrall took over Botany Mill at East Morton, and Michael assumed responsibility for Lee Syke and Ebor, assisted by his sons George, Edwin and Alfred. He originally planned to concentrate spinning at Lee Syke and weaving at Ebor but by 1866 he was sufficiently confident to build a second weaving shed at Ebor, doubling the mill's rateable value. His business boomed in the years after the railway opened and in 1869 a third weaving shed was built at Lee Syke.[14] Hartley Merrall also took the opportunity provided by the opening of the railway to add a weaving shed at Springhead.[15]

Another promoter of the railway was the firm of John & J.N. Craven. John Craven, son of Hiram, was not a textile manufacturer and lived at York, but the family still owned the land in the Worth valley on which stood the four textile mills – Springhead, Mytholmes, Higher and Lower Providence – which Hiram had done so much to develop. The building of the railway led to a rapid appreciation in their value. In 1863 John Craven managed to find a tenant for Mytholmes Mill, most of which had been empty for seven years.[16] He was Edwin G. Hattersley, for whom taking the lease was part of

An aerial view of Ebor Mill.

A plan of the Ebor Mill site. Spinning mill 1 was originally driven by a water wheel, and dates from 1819, with the upper portion added by Cravens and Sugden c.1830–50. There is the outline of a gasometer built in 1847–48, later demolished, which can be seen in the field on the right of the aerial view above. Merralls added Spinning mill 2 and Weaving shed 1 around 1852–53. The next development, c.1867–70, was associated with the opening of the Worth Valley Railway and comprises Weaving shed 2, Engine house 2, the Warehouse and the Storeroom. The last phase began following a fire in the spinning complex at Lees in 1885, leading to the building of the vast Spinning mill 3, the boiler house and the economiser.

a plan to move the spinning section of the family business from Keighley to Oakworth. In 1869 Hattersleys took the lease of Higher Providence Mill[17] and sometime before 1875 occupied Lower Providence as well. This was a coup for Craven, who had had the latter completely rebuilt as a speculation in 1867. Hattersley became a director of the railway company soon after taking Mytholmes, and attended nearly every committee meeting between then and the opening in 1867. Another new director was James Haggas, whose business moved from Damems to Crossroads in 1868.[18] In 1869 Thomas Bland was tempted away from Becks Mill in Keighley to Ivy Bank Mill in Haworth. The mill, built in 1860, was steam-powered from the start, so the only change he needed to make was to add a warehouse in 1870.[19]

The original plan was to continue to Lowertown, instead of terminating at the present Oxenhope station – a bridge over Oxenhope Beck was clearly designed to carry a railway. Lack of money may have been the reason for the abandonment of this proposal, but it has been suggested that George Greenwood, chairman of the railway company in its early years, used his influence to ensure that the line benefited his own Oxenhope Mill rather than those of other manufacturers. Such manipulation was not unknown. The railway also stimulated Oxenhope. During the late 1860s many local manufacturers extended or relocated their businesses. In 1866, for example, John Bancroft took extra space at Oxenhope Mill but two years later he rebuilt Charles Mill, even though it was some distance from the new railway. He died in 1869 and his son, Joseph Riley Bancroft, then entered a partnership with William Binns and Thomas Parker.[20] Feather and Speak,

Ebor Mill showing the 5-storey spinning mill constructed by Merralls. The chimney rises behind the earlier spinning mill built by Townend & Co., which dates from 1819. Merralls ceased trading in 1965, when it was taken over by Airedale Valley Springs.

PHOTOGRAPH: CARNEGIE, 2009

of Holme Mill, disposed of Lowertown Shed to Joseph Whitaker between 1854 and 1858, before the railway was promoted. In 1862 Joseph Whitaker added a warehouse and, two years later, offices to Lowertown Shed.[21] He died before the opening of the railway but the business was continued by his sons. Lowertown was a hive of activity: Feather Brothers and Luty moved from Wadsworth House to Lowertown Mill which they had greatly extended by 1830.[22] Henry Bailey, a partner in Gauthrop and Bailey, rebuilt Dunkirk Mill in 1870[23] and in the same year was listed as the tenant of nearby Brooks' Meeting Mill on the other side of Oxenhope Beck.

The period was one of great activity for the employers but there were mixed experiences for the workers. In Haworth the mechanisation of weaving and combing was practically complete by 1861, so the unemployment of the few remaining hand workers was more than compensated for by the improved prospects provided by the expansion of Merralls and the arrival of Bland and the Hattersleys. In 1861, 1,021 people were employed in the textile industry, in 1871 1,444. In Oxenhope the change was rather more slow. There were 178 hand combers and 99 handloom weavers in 1861, and in

Oxenhope station. There are stories that the railway was originally intended to go right into Lowertown, but that the station was sited just outside Oxenhope Mill because the committee chairman was George Greenwood who owned it. This photograph dates from around 1900, when the railway was at its most prosperous.

Dunkirk Mill, Oxenhope. This photograph, which dates from c.1900, shows the mill as rebuilt by Henry Bailey in 1870, but it is mainly associated with the Dewhirsts, who made cotton banding. Unusually the firm installed a water turbine and diversified into corn milling. The engine house is in the foreground, and the manager's house can be seen attached to the end of the spinning mill.

1871 only 8 hand combers and 9 handloom weavers. Even the improvement in trade stimulated by the railway could not absorb these losses: Oxenhope's textile workforce dropped from 1,275 in 1861 to 1,014 in 1871.[24]

The depression and the Midland takeover

The years after 1857 were some of the most prosperous for the worsted industry, so the long delay in completing the Worth Valley Railway robbed Haworth's manufacturers of their best years. A trade depression began in 1875 and lasted for the rest of the decade. Its most prominent victim was Hartley Merrall junior at Springhead, who in 1875 failed dramatically, being able to pay his creditors only 10s. in the pound.[25] The following year almost saw another spectacular bankruptcy. In 1869, on the death of Richard Butterfield, his firm leased Bridgehouse to the mill manager, John Ramsden Redman, a most capable man who had been the secretary of the Keighley and Worth Valley Railway Company. He formed a partnership with Richard Holt and bought out Butterfields, but Holt involved himself in other speculations and went bankrupt in 1876. By this time the partnership had been dissolved but Redman had to fight a long legal battle to survive.[26] By 1878 the depression was so severe that Haworth's manufacturers got together and agreed to cut wages simultaneously,[27] the apparent alternative being to throw people out of work. This would have increased the poor rate, most of which was paid by the manufacturers. Haworth's textile workforce fell from 1,444 to 1,279.[28]

Oxenhope also suffered. Gauthorp and Bailey disappeared and Harrison Lee Roberts, who took over Brooks' Meeting Mill from Bailey, went bankrupt in 1879.[29] Bancrofts hurriedly withdrew from Oxenhope Mill, which was empty in 1876, and many of the small mills went out of business. Roydhouse, no longer a textile mill, was variously a machine shop and a tannery, while Midgeholme and Throstle Nest were both on the part of Leeming Water which in 1880–81 was drowned by a reservoir intended, somewhat ironically, to supply water and power for textile mills in the Worth valley. Scar Hall also closed and is not mentioned again, while Bull Hill went out of use when George Emmott Pawson moved his machine shop to Wadsworth House Mill. This in turn ended textile production at Wadsworth, the spare space being occupied by Thomas Parker's wool warehouse. The result was another fall in textile employment, to 829. The building of Leeming reservoir did not provide much alternative employment: of the 86 labourers only twelve were born in Haworth township.[30]

Another victim of the depression was the Keighley and Worth Valley Railway Company itself. Initial estimates put the cost at £36,000 but compensation claims inflated the expenses well beyond that figure. Some £60,000 of debentures and £34,000

Leeming Reservoir. This was what was known as a 'compensation' reservoir, as it was built to replace the water lost to the local mill owners after their original supply was diverted to provide water to Keighley.

of preference shares were issued, and eventually £130,000 was raised. The original prospectus estimated annual revenue at £4,000, but because of the depression the average for the first ten years was just £2,000. The Company was unable to pay a dividend, because the surplus had to offset the debts. Fortunately a rival to the Midland Railway appeared, in the form of the Great Northern Railway which proposed to extend from Bradford and Halifax to Keighley, via the Worth valley. This proposal forced the Midland to enter into negotiations with the Keighley and Worth Valley Railway, to prevent it selling out to the rival company. In 1880 a lease was agreed, by which the Midland paid the Worth Valley a yearly rent of £4,200 for the use of the line. In 1885 the Midland absorbed the Company, paying the shareholders £150 of Midland stock for every £100 of Worth Valley shares. The Midland also took over the company's debts and agreed to include dividends which had been withheld, so this was a remarkably good deal for the shareholders.[31] There were complaints about cynical manoeuvring by the Midland Railway, but the truth was that such branches rarely brought much profit to their promoters, the main benefit being the provision of better communications for the local community.[32] In this case not only did the manufacturers' businesses benefit but the shareholders, who were mostly the manufacturers themselves, made a handsome profit.

The textile revival

Among the possible causes of the depression was complacency among the manufacturers, for their reputation for mechanical invention had passed overseas mainly to the USA, and they were slow to appreciate that the taste for brightly coloured crinolines and light fabrics, which the 'fancy goods' trade satisfied, had been superseded by a preference for more sombre styles requiring heavier cloths in blacks and greys. The French took advantage and soon usurped the position that English manufacturers had once occupied. But with the end of the depression in the late 1870s Haworth did not seem to do too badly. For example, Hattersleys were spinners and, less affected by the changes in the fashion market, took advantage of Hartley Merrall's bankruptcy to add Springhead Mill to their portfolio. Blands specialised in heald and genappe yarns which insulated them from the problems besetting the worsted cloth market. After the death of Michael Merrall in 1881, his sons George, Edwin and Alfred restructured the business, turning the weaving side over to making worsted linings for men's coats. In 1885 a serious fire at Lee Syke prompted more changes. The fire had destroyed the old mill which housed all the spinning equipment, paralysing production at Ebor as well as Lee Syke. To prevent a repetition Merralls had spinning machinery installed at Ebor in addition to the rebuilt facility at Lee Syke, all of the most up-to-date type.[33] At Ivy Bank, Blands extended their mill in 1885,[34] while at Bridgehouse Redman seemed to have overcome his earlier problems.

Oxenhope also experienced better times. Kershaws modernised Sykes Mill, while Dunkirk Mill entered a period of modest prosperity when Dewhirsts, the cotton

band makers, moved there from Fisher's Lodge. They rebuilt it and later added a steam engine.[35] In 1870 Thomas Parker left Charles Mill and moved to Wadsworth House and though in 1881 Bancroft lost his other partner, William Binns, he felt strong enough to continue alone. The width of Charles Mill was doubled and a steam engine put in.[36] As William Greenwood aged his business had stagnated, but the enthusiasm of his nephew James Frederick Greenwood gave it a new lease of life. After a flirtation with Oxenhope Mill when Bancroft vacated it, Greenwood moved to Brooks' Meeting Mill in 1879. A weaving shed was added to the original spinning mill and in 1885 he replaced the steam engine with a newer and larger one. Sometime after 1887 water power was eliminated altogether and a modern horizontal tandem compound engine substituted.[37]

Even the one major disaster turned out to be a blessing in disguise. In 1882 Whitaker Brothers went bankrupt, but their Lowertown Shed did not remain empty for long. The mill and the site were purchased by Crabtree Brothers in 1884, in what may have been a speculation. They were building contractors and scarcely a year later let the property to Merralls, who immediately began to expand the accommodation and increase the engine power. In 1887 Merralls bought Crabtrees out and the following year put in extra power and built a new weaving shed.[38] By 1891 the number in textile employment in Oxenhope was 1082, back to the 1871 level.

In Stanbury, though, there was little change in the workforce between 1861 and 1871. As with Haworth, most of the handloom weavers and combers had disappeared by 1861, though some cloth was still woven in farms up by the moors. The last handloom weaver was Timmy Feather of Buckley Green, who died in 1910. He achieved almost iconic status and no book about the area was considered complete without some reference to him. Yet, in contrast to Haworth, the subsequent decade witnessed no improvement in trade, and there was a slump in employment during the depression. There were 251 textile workers in Stanbury in 1861, 260 in 1871 and 206 in 1881.

Two mills did very badly. In 1861 Ponden was occupied by the firm of Williamson Brothers but they left in 1862. The owner, Robert Heaton, then had great difficulty in finding a steady tenant – the mill was empty between 1867 and 1869. In 1870,

This photograph from 1870 shows Ponden Reservoir under construction. Ponden Hall can be seen in the background. Building the reservoir led to the suspension of textile production at Ponden Mill for almost a decade. The reservoir stored 'compensation' water for the textile mills. Nearby Stanbury, which was almost surrounded by reservoirs, did not get domestic piped water until 1946.

© KEIGHLEY NEWS

as work on the Ponden reservoir began, Keighley Corporation bought the mill and all production stopped.[39] At Hollings Mill both the mill buildings burned down in January 1864 and rebuilding had hardly been completed when in December 1865 they were gutted by a second fire. So sanguine were the times that another restoration had been completed by the end of 1866. In 1871 William Turner, the occupant, was employing 100 workers but in 1878 he became a victim of the depression and the mill was sold in November to George Hartley Merrall. George was no more successful than his father at Springhead or his predecessor and went bankrupt in 1880 with liabilities of £3,500. The sale notice shows that Merrall had added a 'small and compact weaving plant' at a time when manufacturing was suffering much more than spinning.[40]

Lumbfoot had a rather chequered career in the 1860s due to flooding. Butterfield's improvements, of two extra storeys to the spinning mill and an extended weaving shed, were destroyed when floods swept away the mill dam in 1867. The previous year James Wright had become manager: in 1867 the undertaking was leased to his firm, James Wright Brothers, and shortly afterwards was sold to them outright. The firm was still trading at the end of the decade.[41] The Williamsons had abandoned Ponden but retained Griffe where, despite a flood in 1864 which caused considerable damage, they added a warehouse and operated on a sound footing for several decades.[42]

Stanbury folk were quite certain that the misfortunes of their textile businesses were due to the lack of a railway. With the return of prosperity elsewhere after 1880 proposals were made for a line from the Worth Valley Railway near Haworth via Stanbury to Colne.[43] Keighley Local Board of Health approached the Great Northern Railway directors as early as 1882,[44] and in November 1884 the GNR line from Bradford and Halifax via Thornton was opened, joining the Worth Valley Railway near Ingrow.[45] In March 1885 the GNR proposed a line from Haworth via Stanbury and Wycoller to

Colne, and public meetings were held at Scartop, Stanbury and Trawden. The question of the best route caused considerable argument, but enthusiasm in the Worth valley and at Colne continued undimmed. There were other projects, too: in 1888 five meetings were held about a North West Central Railway, to link Preston with Keighley. They were attended by Jonas Sugden, John Haggas, Edwin Hattersley, Percy Redman, Francis Williamson and Thomas Wright on behalf of their firms.[46] In November 1889 a serious plan was put forward for a line from the northern end of the Lees Moor Tunnel on the GNR via Haworth and Trawden to Colne. It would cost £150,000 and a parliamentary bill received royal assent on 14 August 1890, but the project was never implemented.

The Midland Railway's opposition was a major reason for the long delays and failure to carry these schemes into effect. The company's directors saw that a line from Colne down the Worth valley would adversely affect traffic on their Colne–Skipton–Bradford route. Neither were they greatly impressed by the claim that at Stanbury there were

Flappit Spring Quarry is on Blackmoor. There are other quarries in Haworth hamlet, at Naylor Hill and on Penistone Hill, as well as at Nab Hill in Far Oxenhope. The stone is Kinderscout Grit and was used in building, paving stones and walling. Keighley bluestone, which is used for road metal, is mined at Bracken Hill edge near Ponden Clough in Stanbury. Cedric Gillson of wind turbine notoriety owned the Naylor Hill Quarry, and his eagerness to replace the sort of steam crane in the picture with a wind-driven electrical one can easily be understood.

'vast beds of good stone which cannot now be worked owing to their inaccessibility but which at once become profitable were the new scheme to be carried out'. There had been a short-lived Stanbury Coal, Iron and Lead Mining Company between 1863 and 1882, and the Midland had heard this sort of thing before.[47] Nor was their scepticism unjustified. Local opinion seems to have been that mining was just a diversion for young men tired of female company.[48] Beyond a flurry of excitement when coal was mined for a short time at Hob Nook on the edge of the moor in 1873, and some desultory activity at Height in the Sladen Valley, nothing substantial was ever achieved.[49]

This distrust was reinforced by the Midland's experience at Oxenhope, where it had expected considerable profits from the stone quarries. In 1861, 65 people in Oxenhope were employed in the extractive industries, mostly in the quarries. In 1871 the figure was the same; in 1881, 74; and in 1891, 69. This business brought little benefit to the Midland because the quarries were on the opposite side of the watershed between the Worth Valley and Calderdale, so it was easier to cart the stone down the Luddenden valley, where most late nineteenth-century housing was built of it.[50] The quarries on Penistone moor brought a little more profit, but even there most of the stone which was not absorbed by local building operations was loaded at Haworth rather than Oxenhope. In 1892 Midland removed the rickety, wooden viaduct so that the railway crossed the worth at a lower level which necessitated the construction of a tunnel at Mytholmes through the spur between the Worth Valley and Bridgehouse beck. Apart from this the company made no further attempt to exploit the Worth valley further.[51]

The failure to build the railway was just one aspect of a disastrous decade for the Stanbury mills. Only Lumbfoot came through unscathed. At Griffe the Williamson Brothers went bankrupt in 1884 and by 1890 the mill was completely empty. In 1884 Hollings was taken by the Bradford firm of Townend Brothers, who also bought Ponden from Keighley Corporation in 1888. Their ambitious plans were thwarted by a disastrous third fire at Hollings in 1889. Its employees believed the mill to be haunted by Thomas Lister, the cotton spinner, who had committed suicide. The next owner, Thomas Greenwood, razed the remnants to the ground.[52] Textile employment in Stanbury fell from 206 in 1881 to 158 in 1891, during a period which was the most prosperous at Haworth and Oxenhope.

Turn of the century blues

A further reason for the failure to extend the railway to Colne was another depression in the worsted trade, beginning in 1891 when the United States proposed the notorious McKinley tariff, designed to place heavy duties on imports of wool and textiles. There was also trouble in Australia following some sensational bank failures. The result was savage competition in the home and foreign markets. At Haworth the worst-affected was Merralls, for the chief market for their worsted coatings was the USA. The new tariff threatened to destroy the large profits anticipated by Merralls as a result of their investment. Although another fire in the Lees spinning complex in 1891 destroyed their new weaving shed,[53] Merralls went ahead with plans to expand weaving facilities at Oxenhope. A new shed was built in 1891 and doubled in size in 1896. But competitiveness was to be maintained by wage cutting, and this led to a series of strikes because the workers, not unnaturally, thought that if the firm could invest there must be money to pay them as well.[54]

Trouble began in 1888, when a strike failed to prevent Merralls cutting piece work rates for weavers. A further reduction in 1891 was also resisted successfully, but in July 1893 400 weavers went on strike, and Merralls responded by locking out the entire workforce of almost 4,000 people. After a fortnight the company capitulated, largely due to the influence of the West Riding Weavers Association, but for the workers it was a pyrrhic victory. The firm's underlying aim was to introduce a system where each weaver looked after two looms. Those who objected were forced to wait for their warps until all the two-loom weavers had been satisfied – which meant that although they got the old price for their pieces, they could not weave so many. A second strike, in September, was soon engulfed in the great coal strike of that year.[55]

After 1893 trade improved and Oxenhope prospered. Bancrofts and Kershaws did good business, and in part of Old Oxenhope Mill production continued until old William Greenwood died in 1893, at which point his nephew concentrated the business on Brooks Meeting Mill.[56] Merralls added a spinning mill to the weaving shed at Lowertown.[57] There were even unsuccessful attempts to revive the North West Central Railway

This image shows the entire Bridgehouse Mills complex at its greatest extent, in 1900, with the Worth Valley Railway running along the right-hand side just after Redman's bankruptcy. Sadly, little remains from the time of the Greenwoods except the frontage of the 1746 house on the extreme left. Both the Greenwood mills have gone and the earliest section is the section bottom centre with its entrance which was put up by Butterfield around 1850. Note that there is both a water wheel and a chimney, showing that both water and steam power were being used.

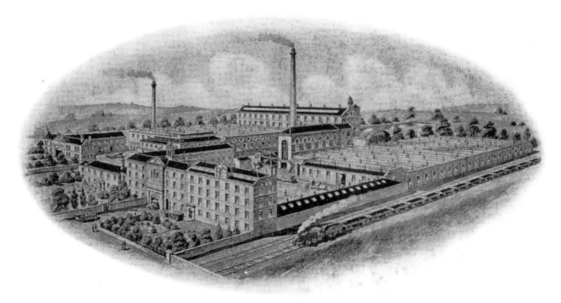

project, but Stanbury's fortunes continued to fade especially after Townends, who had moved to Griffe Mill, decided to sell both Griffe and Ponden in 1898.[58]

By 1900 the good times were definitely over, with the final implementation of the controversial tariff proposals in America. In 1900 Redman & Sons failed and, though the creditors were paid almost in full, it was not possible to continue the business.[59] Nobody was able to turn Bridgehouse into a paying proposition. In 1902 a firm called Haworth Worsted Spinners took over the mill, but it failed in 1905 owing £5,000, and the mill was then bought by a Bradford company which leased space to different firms.[60]

From 1908 a series of major commercial crises afflicted the industry, and in 1910 there were strikes among the spinners at Ponden and Lumbfoot which forced an increase of 3d. a week. In 1911 Haggases sold Crossroads Mill to Gates of Bradford, but no sooner had they done so than a serious fire gutted most of the building. In 1912 a fire at Bridgehouse destroyed the southern end occupied by Snowden and Seeger – fortunately they were insured and an undamaged part of the mill was empty, so they were able to resume business fairly rapidly. In the same year Wright Brothers at Lumbfoot failed,[61] and in March 1912 another serious coal strike dislocated business.

Oxenhope did not suffer as badly. J. F. Greenwood had built up a solid business at Brooks' Meeting Mill, while Kershaws at Sykes had a fully integrated mill where they combed their own wool – the premises had 6,000 spindles and 56 powerlooms. Merralls completed their building programme with a new engine house to accommodate a horizontal tandem compound engine, while among the spinners Feather Brothers added nearby Holme mill to Lowertown, giving them a combined total of 9,000 spindles (more than double the number run by Bancroft at Charles Mill, with 4,200).[62] Dunkirk put in a water turbine which could be used to power both textile machinery and the corn milling facility which Dewhirsts had added.

Between 1901 and 1911 the population of the township dropped by nearly a thousand, as large a fall as in the bad times of the early 1850s. The worst problems were experienced in Haworth, which lost over 700 people, mainly due to the failures at Bridgehouse. Even Oxenhope lost around 300. In Stanbury, despite Lumbfoot's difficulties, there was a slight rise, because production resumed at Griffe and Ponden on a small scale. Everywhere employees were now more vulnerable to periods out of work and to wage cuts than they had been. The old confidence had gone and the industry was fraying at the edges.

13 An industrial community

The workforce

In 1871 the population of the township of Haworth was 5,943, fewer than a hundred more than in 1861, but the next decade saw a much larger rise, of some 800, to a total of 6,794. The 1891 census showed an even bigger jump to 7,988.[1] Subsequent totals are difficult to calculate because later censuses are not arranged by township, but estimates suggest that the 1901 figure was similar to that of 1891, and that of 1911 about a thousand fewer. This pattern reflects the fortunes of the textile industry, as described in the last chapter. Analysis of the occupations given in successive censuses indicate that the proportion working in textiles was lower than that before the depression of the early 1850s, but the industry remained dominant throughout the period, accounting for 68 per cent of the workforce in 1861 and 1871, 63 per cent in 1881, and 67 per cent in 1891.

The reduction in the 1880s was due to structural changes in the woollen industry. Machine woolcombers were usually men, and the job was well paid, but mechanisation reduced their numbers greatly. Weaving, on the other hand, had been a mainly male occupation, but latterly women were preferred. In mid-century children of nine or ten started as doffers or piecers and then progressed to looking after spinning frames. When they were older they moved on to drawing, twisting or weaving. Employers favoured adult women because their wages were lower than those of their male equivalents. Promotion prospects for men were poor, although they could become overlookers, mechanics, woolsorters or warehousemen. By 1891 the census showed a notable imbalance between the sexes as men moved away in search of work. In 1861 Haworth had 2,934 males and 2,920 females, but in 1891 the figures were 3,766 and 4,222 respectively.

Statistics are rather fragmentary but they show that natural increase contributed substantially to the population increase. In almost every year for which totals can be reconstructed, births exceeded deaths and in some years by a considerable margin (for example, in 1878 a surplus of 56, in 1888 of 60, and in 1896 of 76).[2] In-migration also played a significant part: analysis of the origins of marriage partners shows that in 1861 70 per cent were born within the township of Haworth, but by 1891 this figure had fallen to 54 per cent.

There were three important groups of incomers. One came from Warwickshire. The 1871 census lists 134 people born in that county, of whom no fewer than 91 came from Coleshill, between Birmingham and Coventry, and 35 from Coventry itself. The reason for this seems to have been a temporary crisis in the Warwickshire hosiery trade. Another group came from Wiltshire, and moved to Yorkshire because of a very deep agricultural depression in the late nineteenth century. In 1871, 52 Haworth people were Wiltshire-born, but in 1881 the figure had increased to 132 and in 1891 it was still 122. In 1871 there were nine family groups, and in 1881 some 33 families or individuals who were not in the previous census. In 1891 there were 21 families or individuals not present in 1881, indicating that large-scale migration was still in progress. The main origin of these families was the village of Dauntsey, between Chippenham and Swindon, which accounted for 24 individuals in 1871 and 36 in 1881, when there were also thirty from its neighbour, Brinkworth, and ten from Christian Malford some six miles away to the west.

The third group came from nearer home. Lead production in the Yorkshire Dales fell very rapidly, from a peak of 12,406 tons of ore in 1857 to just 20 tons in 1913. Swaledale was among the areas worst affected and there was extensive out-migration. Most of the early emigrants to Haworth came from the Reeth area, but by 1881 the economic collapse had extended along the valley, and migrants came from Healaugh, Gunnerside, Low Row, and Muker. Four Muker families came to Stanbury, including the Hutchinsons who settled at Royds Hall in 1872. They came to work in coal-mining, but the Stanbury Mining Company soon failed and they had to find alternative employment.[3] Subsequently the large mines at Old Gang, on Melbeck Moor, wound down. This, too, had an immediate impact: in 1891 the largest group of migrants from the lead mining area, some sixty people, came from Arkengarthdale, close to Old Gang.[4]

Most English counties were represented in the 1891 Haworth census but the extent of migration should not be exaggerated. Of the 1,233 non-Haworth spouses, 997 were from other parts of Yorkshire and 92 from Lancashire. All the other counties combined totalled 113. Fourteen people were born in Scotland, only ten from Ireland, five from Wales and one each from the Isle of Man, Hong Kong and Switzerland. The small number from Ireland is particularly striking when compared with the large influx into neighbouring Keighley. The lump may have been leavened but locally born people still formed the great majority.

Another change was a shift in the location of population, as indicated in the table below:

Percentage of total population living in the four hamlets of Haworth township

hamlet	1861	1891
Haworth	41	56
Near Oxenhope	15	14
Far Oxenhope	34	24
Stanbury	10	6

The main reason for these changes was the economic dominance of the Merralls at Lee Syke and Ebor, just outside Haworth. The simultaneous development of Crossroads to serve the Haggas' mill and Sugden's Vale Mill attracted workers to the same area. Beginning in the late 1870s and continuing through the 1880s a swathe of housing, known as the Brow, was built. Two new roads were constructed – Station Road and Victoria Road – and soon connecting streets of speculative building filled in the hillside below the Oxenhope road from Mill Hey in the north to Brow Road on the south. After Blands took Ivy Bank Mill in 1870 the steady increase in the workforce generated more industrial housing in the area between Ivy Bank Lane and Stubbing Lane. A third development emerged on the other side of the lane, climbing Coldshaw beyond the Old Hall. This was technically in Near Oxenhope and explains why the growth of that hamlet kept pace with that of Haworth.[5] By 1890 housing extended all the way from Crossroads to Top Haworth. In 1861 there were 636 houses in Haworth hamlet; but in 1891, 1041 – and that did not include the Coldshaw area. The new housing was overwhelmingly working class: according to the 1891 census there were 1099 occupied houses in Haworth Urban District, of which forty had only one room, 202 two rooms, 295 three and 272

A view of Little Street, off West Lane. These are fairly typical early nineteenth-century cottages, with the blackened millstone grit walls that could make Haworth look so grim in wet weather.

PHOTOGRAPH: CARNEGIE, 2009

Main Street, looking up the hill. Note the blackness of the millstone grit, which stands out in comparison with the cleaned building. Note also the row of weavers' windows in the top storeys of these houses.

PHOTOGRAPH: CARNEGIE, 2009

four. Only 289 had more than four rooms. As Benjamin Frith remarked, Haworth had become 'a miniature Manchester'.[6]

Essential services

Servicing these new houses was the responsibility of the Haworth Local Board of Health. Jealous of its independence, and determined to spend as little as possible, Haworth LBH became a byword for incompetence. For example, once the Churchills reservoir was fully operational the Board took no further interest in water supply. In 1869 Keighley Corporation sought powers to build reservoirs at Ponden and Watersheddles, with pipes passing through the area of Haworth LBH. Oakworth Local Board's opposition to the bill was bought off when Keighley agreed to supply it with as much water as needed, at the cheap price of 5d. per 1,000 gallons. Haworth simply sought reassurances that their springs would be safeguarded and that it should not be compelled to take Keighley water in future.[7]

The folly of this attitude was exposed when, in the mid-1870s Haworth suffered chronic water shortages which in 1880 forced it to build a second reservoir at Hough End.[8] The reservoir was financed by a loan of £2,050 from the Local Government Board,

Leeming Reservoir, photographed from Leeming. Opened in 1881, the reservoir supplies Bradford, not nearby Oxenhope, which is out of sight down in the valley beyond the dam. The reservoir and its surroundings were described as important features of the Leeming Conservation Area in a local authority assessment in 2009.
© BRADFORD LIBRARY

which should have been repaid in annual instalments from the general rate. Haworth defaulted on the repayments and in 1887 all further loans were refused until the money was refunded. The Board's reaction was to offload the entire cost onto the water rate, with heavy surcharges.[9] By this time the increase in population had produced further shortages: the water was turned off daily from 7 p.m. to 7 a.m. and 'swilling' banned even in mid-winter.[10] To cap it all, the reservoir was leaking in such a mystifying fashion that the Board called in a water diviner to find out where the missing liquid had gone![11] This inspired some entertaining doggerel:

> 'Upon my Word! this will not do
> My friends,' said Mr Harper*
> 'About a thing in a regular way
> I would not be a carper,
> But if I *am* a little sharp,
> The ratepayers will be sharper.'

> The noble Redman's eyes flashed fire
> As though intent on slaughter.
> He scorned to think the Board would do
> A thing it didn't oughter
> How would the people keep alive
> Unless they found the water?

> 'But really now,' the first one said
> Consider what you're after,
> Ten pounds laid out on crooked sticks?
> Could anything be dafter?
> Your anxious toil won't earn you much
> But blunt remarks and laughter.'

> 'Oh stop your prate,' the Redman† cried
> 'We might have been a prigging,
> Whereas the money's been laid down
> For some scientific twigging.
> Which no one will begrudge when they
> Good water are a swigging.'

The truth was that Haworth did not have a sufficient catchment area for the water the inhabitants needed and the Board was only saved from having to take Keighley water at extortionate cost by the latter's 1892 project to extend the time limit for the construction of the Sladen Beck Reservoir. This time Haworth did not miss its chance and negotiated with Keighley to supply water at 6*d*. per 1,000 gallons whenever there

---

* Frank Harper, pastor of West Lane Baptist chapel from 1868 to 1888.

† Harry Redman, a son of John Ramsden Redman, owner of Bridgehouse Mill.

was a shortage, in return for dropping opposition to the bill.[12] Neither Oxenhope nor Stanbury was any better. In 1863 Oxenhope acquired a local board of health, which watched with complacency as Bradford Corporation constructed reservoirs in its area. The question of a public water supply did not become an issue until the council elections of 1904 and even then nothing was done. As late as November 1913 Oxenhope was still hesitating between taking water from either Bradford or Keighley or constructing its own reservoir.[13] Stanbury believed its wells to be sufficient and when it became part of the Oakworth Local Board area in 1869 the latter made it a special outer district which was not obliged to pay a water rate.

All the houses and streets of both new and old Haworth had to be provided with gas lighting. In 1865 Main Street, Bridgehouse and Mill Hey were illuminated for the first time and by 1870 every considerable thoroughfare was lit, but the lighting was irregular and lamps were often unlit for no apparent reason. In 1872 the Board obtained a local act allowing it to buy the Gas Company's plant for £6,300.[14] The change of ownership produced very little improvement. For a week in January 1875 the whole of Haworth was in darkness, the lamplighters having been told not to light the lamps if there was insufficient gas in the holder. The following winter George Merrall was complaining that the lamps were little more than buttons and the stench was awful.[15] As late as 1890 the light was hardly sufficient to read by and William Rhodes of Mill Hey complained that the smell gave him sick headaches.[16]

This building, now a private house, was the offices of the Oxenhope Urban District Council from 1863 to 1938, and prior to that it was a library.

A major cause was that £12,000, double the original purchase price, had had to be borrowed to renovate the plant, which was then mismanaged in an attempt to save money.[17] The inefficient clay retorts were replaced by cheap iron ones which soon proved to be inadequate, and only then did the Board put in proper brick retorts. The poor quality of the gas was blamed on the Board buying an inferior type of coal in another misconceived economy measure.[18] The purchase of a scrubber in 1877 silenced the grousing for the moment but the quality soon declined again.

Another complaint was the cost. At 4s. 6d. per 1,000 cubic feet it was almost twice the price of Keighley's 2s. 8d. Keighley had a larger population, and the more gas that was produced the cheaper it became. Haworth was small, so in order to obtain the same customer base the Local Board of Health had to look outside its boundaries. During

The gas works and Haworth Brow, 1966. The Haworth Gas Company was founded in 1857 and was then taken over by the Urban District Council in 1872. The increased consumption required a second gasholder, known locally as 'Ackroyd's Monument', which can be seen on the right. Thomas Duerden later described it as an 'eyesore.' In the background on the skyline are houses at Haworth Brow.

the 1870s pipes were laid to Lees, Stanbury and Oxenhope. The dilemma was that if gas consumers alone had to service the loans raised to provide the extra capacity, the price would remain high and people would not take the gas. If the price was pitched low enough to attract extra customers there would be deficits which would have to be funded from the general district rate until the number of consumers was sufficient for the undertaking to benefit from economies of scale. Most of the general rate was paid by the manufacturers who had their own gas plants and saw no benefit in the extension of the public gas undertaking.

The position became acute in 1879, when Lees decided to take gas from Keighley instead of Haworth.[19] In 1883 Frank Harper persuaded the Local Board to reduce the price to 3s. 6d., but the gas accounts showed losses of £700 in both 1885 and 1886. This was because a second gasholder had to be built, known locally as 'Ackroyd's Monument' after James Ackroyd, the estate agent who was largely responsible for its construction. After a violent tirade from Harry Redman at the 1887 loan hearing[20] the Board lost its nerve and the entire cost of servicing the gas loans, now £15,000, was put back on the gas rate, forcing the price back to 4s. 6d. When the gas fiasco was added to the fatuous behaviour of the Local Board over water supplies, most people would have agreed with

William Rhodes who wrote that 'We are ruled by a set of wrangling, in competent, self-advertising nincompoops, whose policy – when they have one – is of a vacillating, despotic kind, which as a rule, ends disastrously.'[21]

A breakthrough came as a result of a major row with Oxenhope. When the pipes were first laid the number of consumers was small and a connecting main of 4-inch diameter was considered sufficient. By 1890 the demand was running ahead of supply and the amount of gas reaching individual consumers was far too small. A new 9-inch main was needed. The Haworth Local Board was unwilling to put the cost on the rates and the manager was instructed to raise the pressure instead. This was not only dangerous, but also increased the cubic footage passing through the meters at the boundary between Haworth and Oxenhope. This raised the cost to Oxenhope, which threatened to take Keighley gas instead. Redman and his supporters were then overruled, the new main was constructed, and the price was reduced to 3s. 6d. The result was magical: quality improved and there was a 30 per cent increase in the amount of gas taken, so that by 1901 the price was down to 2s. 10d. Shortly afterwards the owners of Bridgehouse Mill calculated that they could get cheaper gas by taking it from the public supply rather than their own plant, and Haworth Urban District Council was then able to reduce the price to 2s. 3d.[22]

While the water and gas pipes were being laid, Haworth was also acquiring a sewerage and drainage system by piecemeal extension – but solving one problem created another.

A pleasant winter scene of the Bridgehouse Mill Goit on Bridgehouse beck.

THE GOIT, HAWORTH, IN WINTER.

Emptying cesspools and middensteads did not get rid of the refuse and sewage, most of which was unsuitable for manure. The outfalls were extended so that the waste could be dumped in the river, but after the Rivers Pollution Act of 1876 there was pressure to clean up the Worth. In 1878 Haworth was asked by Keighley to join a conservancy board, but the Local Board refused to participate. In May 1879 the Medical Officer of Health was ignored when he drew attention to the new sewer in Mill Hey, which was illegally discharging the sewage of 74 houses straight into the river, and in 1881 trouble was encountered with the outfall into Bridgehouse Beck, again from the Mill Hey sewer.[23]

As late as 1892 Haworth refused to send representatives to a meeting about improving water quality in the Aire, a plan dependent on action to clean up its tributaries. Frank Harper dismissed the whole matter with the remark, 'The less we have to do with Keighley the better I think'. Oxenhope was also far from supportive, resolving that 'they could let it rest awhile'.[24] By this time both Keighley and Oakworth had sewerage schemes and in July 1892 Haworth received a curt letter from the Local Government Board asking what action it proposed to take. There was no suitable flat land for a sewage farm, so for two years the Local Board conducted desultory investigations of possible sites outside the township.[25]

Then, a new development presented what seemed an ideal solution. The 1894 Local Government Act allowed the merging of neighbouring sanitary districts if this would lead to an improvement in facilities. Lees and Crossroads were at this time part of Bingley Rural District, because they were in the old Bingley parish, but there was a better case for them to be included in Keighley or Haworth. Lees had a sewage farm in the valley which could solve Haworth's sewage problem, while 106 children from Haworth Brow attended Lees School because of the difficulty of reaching the Haworth schools, at the top of the old village on the other side of Bridgehouse Beck. Although a petition against joining Haworth received overwhelming support from the inhabitants of Lees and Crossroads,[26] the Local Government Board decided that amalgamation should go ahead.

Haworth UDC still delayed and was cited before the Keighley Police Court for breaching the Rivers Pollution Act. It was fined a nominal £10, but the clerk to the council was told that stiffer penalties would be imposed if action was not taken. This forced the Urban District Council to come up with a plan for extending the Lees sewage farm, but the loan application for £12,000 was rejected because it involved a chemical treatment system, and the Local Government Board did not favour such methods.[27] The land available at Lees for a filtration system was insufficient, so in that sense annexing Lees had been futile.

A year later, Haworth entered into negotiations to acquire land owned by the duke of Devonshire, on the opposite side of the Worth in Oakworth.[28] Protracted haggling over the price ended in arbitration in 1902, a contract was let in 1903, and the sewage farm was finally completed in spring 1905.[29] By this time Haworth UDC had again been prosecuted before Keighley Police Court, and fined £50 with costs. Robert Clough, chairman of the sessions, commented that he 'did not think they could find a more gross case of indifference to a public Act of Parliament than in the offences of the Haworth Urban District Council.'[30]

Victorian values

The received wisdom is that the Victorians lived in large three-generational households, comprising parents, children and grandparents, the last being too old to work and supported by their children. This has been contrasted with today's small households, with only two generations, and the old folk being provided for by the state through the pension. But were Victorian families really like that? In Haworth the average household size in 1891 was 4.5, and those with over ten people were very few. Similarly, of the 1,285 households in 1861, only 135 had three generations, and in 1891 there were 132 out of 1,831.[31]

Households with ten or more people, 1861–91

census year	total households	ten or more people	percentage
1861	1,285	31	2.3
1871	1,370	39	2.8
1881	1,550	54	3.4
1891	1,831	50	2.7

In some respects census analysis of this sort distorts reality, because it is a snapshot of a community at a single moment. Only 7 per cent of households included three generations, but many other people would have remembered living with grandparents. Another reality about Victorian life, is that in all four censuses *combined* there were only five people over 90 and at no time did the number over 65 exceed 5 per cent. People died relatively young. Household size and family size are not the same thing – households included lodgers and other relatives, but the family cycle included children who had died between censuses. An example is provided by the family of Thomas Feather, a clockmaker who was listed in the 1861 census with his wife and five children. Ten years later he and his wife had eight children listed, but the youngest of the original five has disappeared, probably dead. In 1881 there are four children and in 1891 three so, although there were *nine* children in all, none of the censuses shows the complete family.

Many children died young. The available figures confirm the Medical Officer of Health's gloomy reports. In 1887, for example, 21 children in Haworth died before their first birthday (a death rate of 190 per 1000 live births) and thirteen died by their fifth year, so between a quarter and a third of the population died in their first five years. Other years for which totals can be reconstructed are similarly depressing. Between October 1893 and September 1894 there were 176 births, and 32 deaths of children under the age of one, giving an infant mortality rate of 181 per 1000. In 1902 the rate

From 1895 to 1928 when it moved to the Parsonage, the Brontë Museum was established on the upper floor of the building in this photograph. At that time the ground floor was occupied by the Yorkshire Penny Bank. Now it is the premises of the Haworth Tourist Information Centre and the former museum space is used for exhibitions. Note the wear to the brickwork on the right of the upper-floor window, where the sundial used to sit.

PHOTOGRAPH: CARNEGIE, 2009

was 188.8.[32] This was well above the national figure, which about 140 – or roughly fourteen times the modern figure. Haworth's continuing poor performance on water supply and sewage disposal was undoubtedly one of the causes.

The picture which emerges is of large two-generation families. Very few women married before 23 or 24, so they usually had about sixteen fertile years for child-bearing. If the usual pattern of births was maintained – closely spaced at first and then with wider intervals as the woman aged, that meant eight or nine babies. Of these, at least two would be likely to die before their fifth birthday, leaving six or seven to reach their teenage years or adulthood. This is what happened with Thomas Feather. The incomplete evidence means that it is difficult to determine patterns in the treatment of the elderly, but it is clear that the great majority of people over 65 were not included within extended households. Among the immigrant communities, neither those from Warwickshire nor from Wiltshire included anybody over 65 at the time of their arrival in Haworth, and there were only two older people from Swaledale. Statistically there should have been about fifteen over-65s. among the three groups – presumably the old were simply left behind.

Many working families could not afford to look after their old folk and needed other forms of assistance. Joseph Brett Grant, a very practical clergyman, founded a branch of the Yorkshire Penny Bank at Oxenhope in 1859 and for many years afterwards the annual presentation of accounts formed part of the Shrovetide celebrations at the church. Haworth followed Oxenhope's example and within twelve months had its own branch of the Bank. The late nineteenth century was the heyday of the friendly societies. Although some joined the Freemasons, many preferred to avoid the extra obligations which freemasonry involved, and opted for societies which encouraged saving, such as the Oddfellows or the Ancient Order of Shepherds (which replaced the Foresters in local affections).[33] In 1877 over 500 people took part in a demonstration organised by the friendly societies.[34] All flourished more in Oxenhope than in Haworth. In 1898, for example, the St Mary the Virgin Oddfellows' Lodge at Oxenhope had funds totalling £2,083 7s., but the Haworth Woodlands Lodge languished with only £364 16s.[35] This contrast gave rise to the witticism that in Oxenhope every baby's bottom was spanked with a bank book but Haworth was the place where they put muck on the church tower to make it grow – the tower was raised when the new clock was installed, and again when the church was rebuilt.[36]

Most savings were devoted to sickness, unemployment or funeral benefits but some went into a widows' and orphans' fund. The 1891 census describes 102 people as living 'on their own means', of whom fifty were over 65. There was a preponderance of women: 32 of the 50 over-65s, and 46 of the 52 who were under 65. Most were widows, living on pensions from a friendly society. Considerations of expense may have been a factor in determining the number of families able to look after older relatives, but that should have meant a greater proportion of older people lived in family groups in 1891 than in 1861. In fact, even in 1861 only 71 of a total of 196 people over 65 lived in a three-generational family. By 1891, the figure was 77 out of 343 over-65s. In contrast, in 1861 some 55 individuals over 65 were apparently self-supporting, if lone individuals, couples (married or siblings) with at least one partner over 65 are included. By 1891 the figure had risen to 134, almost twice the number in three-generational households.

So what was really happening? When a couple married they usually formed a new separate household, their circumstances depending at least partly on income. The 1891 census shows that some couples took a house with four rooms, some three and some two. Few had larger houses. Whether the husband and wife were both working does not seem to have made much difference. Having made their choice they usually stayed, even if the family increased rapidly. While the children were too young to work this immobility may well have been due to lack of money, but most of these families seem to have remained in the same house even when the number of pay packets increased. This was particularly so among weavers. One household of nine, headed by a married weaver, continued to live in two rooms even though five of them were working. Woolsorters were more likely to choose a larger house initially, but then followed the same pattern as weavers. Outside textile employment, the only group which tended to move to more spacious premises was the shopkeepers.

The real crisis arose if the chief breadwinner died. If the children were old enough to be earning a family could usually survive, without having to cutback too much, and the widow could even afford to remain at home. If the death occurred before any children were old enough to work the position was much more serious. There were three ways of dealing with the problem. A relative who was old enough to work could be invited to live in the household, providing an extra income. In 1861, 138 households contained a total of 220 relatives; in 1891 the figures were 214 and 340 respectively – they included 99 sisters, 42 brothers, 24 sisters-in-law, 20 brothers-in-law, 38 nieces and 27 nephews.

Alternatively the family could take a lodger. In 1861, 82 households had a total of 98 lodgers; in 1891, 128 had 188 lodgers. They accounted for 16 per cent of the total households in 1861 and 18 per cent in 1891. The only group which regularly took relatives and lodgers as a means of augmenting the normal family income were the tradesmen. Within the Haworth Urban District 30 per cent of them did so in 1891, twice the average of other social groups. Most families, however, took in lodgers only when there was a pressing need. The 1891 census lists 183 families where the heads either had no occupation or were 'living on their own means'. Of these, 36 had a total of 33 lodgers and 22 relatives. The third strategy was for the remaining partner, usually the mother, and her children to return to live with parents again. Among the 132 three-generational families in 1891, only 42 had members over 65 who were clearly dependants. In only 25 of these households was there a son or daughter, with spouse and at least one grandchild, present. In contrast, 67 households had a son or daughter without a spouse, or grandchildren without parents. The three-generational family was more important as a refuge for widowed daughters or daughters-in-law than for aged parents.

Some of the old preferred to keep their independence as long as possible. Our earlier acquaintance John Kitson worked as a woolcomber for James Greenwood until 1848, when he fell ill. By the time he had recovered Greenwood was bankrupt and Butterfield, who took over the business, dispensed with handcombers altogether. Kitson seems not to have worked again – he was 67 – but the censuses show that he and his wife lived by themselves until his death in 1864 at the age of 83. John had married twice. By his first wife Grace he had three children but only one, Hannah, survived childhood. After Grace's sudden death in 1827 he remarried to a widow, Betty Turner, who had four children from her previous marriage. Only two of these five children are named in the diary which is the source of Kitson's story. His own daughter, Hannah, married James Wright Greenwood and in 1851 they were living at Haworth Brow. He was a shoemaker and she a handloom weaver. Neither occupation was particularly well-paid and they had three children, none of them working. By 1861 the family had moved to Bunkers in lower Haworth. One of the three children had died but four others had been born, and three of the six were now working. The only stepchild mentioned by Kitson is Hannah Helliwell, who in 1851 was living in Gauger's Croft – her husband James was a woolcomber and she was a powerloom weaver. They had three children, of whom two were working, the daughter as a powerloom weaver and the elder son as an apprentice blacksmith. Hannah is only mentioned once in the diary, and sometime between 1851 and 1861 she died.

Neither family took the old couple in, but that does not mean that they were forgotten. Kitson's diary mentions regular visits from Hannah Greenwood and the 1861 census shows that James Helliwell, his new wife Betty, and their three children were living next door to the Kitsons in West Lane. John had not forgotten his first wife's mother. There were many arrangements like this, where old people made do as best they could, living if they were lucky on insurance money, or with an unmarried son or daughter, or next door to relatives ... or on parish relief if they were not.

The shifts some people resorted to are illustrated by Hannah Binns, who in 1841, a widow of 38, was supporting her father-in-law, a 70-year-old pauper called John Hardaker. Hannah had three children – Joseph (18) and Jonathan (15) were working as woolcombers and there was a daughter Emily (13). By 1851 Jonathan had moved out and John Hardaker had died, but Hannah was now responsible for her brother-in-law, another John, who was described as an 'idiot'. Joseph had become a sawyer and Emily was a powerloom weaver. Hannah had two lodgers: George Sutcliffe, a stone mason, and Robert Pickles, a comber. Sometime in the early 1850s Sutcliffe married the daughter, Emily, and they had a child, Selena (born about 1854), but by 1861 he, too, had died and Emily was also a widow. Her great-uncle John, the 'idiot', was no longer there, and neither were her uncle Joseph or Robert Pickles. Hannah was 58, and had become a linen draper. In 1871 she was still a draper, but Emily was described as 'blind' and Selena was epileptic, so to make ends meet Hannah had taken another lodger, Edward Wright, a wheelwright. In the 1881 census Hannah, aged 78, described as a 'small wares dealer', was still supporting her blind daughter and her epileptic granddaughter, and had another lodger, James Brotchie, a tailor. After Hannah died the workhouse was the likely fate for Emily and Selena. If that was the price of Victorian values, most of us would consider it too high.

Church and chapel   14

Heavenly voices

If bricks and mortar are an accurate reflection, religious organisations were in a thriving condition during the late nineteenth century. There seemed hardly a moment between 1860 and 1910 when some church, chapel or Sunday school in Haworth was not being built or rebuilt. The most prominent high profile changes were those undertaken by the Rev. John Wade, who became perpetual curate of Haworth on the death of Patrick Brontë in 1861. The church was in a state of disrepair, so when Michael Merrall offered £5,000 towards a completely new building Wade gladly accepted. In 1879 the old church was demolished, except for the tower, and the new one was consecrated in 1881. A large new Sunday school was added in 1904.[1]

The various denominations expanded their accommodation to meet the demand from the inhabitants of 'new' Haworth, extending from Stubbing Lane, through Mill Hey, to Brow, Lees and Crossroads. New chapels were built by the Wesleyan Methodists at Lees (1867); at Bridgehouse (1883, extended 1892), paid for by Frederick Butterfield of New York; and Lowertown (1891). They also extended existing chapels at Marsh (1873) and Sawood (1895). Other denominations were also active. The Primitives built a grand new chapel in Mill Hey (1871) and at Crossroads (1882); the Baptists at Scartop built a chapel in 1870; and even the Church of England, slow to respond, built a mission church at Lees in the 1890s which was then replaced by a new church, St James at Crossroads, in 1909.[2] The building of Sunday schools was no less important: new or extended schools included those of the Wesleyans at Bridgehouse (1892); the Primitive Methodists at Marsh (1873); Horkinstone Baptist chapel (1863); Lowertown Wesleyans (1897); and Sawood Wesleyans (1895).[3]

This building had to be funded. The main income of most churches and chapels came from pew rents, supplemented by 'anniversaries', or annual collections on specific Sundays for the different groups they supported. The system was financially inelastic and socially divisive. Elsewhere by 1900 many were abandoning it in favour of bazaars, which were considered more egalitarian and raised as much money in four days as pew rents in a whole year. But 'bazaar culture' had only a limited impact on Haworth. The

OPPOSITE

The east end of the parish church, viewed from Main Street.

PHOTOGRAPH: CARNEGIE, 2009

181

Oxenhope Wesleyan Methodist Chapel, Lowertown, photographed in 1910. Opened in 1893, this building replaced the original chapel of 1806. With its pedimented roof, symmetrically arranged pilasters and centrally placed doorway it is a good example of the opulent, classical rectangular box chapel much favoured by the local Nonconformists. It was taken down in 1970. The present, more modest chapel was built on part of the same site, the remainder being sold for housing in order to defray the cost.

surviving accounts of the Lees, Stanbury and Lowertown Wesleyan Methodist chapels[4] show that pew rents remained the basic source of income. The most obnoxious feature of the system had been the ability of the pewholders to sublet or sell their 'freeholds'. Wade gave the need to extinguish such freeholds as a reason for demolishing the Brontë church. By the 1890s freeholds were a thing of the past. Most churches and chapels had free seats, while the 'five minute' rule, allowing the pews to be occupied by others if the pewholders had not arrived, ensured that nobody was left standing in a half empty church or chapel. Haworth people were financially conservative. New chapels and schools were not begun until much of the money was subscribed[5] and most building was undertaken by denominations with well-heeled supporters.

In 1864 the chapelry was finally separated from the parish of Bradford and in 1867 Wade became the first rector of the new parish of Haworth. In 1884 his stipend was increased by the Ecclesiastical Commissioners to £300 *per annum*.[6] Michael Merrall paid for the new church and his sons for the Sunday school, and one of his grandsons, M.H. Merrall of Law House, endowed the vicarage of St James, Crossroads.[7] Sir Isaac Holden, the Butterfields and the Redmans[8] could be relied upon to fund the Wesleyan Methodists,

Holden and the Hattersley family similarly supported the Primitive Methodists, though much less munificently. Horkinstone was subsidised by the Kershaws, although the Baptists in general did not have the support of wealthy manufacturers.

There are press reports of bazaars organised by West Lane Wesleyans (1866), Lees Wesleyans (1873 and 1876), West Lane Baptists and Oxenhope Church (1877), the Salvation Army (1897) and Mill Hey Primitive Methodists (1902). Only the Lees bazaar helped to finance new building and none of them was to extinguish a debt. Percy Redman lamented the vogue for bazaars, which he found 'sad and degrading', and remembered the time when a Methodist was expected to pay a penny a week and a shilling a quarter. His wife disagreed. She thought bazaars brought people together in unity to promote a common object – the only drawback was that the few who promoted the bazaar did all the work.[9]

In the late nineteenth century there was something of an Anglican resurgence. Even in Haworth, where its members were never more than a third of the worshippers, they were setting the pace. Their churches had towers or spires, which could be provided with clocks. Grant, at Oxenhope, made sure that his new church had one. Haworth church clock dated from the early eighteenth century, and was now worn out, the fingers

St James's Mission Church, Lees. The Church of England was slow in providing church accommodation for the burgeoning numbers of textile workers of the Haworth Brow, Lees and Crossroads area. This mission church was erected in the 1890s almost a decade after the area was colonised by the Methodists and the Salvation Army. It was finally replaced by St James' Crossroads, a little further down the road, in 1909.

moving with the wind rather than the time. In 1870, on the initiative of a parishioner, Joseph Wright, it was replaced by a new clock constructed by the Bingley clockmaker, Silas Cryer. Faces were provided on all four sides, with gilded hands and numbers on a dull red ground. The tower was raised by nine feet so that the clock could be clearly seen all over the village and a set of Westminster chimes attached to the bells. Local time was Anglican time both summer and winter.[10]

Towers could also house bells, which called Anglicans to worship in a public way that Nonconformists found difficult to rival. Haworth's tradition of change-ringing continued. The best known ringer of the day was James Riley, who recalled how 'mischief makers' would secure the tower door and then burn cayenne pepper, forcing the ringers to take refuge at the top until someone let them out.[11] The standard had fallen since Brontë's time, when there had been the great full peals of 5,040 changes in 1849 and 1853; in 1869 a special ring of 2,500 changes was cut short when the tenor bell rope broke![12] In 1899 W. Whitham of Moorhouse paid for a peal of six bells to be put into the tower of St Mary the Virgin, Oxenhope,[13] which soon acquired a reputation superior to that of Haworth – when a full peal was executed at Haworth in 1903 all the ringers except Riley came from Oxenhope.[14]

The death of Brontë removed the last obstacle to the introduction of High Church services of a ritual and devotional nature. The first edition of *Hymns Ancient and Modern* was published in 1861 and at Advent 1862 Wade began using it at Haworth. By 1864 a visitor to Oxenhope could report that the 'psalms were chanted to Gregorian tunes and the hymns were those from *Hymns Ancient and Modern*'.[15] When the new parish church at Haworth was consecrated the 'very efficient mixed choir' of Brontë's time was replaced by an all male one, robed in surplices and cassocks, boy trebles and male altos taking the place of women.[16] The *Keighley Herald* of 17 March 1882 recorded that the following Sunday morning service would have three psalms, chanted to settings by Woodward; the Benedicite (Beethoven), Jubilate (Spencer), Kyrie and Gloria (Merrall) and Credo (Cooper); but only two hymns. In 1895 the *Keighley News* noted that the voice of the principal treble, J. Boocock, 'was of exceptional sweetness and quality'. On Easter Day 1897 all the settings were taken from Stanford in B flat, with the anthems 'I will tell you a mystery' and 'Worthy the Lamb' from the *Messiah*.[17] The opening of the new church brought many gifts, adding greatly to its beauty. Among them were no less than ten stained glass windows, one in memory of Charlotte Brontë was executed by the famous London firm of Clayton and Bell. Oxenhope could not match this number – most of its windows were small – but when Grant died in 1879 three were donated in his memory.[18]

All this activity brought accusations of incipient Romanism but Wade and Grant were not regarded as extreme high churchmen.[19] There was more doubt about W.H. Gunyon, vicar of Oxenhope from 1892 to 1925. The evangelical E.C. Bowring noted minor improprieties – the placing of flowers on the altar and wafers instead of ordinary bread at communion – but another correspondent claimed that Gunyon was a member of the 'romanising' English Church Union, advocating the use of wakes, altar lights, the confessional, fasting communion, making the sign of the cross and bowing to the altar.[20]

In some parts of the country Nonconformists began building Gothic Revival churches, but not in Haworth. All the new and rebuilt chapels were traditional classical rectangular preaching boxes, so they had no towers for bells, and galleries blocking the windows made stained glass pointless. Music was peripheral to their services, though moves were made to chant the Lord's Prayer, introduce a vesper and sing the amens. There were rumblings of discontent among the older generation, one of whom remembered 'the days now gone apparently for ever when a stirring hymn was sung to a grand old tune, in which the whole congregation would join with heart and soul and voice.'[21] In other ways the Nonconformists could compete – there was no objection to organ music and the chapel arrangement was advantageous, because whereas in the Anglican churches the organ was usually positioned to the side of the chancel or in a gallery, to focus attention on the altar, in the Nonconformist chapels the organ had pride of place behind the table from which the minister conducted the service.

The interior of Hawksbridge Baptist chapel. In Church of England buildings the organ was usually sited at the side or in a gallery so that the central focus was the altar. Nonconformists had no such inhibitions. Their organs were placed centrally and often dominated the interiors of their chapels. This is a typical example, with its pipes towering above the minister's desk.

West Lane Baptist chapel. Originally built in 1752, it was enlarged in 1775 and rebuilt in 1844. It has hosted a very successful Gilbert and Sullivan opera society which has given one of the operas every year since 1964.

PHOTOGRAPH: CARNEGIE, 2009

St Mary the Virgin at Oxenhope acquired a new organ in 1861, replacing it with a larger one in 1876. The new parish church at Haworth was provided with one in 1883.[22] West Lane Wesleyans replaced their existing organ in 1865 and again in 1905. Most organs were mechanical ones – blown by hand – but that at Bridgehouse (1905) worked on the hydraulic principle, with a supply of water obtained from the public supply.[23] Other new or improved instruments included those at Mill Hey Primitive Methodist chapel (1870), replaced with a grander one in 1908;[24] Hawksbridge Baptist Sunday school (1889); and Horkinstone Baptist chapel (1890);[25] Lowertown Wesleyan (1891, replaced 1907); Marsh and Sawood (1892); as well as Lees, Stanbury and Scartop Wesleyans and Hall Green Baptists.[26] That left only the West Lane Baptists with their original instrument, which was not to be replaced until after the First World War. Organ competition was expensive: Sawood's relatively modest two-manual cost £100, Hawksbridge's larger one £150, while West Lane Wesleyans grand three manual 1905 organ set the chapel back £450.[27]

The scope for music within the structure of nonconformist services may have been limited but there was no reason why their choirs should not sing anthems or even complete cantatas, which soon began to dominate the 'services of song' held to raise funds. The cantata competition was in full spate by the turn of the century. In 1897 the West Lane Baptists gave *Joseph and his Brethren* and in 1900 West Lane Wesleyans performed *The Two Seasons*. *From the Manger to the Cross* received airings from the Horkinstone Baptists in 1905 and the West Lane Wesleyan Methodists in 1908.[28] In 1913 and 1914 *The Gentle Shepherd* and *Our Blest Redeemer*, both by Whitty, were given by the Stanbury Wesleyans and the West Lane Baptists while the West Lane Wesleyans introduced Gaul's *Ruth*.[29] For sheer variety, however, none could rival the Bridgehouse Wesleyan choir. Between May 1911 and November 1912 they gave Stainer's *Daughter of Jairus*; *Joan of Arc, Maid of Orleans* by Gaul; *Jonah* by Jamoneau; and Sterndale Bennett's *The May Queen*.[30]

At Haworth parish church in 1898 the choir performed the most enduring cantata of all, Stainer's *Crucifixion*, which it subsequently performed at every Eastertide alternately with Lee Williams' *Gethsemane*, down to 1914.[31] The other great favourite, Maunder's *Olivet to Calvary*, was first sung by the Lees Wesleyan choir in 1905 and was soon recognised as the chapel's speciality.[32]

Did this emphasis on opulent building and devotional rather than evangelical services increase the number of the faithful? Absolute figures are unobtainable because the denominations calculated their memberships in different ways, but it is clear that for thirty years from the early 1860s all the congregations in Haworth were growing. The great successes were the establishment by Grant of a solidly based Anglican community in Oxenhope, where there had been none before, and the rise of the Primitive Methodists who doubled their membership in Haworth during the 1880s. After the early 1890s membership was more volatile, and by 1905 complaints were heard about a lack of spiritual commitment, though the actual decline in numbers was – with the exception of the Wesleyan Methodists – small. In 1890 the Wesleyans of West Lane and Bridgehouse had 405 members between them, but in 1914 only 220, yet both had rebuilt twice and had played major roles in the flourishing of musical activity.[33] Was the fall in numbers the consequence of a less rigorous approach to worship?

In this regard, the experience of the Baptists is informative. Many Particular Baptists were softening the harsher features of evangelical Calvinism. Like their Anglican and Wesleyan Methodist confreres, some pastors absorbed the new critical approach to the Bible brought about by Darwin's *Origin of Species* and Ernest Renan's *Life of Jesus*, both published in 1870. The greater emphasis on more elaborate musical forms was part of the change. But other Baptists totally rejected 'the new learning'. Under its High Calvinist minister, Joseph Thornton, Hall Green espoused Strict Baptist tenets and though after his departure in 1862 the chapel remained without pastoral guidance until 1903, its members continued down the path he had marked out for them. When in 1886 the Baptist Union failed to denounce departures from the *1689 London Particular Baptist Confession of Faith*, Hall Green left the organisation and turned its back on the other chapels, including that at West Lane.[34]

Was Hall Green right? The real problem was too much competition and a declining population. In 'old' Haworth the Wesleyans lost a three-way struggle with the Anglicans

Salvation Army Exposition. The Salvation Army opened its barracks in Hall Green in 1882. Its willingness to go to the people, its army style parades and 'knee' drills, and its penchant for brass band music, appealed to many in late nineteenth-century Haworth. The picture shows the founder 'General' Booth, and the two ladies (left and right) are wearing the distinctive Salvation Army bonnets.

and Baptists, the latter having increased membership from an average of 189 in the 1880s to 237 in 1914. Their success was partly due to the long pastorate of the deeply respected David Arthur (1888–1925) and partly to money from a trust left by the temperance enthusiast, Thomas Parker, which enabled them to appoint two assistant pastors.[35] The experience of the West Lane Baptists showed that new chapels and organs were not necessary for success nor were they essential for taking a full part in the music making. In 1883 the Salvation Army established a barracks at Hall Green and many were tempted by its open air meetings and drills.[36] There was now a four-way struggle for membership in this industrial community in 'new' Haworth on both sides of Bridgehouse Beck. Again the Wesleyans lost ground, and their desertion of evangelical ways may have played its part. In Oxenhope, where neither the Primitive Methodists nor the Salvation Army gained a foothold, the old balance was maintained. Lowertown Wesleyans had almost the same membership in 1914 as in 1892.[37]

The Nonconformist conscience

The Baptists continued to agitate for the disestablishment of the Church of England. There was a Liberation Society lecture at Hawksbridge in 1875 in which the Reverend

J.H. Taylor of Bingley maintained that national establishments were unjust, politically mischievous, damaging to the established churches in the long run and injurious to religion in general.[38] There was little support from the other denominations. The Wesleyan Methodists came out against the Liberation Society in 1861 though individual Methodists could rock the boat – in 1883 Wade complained to the Rev. J. Emberton, the Wesleyan minister, about a poster advertising a Liberation meeting in the West Lane Methodist Sunday schoolroom. Emberton hastily disassociated himself from the trustee who authorised it and the meeting took place in the Drill Hall instead.[39]

There was a feeling too that the Church of England was hostile to a national system of education.[40] The 1870 Education Act provided for the establishment of a school board, elected by the ratepayers and with powers to levy a rate, wherever there were insufficient places for all local children. In Haworth the Baptists immediately advocated a school board, believing that religious instruction should be confined to Sunday schools and seeing a board system as a way of breaking the Anglican and Wesleyan monopoly over day school instruction. The Anglicans argued that Haworth already had enough school places, so a board was unnecessary. The Wesleyan Methodists, financially weaker than the Church of England, concluded informally that a school board would be a means of maintaining influence,[41] but some wanted to keep control of their own schools. The Haworth Wesleyans refurbished their school in 1872 and Wade received a letter from W. Maltby, the Wesleyan minister, informing him that they would be putting up their fees. He asked Wade to increase his at the same time, lest the Wesleyan school should lose pupils to the cheaper National School, become unviable and have to close, which would lead to the imposition of a school board. Wade did not want this, so both schools raised their fees from 3d. to 4d. a week in 1875.[42]

The issue was finally forced by the Baptists, who closed their school at Horkinstone in 1879 and created a shortage of places at Oxenhope. They claimed that they were losing £50–£60 a year but suspicions were voiced that this was a deliberate ploy to make the creation of a school board inevitable.[43] The first school board election again exposed the ambivalence of the Wesleyan Methodists. There were to be seven members and to prevent the Anglicans, who had put forward four candidates, from gaining a majority on a split vote an 'unsectarian' meeting decided to limit nonconformist nominations to two Methodists and two Baptists. The Baptists duly nominated Hophni Bland and J.F. Greenwood and the Haworth Methodists put forward J.R. Redman. Oxenhope Methodists found themselves in a dilemma. Neither of their preferred candidates, John Parker and J.P. Heaton was prepared to stand. Stanbury Methodists proposed William Craven as an alternative but Oxenhope preferred to support a third Baptist, William Kershaw junior. This move so incensed Stanbury that Craven persisted in his candidature, threatening the Nonconformist strategy. In the end, Kershaw topped the poll and Craven and the fourth Anglican were at the bottom, but the affair reflected no credit on the Methodists.[44]

The aim of the Baptists to eliminate voluntary schools altogether was powerfully aided by the geography of the district. The first problem was at Stanbury, where 76

The Old School, Stanbury. Founded in 1806 by the Baptists, its master was funded by interest on shares in the Leeds and Liverpool Canal. The first master was Abraham Sunderland, and a descendant John Sunderland was the last. He was kept on as the first master of the Board school that replaced it in 1882.

PHOTOGRAPH BY COURTESY OF JACK LAYCOCK

places were needed but there was room for only 60 pupils. The school was a Baptist foundation and the trustees willingly allowed it to be replaced by a board school in 1882, built on land bought from the Haworth church trustees. The first master of the new school, John Sunderland, had been the last teacher in the old – he was a descendant of Abraham Sunderland, its first master, who was mentioned by Emily Brontë in a diary paper written when she was sixteen, and he continued to hold evening classes in the original 1805 building for some years.[45] In Haworth itself the National and Wesleyan schools were at the top of the old village so children in the newer housing in the valley had to climb an extremely steep hill, a problem especially for infants during the often bitter Haworth winters. The position was even worse at Haworth Brow, where many parents sent their children to Lees Wesleyan School. This led to rows between the Haworth and Bingley School Boards about who was responsible for the extra expense. Haworth flatly declined to pay anything while there was still room for the children in Haworth schools.[46]

By 1885 Haworth National School was full and in 1891 Wade closed the infants' school to make more space for older pupils, substituting a much smaller infant class within the main school.[47] Some 102 infants had attended the National School, and they could not all be accommodated. This added to the pressure on the Haworth Wesleyan School, which was larger and had plenty of room, but was once more in financial difficulty. The need for a new school in a more suitable location was obvious and the Wesleyans should have accepted the inevitable with good grace, but instead they dug their heels in. This led them to be accused of forcing children to walk from Haworth Brow to the top of the old village because they needed the fees.[48] In 1889 the Mill Hey Primitive Methodists agreed to allow the Board to use part of their Sunday school as an infants' day school, as a temporary measure.[49] In 1892 rumours began to circulate that the Wesleyan school was to close but the trustees clung on until 1895,[50] after the opening of a new school large enough to accommodate all Haworth children. Situated in a central location at Butt Lane, the new Central Schools drew so many pupils away from the National School that it too was forced to close. The first headmaster appointed by the board was Arthur Hirst, who had come to Haworth as master of the Wesleyan School in 1887 and was to remain until 1922.[51]

At the first meeting of the Haworth School Board in 1879 a letter had been read from the Horkinstone Baptists, offering to lease their school premises in Oxenhope to the board at £15 *per annum*. The offer was accepted,[52] but Horkinstone was a remote location and, pushed by the Board of Education, the School Board soon built a new infant school in Oxenhope itself, which also took the infants from Horkinstone and Hawksbridge. Horkinstone continued as a board elementary school and regularly achieved the best results in the area, helped not a little by the generous attendance prizes donated by Kershaw Brothers whose premises were nearby.[53] The Board's new infant school was never full because Lowertown Wesleyan and Oxenhope National Schools continued to maintain their own infant departments.[54]

The Oxenhope Wesleyans behaved with characteristic obtuseness. Their Lowertown

Butt Lane schools, 1901. The National school and the Wesleyan school were both in Top Haworth, which created problems for children living in Haworth Brow and Mill Hey who had to climb the steep hill even in mid-winter. Haworth Central Schools, which opened in 1897 and replaced them, were far more accessible and free! The problem reappeared with the building of Hartington, but today the problem of distance is alleviated by the ubiquity of buses and particularly cars.

building was inadequate but the trustees refused to respond to an inspector's criticism of the unpleasant smells which pervaded the school. They claimed that this was the result of emissions from neighbouring factories, instead of inadequate ventilation, drainage and sewage disposal arrangements. Only the decision in 1895 of the Wesleyan Methodist Conference at Plymouth, to dispose of all their schools, forced Lowertown to hand control to the Board.[55] It is perhaps significant that at a time when they were unwilling to make even basic repairs to their day school, the Oxenhope Wesleyans could raise money for a new chapel and a new Sunday school. The closure of the Wesleyan School was followed by the opening in November 1896 of an entirely new board school, which had the typical plan of a central hall with classrooms around it: 'The classrooms are fitted with continuous desks with a separate seat for each scholar, and the floor is raised into platforms in order that the teacher may have complete control of the class.'[56]

The National School managed to avoid Board control, largely thanks to Gunyon's determination. The old Free Grammar School was another problem. Under Grant's successor, William Summerscales, the school had reverted to teaching reading, writing and simple arithmetic. The next master, William Patchett, who came in 1864, tried to revive a classical curriculum – but he never had more than fifteen pupils and by 1886 a mere eight. The Charity Commissioners decided that the school should be dissolved and the master pensioned off. A Scott Trust was created, to oversee the use of the remaining money in providing scholarships for local students at suitable secondary schools in the area. Under the initial plans, four of the seven trustees were to be nominated – one each by the Haworth School Board, the Haworth National School, the Haworth Wesleyan School, and the Keighley Endowed Schools and three co-opted of whom one was to be a woman. The Baptists, led by J.F. Greenwood, one of the trustees, were in favour, because the scheme would break the Anglican hold over the endowment and ensure that successful students received a good education in efficient schools. The other denominations were furious. Some Board members had little time for academic education and all resented the spending of the money outside Haworth. Greenwood was accused of masterminding the plan, but when he challenged them to find a viable alternative they failed to do so. The Charity Commissioners' scheme was adopted, though with six representative governors rather than four. There can be little doubt that Greenwood was influenced by the success of his sister, Marion, who had been one of the first intake at Bradford Girls' Grammar School in 1875 and in 1879 won a scholarship to Girton College, Cambridge. She gained a double first in the Natural Science Tripos and went on to teach at Girton and Newnham.[57]

In 1902 a new Education Act abolished local school boards and handed their powers to local authorities. The Haworth Board was replaced by a committee of the West Riding County Council, covering the whole of the Worth valley. The demise of the School Board was greeted with what became a regular lament about the decline of local accountability. J. F. Greenwood, its most active member, complained that he would find it difficult to combine visits to Wakefield with his business commitments, but received little sympathy. When the School Board had been established J. R. Redman had tried to calm the fears of the Wesleyan Methodists by playing down the impact of the school rate, but Anglican calculations suggested that if all the voluntary schools were replaced a rate of 2s. 4d. would be needed.[58] In 1900 the school rate was 2s. 2d., one of the highest in the country, and the Board had accumulated debts of over £26,000 as a result of the ambitious school building programme.[59] Anything that spread the rate burden more equally over the West Riding was welcome to the ratepayers. The Baptists could console themselves with the thought that voluntary provision in the area was largely ended, and the Anglicans could say that they had given the ratepayers fair warning. The Wesleyans had lost both their schools without gaining any of the credit for the improved system.

Social issues also concerned the churches. For example, though Haworth people had a reputation for abstemiousness – Babbage noted in 1851 that 'dram' drinking was far below the average for similar industrial communities – there was an active late nineteenth-century temperance movement. In 1867 the West Lane Wesleyan chapel founded the first Band of Hope, which committed its members to strict teetotalism,[60] and other Wesleyan Chapels founded their own bands, notable enthusiasts at Oxenhope being John Pighills and George Humphreys, the Lowertown schoolmaster. The Baptists and Primitive Methodists soon joined the movement, though the latter found that the demon drink even tempted local preachers: in 1887 the circuit committee minuted that, 'Brother B. Emmott be removed from the plan as he has severed himself from the society by continuous non-attendance at class and constant attendance at the public house.'[61] By 1890 the Wesleyan Bands of Hope alone numbered over 500 members. Pressure from the temperance lobby even compelled Wade to form a Church Temperance Guild. In May 1893, after a stirring address from him, an audience of 150 were treated to ditties such as 'The Robin's Temperance Song', 'Buying Beef instead of Beer', 'The Voiceless Chimes', 'The Drunkard's Wife', 'Rosa's Last Words', 'How the Money goes', and 'Paddy's Last Pledge'.[62] By 1897 the Guild had 211 temperance members and 149 total abstainers.

This rare unanimity between 'Church' and 'Chapel' led to the celebration of Temperance Sunday at the beginning of Advent each year from 1897. Four years earlier, a resolution of the local Primitive Methodist circuit, welcoming the local option on extinguishing drink licenses, was echoed by the Wesleyans and the Baptists, and all religious organisations supported the drive to close public houses on Sunday.[63] The reason for the high profile of the movement, but also for its limited impact, was that its strength was in the Sunday schools. An examination of the membership figures shows that the majority of those signing the pledge were children. Of 357 on the roll of the West Lane Band of Hope in 1870, a hundred were Sunday school teachers and two hundred were children. In 1879 the Lowertown Bands of Hope had 69 children between seven and 14, and forty young people between 14 and 21, but only 38 adults.[64] Those beyond the influence of the religious organisations were unaffected, and considerable sections of chapelgoers had also failed to take the pledge.

Competition between Sunday schools was strong. From 1860 to 1900 the local papers reported the sums raised at each church or chapel Sunday school anniversary, which stimulated a rivalry to see which could achieve the most. Haworth parish church regularly topped the list, its best effort being £100 in 1885, but the total sums raised by the Baptists and Wesleyan Methodists both eclipsed the Anglican takings.[65] The Whitsuntide processions were ever more grand. All the denominations paraded around the village, taking care to visit the homes of the manufacturers who supported them. The Anglicans made a great show, with a procession headed by Wade and Grant in their ecclesiastical robes and concluding with tea, sports, amusements and dancing, which far outshone the more sober entertainment put on by the strait-laced Nonconformists. The competition was generally good humoured, though by 1897, with eight processions (four of which were headed by a brass band) there was considerable congestion: 'It took four policemen to clear a road for the Parish Church whilst the other seven had to do the best they could,' complained a correspondent of the *Keighley News*, 'I wonder whether the police did justice ... in allowing the Haworth Public Brass Band to smash into the ranks of the Salvation Army.'[66]

The processions and the temperance agitation continued into Edwardian times, but in the Sunday schools neither the concentration on purely religious instruction nor the emphasis on temperance had much influence on membership. Surviving figures for the Haworth and Oakworth Wesleyan Methodist circuit and for the Baptist chapels suggests that Sunday school trends followed those of the chapels. Between 1890 and 1914 the Wesleyan Methodist circuit numbers fell by about 400, whereas membership among Horkinstone and Hawksbridge Baptists remained static and West Lane Baptists increased in line with chapel membership.[67] As the Wesleyans acknowledged, the problem was a lack of spiritual commitment – in 1900 some 230 of the Wesleyan Sunday school scholars moved to junior society classes, less than 10 per cent of the total. By 1914, after strenuous efforts, this figure had only improved to 14 per cent.[68] The heart of the temperance movement was where it had long been – with the Baptists, not the Wesleyans, and most prominently with Thomas Parker, nephew of Thomas Parker the noted tenor. Parker junior was a broker and dealer in old oak; at one time, surveyor of the Local Board of Health; and at another time an elected member. In 1855 he opened a temperance hotel at the top of Main Street, twelve years before the foundation of the first Band of Hope. As a Baptist, he would not to take the sacrament until unfermented wine was introduced, and though a staunch Liberal he refused to cross the threshold of the Liberal Club because it had an alcohol licence. One of the sights of Haworth was Parker in his old age, sitting outside his hotel on an oaken chair with his shaggy dog by his side. When he died in 1898 he left money in trust to the West Lane Baptist chapel and endowed a temperance lecture to be given each year on Rushbearing Sunday.[69]

Goths and Vandals

In 1879 the rector of Haworth, John Wade, accepted £5,000 from Michael Merrall to pay for the demolition of the old church and the building of a new one in the then fashionable Gothic style.[1] The decision was controversial. At a large protest meeting, held in the Drill Hall in May 1879, T.T. Empsall, president of the Bradford Historical and Literary Society, and Dr Maffey and E.P. Peterson, also of Bradford, spoke out against the plan. Letters opposing the demolition were read from Haworth's largest landowner, General Emmott-Rawdon; the lord of the manor, W.B. Ferrand; and Isaac Holden, the textile manufacturer. But the project went ahead, and in 1881 the new church was consecrated

Haworth old church. This early photograph shows the 'Brontë' church from the graveyard side. There is no clock visible, which shows that the photograph was taken before 1870. The clock provided by Isaac Smith only had a face on the Main Street side. The expanse of graves, the lack of trees and the misty nature of the picture emphasise what many regard as the unpleasant conditions in which the Brontë sisters lived.

The new Haworth church. The construction of the church was opposed by those who revered the memory of the Brontës and the rector of the time was execrated for his part in the demolition of the old church. However, closer examination of the circumstances exonerates him from most of the charges. The new church was paid for by Michael Merrall, the textile manufacturer, and opened in 1881, just before his death.

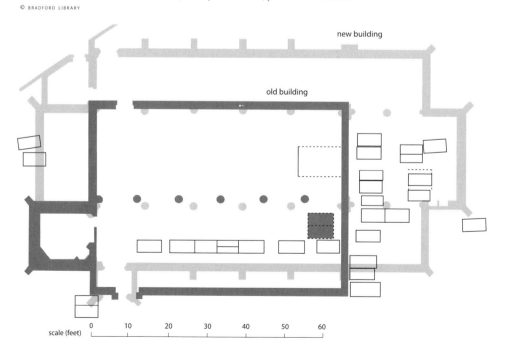

by the bishop of Ripon. All that was left of its predecessor was the tower.

For those outside Haworth, Wade and his supporters seemed to typify Arnold's 'Barbarians'. In 1888 the *Herald and Courier* called him a vandal, and an article in the *Star* the following year suggested that he was motivated by jealousy of the achievements of the three Brontë sisters. In literary terms that was untrue, and Wade was later a founder member of the Haworth branch of the Brontë Society, but he certainly wanted to introduce a different style of churchmanship. Brontë had been an Evangelical, for whom the pulpit was the focus of interest, but for a High Churchman such as Wade ritual centred on the altar, so the east end took on a greater significance.

He was aware of the clash of interest between those who sought to keep the church as Brontë and his daughters had known it, and his own desire to reorder it. In 1869 he eagerly took up a proposal for a new church on land nearby, but examination of the deeds revealed that the endowments related only to a building on the existing site. He then tried to alter the old church. In 1834 a gallery at the east end had been put up to accommodate the organ. The space beneath was so low that it was difficult to stand upright at the altar rail. In 1872 Wade had the gallery taken down and the organ placed on the floor at the north east corner. This gave a more fitting setting for communion, but his proposals for further extensive changes produced objected on the grounds of cost, because the Grimshaw aisle was in a tumbledown condition, the floors of the box pews were rotten, and all the fittings would have to be removed to allow a layer of concrete to be laid, to insulate the church from rising damp. A more viable solution would be to make a completely new start on the existing site. Even Wade's critics accepted that change was inevitable. Empsall argued for a 'judicious restoration', while Peterson suggested demolishing the Grimshaw aisle and a return to the fifteenth-century plan, but with Victorian pews and a three-decker pulpit. The effect would have been pleasing but, shorn of its galleries, aisle and high box pews, the church would no longer resemble that in which the Brontës worshipped. In any case, the church had been rebuilt in the early seventeenth century, and the plans confirm that Grimshaw's extensions had not even left much of the early Stuart church.

The opposition could muster almost no support in Haworth itself. Wade's congregation was solidly behind the change, while George Sowden, who became vicar of Hebden Bridge, later wrote that 'it was the very ugliest building inside that ever I saw

Rev. John Wade succeeded Patrick Brontë as perpetual curate of Haworth in 1861. He was rector from 1867 to 1898, and was responsible for the building of the right-hand wing of the parsonage. Wade is remembered largely for his controversial part in the replacement of the Brontë church by the present one in 1879–81.

PHOTOGRAPH BY COURTESY OF JACK LAYCOCK

Old Oxenhope House as it was in 1900. This was the home of William Greenwood junior, the textile manufacturer, until his death in 1893. Patrick Brontë was on good terms with him even though he was a Particular Baptist. He could be relied on to support subscriptions for church projects if Brontë made a good case for them, such as the increase of the three bells to a peal of six, and he was one of the very few in Haworth who regretted the demolition of the old church in 1881. Greenwood was a life-long bachelor and Brontë was a widower, so stories have circulated regarding his visits to Old Oxenhope where he was entertained by Greenwood and his sister Sarah who kept house for him. As Brontë must have been a good thirty years older, such rumours should be taken with a pinch of salt.

… Nothing in the world would have reconciled me to go on ministering for a life-time in the old building as it was.' At the hearing in the consistory court not a single pewholder opposed the faculty which would allow the work to proceed. There were some murmurs from Nonconformists, such as the manufacturer William Greenwood, who had known Brontë well and regretted the passing of the old order, but nobody would help to pay for repairs. Furthermore, there was still a good deal of hostility towards anything apparently emanating from Bradford – the Anglican estate agent, James Ackroyd, was only narrowly dissuaded from proposing a motion repudiating 'interference on the part of any outsiders, whether antiquarians or other quarians'.

Haworth was arguably more at risk from Philistines rather than Barbarians. The Mechanics' Institute encountered bad times, as evening classes proved increasingly difficult to organise. An art class met intermittently, and work was submitted for examination to South Kensington for a number of years;[2] a building construction class appeared briefly; and Harry Greenwood gave lectures on English history and grammar; but attempts to start classes on scientific subjects failed. Dressmaking evoked little interest (the number of women members was always small) and there was never enough money to support visiting lecturers. James Ogden observed that when he was curator he spent his time stopping boys from throwing bottles out of the window and from boring holes in the floor with a red hot poker.[3] One problem was the cramped accommodation.[4] The Institute had moved to premises over the Yorkshire Penny Bank,[5] but gymnastic and dancing classes, very popular at neighbouring institutes, could not be held through lack of a hall, while anyone wanting a game of billiards had to adjourn to the Conservative or Liberal clubs because there was no table.[6]

With the death of Michael Merrall in 1881 the Institute became moribund. Wade, who for some time had considered starting a church institute,[7] took the chance to do so, and Merrall's son, George transferred his allegiance to the new Lees and Crossroads Institute, nearer to his works. The social functions of the Institute disappeared, and attendances at the AGM slumped to fewer than 20.[8] Haworthites apparently preferred ham teas and entertainments in their own churches and chapels – though it is significant that the same pattern, of initial enthusiasm giving way to lethargy and collapse – can also be traced at Oxenhope and Stanbury. The introduction of evening classes at the new Haworth Central Schools in 1897 ended any aspirations to an intellectual function that the trustees of the Institute may have held.[9] The only part of the Mechanics' Institute which had wider public support was the reading room, where the members could look at newspapers and borrow library books.[10]

In 1898 a trustee, George Rushworth, proposed that the institute be wound up and the remaining funds, which he calculated at £550, be given to the Urban District Council towards the building of a free library. He suggested certain conditions: the library should be on the *west* side of Bridgehouse Beck; and the council should adopt the Free Libraries Act, allowing it to devote a penny rate to the provision of library facilities. In Haworth in 1898 a penny rate would yield approximately £70 which, Rushworth calculated, was enough to pay a curator, cover maintenance costs (£26), and newspaper subscriptions (£20 4s.), leaving £20 for book purchases.[11] The proposal was greeted with open scepticism or outright opposition by many councillors, especially those representing Lees and Crossroads, which now had their own Institute and library. They persuaded the council to insist that if a penny rate was approved, the Institute trustees must accept a suitable site anywhere within the old Haworth Local Board district. Reluctantly the trustees agreed.[12] As the opponents of the free library knew, the cost of buildings would be nearer £1,500 than the £500 on offer and, though a committee was formed to raise the money, the target proved to be unattainable.[13] In May 1901 the committee approached the Scottish-born steel millionaire and philanthropist, Andrew Carnegie, whose generosity had already funded library buildings in many British towns. Carnegie's answer, in July 1902, was an offer of £1500 subject to the council providing an annual endowment of £100. A penny rate would only amount to £70, but it was hoped that interest on the £550 from the Mechanics' Institute would make up the difference. There was still the question of a site. As soon as Carnegie's answer was received, George Merrall offered land at Ebor Lane Top, free of charge.[14]

Unfortunately, this was on the edge of the district and on the *east* side of the beck, not far from the Lees Institute. The chairman of the committee, the rector of Haworth Rev. Thomas Story, considered this site very unsuitable, but since Captain Emmott was demanding £175 for the ideal site in Butt Lane and the committee had only raised £55, the offer was accepted. The Institute trustees were unhappy and when Emmott reduced his asking price to £35 they withdrew their offer. There was stalemate. Supporters of the Ebor Lane site, and those who did not want a library, claimed that a decision had been taken in favour of Ebor and that the approval of a penny rate, which had now accumulated to over £400, was conditional upon their agreement. If the council chose Ebor it would lose the Mechanics' Institute money and fall short of the £100 Carnegie wanted. The Butt Lane site, on the other hand, would not benefit from the penny rate. Story declared that it was 'the politics of Mudfog'.[15]

At the 1903 local elections James Ackroyd and John Hudson campaigned for a free library and were returned at the head of the poll. They proposed a site in Belle Isle Road, which was nearer to Ebor than Butt Lane, required users from both Haworth and Lees to climb one hill; and was on the *west* side of the beck only which would satisfy the Institute trustees. To meet the objection from Lees and Crossroads that they already had a library, it was proposed that there should also be recreation rooms and basement slipper baths. But the plan was ill-conceived, for it would cost a further £1,000, which the council would not countenance, and rumours soon circulated that the site was 'rat infested'.[16] In 1906 a frustrated Ackroyd returned to the idea of a straightforward library, on the Belle Isle site, but a local plebiscite rejected the scheme by 660 votes to 550. Thus, Haworth had neither a free library nor a mechanics' institute.[17]

The members from Lees and Crossroads, still smarting from being forced to contribute to Haworth's sewerage scheme, had been a major obstruction, but outright philistinism played its part in this fiasco. James Redman, the monumental mason, believed there was little demand for a library, and James Doughty called the idea an 'expensive luxury'. James Greenwood considered that Sunday school libraries were sufficient, though they only stocked children's books, and J.H. Pickles, the Wesleyan Methodist school superintendent at West Lane, agreed. Barwick Midgley was opposed to all secular libraries, which he believed took people away from religion. He thought 'the free library in Keighley ought to be a lesson for Haworth. It puzzled him to know why ministers were so in favour of the scheme. They were not serving the interests of the Sunday School libraries.'[18]

Brass bands and cricket

Yet it would be wrong to assume, on the basis of the demolition of the church that the Brontës knew and the failure of the free library scheme, that Haworth was a cultural desert. Indeed, considering the limited time that the workers had available, the level of activity was quite remarkable. There were entertainments almost every weekend during the winter, though the culture was 'popular' and introverted. As with many Pennine industrial communities, Haworth had its own variant of Yorkshire dialect which marked it off both from its neighbours and from the world at large. Dialect was the preferred form of speech for the working classes and professional men as late as the inter-war years and was used by Emily Brontë to build up the character of Joseph in *Wuthering Heights*. Halliwell Sutcliffe claimed in 1904 that you could not get to know the people without 'an under knowledge of the old Haworth speech and ways of thought'. Haworthites liked dialect stories, plays and verses interspersed with songs. The works of the local humorist William Wright (Bill o' th' Hoylus End) and John Hartley, the Halifax vernacular poet, were particular favourites.[19] In 1875 Wade complained that the National School

> could not turn out children with the least sign of a lady or gentleman about them. They were taught to read correctly in the school, but immediately they were outside they talked in the broad vernacular of the place. They were frequently pointed at by strangers who made the remark, 'That's Haworth'.[20]

So although there was no lack of 'culture', everything was organised on sectarian lines, and the resources on which each denomination could call were limited. Organs were within financial capacity of individual churches and chapels, and competition ensured that each was bigger and better than its predecessor. Similarly, each was capable of organising a choir which could beautify its services and was competent to perform small scale cantatas, but none could readily perform large-scale oratorios such as *Messiah* and the *Creation*. A shining exception was the Haworth brass band which, here as elsewhere in the region, had deep roots among those working in textile mills and mines. Enterprising manufacturers encouraged their employees to form works bands. John Dawson Hopkinson, the best player Haworth ever produced, completed his career before the Haworth band was formed. According to his obituary in the *Leeds Intelligencer* of 11 August 1860 he was formerly the leader of the band belonging to Lister Marriner's Keighley works, which was the most famous in the area and won the great Crystal Palace brass band contest in 1862. Hopkinson later played in the band attached to Wombwell's menagerie, which toured round the fairs – the pioneer films of Mitchell and Kenyon show that this was still flourishing in the Edwardian period.[21] Hopkinson's reputation was achieved in a very short time, for he was only 28 when he died.[22] Another member of Wombwell's band was W.H. Whitaker, later well known as a choral conductor. He organised a string band which often provided the music at Nonconformist gatherings in Oxenhope.

The original founder of what became the Haworth brass band was John Heaton of Ponden. The first reports of the instrumentalists playing together date from 1854 and in 1856 they were invited to play in Haworth at the peace celebrations marking the end of the Crimean War. After Heaton's death the Ponden band survived precariously, rehearsing at Dry Clough, until Hartley Merrall junior encountered a group of them 'busking' on his way to church around 1860 and decided to form a band based on his textile works at Springhead. The first leader was James Bancroft, one of the original Ponden players, and the first conductor was William Turner of Oakworth. The band quickly achieved an excellent standard, winning awards at Keighley, Skipton and Trawden and even competed at the Crystal Palace Band Mecca in 1863.[23]

When Hartley Merrall's business failed in 1875, the band lost its patron, and with the textile industry deep in depression its future looked black. The band was rescued largely through the efforts of John T. Robinson of Currer House, who organised a meeting at the *Black Bull* attended by many influential gentlemen. Some £200 was raised by subscription, enough to purchase instruments, scores and musical accessories, and to provide new uniforms for the band members. Bancroft remained the leader until his retirement in 1899. There was no lack of engagements. In later Victorian times no event was complete without a brass band in attendance. Wade realised the value of such contributions, and regularly secured the services of the Springhead band, and its

successor, the Haworth brass band, for the Anglican Whitsuntide processions. By the end of the century competition was intense – in 1898 there were four bands at the Whitsuntide event in Haworth and another in Oxenhope.

For most of its existence the Haworth band has been a good 'village' band. Its nickname, the 'bread and cheese band',[24] emphasised the absence of the sort of money which enabled the big company

The grave of John Dawson Hopkinson, a locally renowned musician and bandsman. His career largely predated the Haworth Brass Band, but he was a member of the brass band organised by the Marriner textile family of Keighley which won the prestigious Crystal Palace contest in 1862. He died aged just 27.
PHOTOGRAPH: CARNEGIE, 2009

The Haworth Brass Band, photographed at Longlands, the home of George Merrall. The band began as the Ponden Band in 1854 and then became the Springhead Band in 1861 under the patronage of Hartley Merrall junior. When he went bankrupt in 1878 it was saved by Mr John T. Robinson of Currer House, who organised a subscription on the band's behalf. Now known as the Haworth Public Brass Band the money was spent in providing the instruments and uniforms seen in the picture.
PHOTOGRAPH BY COURTESY OF JACK LAYCOCK

bands to attract and pay top-class players. The band's best period began in 1910, when the committee managed to secure the services of John Paley, formerly with the famous Black Dyke Band, as its conductor. The result was a remarkable string of successes. During 1911 prizes were won at contests at Ilkley, Lees Moor, Stanley, Rochdale and Morecambe, where the Band won a fifty guinea cup, and in 1912 there were further triumphs at Huddersfield, Rochdale, Keighley, and Morecambe again, and also at the big contest at Belle Vue, Manchester.[25]

There is a story that when the members arrived home from their Belle Vue triumph they wanted to celebrate in the traditional way, by marching up from the station to the *Black Bull* playing as they went. The train reached Haworth at two in the morning and some members were worried that they would wake people up, so they agreed to take their boots off and march in their socks![26] In 1913, apart from contests, the band was engaged for concerts on Blackpool and Morecambe piers and at Nelson, but in the following year the outbreak of war led to the departure of Paley and, eventually, to the loss of many band members.

The founder of Haworth cricket club was Crawshaw Dugdale,[27] who was born at Accrington in 1837 and was an active player in his youth. By the time he arrived in Haworth as assistant to Dr Ingham in 1863 his best playing days were over but his enthusiasm was largely responsible for the adoption of the game in the village. The scores achieved by the club in the early years were small – rarely exceeding a hundred runs per innings – which suggests a bumpy pitch. The manufacturer James Frederick Greenwood had his cricket career cut short when he sustained a pair of black eyes from a short-pitched delivery during a match at Bents Farm.[28] Most games were played on an *ad hoc* basis, the strength of the club being shown by the fixture list rather than the

Haworth Church Cricket Team. The earliest cricket team represented all Haworth, but when the number of players grew too large it divided along sectarian lines. Haworth Church was the strongest team before the First World War, winning the league in 1909, but it disbanded after the 1938 season and was never revived.

results. There were other, more ephemeral, local clubs, such as Haworth Garibaldi, Haworth Brunswick and Haworth Albion. In the early years there was a flourishing club at Stanbury, at least as good as Haworth, but it disappeared as Stanbury's population fell with the decline of the textile trade Oxenhope did not have its own club until 1881.[29]

In the 1890s the increasing popularity of the game led to two major new developments. The number of clubs increased, but the original Haworth club divided along sectarian lines into teams representing Haworth Church and Haworth Wesleyans. There was a similar division in Oxenhope with the addition of a third team based on Horkinstone Baptist chapel. The second development was the appearance of organised leagues. Haworth Church, the strongest team, competed regularly in the West Bradford League, winning it in 1909.[30] The others contented themselves with playing in the Keighley and District League. Just before the First World War the Oxenhope Wesleyans began to challenge the supremacy of Haworth Church. Greenwood described how when the former was founded in 1899 the players had to change in a hencote. They then bought a tent and when the decision was taken to play in the West Bradford League in 1909 a series of 'at home' entertainments raised £20, enabling the club to build a proper pavilion. It opened in 1913, the first year in which the team achieved better results than Haworth Church.[31]

Though the teams bore sectarian labels, ambitious cricketers tended to migrate to the most successful ones whatever their own religious leanings. In Haworth this benefited the Church team. Arthur Hirst, successively headmaster of the Haworth Wesleyan and the Haworth Central Schools, was a keen cricketer and played for Haworth Church while he was good enough for the West Bradford League, but then transferred to the Wesleyans.[32] Charlie Wildman, a well-known Nonconformist choirmaster between the wars, played regularly for the Haworth Church team. In 1910 he took 8 wickets for 8 runs, playing for them against Crossroads.[33] Cricket was in his blood – during the 1882 season his father John took 54 wickets for 215 runs, or 3.98 runs per wicket![34] In Oxenhope similar pressures worked in favour of Oxenhope Wesleyans. By the end of the period Oxenhope Church confined its activities to a junior team and the Horkinstone team had disappeared altogether.

An alternative culture

One of the most striking developments in late nineteenth-century Haworth was the success of the co-operative movement. In 1861 co-operative societies were founded at Haworth, and at Lees and Crossroads, just a year after that at Keighley.[35] Hostility from established tradesmen created difficulties at the start but once these were overcome the societies flourished. In 1882 Lees and Crossroads added a second shop at Lees to the original one at Crossroads. Haworth's central store was in lower Main Street but in 1866 it added a branch in Mill Hey[36] and later another at Townend. The Oxenhope Industrial Cooperative Society was founded in 1868[37] in premises at Scar Hall, Leeming, and the

Lower Haworth Main Street. This picture, dating from around 1917, shows the Cooperative Society main shop at the bottom on the right-hand side. The four cottages next to it were also owned by the Cooperative Society. In 1933, at its most prosperous, Haworth Cooperative Society had grocery, drapery, outfitting and boot and shoe departments along with three butchers, three greengrocers, two boot repairers and a printing department. It also owned Old Hall Farm and Bankfield Quarry. Note also the simple but elegant gas lamp on the left-hand side and the uneven cobbles which were so to annoy motorists such as the Rev. Charles Manchester.

137 MAIN STREET, HAWORTH.

Lower Main Street showing the old Co-operative Society Headquarters (*centre*), which opened in 1861 only a year after that in Keighley.
PHOTOGRAPH: CARNEGIE, 2009

Uppertown Cooperative Society, which confusingly served Lowertown as well, four years later.[38] The Haworth society established a branch store in Stanbury in 1877 but that village had to wait until 1890 for its own independent society.[39] By this time the Haworth, Oxenhope and Stanbury societies had approximately 1,500 members between them, which assuming one member per household accounted for 82 per cent of all households.[40]

The founders of the earliest co-operatives wanted to provide an alternative to the system whereby employers could compel the workforce to buy food and other necessaries from the factory shop at exorbitant prices, despite Merralls being prosecuted in 1898 for breaking the 'truck' Acts,[41] but the battle had effectively been won by the end the century, and the more positive benefits of co-operation had gained in strength in the meantime. People realised that the increased purchasing power of the societies could be used to force prices down. In addition, those who owned shares in a society could influence its policy,[42] and also had a good investment with a steady profit from the dividend on purchases, which was usually between 2*s*. and 3*s*. in the pound. At first only those buying shares received the dividend, but by the 1890s most societies felt able to limit the number of shares any individual could hold and started to pay out on all purchases, though at a lower rate.

Initially most societies concentrated on groceries and clothes, but later a meat department might be added. Press reports suggest that this was a more difficult commodity to handle and needed considerable managerial skill. Problems in the meat department were largely responsible for a fall in Haworth's dividend to 1*s*. 7*d*. in 1892. The secretary was dismissed but his successor, Haydn Parker, restored the situation and won a testimonial for his work eight years later.[43] Smaller societies, such as Oxenhope, had even greater difficulties. At first the Industrial Cooperative obtained meat from Uppertown, only starting its own operation in 1882. This did not pay and in 1889 the society reluctantly renewed its connection with Uppertown. A second attempt at independent purchasing in 1892 was more successful. The traditional fare at Christmas was pork, and both the Oxenhope and Stanbury societies ran clubs to help families pay for the celebratory meal. The consumer could spread out the costs and the farmers knew how many pigs had to be fattened for the table.[44] Larger societies, such as Haworth and Lees, also had boot and shoe and hardware departments. Coal deliveries were more complicated to organise. In 1864 Lees, Oakworth and Haworth formed a joint enterprise but by 1873 each felt strong enough to become independent. A similar arrangement between the two Oxenhope societies was terminated in 1882.[45]

The co-operative principle was flexible. All the local societies took shares in the Cooperative Wholesale Society, and could also participate in regional specialist societies. The most widespread joint enterprise dealt with flour. At different times the local cooperatives were members of flour societies based on Hebden Bridge and Halifax. The Keighley Society was large enough to have its own ironworks,[46] in which Haworth took shares so that it could open an ironmongery department which provided mangles (a Keighley speciality), and gas cooking and lighting equipment. The records of the Oxenhope Industrial and the Stanbury societies show that they also had 'outside' shares – for example, Oxenhope had an interest in the Leicester Boot and Shoe Cooperative.

Co-operative societies performed other functions. Oxenhope Industrial ran a penny bank from 1899 and Uppertown had an accident insurance fund.[47] Haworth formed a small savings bank.[48] Many offered insurance against sickness and unemployment. Some provided burial funds and had their own funeral parlours. By the early twentieth century the Haworth society held a children's festival and a gala each year, and Oxenhope a children's treat. At the 1906 Haworth gala there was a tragic accident when, during an exhibition of parachute-jumping from a balloon, Lilian Cove's parachute failed to open and she fell to her death. In 1905 the Haworth society founded its own library. The five

Victoria Hall belonged to the Oddfellows Friendly Society which originally met at the New Inn Stubbing. Ramsey Macdonald spoke there when he visited Haworth. An alternative venue for visiting speakers was the Cooperative Room in their Main Street premises.

© KEIGHLEY LIBRARY

original readers had increased to 87 by the end of the year and when the free library was voted down a reading room was opened in the Baptist school room. During 1909 alone 118 books were purchased.[49]

In 1895 Philip Snowden, a native of Ickornshaw and later the first Labour chancellor of the exchequer, came to Haworth for the opening of the Independent Labour Party rooms. Soon afterwards he addressed a large audience in the Oddfellows' Victoria Hall, on the principles of socialism.[50] This presented the cooperative societies with a dilemma. The strong Liberal influence in the local movement originally made the societies chary of direct political involvement,[51] but as time passed the common ground with the ILP at national level grew and in 1899 the Cooperative Movement, along with the trade unions and the Fabian Society, joined the Labour Representation Committee. This was not popular in the Keighley area and the visit of Ramsey Macdonald, the future Labour prime minister in 1899 during which he spoke at the Victoria Hall may have been an effort to whip up more enthusiasm.[52]

Snowden left in 1902, to concentrate on winning a parliamentary seat, while the abolition of the Haworth School Board ended any direct influence of the local Labour Party on educational affairs. On Haworth Urban District Council between 1895 and 1907 there had been three wards: Old Haworth returned five members; Near Oxenhope one; and Lees and Crossroads three. Councillors served three-year terms, and by 1903 a Labour member was usually returned for old Haworth at each election, giving them three councillors – Allen Woodman, Fred Quarmby and James Smith – by 1906. However, from 1907 there were six wards, each returning one member at each annual election (giving a total of 18 councillors).[53] This established an impregnable Liberal majority, drastically reduced the number of Conservatives, and eliminated Labour representation altogether.

A parallel development was the formation of the Haworth Brotherhood, an interdenominational organisation which invited visiting lecturers to speak to joint church and chapel audiences on issues of the moment. Initially there seemed a good chance that socialism would be admissible as subject for debate. Snowden, one of the founders of the Labour Church in Keighley, believed passionately in Christian Socialism and Macdonald's visit was officially for a Labour Church service.[54] There was a strong undercurrent of support in many congregations, particularly those of the Primitive Methodists and the Baptists. Harrison Wallbank, a leading Haworth Socialist, was a Sunday school teacher. Among the lectures at the Co-operative Assembly Rooms were those by the Reverend Richard Roberts, who asked 'Christian Socialism. What is it?', and Frank Harper, Baptist minister at West Lane from 1868 to 1888 and president of the Haworth Co-operative Society during the 1890s, lectured on 'Socialism and Individualism' and 'Land, labour and capital'.[55]

When Arthur Henderson, another ILP leader and a Methodist lay preacher, addressed the Brotherhood on the evils of drink he was heard with approval but when he spoke about the principles of socialism there was a furore. James Pedley complained that the pulpit was being used as a vehicle for party politics, but James Smith, the leader of

Haworth Independent Labour Party, pointed out that the fare Pedley wanted – sermons on self help, temperance and technical education – were part of the Liberal Party platform. His demonstration of the political bias contained within the Brotherhood's lecture programme was not lost on the largely Conservative Anglicans whose interest rapidly waned as a result. Rivalry grew. The ILP soon had its own institute in Earl Street,[56] but in the chapels any talk of socialism was anathema.[57] Antagonism was particularly sharp in Oxenhope, where by 1912 attendance at Brotherhood meetings was almost exclusively Wesleyan.[58]

Mouldgreave Barn. This is good example of an eighteenth-century detached barn. The earliest houses had barns attached but in the eighteenth century detached barns were preferred. They could be used for a number of purposes; the one at North Ives, for example, was a Quaker meeting place in the early eighteenth century.
BY COURTESY OF STEVEN WOOD

We can tell that this view dates from before 1897 because there are no schools in Butt Lane. Bridgehouse Mills are at the bottom right but cannot be seen for the trees. Ivy Bank Mill, however, is visible on the bottom left. To the right of Ivy Bank's chimney is the Drill Hall used by the Haworth Volunteers. Main Street climbs the hill at the back with Haworth church in the distance on the right skyline. Notice the amount of smoke from houses as well as mill chimneys which is obscuring parts of the photograph!

Armageddon   16

The Haworth Volunteers

In 1859 relations with France deteriorated to such an extent that there was an 'invasion' scare. This episode has long been forgotten, but the government was sufficiently worried to make plans for a permanent countrywide volunteer defence force. During 1860 companies were formed at Leeds and Bradford and an 80-strong Keighley company held its first open air drill in December of that year. Keighley was soon recruiting more widely and at the end of May 1861 their Rifle Volunteers marched to Haworth and back as part of a publicity campaign.[1] In March 1866 a meeting was held in the National School at Haworth with a view to forming a separate Haworth Company: 46 men had already been enrolled and fourteen more expressed interest, so the lord lieutenant consented to the formation of the 42nd Haworth Company of the West Yorkshire Rifle Volunteers. Three weeks later a second meeting was held, to choose uniforms.

Predictably enough, the officers were drawn from the professional and merchant classes: the captain was George Merrall; the second in command, Lieutenant Sugden, was a member of the Vale Mill family; and the ensign, George Hartley Merrall, was son of Hartley Merrall junior of Springhead. Dr Ingham was the surgeon and Grant the chaplain. None of them had any practical experience, so Captain Marriner of the Keighley Corps loaned them a staff sergeant once a week for drilling until the War Office appointed one for Haworth. In July the Company, led by its own Rifle Band, attended its first church parade at Haworth, and at the end of the month a gala was held during the Rushbearing Feast to raise money for the new force.[2] There was regular drilling, but despite commendatory remarks from the adjutant, the Haworth Volunteers compared badly with the companies from Skipton, Keighley and Bingley. In 1869, twenty of the 66 recruits were classed as 'non-efficient' (compared with twelve in a hundred at Bingley, seven in 65 at Skipton, and just four out of 82 at Keighley). The following year's returns showed only a slight improvement.[3]

One reason was the lack of a place to drill when the weather was bad. In April 1870 a rifle bazaar, held to finance the building of a drill shed, raised £662 13s. 10d. and in August 1871 Major General Green-Emmott-Rawdon of the Bombay Staff Corps, the largest landowner in Haworth, approved the immediate erection of a drill hall on his land.[4] In 1867 a rifle range was opened on the moor between Flappit Spring and Manywells Height, and regular annual competitions for the Ladies Challenge and Recruits cups did much to improve the standard of firing – in 1873 Haworth only narrowly lost a rifle contest against Keighley.[5] As a result of army reforms in the late 1870s the volunteer companies were amalgamated, and Haworth became G Company in the 6th battalion of the Duke of Wellington's Regiment. Another change was the institution of annual camps where competitions in drill, firing and field scouting were conducted under the eye of the colonel.

In 1889 M.H. Merrall, son of George Merrall, became captain of the company. Whether or not this was an example of nepotism, he proved to be an excellent choice and during his eleven years in command the force went from strength to strength. Haworth won the battalion's Arnold Foster Drill Shield six times, a far cry from the inefficiency of the early days. Firing improved dramatically: in 1888 Haworth won a rifle contest against Keighley, at Nan Scar, and during the 1890s the company produced a series of crack shots in Captain Wilkinson, Sergeant Kay, Private Boocock and Lieutenant Ratcliffe. In 1895 and again in 1899 the company won the regiment's Bingham Silver Cup for musketry.[6]

After the Boer War of 1899–1902 the Duke of Wellington's became one of the new territorial regiments, designed to relieve the regulars of much of the burden of home defence. When Merrall retired he was succeeded by a professional officer, Captain Cass, who built on already firm foundations. In 1904 the Company won the Bingham Trophy with almost ridiculous ease, scoring 44 points against the 30 of their nearest rivals, and by this time Haworth had won the Arnold Foster Shield so often that it was hardly worth taking it out of the trophy case. Between Cass's arrival in 1900 and his departure following promotion at the end of 1911, there was only one year when the Company did not win either the Arnold Foster Battalion Drill Shield or the regimental Bingham Silver Trophy for musketry. In 1912 Lieutenant-Colonel Clarkson called the Company the most efficient in the whole regiment and, in relation to the number of its inhabitants, Haworth was said to have possessed more prizes at shooting and drill than any other place in northern England. The standard reached by the Haworth Company ranks as the village's most outstanding achievement during the period 1860–1914.[7]

The First World War

When war broke out with Germany in August 1914 the British Expeditionary Force, made up of professional soldiers, was shipped to the Continent to help the French. The Territorials were called up and moved to Lincolnshire, where they took the place of the regular soldiers. In Haworth a relief committee was formed but, typically, it resolved that while it welcomed the council's decision to begin a Prince of Wales Fund for those in need, it preferred to stick to local relief. Only with difficulty was the Oxenhope section persuaded to give the national fund £84 of the £200 raised. Groups of women made

Private Joseph West with Stanbury schoolchildren. The photograph is dated 1915, so it may be from the time in Lincolnshire before the second battle of Ypres.

garments for soldiers and James Frederick Greenwood supplied the material for those in Oxenhope free of charge.[8]

The delusion that the war would be short was soon superseded by grim reality. The Germans overran Belgium and many Belgians fled to England, two families being housed at Lowertown in property belonging to Merralls.[9] The Germans pushed deep into France, and the retreat of the BEF from Mons was described by Sidney Stockman, a former Haworth coal merchant, and Private Gilbert Smith, in their letters home. The first Haworth casualty was Private Henry Bates, killed in action on 24 August 1914.[10] The German offensive was stemmed on the river Marne and the two armies then tried to outflank each other, culminating in the first battle of Ypres in October 1914. Both sides dug in and soon trenches extended all the way from the Channel coast to the Swiss

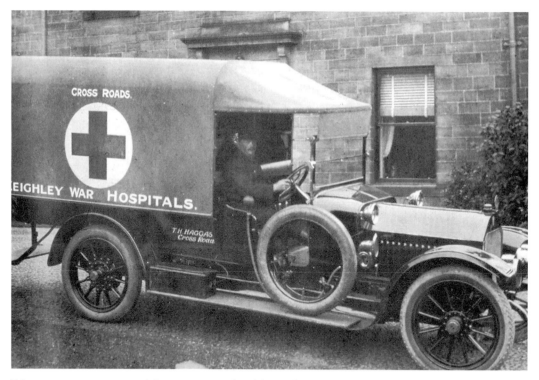

Elaborate arrangements were made in 1914 to prepare the inhabitants for war. This is a typical First World War ambulance. As Haworth was neither invaded nor bombed, it must have been used to transport injured soldiers on leave.
PHOTOGRAPH BY COURTESY OF JACK LAYCOCK

border. The casualties suffered at the Marne and Ypres were so great that the idea of fighting just with a professional army had to be abandoned. Plans were laid to send the Territorials to France as reinforcements.[11] Haworth men anticipated that they would go from October 1914 onwards but their 6th Battalion of the West Yorkshire regiment, part of the 49th Division, did not sail from Folkestone until 15 April 1915.

It arrived in the middle of the second battle of Ypres, in which the Germans fired gas canisters. The Canadians, taking the brunt of the attack, were so badly affected that they were withdrawn from the line and replaced by soldiers from the 49th Division. The Germans had been almost as badly frightened by the gas as their opponents, and were unaware of the extent of the casualties inflicted. This was fortunate, for the Yorkshiremen had never seen a bomb, their training had not included stabbing dummies with a bayonet, and gas was as much an unknown quantity to them as to the Canadians. The arrival of the Territorials and three Indian Divisions enabled the British to extend their front and the West Riding men took part in a limited attack on Neuve Chapelle, which stalled through lack of resources. The British retired in good order and there were no Haworth casualties. They were moved back to Ypres in June and remained there for the rest of the year, through an unpleasant winter with, in December, a heavy bombardment and gas attack during which Sergeant John Bell, son of a Haworth widow, was killed.[12]

At home, efforts to recruit more men were gathering momentum. In March 1915, some six hundred troops marched from Bradford to Oxenhope, to encourage local men to enlist in the 2nd battalion of their 'Pals' regiment, to be based in Keighley. By January 1916 696 men had presented themselves in Haworth, of whom 478 were accepted (a percentage well above the average). The real figure was probably higher, for some men had already joined up at Keighley before the Haworth recruiting office had opened.[13] These new recruits, together with those already at the front, fought on the Somme, a series of related battles lasting from the 1 July 1916 until the end of September. This succession of frontal attacks gained some ground but at a terrible cost. Letters home described the constant activity, but Haworth men did relatively little fighting after the failure of the initial attack in their sector. Much of their time was spent sending out smokescreens to cover operations further south, and in reconstructing trenches destroyed by the Germans. One trench in no-man's land was called 'Bateman's Street', after Lieutenant Colonel Bateman who took command of the 49th Division in April 1916. Nevertheless at least 13 men from Haworth were killed during this period, most of them as a result of heavy shelling.

The battle of the Somme convinced the government that conscription was the only way to maintain manpower. There was a general call up of all men fit to serve, each district appointing a tribunal to judge the cases of those who pleaded for exemption.

Wounded soldiers from the First World War, 1917. The soldiers can be identified by their white lapels. In total eleven Stanbury men were killed, a heavy loss for such a small village. Stanbury Primary School can be seen in the background.

The chairman at Oxenhope was J.F. Greenwood, and the destruction by fire of a large part of his Brooks Meeting Mill was thought to have been the work of aggrieved men who had been refused exemption. Through 1917 the West Riding men had a terrible time. Mrs Bell lost another son,[14] and a dreadful three-day battle in the snow, described in a letter home by Gunner Tom Hollings of the Royal Horse Artillery, two local men were killed and four more (including Tom's brother Rennie) were wounded: Rennie was killed in a later engagement.[15]

Defensive resources far outweighed offensive power, but the generals on both sides seemed unable to learn from their mistakes. The failure of the German offensive at Verdun and the British on the Somme demonstrated that the violent bombardments which preceded the attacks could be extremely counterproductive, alerting opponents and cratering the terrain so badly that progress on foot was drastically slowed.[16] The shrewdest of the British commanders, Lieutenant General Plumer, realised that bombardment tactics would only be effective if a limited target was selected. He successfully attacked Messines ridge, an action which involved the Yorkshiremen and in which Sergeant George Peacock was killed.[17] Haig decided to turn Plumer's modest achievement into an all-out attack, despite warnings that a heavy bombardment around

The ceremony of dedication of the First World War Memorial, 1919. The clergyman is Rev. T.W. Story, the rector of Haworth.

PHOTOGRAPH BY COURTESY OF JACK LAYCOCK

Ypres would destroy the drainage and lead to flooding. Haworth men soon realised the correctness of those warnings. In the early stages of the assault they were in line near Dunkirk. There were no trenches, their front being sand dunes; scouting was done more by swimming than walking; and the men endured continuous shelling for three weeks, and a mustard gas attack, before being withdrawn in mid-August 1917. The initial offensive had ground to a halt but Haig was determined to try again and during September the 6th Battalion was among the resources thrown into the battle. Continuous rain produced flooding worse than even the pessimists had feared and the battlefield became a swamp, but Haig would not give in until the fragmentary remains of the village of Passchendaele, the original target, had been occupied. The victory achieved no strategic objective of any importance. At least 40 men from Haworth township were killed during 1917, three-quarters of them in the third battle of Ypres or Passchendaele offensive. Ultimately the impasse was broken when, on 19 November at Cambrai, the British launched the first ever offensive using tanks – during it a Haworth man, Sergeant Major E. Peacock, was wounded.[18]

The collapse of Russia allowed the Germans to move troops from the Eastern Front and under generals Hindenburg and Ludendorff they planned one last great offensive. April 1918, a terrible month, saw the 6th Battalion on the eastern edge of the Ypres salient, fighting valiantly under Lieutenant Colonel Bateman. The Battalion then went into reserve but was recalled twice more. Casualties were heavy, but they kept their formation. That was not the case with the Northumberland Fusiliers, which had Haworth men in its ranks.[19] They were completely overrun and many were taken prisoner. Fighting continued into the autumn, some of the heaviest casualties coming in the weeks just before the armistice was concluded on 11 November. Some unhappy families in Haworth heard of the death of loved ones only after the news of peace had been received.

Most of those on the Western Front in 1918 were conscripts. The Duke of Wellington's Regiment was sent to Italy, to help to shore up the Italian Army in the aftermath of its defeat at Caporetto. Sergeant Goodchild wrote complaining of the lack of publicity for the way the regiment had spearheaded the attack on the Austrian lines behind the river Piave in the closing months of the war. Private Peel from Stanbury was killed and Private Denby from Haworth was wounded. Captain John Hodgson, born in Stanbury, started the war as a Red Cross worker and then joined the Royal Naval Air Service. By January 1918 he was a full lieutenant and helping to harass the enemy in the Straits of Otranto.[20] Some Haworth men went even further afield. Corporal W.H. Beasley was killed at Gallipoli and the tragic *Mrs* Bell lost a third son there.[21] The Methodist roll of honour contains the names of men who served in Mesopotamia and Salonika. Bombardier John Finan took part in the retreat from Mons in 1914, the relief of Kut in Mesopotamia in 1916, the conquest of Palestine in 1917, and the final drive to victory on the Western Front in 1918.[22]

Altogether 193 men from Haworth township lost their lives: 105 from Haworth, 38 from Oxenhope, 11 from Stanbury, and 39 from Lees and Crossroads, a terrible price to

The war memorial in 1920. Originally the war memorial only commemorated the dead in the First World War in France, but the names of those killed in other theatres and in the Second World War have been added on the other faces.

FROM THE COLLECTION OF STEVEN WOOD

pay for victory. The West Lane Methodist roll of honour shows that thirteen of the 84 members who enlisted were killed – a rate of roughly 1 in 6.[23] Haworth's war was a war of ordinary soldiers, and there were few commissioned officers. J. Stuart Arthur, son of the Baptist pastor, was commissioned as a second lieutenant in 1915, and Walter Robinson, Haydn Scarborough and Joseph Maude were promoted to the same rank in June 1917. Maude ended the war a prisoner. Both Robinson and Scarborough lost their lives.[24]

On a more positive note, John Hodgson was awarded the Distinguished Flying Cross; eleven men received the Military Medal; and eight gained Distinguished Certificates of Merit. Lewis Barnes of Stanbury started the war as a private and ended it as a sergeant, and Joe Bates won a bar to his MM. Three won foreign decorations: Joe's brother, Lance

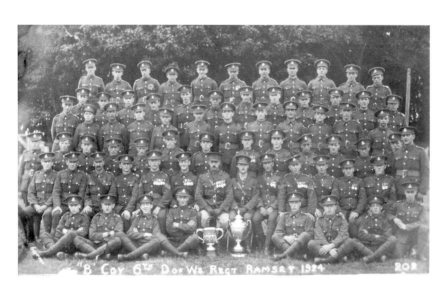

B Company of the 6th Duke of Wellington's Regiment, 1924. The company first fought at the second battle of Ypres in May 1915 and later in Italy. It should be carefully distinguished from the so called 'Pals' regiments which were made up of conscripts.

PHOTOGRAPH BY COURTESY OF JACK LAYCOCK

Corporal Samuel Bates of Oxenhope, received the French Medalle Militaire; Sergeant Major Ellis Ratcliffe of Lees added the Croix de Guerre to his DCM; and Hodgson the Italian Medale d'Argent and Blue Ribbon to his DFC.[25]

The Second World War

Few who celebrated the peace in 1919 could have imagined that within two decades they would be at war with Germany again. During the years before war broke out in September 1939 there had been growing apprehension about the likelihood of mass air raids, and here, as everywhere else in the United Kingdom, an Air Raid Precautions unit [ARP] was formed. Fire-fighting demonstrations were held at the Salvation Army Hall, a Home Guard company was enrolled, and a Royal Observer Corps post was established on Blackhill. In anticipation of bombing, the evacuation of children was implemented – sixty were brought to Oxenhope from Bradford, but most soon went home again when nothing happened. The blitzkrieg through Belgium in the spring of 1940 brought another flood of refugees, but this time they stayed in Keighley, though Haworth entertained children evacuated from Guernsey. Those watching and waiting had little to do, for Haworth was not bombed and there were no fires to be put out. The personnel manning the post on Blackhill counted 129 different types of aircraft, several V1 flying bombs and two V2 rockets, but the nearest Haworth came to the war was when a flying bomb fell on Sowerby Bridge.[26]

The ladies of the Haworth Women's Voluntary Services were soon busy preparing parcels for soldiers serving abroad, which included clothing, cigarettes, chocolates, sweets and chewing gum. At first the parcels were sent only to those on active service but as the war developed the scheme was extended to prisoners of war.[27] The money for the parcels was raised by concerts and bazaars, and local people also contributed to the Red Cross scheme of a penny a week to help the wounded, and that too was later extended to prisoners of war. In the First World War there were no really serious shortages until the German U-boat offensive of 1917, but this time they were anticipated from the beginning. Food was rationed and everyone was urged to dig for victory by growing their own. Clothing was also rationed, and attempts to evade the controls were punished rigorously. Donald Maude, managing director of Brooks Meeting Mill, was fined £250 in 1943 for giving out spare bits of cloth to his workers, a common practice in textile mills.[28] Nothing was to be wasted. Salvage schemes were started and war savings campaigns were publicised.[29] Other schemes personalised, or localised, the war effort. At the height of the Battle of Britain the Spitfire-Hurricane Fund encouraged every town to raise money to build a plane. Locally, whist drives and concerts were held. In August 1941 street groups were collecting money for small arms and munitions, in March 1942 (at the height of the Battle for the Atlantic) there was Warship Week, in 1943 Wings for Victory, and in 1944 it was the turn of the Merchant Navy.[30]

The Government requisitioned all textile mills, instructing each as to what it should produce. For example, the firm of William Greenwood junior, which operated Brooks'

Meeting Mill, made naval uniforms for use in minesweepers, and part of their storage space was commandeered. Each firm was allowed a percentage of free work: Brooks' Meeting received some orders from Latin America. Profits were strictly controlled. Every company was allowed £1,500 for each working director and an additional sum calculated on the profits of the best of the last three years before the war. Greenwood's was unfortunate, for there was only one working director and none of the three years previous to the war had shown an operating profit. This only left £1,500 for reinvestment.[31]

There was conscription from the beginning of the war, and all able-bodied men were called up. By 1943 there were 200 men from Oxenhope eligible to receive parcels and proportionate numbers from Haworth and Stanbury. The progress of Haworth's war can be followed from the printed casualty lists in the *Keighley News*. The dubious distinction of being the first recorded Haworth victim went to Sapper Thomas Clay, killed by a bomb near Abbeville on 21 May 1940 during the German offensive which preceded the evacuation from Dunkirk Three more are listed as killed and four others ended as prisoners of war.[32]

Many Haworth soldiers went to the Far East. Private Robert Toothill was reported missing after the Japanese attack on Hong Kong and more were involved in the surrender of Singapore. Anxious families had to wait many months to learn whether husbands or sons had been killed or were languishing in Japanese prison camps. Paymaster Commander Adrian Pigott RN of Crossroads described what he called the 'The Last Week of Freedom in Java', together with the Japanese attack, and his eventual escape to Australia. Lance Corporal Wormald was killed in Burma during the fighting around Imphal.[33]

Few Haworth men served with Wavell in the Middle East, but more fought under his successor, Auchinleck. Angus Martin was injured in January 1942, and Jonas Denby of the Green Howards and Albert Peacock lost their lives in the Gazala campaign. The next identifiable losses took place in January 1943 under Montgomery, during the pursuit of Rommel after El Alamein, and there was a Haworth presence in the attack on Sicily and the long haul up the Italian peninsula. Gunner Jack Smith was awarded an Oak Leaf for his service there.[34] Montgomery left Italy to take charge of the successful D Day landings in Normandy in June 1944. Sergeant Joe Edmundson commanded the tank which protected the headquarters of the Guards Armoured Division from Caen through to VE Day. Private R.O. Webb of Oxenhope also fought throughout the campaign and was awarded a Certificate of Merit by Montgomery.[35]

Some Haworth men enlisted in the RAF and Pilot Officer Jack Finding of No.83 squadron was awarded the DFC for flying a damaged plane back to England and crash landing it safely. Another DFC was won by Flight Lieutenant James Thomas Reckie Taylor, who made 45 successful sorties. Flight Sergeant J.R. Dutton was mentioned in dispatches for gallant and distinguished service in North West Europe. Three others were killed in action during the dying months of the war. When Flight Sergeant Basil McCracken-Hamilton, who was born in Haworth, went to collect his DFM from the king, he was accompanied by his father Dr McCracken-Hamilton, the only member of the RAMC to win his 'wings' in the 1914–18 war. Flight Sergeant George Jarvis served four years in the south of England and one in the north, being passed grade 1 fit at the age of 65, but he was not allowed to go overseas. In the First World War he had served in France and Belgium and before that in South Africa, Burma, India, Malta and Egypt! Haworthites were also in the Navy. John Peacock and Ronald Cox served on the destroyer HMS *Wilton* in the western Mediterranean: a letter home described operations at the time when Rommel and von Arnim were attempting to defend Tunisia.[36] Driver Keith Bentham RASC and Craftsman Lewis Binns, both of Stanbury, bumped into each other in the Middle East. Such an event was considered unusual, though such meetings were commonplace on the Western Front in the First World War. Casualties in the Second World War were much lighter than in the first, though the toll was great. Haworth lost 43 dead, Oxenhope sixteen and Stanbury one, a total of sixty. In the First World War regiments were associated with often quite small and particular geographical areas, whole streets suffered losses and collective grief. Twenty-five years later, that was much less likely.[37]

Both wars involved tremendous dislocation and placed huge demands on the Home Front as well as those on active service. There was terrible loss of life in the Great War, and a degree of national and community trauma, but this, surprisingly, did not change the direction in which Haworth developed. The important changes in the period after 1918 were due to other factors. In his book *The Strange Death of Liberal England* George Dangerfield argued that the seeds of the inter-war collapse of the Liberal Party lay in the period before the First World War, when it seemed to be at its strongest, and the failure of many of the traditional industries during the 1920s and 1930s was due primarily to global economic factors. The next two chapters trace the decline of the textile community and follow that downward spiral all the way to the early 1970s.

VE (Victory in Europe) Day, 1945. This photograph shows flags and bunting in Sun Street in June 1945 when the fighting ended in Europe. The casualties were not as bad as in the First World War – Haworth UDC lost 43, Oxenhope 16 and Stanbury 1 – but still distressing especially for the families of the dead.

PHOTOGRAPH BY COURTESY OF JACK LAYCOCK

Lower Laithe Reservoir, also known as Sladen Beck Reservoir, photographed when newly opened in 1925.

An inter-war view of Bridgehouse Lane. The railing around the war memorial can just be seen on the left. Hall Green Chapel is obscured by the houses in the centre left and lower Main Street is in the haze at the back of the picture.

Decline and fall 17

An Indian summer

The Haworth of the inter-war period may not have been quite the 'Home fit for Heroes' that many of the returning soldiers anticipated, but it was a far better place than in Victorian times. The sobering experience of war and the rise of a new generation ended the infighting of earlier years. James Ackroyd was his usual argumentative self but he found little support and when he decided to call it a day in 1923 after a period of service lasting nearly fifty years, a new era had definitely dawned.[1] Much of the credit for the novel spirit of cooperation and efficiency must go to Thomas Duerden. One of the first boys to gain a Scott scholarship to Keighley Trade and Grammar School, he later built up a successful business as a wholesale grocer.[2] He was first elected to the Haworth UDC in 1911, and in 1914 was appointed chairman, an office which he held for the remainder of the council's existence.

At last, solid achievement could be demonstrated. Although rates increased everywhere because of wartime inflation, in 1916 Haworth had the lowest in the area[3] and it maintained that record for the entire period of its independence. But that did not imply neglect, for Duerden could point to a sharp improvement in public health which he put down to the reorganisation of scavenging. In 1916 the council took over responsibility for the cleaning of ashpits and privies from the Brow and Lees and Crossroads areas; in 1925 the sewage works was modernised; and in 1926 a motor lorry was bought for the removal of waste.[4] All this was done with economy, though in 1930 threepence was added to the rate to pay for sewers and drains to the new houses on Coldshaw. The provision of gas was turned into a success. There were complaints after the war that many of the street lights, extinguished to comply with blackout regulations, were not being relit as an economy measure; in 1923 the quality of the supply to Marsh declined temporarily; and in 1927 a similar deterioration at Lumbfoot forced the council to install a new main.[5] But these were minor problems, and the reputation of the undertaking remained high. The price was lower than in any neighbouring authority and production increased. Duerden attributed the success to Frederick Greenroyd, who became gas manager in 1903, but the efficient administration continued after his departure in 1923.

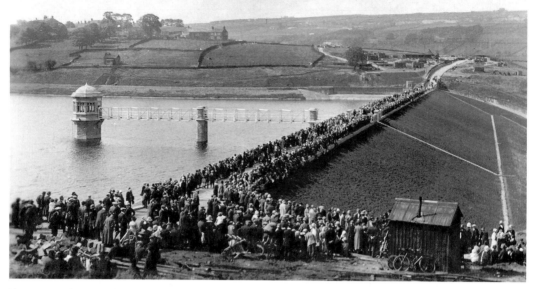

The opening of Lower Laithe (Sladen Beck) Reservoir, 1925. Haworth arranged to get cheap water from Keighley in return for allowing the pipes to cross its land.

Thus, in 1926 production increased by 2 million cubic feet, and in 1932 the Ebor and Lee Syke Mills decided to take council gas.[6] Lees and Crossroads, which had opted out in 1879, now found their gas and water dearer. The equalising of prices throughout the district was considered but rejected as too expensive. Even the Lees and Crossroads representatives agreed that was correct, and Haworth UDC could only support their complaints about the bad quality of the gas supplied from Keighley. A new 9-inch main was installed in 1923, and the quality improved, but Lees and Crossroads still paid considerably more for their gas.[7]

Water supply continued to be a problem. Increasing consumption throughout the Worth valley, and postwar price inflation, forced Haworth to renegotiate its agreement with Keighley. Henceforth it paid ninepence per thousand gallons, and 1s. 3d. per thousand gallons for anything over 2.5 million gallons. This led to wild fluctuations in the water rate. In wet summers Haworth did not need any Keighley water but in dry ones such as 1925, 1928, and 1929 the council had to take considerable quantities, causing rate rises of up to fourpence in the pound.[8]

The UDC reacted sharply to threats to its independence. In 1915 it opposed an application by Keighley Corporation for an order allowing it to supply electric light to the surrounding urban and rural districts, and succeeded in securing the exclusion of Haworth.[9] Electricity cables were installed in the early 1920s but the urban district council's own sub-station was not operative until April 1926.[10] Normally the council bought electricity from Keighley, but once it had a sub-station it could switch to an alternative supplier, such as the Yorkshire Electric Power Company, if Keighley was difficult. Public lighting quickly moved quickly from gas to electricity and by 1931 Haworth was so well lit in winter that one observer reckoned it looked like fairy land.[11]

Householders were slower to take supplies because they had to wire their houses at their own cost, so initially the undertaking experienced serious financial problems, but by 1935 it was breaking even at a price of around 4½d. per unit, much the same as in neighbouring authorities.[12] Another innovation was the introduction of the telephone. The firm of William Greenwood junior appear to have been the first to install one, in 1920, when it linked its warehouse in Brook Street, Bradford with Brooks Meeting Mill, which had the number Haworth 1.[13]

The most expensive initiative in the inter-war years was the provision of parks and recreation grounds. The people of Lees and Crossroads purchased land for a recreation ground as a memorial to those who had died in the First World War and in 1927 the council took it over, the following year purchasing additional land opposite Crossroads Co-op. In 1929 the council obtained a loan of £4,820 to landscape the site, with a relaid bowling green, a small stone toolshed, hard courts to replace the two grass tennis courts, an ornamental shrubbery and, on the lower level, a playing field. A children's playground and paddling pool were added in 1935 and 1937 respectively.[14]

In 1920 the council tried to purchase land in Haworth for a park and recreation ground. Negotiations with Captain Emmott to purchase 7½ acres in Butt Lane from the Rawdon estate were at an advanced stage when the 1921 financial crisis led to the cancellation of all loan applications. Three years elapsed before the scheme was revived. The scale of the proposals, requiring an estimated £9,500 for purchase of the land and development, disturbed the Ministry of Health, which did not sanction the loan until the following year. Work began in November 1926 and the park, cleverly landscaped by Albert Sunderland, its first superintendent, to take advantage of the sloping site, was opened in May 1929. In August 1930 more land behind the Central Schools was purchased for playing fields. The park included two hard tennis courts, a bandstand, a terrace, two shelters and a greenhouse. A bowling green was added during 1935 and a children's playground in 1936.[15] The completion of the park marked the realisation of a scheme close to Duerden's heart. By 1913 Haworth people realised that in rejecting the free library and allowing the mechanics' institute to fail they had made a mistake. Plans to revive the institute, which was re-established temporarily in the Liberal Club, were halted by the war, but after 1918 the idea was taken up with enthusiasm by Duerden. In 1925 the new Public Institute building in Butt Lane was opened by Lord Haldane.[16] Haworth then had educational and leisure facilities which were the best in the valley.

At Oxenhope by 1920 the provision of a proper water supply was imperative. An inquiry showed that 399 households were supplied by a variety of private owners, 25 used pumps and 144 obtained their water from wells. After years of stalling, Oxenhope UDC agreed to construct a reservoir at Buttergate Sykes. The cost was estimated at £12,000 and calculations suggested that springs would provide 55,000 gallons daily, enough to supply the 569 households with about 15 gallons a day. The sewerage facilities were also improved in 1926, though there was much grumbling over the cost.[17]

In Oxenhope there were much earlier plans for recreation grounds, though they came to nothing. In 1884 a fund was established for that purpose, using compensation money

Opening of Haworth Park Bowling Green. Haworth Park was completed in 1929 and the bowling green was added in 1935. A children's recreation ground was added in 1936. The park landscaping, which cleverly took advantage of the slopes, was the work of Albert Sunderland, the first superintendent. The facilities were universally regarded as the best in the area. Thomas Duerden, chairman of Haworth UDC 1914–38 is seen cutting the tape. The costs of the park may have been a factor in Haworth's loss of independence; Oakworth gave as one of its reasons for preferring Keighley as not wishing to take responsibility for the outstanding loans.

PHOTOGRAPH BY COURTESY OF JACK LAYCOCK

obtained from the extinguishing of freeholders' rights on Sawood Little Moss, but the management committee held onto the money for nearly fifty years. An abortive attempt was made to use the fund in 1897, to mark the queen's diamond jubilee, and in 1921 the freeholders refused to support a council plan for a recreation ground, maintaining that the time was not propitious because of high inflation. In 1924 A.J.P. Heaton offered to sell the council a suitable piece of land, provided that the purchase money came from the freeholders' funds. He would then use the money to lay out the grounds. Unfortunately the scheme collapsed after arguments about the inclusion of lavatories. This led the council chairman, J.F. Greenwood, who was also chairman of the freeholders' committee, to resign from the council in a fit of pique. He was only coaxed back with difficulty. Agreement was not secured until 1931 and even then the council was daunted by the cost of providing a bowling green and arranged for a public subscription.[18]

Soon after the Great War a private water supply was provided for Stanbury by Charles Bairstow, its largest landowner. He had inherited the Taylor properties through his wife. In other respects the village remained the most backward part of the old township. In 1935 a public health report claimed that the houses were badly arranged, the drainage was unsatisfactory, there was no sewerage scheme, and yards were generally unpaved.[19]

Amalgamation

Although there were many social and environmental problems in the upper Worth Valley between the wars, the urban district councils functioned comparatively effectively. The childhood memories of people who grew up in Haworth during the period paint a picture of a semi-rural idyll. So when plans were put forward to amalgamate the urban districts into larger units they met with almost universal hostility. To this day Haworth people bemoan the loss of their prized independence and blame Keighley for what happened. It is therefore important to stress that the changes were prompted not

County Borough
proposed by Keighley

SILSDEN UDC

KEIGHLEY
RDC
West and
East Morton

KEIGHLEY RDC
Sutton

Steeton

KEIGHLEY MB

OAKWORTH UDC
includes Stanbury

HAWORTH

OXENHOPE UDC

Original Municipal Borough

added to Skipton RDC, 1938

added to Keighley, 1938

retained its independence

by Keighley Corporation but by the reorganisation of local government nationally in the late 1920s.

The 1929 Local Government Act had two main aims. The first was the abolition of the post-1834 system of poor law unions and the substitution of a system of unemployment exchanges, operating under a national framework and administered by county councils. The Haworth representatives on the Keighley Board of Guardians, like their colleagues, were appalled. They believed that supervision by elected representatives was an important democratic safeguard and considered that local people understood the needs of the poor and unemployed in their own communities better than any department in Whitehall. Ironically these were exactly the arguments which had been advanced against the new Poor Law in 1837. Few agreed with them and those in receipt of relief were glad to see the end of a system which they found demeaning in the extreme. Nonetheless the guardians were right insofar as the change certainly marked a move away from local accountability towards national uniformity.[20]

The other main aim was to simplify the geographical structure of local government by abolishing very small authorities and amalgamating them or annexing them to larger neighbours. Each county council was required to review all the districts within its boundaries where a penny rate brought in less than £100. The West Riding County Council duly embarked on such a review, holding meetings with the interested parties. None of the small urban district councils in the Worth Valley wanted any sort of change. Their first instinct, indeed, was to boycott the meetings and they only participated on learning that maintaining the status quo was simply not an option. Keighley Corporation proposed that it should extend its boundaries by adding Haworth, Oxenhope and

Oakworth Urban Districts and Keighley Rural District (Morton, Morton Banks, Silsden, Steeton and Sutton) to the borough. The scheme was opposed by all the Worth Valley authorities and by the county council, which proposed a straightforward amalgamation of Haworth, Oxenhope and Oakworth Urban Districts. Haworth welcomed that idea and Oxenhope accepted it with resignation. The key was Oakworth, because without it the new authority would not be viable.[21]

Oakworth's chairman, Joseph Hill, examined the issue with great care and concluded that the interests of his district would be best served by joining Keighley.[22] Keighley already supplied its gas and water (so joining with Haworth would not entitle Oakworth to take the latter's cheap gas), the electricity came from Keighley, the bus services were run by Keighley, the Keighley fire brigade attended all Oakworth fires, and many Oakworth people were employed in Keighley, which was also the main shopping centre. The drainage problems at Stanbury have already been mentioned, and Hill was aware that a proper sewerage system was needed at Laycock. Joining Keighley would solve the problem, because a sewer could be linked to the Keighley system at Braithwaite, less than a mile away.

Hill also saw difficulties in a union with Haworth, its council offices were poky and cramped but in the most convenient place and he expected a demand for expensive new offices. He was worried about the £14,000 loan burden that Haworth had incurred in the creation of parks and recreation grounds. Poor communications also gave cause for concern: Haworth, Oxenhope and Oakworth straddle three valleys and travel along them was far easier than between them, so much so that joint meetings between the three councils were invariably held in Keighley. In 1932 Oakworth Council School for

An early Haworth bus. The first regular bus services began in 1925, and by 1961 there were 64 services a day between Haworth and Keighley alone. Private ventures had preceded such services, however, and continued to operate local services. The Bronte Bus Company provided routes between Haworth, Oxenhope and Stanbury, and smaller outfits such as 'Old Bill' motors (one of whose buses is pictured here) filled in any 'holes' which were left.

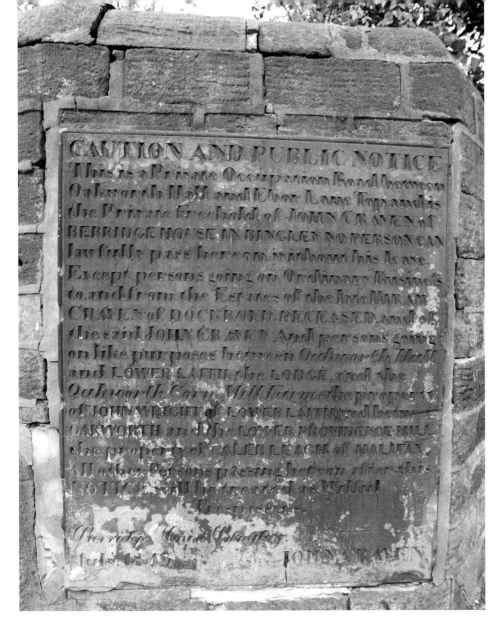

The toll sign on Ebor Lane. Until 1934 there was no public road connecting Haworth with Oakworth. This was a private road with one tollhouse at the top of Ebor Lane, a second at the bottom of Mythomes Lane and a third in Oakworth.

example, was too full to take children from Laycock, so the Worth Valley Education Committee decided to send them to Haworth. The only way was for them to travel into Keighley and then out again through Ingrow and Crossroads.[23] Communication between Oakworth and Haworth could only be made across private property, most of it belonging to the mills, which charged tolls for the upkeep of their roads. Providence Lane was adopted in 1934 and Vale Mill Lane the following year, when the county council was finally persuaded to contribute to their maintenance, but as late as the 1960s neither could be negotiated by buses.[24]

Hill's arguments convinced his colleagues on Oakworth Urban District Council, but an anti-Keighley campaign orchestrated by Thomas Duerden of Haworth led to

Hill's defeat in the 1935 council elections. Oakworth ratepayers' fear was that as part of Keighley the local representatives would be a small minority, whereas in Worth Valley council they would have much more influence. The urban district council demonstrated its dismay by re-electing Hill as chairman even though he was no longer on the council![25] An inquiry into the West Riding proposals, including the rival plans of Keighley and the county council, was held at Wakefield during August and September 1935. The inspector eventually recommended a modified version of the Keighley plan, whereby the borough would be extended to include Oxenhope, Haworth, Oakworth, Morton and Morton Banks, but not Steeton, Sutton and Silsden.[26] In the spring of 1938 the urban districts of Haworth, Oxenhope and Oakworth were dissolved, and the three areas were united with Keighley. For Thomas Duerden there was one consolation: he was deservedly elected the first mayor of the enlarged borough in 1938–39. His death in 1943 was a great loss to the civic life both of Haworth and of Keighley.

In retrospect the logic for amalgamation is compelling, for the 'independence' of Haworth was largely illusory. Apart from producing its own gas the urban district already relied very heavily on other authorities and agencies for most services – and in the case of gas union with Keighley allowed the closure of Haworth gasworks which Duerden himself called an eyesore.[27] After amalgamation Keighley connected the water and sewerage systems of Oakworth and Haworth into its own networks, modernising facilities at Laycock and Stanbury (though completion of the latter was delayed by the Second World War). Oakworth already took its water from Keighley and connecting Stanbury, which was very close to the reservoirs, ended the need for private supplies there. Oxenhope had separate sewerage arrangements but it benefited from the Keighley water system because, although the hamlet was self- sufficient, the capacity of its reservoir was a mere six days, which was a major threat in dry years.[28]

The old urban district areas benefited in other ways. There had been some services for which they previously could not or would not pay. A notable example was fire protection. The Haworth brigade was notoriously inefficient. In 1889 Townend's Mill burned down because the brigade arrived with a hosepipe so full of holes that it could not raise a jet of water higher than the first storey. The position was little better in 1925. The equipment was usually carried in the van of a friendly greengrocer, but a fire broke out at the hairdresser's in Main Street while he was away at market. The equipment had to be loaded onto a handcart and dragged up the street. Not surprisingly, the shop was destroyed. At Oxenhope in 1916 the Keighley brigade refused to turn out for a fire at the spinning mill of the council chairman, James Frederick Greenwood. After this the Oxenhope UDC began to pay Keighley Corporation the equivalent of a penny rate for full fire cover. The independent Keighley fire brigade now provided cover for the whole of the extended borough, though during the war it was brought under government control and from 1947 the fire services were reorganised nationally. There was now a proper motorised service with a fully manned sub-station, and in 1958 the Haworth firemen won the County Fire Stations Efficiency Competition![29]

Haworth's poor record on public health was another factor. In 1934 the medical officer

Looking down Haworth Main Street. An early twentieth-century view looking down the street from a vantage point below The Black Bull. Much of it is still recognisable today.

of health for the Craven districts showed that in Haworth the birth rate was 10.4 per 1000, below the Craven average of 12.7 and far short of the national figure of 15.0. But the death rate was 16.5 (contrasting with 13.7 in Craven and 12.0 nationally). Infant mortality was 80 per 1000 live births, a long way below the appalling figure of 180 at the beginning of the century, but well above Craven's average of 66 and the national figure of 62.[30] Haworth was unable to provide the health services which a modern community needed, and had little vision. As late as 1914 its contributions to the Victoria Hospital in Keighley were by voluntary subscription, not the rates, and Haworth Council refused to pay a school nurse on the grounds of expense. Union with Oxenhope and Oakworth would have brought little improvement, but Keighley was large enough to provide a full range of health care, including school medical services and maternity clinics.

The decline of the textile trade

Life in Haworth between the wars may have been pleasant for those who had jobs but it was less acceptable for the many who were out of work. The main employer, the textile

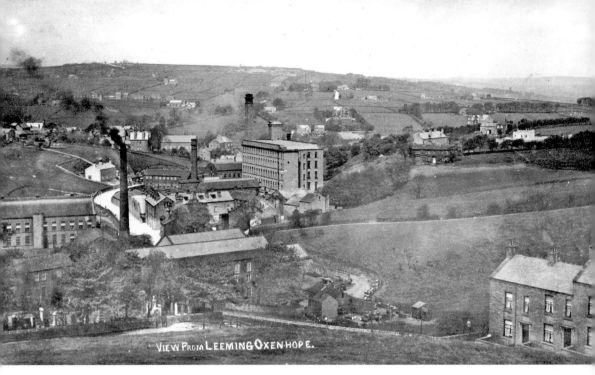

Oxenhope from Leeming, 1900. Mills still dominate the scene in the Edwardian era. Lowertown Mill (formerly Lowertown Shed) is in the centre of the picture. It was bought by Merralls in 1887 and then passed into the hands of Hield Brothers who operated it until 1980. The mill finally closed in 1988. Holme Mill can be seen on the bottom left.

industry, was increasingly vulnerable and economic decline began to have very serious consequences for communities such as Haworth. There were frequent fluctuations in trading conditions and Haworth, because it was smaller and geographically marginal, suffered more severe swings than many other districts. The lesser firms in Oxenhope and Stanbury found that the slightest error of judgment could be fatal. The 1921 commercial crisis brought about the downfall of Kershaw Brothers and Sykes Mill was taken over by John Clough & Co. of Ingrow. Butterfield & Wallbank made a fresh start at Griffe in 1917 as Wallbank & Sons, putting in a new gas engine, but by 1923 they had been replaced by Whalley & Haggarth. In 1926 the mill was up for sale again and production finally stopped in 1928. At Lumbfoot, after the failure to sell the mill in 1915, a number of different firms attempted to keep it going but the last, Andersons, also ceased trading in 1928. The contraction also affected related trades. At Wadsworth Mill, Pawsons stopped making spindles and flyers for textile machinery, and between 1922 and 1927 George Emmott-Pawson turned to making springs for gramophones there. This continuing adaptability, enabled the firm to operate in the old mill until the beginning of the twenty first century. Even the larger businesses were forced to retrench. Merralls sold their Lowertown Mill to Hield Brothers of Crosshills in 1928 and the Great Depression of 1929–31 led to large-scale redundancies over the whole area. At the peak of the crisis in October 1930, over 2,000 people were registered as unemployed by the Haworth office.[31]

After the Second World War there was a period of apparent prosperity. Once the years of post-war austerity passed the country had a decade of full employment,[32] but even as Macmillan was telling the nation that it had 'never had it so good' the clouds were gathering. By 1959 the home market was saturated, but exporting goods was ever more difficult because of competition from other countries. Textile manufacturers complained even through the good times that the necessary skilled workforce was disappearing. The old apprenticeship system collapsed, the school leaving age was raised first to 15 and then 16, and the brightest stayed on to university. The alleged British preference for academic education over practical subjects was blamed, but annual returns show that the overwhelming number of vacancies in the textile and light engineering trades were for women, who had traditionally performed the cheap and relatively unskilled jobs. Now girls were finding better paid work elsewhere, while older women only wanted part-time jobs to fit in with their domestic commitments. That was little use to the textile trade. Some mills, like Merralls, resorted to immigrant labour but recruiting expenses were a deterrent.[33]

Wreck of Old Oxenhope Mill after the fire of 1962. The original mill on this site was built for worsted spinning. When he took over in 1833 William Greenwood junior appears to have put in power looms. Production continued until his death in 1893 when his nephew, J.F. Greenwood, moved the entire business to Brooks Meeting Mill. The mill was actually owned by John Anderton Greenwood (not William) and he let it to Whitaker, Feather and Radcliffe, who then bought it on his death in 1921 and stayed until 1960. It was then briefly occupied by G.W. Thomas until 1962. This photograph shows the wrecked spinning mill.

Fire at Lee Syke Mill. This fire in 1965 was the biggest ever seen in the Keighley area, and despite the efforts of 25 engines and 140 firemen the whole of the spinning mill was entirely gutted. It took place just after the firm had retooled, and effectively destroyed its viability. The centre was the original site of the first mill built by the Merrall Brothers in 1844, though many times altered afterwards. There had been at least two earlier fires. At their most prosperous in the late nineteenth century, the Lee Syke mills occupied both sides of the roads. The Merralls also owned Ebor Mill in the valley and Lowertown mills at Oxenhope.

© KEIGHLEY NEWS

The consequences were predictable. During the 1960s, as the boom of the '50s ended, there was a series of closures and mergers and by 1974 the textile trade was a shadow of its former self. In the immediate post war years, Dr Anna Bidder, Marion Greenwood's daughter, tried hard to revive the fortunes of William Greenwood junior, but the end of the firm came when it sold Brooks' Meeting Mill to Heaton and Rushworth. In 1894 John Anderton Greenwood had vacated the mill at Old Oxenhope, and let it to Whitaker, Feather and Ratcliffe. It was bought by them at his death in 1921, and they stayed there until 1960. The mill was then briefly occupied by G.W. Thomas Ltd but burned down in 1962.[34] In 1960 the chief firm in Bridgehouse Mill, G.F. Denby and Sons Ltd, relocated the manufacture of their rayon and nylon dress goods to Bradford.[35] A high-profile casualty was Merralls. After the death of M.H. Merrall in 1957 the firm embarked on an ambitious modernisation plan, which involved scrapping all its old machinery. The retooling had hardly been completed when there was a disastrous fire at Lee Syke in 1965. Despite the efforts of 25 engines and 140 firemen the mill was gutted in the biggest mill blaze ever seen in the Keighley area. The company was then taken over by S. Jerome & Sons (Holdings) Ltd of Shipley.[36]

Nor were more modern businesses immune. As late as 1963 an article in the *Keighley News* was celebrating the success story of Hield Brothers. They had started in 1922 with a capital of £25,000 in a small weaving plant at Crosshills and now had capital of £1 million and working assets of £2 million, owning mills at Oxenhope, Morley, Bradford and in Canada. Only three years later, the original shed at Crosshills was closed down and in 1971 the Oxenhope site was also abandoned.[37] Another major casualty was Hattersleys. In 1966 there was a serious fire at Mytholmes Mill, which was not rebuilt. Production had already ended at Upper Providence Mill and by 1971 it had also finished at the other two mills on the Oakworth site. Today only the chimney of the former Lower Providence Mill remains, like Ozymandias's shattered visage in the desert sands, to remind the passer by of the mutability of all human affairs.[38]

In 1972 production stopped at Dunkirk Mill. A new firm called Bancroft and Sunderland was formed in 1956. It owned Eagle Mill in Keighley, Charles Mill in Oxenhope, and Ponden Mill in Stanbury but in 1973 decided to concentrate the business at Eagle Mill. Operations ceased at Charles and when Ponden Mills closed textile production ended in Stanbury.[39] Of course some firms struggled on. Ivy Bank was a working textile mill until 1977 but in 1997 the building was gutted by fire. Ebor was used by Jeromes for spinning until 1988, when they sold it to Airedale Springs and moved to a new purpose-built spinning mill in Keighley.[40] There were new businesses such as Cullingdale Weavers, Herbert Holmes Ltd of Marshlands, and the quilt-making enterprise at Ashmount,[41] but the textile community was now only a memory.

Census figures for Haworth civil parish show a downward trend, from 4,599 people in 1921 to 3,526 in 1971.[42] Textile production was shrinking steadily throughout the whole

Fire at Mytholmes Mill. Hattersleys were originally Keighley textile machine makers but they expanded into worsted spinning when the Worth Valley railway was built, buying Upper and Lower Providence, Springhead and Mytholmes mills. This fire in 1966 contributed to their decision to cease worsted spinning altogether. For a time they made garden machinery at their Keighley works but finally closed down completely in 1982.

period. At the time of the 1965 fire Merralls had a workforce of 170 at Lee Syke, but only a fifth lived locally. Hattersleys employed a mere 80 people when the firm closed down. At Oxenhope, though, the population remained relatively stable and actually rose, from 3,382 in 1961 to 3,544 in 1971.

Haworth's experience was not unique. It seemed somehow appropriate that in 1974 Keighley was swallowed up by Bradford just as Haworth had earlier been swallowed by Keighley. All those services of which Keighley had been so proud had passed out of its hands or had fallen by the wayside. Electricity had been nationalised; water and sewerage services were the responsibility of the Craven Water Board (and even that disappeared a decade later); municipal transport was superseded by services operated by the new West Yorkshire Passenger Transport Authority; the National Health Service had taken over all the local medical facilities; Victoria Hospital had been replaced by Airedale Hospital at Steeton; and even the fire brigade was part of a national system. During the mid-1960s the Labour government began to plan for a comprehensive reorganisation of local government and in 1967 the Redcliffe-Maud report recommended the abolition of the two-tier system of county councils and districts and its replacement by unitary and regional authorities. In certain parts of the country, though, metropolitan authorities were to be created.

After 1970 the new Conservative government, though it stepped back from the unitary system in most 'shire' areas, accepted the case for the creation of metropolitan counties and boroughs. Under the 1972 Local Government Act the West Riding was abolished and a new West Yorkshire County Council was created, centred on the Leeds/Bradford conurbation. Within it were a series of metropolitan boroughs. One of these was Bradford, but its boundaries extended far beyond the old area of Bradford City Council, to include not only Keighley – and thus Haworth – but even Silsden and Ilkley. From 1 April 1974, therefore, Haworth became part of the Metropolitan Borough of Bradford. The wheel had come full circle. Seven hundred years earlier, Haworth had been a sub-manor of the manor of Bradford, and a chapelry in the sprawling parish of Bradford. The social and economic changes of the sixteenth and seventeenth centuries led to the dissolution of the manorial link, while the restructuring of the churches in the eighteenth and nineteenth centuries broke the connection with the parish. For a brief period of some seventy years Haworth had been administratively independent. Now, after a 37-year marriage with Keighley, it was once more in Bradford's embrace.

Paradise lost?   18

The Sound of Music

After the First World War 'business as usual' returned for the Anglicans and Baptists. Oxenhope's bells were raised to a full peal of eight [1] and when the National School burned down in 1925 the parish soon raised money for a replacement. In 1928 Haworth built a new rectory in West Lane, and sold the old parsonage to the Brontë Society.[2] The Baptists were also rebuilding. Just before the war they had added a chapel to the Sunday school at Hawksbridge, the only Gothic nonconformist building in the township, and in 1927 the Horkinstone Baptists moved to a new chapel in Denholme Road, Oxenhope.[3] There was even a newcomer or, rather, a belated return on the oldest of them all. In 1917 the Roman Catholics established a mission in Haworth and in 1922 it was upgraded to parish status with the Father J. Twomey as its first priest.[4]

For the Methodists the 1920s were less hopeful, since membership of the Haworth and Oakworth circuit had fallen from 807 to 628 between 1913 and 1918.[5] The revival meetings, planned to repair the damage, involved a flood of music. The steady flow of cantatas recommenced to which all the denominations contributed, and between 1919 and 1939 the *Keighley News* reported 57 of them, or nearly three a year, *Olivet to Calvary* and *The Crucifixion* being much the most popular. Large-scale works such as oratorios had been rare before the war, and a choral society founded in 1892, under the patronage of Alfred Merrall, only lasted three years.[6] But the success of *Judas Maccabeus* at the West Lane Baptist chapel in 1909 may have inspired the Methodists to inaugurate the series of oratorio concerts in which other choirs were invited to take part. *Elijah* and *Messiah* were very successful, though they were performed on successive days in 1911.[7] In 1915 Fred Smith took over at West Lane Methodists. During his time a full range of oratorios was performed; Haydn's *Creation*, *Elijah* and the lesser known *St Paul* by Mendelssohn, and four Handel oratorios, *Messiah*, *Judas Maccabeus*, *Samson* and *Joshua*. The augmented choirs regularly exceeded a hundred voices and many of the soloists graced the national stage. Elsie Suddaby, Muriel Brunskill and Roy Henderson were all household names. Another soloist, Darrell Fancourt, later made a career in Gilbert and Sullivan as a stalwart of the D'Oyly Carte Opera Company. There were home-grown talents too,

Mechanics' Institute. The revival of the Mechanics' Institute was largely the work of Thomas Duerden, chairman of the Urban District Council from 1914 to 1938. This building in Butt Lane opened in 1925, but it had lost its usefulness by the 1960s.
PHOTOGRAPH: CARNEGIE, 2009

including Frank Smith, a talented tenor who later broadcast with the BBC. Similar programmes but with local soloists were put on by Oxenhope Methodists under the direction of Willie Moore.[8] The greatest coup was achieved by the Baptists, whose 1927 and 1928 concerts included Isobel Baillie, one of the finest English singers of the twentieth century.[9] That a places as small as Haworth could attract performers of such calibre was extraordinary. Did these triumphs benefit the Methodists in membership terms? Numbers did stabilise at 550–600 but that experience was common to other denominations whose musical offerings were more modest.

With the retirement of Willie Moore and the departure of Fred Smith to Oakworth in 1929 a different kind of music emerged. Operettas were first mentioned in 1912 but most were clearly designed for performance by Sunday school children. Performing secular stage works was a sensitive issue: in 1922 a notice appeared outside the Long Lee Primitive Methodist chapel inviting complaints about its children's operetta.[10] The Church of England had a more relaxed attitude. In 1926 Haworth's choirmaster, Lewis Scargill, put on the operetta *The Quaker Girl* by Lionel Monckton. Its success led to the formation of Haworth Amateurs, who staged two more Monckton works, *The Dancing Mistress* (1927) and *Lady Molly* (1928), followed by a Viennese concoction, *The Last Waltz* (1929). For the Society it almost *was* the last waltz. Following the performance of Lionel Monckton's best known piece, *The Arcadians*, in 1930 the society had to disband because there was nowhere to perform.[11] The only suitable venue, the Brontë Cinema, installed equipment for the new talking pictures, making it useless for stage performance.[12]

The vicar of Oxenhope, Wellesley Greaves, was a Gilbert and Sullivan enthusiast and he was largely responsible for the foundation of an amateur operatic society based on Oxenhope church. He played Sir Joseph Porter in *HMS Pinafore*, the opening show, and produced the second, *The Mikado*. Although he went to Hebden Bridge in 1931 there was a production each year until the outbreak of the Second World War. Operettas

'Dogs of Devon', 1933. During the 1920s the Haworth Amateurs performed a number of Lionel Monckton's popular operettas at the Bronte Cinema under the baton of the church choirmaster, Lewis Scargill, but the conversion of the cinema to the 'talkies' made it unsuitable and forced the denominations to adapt to more limited premises. Here is the church company which performed 'The Dogs of Devon' in 1933.

PHOTOGRAPH BY COURTESY OF JACK LAYCOCK

require an orchestra. The Marsh Orchestra, founded in 1922, played regularly for the Oxenhope shows.[13] The string players may have used violins made by Kershaw Barrett, the stone contractor, at his workshop in the old Free School building.

Later in the 1930s there was a further decline in chapel membership. At West Lane Baptist chapel the death of David Arthur in 1925 was followed by considerable volatility in numbers. There was also a sharp decline in the Strict Baptist congregation at Hall Green.[14] The response of all the religious organisations was to expand leisure activities even further, to raise money and to try to attract new members. 'At Homes' were held, tea parties which were accompanied by an entertainment of songs and sketches. By the end of the decade there was a drama group and an annual pantomime for the children at practically every church and chapel in the district.

After the Second World War these activities revived. Oratorios were regularly performed, Oxenhope resumed its Gilbert and Sullivan shows in 1947, and after a successful concert version of Edward German's *Merrie England* at Hawksbridge in 1946, the West Lane Baptists produced the *Pirates of Penzance* in 1947, the first in a string of Gilbert and Sullivan successes. In 1950 a society was founded at Lees Wesleyan Methodist chapel, starting with yet another 'G & S' production, *Ruddigore*.[15] The Moorlands Philharmonic Orchestra was formed by J. Rushworth Wildman in 1945, and the following year he started a choral and orchestral class at the Haworth Evening Institute.[16] He wanted to perform operas but there was no suitable venue, so had to content himself with oratorios or concert versions: Haydn's *Mass in D* (1945), *Maritana* (1946), *Il Trovatore* (1947), *Lohengrin* (1948), *Faust* (1949) and *Tannhäuser* (1950).[17] Pantomimes reappeared and there was an average of eight plays a year.

The flowering of music and drama reached a climax at the time of the Festival of Britain. In addition to the usual fare, Wildman held concert performances of *The Bartered Bride* and *Il Trovatore* and a version of *Hiawatha's Wedding* with a choir of over 200 voices drawn from Haworth, Todmorden, Skipton Ladies and Glusburn Male Voice Choir. He also took part in a monster dramatic version of *Messiah*, scripted by Canon Dixon, the rector of Haworth, which included pieces from *Elijah*, *Olivet to Calvary*, *Bach's Passion* (the report does not say which) and well known quartets.[18] Smith Midgley and Norman Feather guyed the current fashion in their show 'Pantomania' and Haworth Parish Church Choir went off to the Harrogate Choir Festival, where it won first prize and an invitation to sing evensong at St John's Smith Square, London.[19]

Yet by 1960, not much of all this survived. In 1954 the choral and orchestral class at the Evening Institute closed.[20] There were no more operatic concert versions and the Moorland Philharmonic vanished. Lees Gilbert and Sullivan society disbanded in 1956, Oxenhope in 1957, and West Lane abandoned Gilbert and Sullivan for *Rose Marie* in 1958 and then folded. Their principal soprano, Margaret Newsome, was already ill and her death followed in 1960. She was only 39.[21] The oratorios stopped and if cantatas were still being performed they were not reported. Pantomimes and plays were also fading. In 1958 an open letter from Ingrow drew attention to the rival attractions of the cinema and TV and appealed to church drama groups to patronise each other's shows, harmonise performance dates, and make sure they were not doing the same plays.[22]

The collapse

A major reason was the decline of the religious organisations which provided most of the singers and also the premises. Although West Lane Baptists were involved in the founding of a new chapel at Bracken Bank in Keighley in 1956, the slide in their numbers continued.[23] The annual temperance lecture was still held, though as early as 1927 its patron, Parker, was described as an 'eccentric' old man. Temperance was discredited by the failure of prohibition in the USA and assumed a much lower profile. Kenneth Grant, who gave the 1959 lecture, had worked in the Temperance Department of the Methodist Connexion,[24] but now his department was called Christian Citizenship and temperance was only one of seven sections. By 1930 the Whit Walks, so important a feature of Victorian and Edwardian Haworth, had been abandoned by all except the Baptists. They continued walking until 1953 when the walkers were soaked by a violent thunderstorm.[25] They did not try again. Sunday, once a day of religious observance, became a day of recreation. In 1943 the bowling greens in Keighley parks were opened on Sunday afternoons as a war time concession, in 1946 the Parks Committee extended

This new chapel at Hawksbridge replaced the old one in 1923, ironically just before the collapse in membership. It is the only nonconformist chapel in the township to make any concessions to the gothic revival style that was typical of the architecture of Anglican churches of the time and was imitated by many nonconformists elsewhere.

© BRADFORD LIBRARY

this to all games and to Sunday evenings and by 1948 there were band concerts too. Sunday cricket had to wait until 1958.[26]

A decline in Easter Communicants at both Haworth and Oxenhope suggested that the malaise was spreading to the Anglicans. Oxenhope National School burned down for a second time in 1955 and in 1965 the prohibitive cost of repairs led to the demolition of the Haworth 'new' Sunday school, built in 1904.[27] Neither was replaced, though at Oxenhope the Council School was redesignated as the one church school in the township. The gravest difficulties were experienced by the Methodists. As early as 1932 there were plans for a merger between the Wesleyan and Primitive Methodist Haworth and Oakworth circuits, though the Primitive Methodists resisted until 1947, when union was forced on them by the dissolving of their Oakworth Lane Ends congregation and the sale of the chapel.[28] The combining of the circuits in 1949 led to a rationalisation. There was no need for two chapels in Station Road: Mill Hey closed and the congregation transferred to a refurbished Bridgehouse. Dry rot was found in the chapel at West Lane and the decision was taken in 1950 to demolish it. The Sunday school was repaired at a cost of £5,000 and the primary and library rooms converted into a chapel

Mill Hey Primitive Methodist Chapel. The first chapel on this site was built in 1836, with the current one being constructed in 1870, although it is not clear whether it was added to or replaced the original building. It closed in 1954, and after being occupied by a variety of commercial operations, as evidenced by the faded advertisements and notices for SMS Workshop Supplies and Snowdens' Army Surplus. The building is now derelict.

PHOTOGRAPH: CARNEGIE, 2009

for 130 people. In 1964 Bridgehouse followed suit. In 1970 Oxenhope decided to scrap both its chapel and Sunday school, sell part of the site, and use the money to build a new smaller chapel. Others did not even have those resources. Dry rot finished Sawood in 1952 and Stanbury in 1973, leaving Scartop as the lone beacon of Methodism in the upper Worth valley, where its annual open air charity service remained popular and provided the chapel with valuable publicity and financial support.[29]

These problems were common to every Protestant denomination by 1960, but a simple retreat from Christianity was only part of the story. The Haworth Brass Band had no links with any of the denominations yet it experienced exactly the same misfortunes. It took a little time to reform after the First World War but was lucky to find an excellent bandmaster, Arthur Grace, host of the *Fleece Inn*, and soon rediscovered the form which had brought it pre-war success. In 1920 Paley returned as conductor to win a famous victory at the Keighley Band Contest, where the euphonium and trombone players were given special prizes.[30] Coaching by the famous Halifax trainer, Willie Wood, brought a string of other successes, including first place at Trawden where the soprano player, Walter Sugden, won the gold medal. Another outstanding player was Harold Jackson, who in 1928 (aged 14) won the solo prize for his cornet playing at Trawden.[31]

The facilities in the new park at Haworth were ideal for brass band contests and one was held there each year from 1931, while the band made an excellent showing elsewhere. After the Second World War, with a new conductor, Arthur Rogerson, it regained its high reputation in competitions.[32] Yet by 1955 it was in the doldrums, and the local paper bemoaned the declining popularity of brass band music and the virtual disappearance of village bands: 'Haworth band still manages to struggle on after close upon a hundred years but its older members must sigh for the days when there were fewer distractions for youth.' By 1964 only a dozen or so men regularly turned up to practise in the bandroom above the *Fleece*.[33]

At the time of the 'free library dispute' Lees Institute was held to be the best in the district, but by 1952 it was closed. M.H. Merrall argued for its sale: 'Village institutes seem rather out of date. There are so many other things that can be done by young people. I am not surprised really because all one can do here is play billiards, drink a bottle of 'pop' or read a paper.' The other trustees were reluctant to accept his assessment but a public meeting attracted only 24 people, and the prospects of securing the necessary £300 annual income were very dim. Closure was unavoidable. Haworth Institute eventually succumbed to similar pressures. By 1961 all but one of its classes were on leisure subjects, rather than educational topics, and in 1965 it closed its doors.[34] The friendly societies had the ground cut from under their feet by the National Insurance Act of 1948. The Shepherds soon lost their sheep and although the Oddfellows battled on their insurance work catered for only a small minority.[35]

The most spectacular collapse was that of the co-operative societies, which enjoyed their greatest success in the inter-war years. Lees and Crossroads increased its membership from 548 in 1914 to 777 in 1940; Haworth's rose by 50 per cent, from 1074 to 1543; and in proportional terms Stanbury's growth was even greater from 108 to 288. Dividends remained high, rarely dropping below 2s. 0d. and at Stanbury by 1940 reaching 3s. 6d., earning it a reputation throughout the movement as the small society with a large dividend.[36] In 1933 Haworth had grocery, drapery, outfitting, and boot and shoe departments, together with three butchers, three greengrocers, two boot repairers, a coal agency and a printing department. In 1925 the Society bought Old Hall Farm, and let out Bankfield Quarry on a lucrative lease. Cottages next to its premises in Main Street were bought to be rented out, and in a 1933 advertisement its Board proclaimed that 'It is well known that this Society is one of the strongest in the movement.'[37] Attendance at the annual galas and children's festivals grew steadily: 1927 was declared Haworth's best ever and 1928 saw a record attendance. In 1938 the smallest society, Stanbury, put on a gala and sports in Alderman Middleton's field, with a procession headed by the Haworth Brass Band, fantastic costumes judged in the Council School and a demonstration of magic by Will Raymond.[38]

Yet even before the Second World War problems began to appear at Oxenhope. The two co-operatives there increased their membership but more slowly than the other three societies. Uppertown reached a peak of 616 in 1931, while the best the Industrial could manage was 222 in 1929. Numbers then fell back and in 1938 the Industrial, with 181, had fewer members than before the Great War. Neither society seems to have been well-managed. In 1929 Uppertown bungled a change from their old branch shop in Station Road to a new departmental store, and had to dispose of its farm which had been losing £300 a year. A special meeting on 9 December 1938 accepted that merger with the Keighley Industrial Co-operative Society was the only way to safeguard the investments of its small shareholders, many of whom had put in their life savings.[39] The Industrial was more secure financially but its activities were confined to grocery and drapery, and there was no money to modernise its premises at Scar Hall. The members were reluctant to sacrifice their independence and a special general meeting in November 1938 approved a merger with Keighley by only 24 votes to 17, short of the necessary percentage. But Uppertown's collapse damaged its fellow, and on 7 January 1939 both societies agreed to merge with Keighley.[40]

After the Second World War the other co-operative societies began to experience difficulties due to increased competition and rising expenses. Haworth's membership no longer grew and the society's problems mounted steadily. By 1953 the dividend had fallen to 11d.; in 1951 there was a loss in the butchery department; turnover in the shop at Sun Street fell from £54 per week in 1948 to £35 in 1954; in 1955 the fish and fruit department at Townend was discontinued; in 1956 the Old Hall was sold; and in 1962 the boot and shoe repairing department was closed.[41] Lees and Crossroads enjoyed better fortunes, with membership passing 1000 in 1958, but difficult trading conditions led to a steady fall in dividends. A self-service store was started but its position was undermined by slum clearance, which robbed it of customers from Bocking.[42] Together with Haworth, it merged with Keighley in 1964, and three years later the last survivor, Stanbury, followed suit.[43]

The problem was not confined to Haworth. Soon all the local co-operatives in the Aire Valley merged to form the Keighley and Skipton Co-operative Society, and in 1970 this is turn amalgamated with Bradford. It was decided that all branches taking less than £1,000 a week should close, and efforts would focus on creating supermarkets in the main centres. This meant the end for co-operation in Haworth. A plan to turn the central store in Main Street into a licensed hotel was approved by Keighley Council, but failed for want of a developer willing to work with the Society, and the property was sold in 1971.[44] The only vestige of co-operation surviving is at Oxenhope, where there is still a 'mini-market' at the time of writing.

With so many respected institutions disappearing or getting into difficulties there was widespread breast-beating. A letter in the *Keighley News* asked 'Is Haworth dead'? Another bemoaned the decline of Lees and Crossroads. An article described Stanbury as a village of old people. Only Oxenhope seemed at all sanguine about the future.[45] In 1920 Herbert Butterfield of Oxenhope won second prize in a nationwide competition, organised by the National Reform Union, on the topic 'The Advantages of Individual Freedom over State Interference'. By the time he was appointed Master of Peterhouse, Cambridge, in 1955, after a long and distinguished career as an historian, very little of the self-help philosophy it celebrated was left.[46]

The survivors

References to football before the First World War are rare, but in the 1920s that changed. In 1921 Haworth won the Keighley and District League by such a wide margin that the team became more ambitious and entered the new County Amateur League. In general their performances were poor, their best result by far being third place in 1929, but travelling was difficult when Saturday morning working was still standard, and expenses were heavy. Fourteen clubs played in the first season of 1922–23 but only three of those, Haworth being one, lasted long enough to compete in 1928–29. The onset of the Depression brought financial difficulties and Haworth, having dropped out of the County Amateur League in 1931, joined the new Airedale and Craven League. However, the League charged 6s. 9d. per player, even if they only played one game; that was financially too burdensome and the team disbanded.[47] At a somewhat lower level the local council allowed Oxenhope to use the recreation ground for football and there were works teams from Hattersleys and Hields, neither of which performed with distinction.

After the Second World War the Haworth team was re-formed, beginning with a thumping win in the Keighley and District League in 1947 which, as in 1922, encouraged them to look for stronger opposition. In 1948 Haworth entered the Bradford Amateur League, where it played without marked success until 1955 when it became yet another victim of the malaise affecting everything in Haworth.[48] Oxenhope, being less ambitious, opted for the Craven League and was rewarded with a remarkable series of successes, winning the A division in six of the seven years from 1957 to 1963 and then again in 1966.[49] Between 1955 and 1966 there were some ephemeral clubs but not until 1967 did a properly organised Haworth team join the Craven League. By 1974 both Haworth and Oxenhope were firmly established, though results were somewhat variable.[50]

Between the wars cricket flourished. In the West Bradford League there were three teams from Haworth, one from Crossroads and three from Oxenhope. Oxenhope Church dropped into the Keighley League in 1923 and stayed there, but Crossroads won the West Bradford League in 1925. For most of the '20s and '30s Haworth Church was the strongest of the local teams, winning the league in 1923, 1926 and 1927. Haworth Methodists won in 1934 and Haworth Baptists in 1935, but Oxenhope Baptists had never been a strong team and they folded at the end of the 1931 season. More surprising was the fall from grace of Haworth Church, which came bottom of the league in 1938 and promptly disbanded.[51]

When cricket resumed after the Second World War the Haworth Church team was not revived but otherwise the West Bradford League took up more or less where it had left off. Haworth Methodists won the League in 1945, tied with Crossroads in 1947, and won again in 1948.[52] After 1949 there was the same noticeable decline. No team actually collapsed but the results were nondescript, both Haworth Methodists and a resuscitated Haworth Baptists spending periods in the Second Division. After a particularly bad season in 1963 Charles Manchester, rector of Haworth, half-humorously advocated a united denominational team called 'Ichabod' or 'Integrated Cricketers of Haworth Anglican, Baptist and Other Denominations'.[53]

His suggestion was inspired by the example of Oxenhope. There, the Wesleyans originally played at Haley, but when there was a chance to buy a better and more convenient field near the recreation ground for £700 they proposed a joint effort to raise the purchase money. The team would be called Oxenhope Parish. Neither the Anglicans, whose ground was halfway up Cockhill, nor the Baptists, had been able to produce teams of any calibre and they adopted the scheme with enthusiasm.[54] By 1960 Oxenhope had built up an excellent team which won the West Bradford League in 1960, came second in 1961, and won it again in 1962, 1963 and 1965.[55] The watching Haworth teams drew a different conclusion from the rector. By 1963 they attached more significance to a secular outlook, so in 1970 Haworth Baptists became Haworth West End. Haworth Methodists retained their name longer, perhaps because they won the League in 1972, but eventually they opted for plain Haworth.[56]

Other organisations sought to revitalise themselves and widen their popular appeal. The brass band, for example, regained strength after a successful concert entitled 'Music for All', shared with Keighley Amateurs in 1968. Under a new conductor, John Moor, determined attempts were made to banish the cloth-cap image, despite major financial challenges. The band bought new instruments using a £4000 loan from Keighley Council and its efforts were rewarded with success at Belle Vue, Manchester, when the band came second out of 18 in the competition. It had to hold many concerts in order to pay off the loan and in 1972 lost its rehearsal room for some weeks, using instead a stone shed in a disused quarry. The quarry building had potential and £900 was spent refurbishing it. In August 1972 the band opened its new Sun Street headquarters. Members had to raise £400 to enter the Third Division competition at Fulham Town Hall in 1973, but they won and, though there were heavy debts, the position was brighter than for some time past.[57]

Operetta was also reborn. In 1964 West Lane Baptists revived their amateur operatic society with a performance of the *Mikado*, followed by a long series of Gilbert and Sullivan shows. Oxenhope resumed normal business in the same year, but abandoned Gilbert and Sullivan in 1968 in favour of a more eclectic selection of operettas (*White Horse Inn* 1969, *The Gypsy Baron* 1970 and *La Vie Parisienne* 1971). The market could not sustain two societies in the competitive world of the late twentieth century, and the West Lane Baptists proved to be the stronger, under the guidance of their musical director, Terry Lofthouse, who conducted all of the shows in the period. Even that society needed resources drawn from beyond the Baptist Choir: in 1964 it was billed as 'the Baptist Choir and Friends', and soon all voices were welcome, whether from other denominations or from no Christian affiliation at all.[58]

The changes between 1914 and 1974 had led to the 'professionalising of service'. The urban district councils ceased to exist because they had been unable to provide the level of health and medical care that modern society demanded. As a way of retaining their congregations the churches and chapels tried similarly to provide leisure services, but were challenged by new forms out of their control. In Haworth the first moving pictures were shown by the 'Gem Picture Palace' at the Drill Hall. In August 1912 it put on films of the Empire Day Church Parade in Keighley, to the accompaniment of the Haworth brass band; travel pictures of the Maritime Alps; and two humorous films called 'Bobby

The Hippodrome Cinema, Belle Isle Road, Haworth. The earliest film shows were put on at the Drill Hall in 1912, but in 1913 the Haworth Hippodrome Company was formed which erected this purpose-built cinema in Belle Isle road in 1914. A second cinema, the Brontë, followed in 1921. For a number of years operettas were performed here, but the introduction of the equipment which turned 'silent' films into 'talkies' made it unsuitable for them. The Brontë cinema closed in 1956 and the Hippodrome in 1961. Since then the Hippodrome has had a number of different owners. Between 1988 and 1995 it housed the Museum of Childhood, memorabilia of Victorian and Edwardian times, but it was off the beaten track and a mixture of falling visitor numbers and vandalism forced its closure.

the Bootblack' and 'Foolshead Adventures'. In June 1913 the Haworth Hippodrome Company was formed and in October Haworth's first purpose-built cinema opened in Belle Isle Road.[59] After the First World War home entertainments such as gramophone records and the radio increased the competition and by the 1950s there was access to a professional level of entertainment that no local drama or operetta group could hope to provide. It was no accident that the slump in local entertainment facilities coincided with the growth of television from the early 1950s.

An exhibition of work from the classes at Haworth Evening Institute in 1957 showed that all but one (men's woodwork) was aimed at women: light woodwork, tailoring and dressmaking, soft furnishings, embroidery, and basketry. At Stanbury in 1948 the Evening Institute was superseded by a Women's Institute, which was soon flourishing.[60] The worst problems related to teenagers. Full employment in the 1950s put money into their pockets which they could spend on leisure pursuits. Boys would still play football and cricket but the numbers involved represented only a small fraction of the age group. Both sexes wanted somewhere to meet each other, to listen to music and dance. Religious groups tried hard to provide such facilities during the 1960s. St James Crossroads and Oxenhope Wesleyans ran successful youth groups but in each case membership was confined to families with a Christian affiliation, thus excluding three quarters of the population.[61] In Haworth a successful youth club had been run in the secondary modern school since 1948 and by 1961 membership was 150. In 1968 it came under the management of a community association which replaced the defunct Institute. In his first report the warden maintained that the Association's work was 'absolutely Christian in concept' and he deplored the lack of input by the churches. The rector of Haworth, R.T. Hughes, argued that while individual Christians had been the Centre's keenest supporters from the beginning, at Haworth church they were doing exactly the same as the community centre but on a different foundation. The centre's work was Christian in concept but almost entirely secular in application, but 'Every Church seeks to be a Christian community centre'.[62] Church members were free to support both, but the two groups became rivals for the allegiance of the young and the recruitment of skilled organisers.

Within the changing Haworth community, churches and chapels saw growing lack of interest. Baptist numbers declined so that, although West Lane maintained a respectable congregation, by 1973 Hawksbridge had only 21 members and Horkinstone was in single figures. The Strict Baptists at Hall Green were also dwindling.[63] The Methodists were rather more effective in maintaining numbers: their circuit had around 500 in 1966. Anglican Easter communicants increased slowly from the low point of the mid-1950s, and in 1973 a survey in Oxenhope concluded that 20 per cent of the population still attended church or chapel, 90 per cent would be sorry to see the churches disappear, and 60 per cent thought they did a good job.[64] This seemed to indicate that there was still a niche for them, but the likelihood of a return to their once central role in the community was very small. Their congregations were ageing and more inclined to mourn a Paradise Lost than to make the painful decisions needed for the creation of a New Jerusalem.

The new Haworth 19

The Brontë Society

By the 1890s most of those Charlotte had caricatured were dead, and those aspects of
the writings of Emily and Anne which had offended the susceptibilities of 'respectable'
mid-Victorians had ceased to shock. The time was ripe for those who wished to preserve
the family's memory. The Brontë Society was the brainchild of a Dewsbury journalist,
W.W. Yates, who had been trying to popularise the novels for some years. After a
discussion with John Brigg, soon to be MP for Keighley, he wrote a series of articles
in the *Dewsbury Reporter*, *Leeds Mercury*, *Keighley News*, *Bradford Observer* and *Halifax
Guardian* advocating the formation of a Brontë Society and Museum. At a public meeting
in Bradford a committee of 24 was chosen – ten from Bradford, five from Dewsbury,
four from Haworth, two each from Halifax and Keighley, and one from Oakworth. The
Haworth four were J.H.S Redman and J.F. Greenwood, Mrs Sugden and the Reverend
John Wade. The first president was Lord Houghton, the Lord Lieutenant of Ireland.
The Bradford Free Library and Museum Committee offered to provide a home for any
items collected.[1]

Hitherto most Haworth people had taken little interest in the famous family which had
lived for so long in the village. When Patrick died in 1861 most of his domestic effects
had passed into the hands of his servant, Martha Brown, and subsequently to her two
nephews. In 1889 they had tried to make a bit of money by exhibiting their collections in
a tearoom but few were prepared to pay the entrance fee and they gave up. One brother
emigrated to America; the other moved to Blackpool and the collection went with him.
Yet now that the initiative had been taken by others there was uproar. The *Keighley
News* huffed and puffed about the poor representation of Keighley and Haworth on the
committee. There were dark mutterings about the 'predatory' attitude of Dewsbury.
Haworth opinion was further annoyed by the paper's assertion that, though the Bradford
Free Library offer was 'kindly meant', Brontë relics would be better located at Keighley.
The town was 'connected with the Brontës, had good communications, a park and a
mansion'. Eventually the Brontë Society committee conceded that the most appropriate
place for the museum would be at Haworth. Two rooms above the Yorkshire Penny

Bank were bought and in May 1895 the Museum was opened amid great celebrations. Brontë enthusiasts journeyed from all over the West Riding to be present and some even came from London. At Haworth station the visitors were greeted by a crowd of over 700 and were serenaded up Main Street by the Haworth Brass Band. There was one sour note. At the first AGM of the Society committee had been reduced to twenty. One of those dropped was John Wade, and he was not on the guest list for the Museum opening either. The reason was clear: among those attending was Dr Erskine Stuart who, seven years previously, had made a vitriolic attack on Wade for his part in the destruction of the old Brontë church.[2]

The early history of the society was marked by enthusiasm and penury. At the end of the first year there were 156 members. Many of them had given Brontë memorabilia to the Museum, but few were prepared to contribute money when items of interest came on the market. The Browns demanded £500 for their Brontë collection, far beyond the Society's means, and the items were sold at Sotheby's in 1898.[3] Other opportunities were also missed. For example, in 1906 there was a chance to buy two of Branwell's paintings on the death of Arthur Nicholls.[4] In 1895 Gertrude Holden suggested that the Society should try to purchase the old parsonage, and the idea was repeated in 1898, but nothing was done.[5] There were not enough visitors and the threepenny entrance fee for the Museum did not cover costs. In 1900 there was only £8 in the bank. Nonetheless, the first issue of the *Transactions* appeared in 1895 and the Society gained a charter of incorporation in 1902. Thereafter a steady improvement in its fortunes was evident. The AGMs were held each year in different locations with Brontë connections and by 1907 there were 352 members and the first annual excursion was organised.[6]

The high unemployment before and after the First World War affected membership and visitor numbers but in 1928 the Society received a valuable boost. The rectors of Haworth did not greatly care for living in the old parsonage and in 1926 a new rectory was built in West Lane. The Society was offered first refusal of the old building, at a price of £3,000. Generously, Sir James Roberts volunteered to provide the money. The son of a Haworth farmer, he had been appointed mill manager to William Greenwood at Old Oxenhope in 1866 and then had become a wealthy textile manufacturer, retiring from business in 1918. The Society took possession in 1928 and the parsonage has been recognised as its headquarters ever since.[7] The possession of such a tangible architectural reminder of the Brontë family helped the Society's image. In 1936 there were 405 members but, perhaps more important, in 1934, only five years after opening to the public, the parsonage received 12,196 visitors.[8] This enhanced standing also prompted a flow of gifts and loans of Brontëana.

The Second World War slowed progress, but the return of peace brought a striking surge in interest, with visitor numbers peaking at 56,016 in 1949.[9] There was a steady rise in membership, to 773 in 1955,[10] and by the late 1950s alterations and extensions became necessary. A covered way, a strongroom and a new flat for the caretaker were built. The £12,000 proved insufficient and there was controversy when the extra cost was defrayed by selling land behind the parsonage for old people's flats.[11]

There were further heated arguments when Joanna Hutton was appointed as curator in December 1962. She had been an actress before her marriage and had no experience

The opening of the Brontë Parsonage Museum, 4 April 1928. The purchase of the parsonage by the Brontë Society was made possible by the donation of £3,000 by Sir James Roberts. He was a local farmer's son, went on to become William Greenwood junior's mill manager at Old Oxenhope, and eventually retired in 1918, a wealthy Saltaire textile manufacturer. He can be seen (second from the right) addressing the crowd. Behind him is the wing that had been added to the original parsonage by the Rev. John Wade in 1870.

in caring for manuscripts or artefacts. The Council had already appointed Amy Foster as her archive assistant, but that did not prevent six of its highly respected members resigning in protest.[12] Mrs Hutton's appointment was part of a fresh approach, which included a very controversial redecoration and rearrangement of the parsonage, designed to make it look like an inhabited house rather than a museum. Wherever possible exhibits were brought out of their glass cases and the rooms arranged in the way they would have been at the time of the Brontës. Mrs Hutton's most far-reaching innovation was the conversion of the parsonage cellar into a lecture theatre.[13] Her 5½ years in charge were a triumphant success. Visitor numbers rose from 52,000 in 1962 to 97,000 in 1968 and shortly after her departure they topped 100,000. In 1972 the Society had over 1,000 members and there were 141,000 visitors.[14] Mrs Hutton admitted that she was riding on a rising tide, attributing the increase in 1964 to the TV serialisation of *Jane Eyre*, but she used her media skills to extract maximum benefit from the favourable circumstances. In 1970 alone 11,000 children came in organised parties to see the parsonage and hear about the Brontës.[15]

As a literary shrine Haworth now ranked second after Stratford-upon-Avon and there was a play or a film about the Brontës, or based on one of their books, almost every year. The historical background to the books was not neglected and biographies of all three sisters and their brother Branwell appeared, written by Winifred Gerin. Her husband, John Lock, collaborated with Canon Dixon on *A Man of Sorrow*, a biography of Patrick Brontë.[16] Many of the Society's earliest members lived in the USA and by the 1930s they were about a quarter of the total. Henry Houston Bonnell, a wealthy American, had made an extensive collection of Brontë memorabilia during his lifetime. He died in 1926 and in 1929, shortly after the acquisition of the Parsonage, his widow arranged for it to be given to the Society. She remained a valued member until her death in 1969.[17] There was a very successful exhibition in Spain in 1949, as a result of which 30,000 copies of *Wuthering Heights* were sold. By 1954 the novels had been translated into many languages, including Esperanto, Chinese and Siamese.[18] In 1956 the museum was visited by Jalauddin Ahmed, director of the Sind regional government in Pakistan, who was writing a book on the Brontës in Urdu. In 1971 there were visits by groups from Russia and Japan.[19] When Dr Donald Hopewell resigned in 1974 after 42 years as president, the Society was flourishing as never before. Perhaps the total of 1,841 members and 221,497 visitors of that year would be difficult to repeat, but the future appeared to be secure.

Town into country

Sixteenth-century enclosure had largely ended the communal ownership of land in the area, so that the countryside was not available to Haworth people in search of recreation. In 1779 the moorland in Oxenhope was enclosed and allotted to the freeholders, all that was workable being turned into pasture and most of the rest given over to grouse preserves. The shooting rights were still being let in the 1970s. In Stanbury the unenclosed land belonged to the local freeholders as a group and they too let out the shooting rights.[20] In 1860 a proposal to enclose Haworth Moor was rejected by the Enclosure Commissioners but that was of little benefit to the inhabitants – in August 1862 Sarah Parker, James Waddington, Susan Holmes and Thomas Greenwood were prosecuted for gathering bilberries on the moor. Greenwood was 77 and selling bilberries was a means of supplementing the 2s. a week poor relief which he received. The case generated considerable resentment and in May 1895 the western part of the moor where the grouse were nesting was deliberately set on fire.[21]

Working-class people could not shoot grouse but they could shoot pigeons. Regular competitions were held but by 1900 the sport was dying out, replaced by breeding homing pigeons, a more attractive pursuit than slaughtering the birds.[22] The workers no longer had to farm land but those who had gardens could grow vegetables and flowers. A horticultural show was held in Haworth as early as 1863 and one at Stanbury began in 1865.[23] Most Haworth houses did not have gardens but after the 1917, and the national food shortage, allotments were made available to some. After the war the Land Settlement Facilities Bill allowed county councils to acquire land for leasing as allotments to ex-servicemen. Eighteen acres at Haworth Brow was distributed by the Allotments Association and land adjacent to the park was also used. In Oxenhope land at Uppertown was leased from the trustees of J.P. Heaton, but there were too many applicants, so additional land was acquired from J.H. Beaver.[24] A further impetus was provided by the Second World War, and a third horticultural show was founded at Oxenhope in 1941.[25] The Stanbury show flourished but that at Haworth was more precarious. Between the wars competitions were dominated by Albert Sunderland, but

Haworth Horticultural Society. Horticultural societies were a prominent feature of the inter-war years when the number of allotment gardens flourished. The most successful local society was at Stanbury but Oxenhope did not get one until 1941. The Haworth society began well and then wilted when its most enthusiastic member, Albert Sunderland, became superintendent of the new park in 1929. He is the tall man with a handful of leeks.

PHOTOGRAPH BY COURTESY OF JACK LAYCOCK

when he became Parks Superintendent in 1929 the Gardeners' Society collapsed, only reviving during the Second World War.[26]

By 1914 the rigid division between town and country had started to break down. Much land was acquired by local authorities as reservoir catchments. Thus, parts of Oxenhope Moor were owned by Bradford Corporation. In 1902 there was a quarrel among the Stanbury freeholders over letting the shooting rights and they sold them to Keighley Corporation.[27] Haworth and Brow Moors were acquired by Keighley when it bought the rights of the lord of the manor in 1904 but in 1908 Haworth Council was permitted to purchase the moors from Keighley if the ratepayers agreed. In 1910 a referendum was held but the ratepayers voted against the plan by 340 to 200, out of an electorate of 1,725. Most of the negative votes came from Lees and Crossroads. Keighley kept the moors.[28]

The reservoirs accelerated the destruction of upland agriculture. Life had always been hard for small farmers, when hand combing ceased many tried to combine farming with work in the stone quarries. What finally led to the abandonment of many remote farms was the government regulation of 1905 banning the pasturing of cattle on catchment land, because their dung allegedly fouled the water.[29] Nonetheless, the water authorities were more open in their attitude to public access than were the small farmers, or the landowners trying to make a profit out of grouse shooting. A growing number of people from the neighbouring towns walked in the countryside for relaxation and exercise. In 1906 there was a clash in Walshaw Dean, after Lord Saville had attempted to close off his grouse moor and cut direct links between Wadsworth and Stanbury. In the same year, probably not coincidentally, Haworth Ramblers was formed and their first ramble took them via Top Withens into Walshaw Dean. The best known of the ramblers was Tom Stell: in 1932 a seat was put on Haworth Moor at his favourite spot overlooking the Worth Valley.[30]

Jonas Bradley was master of Stanbury Primary School from 1890 to 1920 and lived in the village until his death in 1943. He is chiefly remembered for his pioneering work on nature study in primary schools. He was also president of the Haworth Ramblers for many years as well as a prominent member of the Brontë Society.

The interior of Stanbury Primary School classroom, looking east in 1902, as it would have been when Jonas Bradley was the master. The desks and chairs are typical of the time, but Stanbury was too small to have the classrooms round a central hall as at Oxenhope. Elizabeth Snowden later remembered how Bradley used to bring brought his many influential visitors to meet the children here.

The ramblers who gained the most from their walks were those knowledgeable about the countryside through which they passed. Jonas Bradley was master of Stanbury Primary School from 1890 until his retirement in 1920 and continued to live in the village until his death in 1943. He joined Haworth Ramblers soon after its formation, and became its president. He undertook pioneering work on the introduction of nature studies into the school curriculum, though at first this was frowned upon and classes had to be held on Saturdays. In 1903 he was criticised for unauthorised expenditure on the photographic negatives used in the preparation of his lessons but the subsequent investigation brought such an enthusiastic report on his nature study scheme that it came to the notice of the British Association meeting at Southport in January 1904. The secretary wrote asking him to assist the committee on observational studies in schools, 'by sending a brief account of his scheme for teaching botany, and any observations he might like to make upon observational studies in primary schools'. Illustrated articles appeared in all the London magazines 'and Stanbury instead of being just a pendant to the Brontë country, became known on its own account'. Elizabeth Snowden remembered his classes vividly, particularly his strictures on stealing birds' eggs and the way he brought his many visitors to talk to them.[31]

Between the wars townspeople made increasing use of the countryside, in various and diverse ways. There was greater awareness of the negative health implications of town living. In the 1870s Keighley Poor Law Union had been in the forefront of resistance to compulsory smallpox vaccination, with the result that vaccination levels were very low. In 1926 there was an outbreak of the disease in the area, though fortunately it was a mild strain and despite a large number of cases, especially among children, nobody died. However, an isolation hospital was established at Upper Height on Stanbury Moor and the Joint Hospital Board heard that once the sufferers got better, they 'were so much improved in health that they did not care to return home if they could help it'.[32]

Enthusiasm and awareness of the countryside among the young was also fostered by the scout and guide movement. A photograph of the proclamation of George V's

Haworth Scouts Pioneer Company. The earliest evidence for scouts in Haworth is their presence in a photograph of the proclamation of the succession of George V in 1910, only three years after the camp held by Baden-Powell on Brownsea Island was held to popularise the movement. Between the wars their most enthusiastic promoter was Rev. G. Hudson-Naylor, vicar of St James Crossroads. He also formed a Girl Guides' company in 1931. The pioneer troop is shown in front of the Navvies Mission hut in West Lane where they held their meetings.

accession in 1910 outside the church gates shows that Haworth had a scout troupe only three years after Baden-Powell's celebrated camp on Brownsea Island. Originally the scouts met in the Navvies' Mission Hall on West Lane but after the First World War interest steadily increased in other parts of the township. One of its most enthusiastic local proponents was the G. Hudson Naylor, vicar of Crossroads. Scouts are first mentioned there in 1922, and girl guides by 1931. A group began at Oxenhope, fired by the enthusiasm of Norman Bancroft.[33] From the mid-1930s to the mid-1960s both movements flourished in the area: in 1962 membership in the Keighley district was over 600 boys and a similar number of girls. John Foster Beaver junior, the County Scout Commissioner, enthused that it was the 'finest district report I have ever heard'. By the early 1970s interest was waning, but the movement was still very influential.[34]

By the mid-1920s walking and hiking in the countryside had become a major popular leisure pursuit among town dwellers, and in the 1930s the first moves towards the creation of national parks and formal long distance footpaths were made. After the Second World War these were translated into reality with, for example, the designation in 1951 of the Pennine Way, part of which passed through the township from Top Withens to the Colne road at Whitestone Clough. For seven years the old church Sunday school in Kirkgate served as a youth hostel but in 1958 Canon Dixon had to ask for its return because of dry rot in the 'new' Sunday school.[35] The Haworth Ramblers had begun by walking in the area around the town, but they soon began to go further afield, to the Yorkshire Dales.[36] Those who came to walk around Haworth – at least in the 'formal' sense – were therefore not its inhabitants but outsiders. Was the Worth Valley simply a rather unremarkable section of the Pennine Way, to be negotiated as quickly as possible, or was it attractive countryside in its own right. Or was it really 'country' at all?

One way in which to judge it was the state of local farming, which in Haworth was purely pastoral and almost entirely limited to cattle. After the Second World War, when the government was prepared to offer subsidies for the first time since the abolition of the Corn Laws a century before, there was renewed interest in farming. An agricultural show was established at Haworth in 1952, although in 1956 it was absorbed into the Keighley Show.[37] In 1960 the Worth Valley Young Farmers Club had a splendid year at Keighley Show, winning the Skipton Region Efficiency Cup and all the first three prizes with cattle in the dairy section.[38] Nevertheless, only a tiny percentage of the local population earned its living from farming, and Haworth's streets of nineteenth-century terraced housing were hardly redolent of country living. Oxenhope and Stanbury were not true country villages either but dormitories for people working in Keighley, Bradford and Leeds. They could try to disguise this, as at Oxenhope and Stanbury with their Women's Institutes (rather than Townswomen's Guilds). There were country amusements such as pony clubs and sailing on Ponden reservoir, and Keighley Corporation labelled Haworth Moor as a 'Country Park'.[39] They could show what the landscape could tell us about Haworth's past before satanic mills darkened the scene, as Reg Hindley did to great effect on his WEA walks.[40] Yet in the end the question to be asked was 'how could the millstone grit of the Worth valley scenery compete with the dramatic limestone dales'?

There was only one answer. When Whiteley Turner wrote his book *A Spring-Time Saunter* which took him and his companions into the Worth Valley in 1904, he subtitled it 'Round and about in Brontë land'.[41] Two years later the Walshaw Dean footpath argument erupted and among the three reasons put forward for keeping it open was its associations with the Brontës. Mrs Gaskell had described the Brontës as living in rural solitude and the sisters were known to enjoy long walks on the moor. The links with the Brontës were exploited by later novelists, such as Halliwell Sutcliffe and Emily Heaton, when they wrote about the area.[42] The implied threat to the literary interest and importance of the area was the main – and successful – argument against the erection of electricity pylons in 1931 and 1965.[43] There were persistent attempts to preserve the unremarkable Top Withens farmhouse even after most authorities concluded that it was not the one referred to in Emily's novel.[44]

There is a story that in 1928 a visitor asked an ancient Haworthite to direct him to the 'Brontë Waterfall'. He replied 'Nay, Ah don't knaw. Ah nebbut knaw one waterfall near here and that's at Sladen Beck over yonder. Happen tha means that?' When the visitor agreed that it might be the one, the man snapped, 'Then why couldn't ta call it that at first? What's ta good of usin' sich new fangled names'? For locals Sladen Beck waterfall was what they knew, but to visitors that name carried no meaning. The artist Ken Jackson gave up teaching to earn a living by selling landscapes of the dales and Haworth. He candidly admitted that the Brontë legend had induced him to live in Stanbury. Selling books about Haworth is easier than for any other village in northern England for the same reason.[45]

Road versus rail

In charting the decline of the local textile industry one major influence has been omitted. The Worth Valley railway had saved Haworth from becoming a backwater like Stanbury. The line was most profitable in the last years of the nineteenth century. Haworth station was enlarged in 1898 and had 24 staff, and in 1900 there were 17 trains a day in each direction.[46] The new century brought a decline which coincided with that of the textile industry. Soon passenger trains ran only in the morning and evening peaks, for commuters, and arrivals and departures from Keighley station did not coincide with main line trains. Complaints were numerous and unavailing.

Other forms of public transport were introduced provided competition. Horse trams were first approved Keighley in 1888 and the little system was electrified in 1904. One line extended to Ingrow. In 1913–16 trolleybuses were introduced on two routes, from Ingrow to Oxenhope and from Keighley to Oakworth.[47] As early as 1906, though, Haworth Council was in discussion with Keighley Corporation about the provision of buses, but there were delays because the borough did not secure parliamentary authority to operate buses until 1912. One pre-war service, from Ingrow to Lees Hill, began in 1910.[48] In 1924 Keighley abandoned its trams and in 1932 its trolleybuses, replacing them with a much extended network of motor buses. A local service to Haworth had been

Haworth Station, 1890. The opening of the Worth Valley railway in 1867 soon proved a boon to the textile manufacturers of the valley and, more recently, to the producers of TV costume dramas. Oakworth Station, which is similar in design, was used extensively in the *Railway Children* and there are also good shots of it in the episode of the ITV Sherlock Holmes series on *The Bruce Partington Papers*, where it is labelled Woolwich Arsenal. Note the footbridge that gave access to Belle Isle Road and which replaced the earlier level crossing.

introduced in 1925 and over the next few years various companies added routes, linking Haworth with Bradford via Keighley and Denholme, and Halifax and Todmorden via Hebden Bridge. By 1961 there were 64 services each day between Haworth and Keighley alone, while locally the Brontë Bus Company ran services between Haworth, Oxenhope and Stanbury.[49]

Yet the real social solvent after the 1920s was personal transport. In a hilly area such as Haworth the bicycle was never a popular form of transport and there is no reference to a cycling club until 1949.[50] Cars were a different matter. In 1903 the council resolved that the speed limit should be 10 mph except on Hebden Road, where 12 mph was acceptable. Haworth had a pioneering car enthusiast, Charlie Merrall, who in 1906 was fined for exceeding the speed limit of 20 mph in Hawksworth and in March 1907 was summonsed because his car had collided with a wagon near Lister Park in Bradford when doing almost 30 mph in a 20 mph area.[51]

Except for rich individuals such as Merrall, car ownership only became a reality after the Second World War. Increasing numbers of visitors came to Haworth in their cars, creating serious problems of congestion and parking in Main Street. The Reverend

The most notorious early Haworth motorist was Charlie Merrall who was fined for speeding in Hawksworth in 1906 and for colliding with a wagon near Lister Park, Bradford when doing 30 mph in a 20 mph restricted area. It would be nice to think that this is him with his pantomime princess bride but it is apparently his brother M.H. (Bertie) Merrall who played an important part in making the Haworth Volunteers such a success and who was the head of the Merrall textile company for most of the first half of the twentieth century until his death in 1957.

PHOTOGRAPH BY COURTESY OF JACK LAYCOCK

Charles Manchester lamented the way the cobbles damaged the springs of his car, with *Delilah*, an entertaining parody of Anne Brontë's poem *The Narrow Way*: *Delilah* was the name of his car:[52]

DELILAH

Believe not those who said
That Main Street hill was smooth;
For it has made Delilah dead,
And that's the honest truth.

Though not the only road
Unto the realms of joy;
Yet when she that way bore her load
She'd all her powers employ

Mend, mend thee for the right!
Cast useless sets away;
Praise be! Before she passed from sight,
Delilah's cause held sway.

To labour and to move,
To flatten and ensmooth;
She moved the Council up above,
Through TV news, forsooth!

If but thy springs approve,
And if, within thy breast;
Thou feel new comfort – give her love,
Delilah's earned her rest.

THE NARROW WAY

(1) Believe not those who say
The upward path is smooth,
Lest thou shouldst stumble in the way,
And faint before the truth.

(2) It is the only road
Unto the realms of joy;
But he who seeks that blest abode
Must all his powers employ.

(5) Arm – arm thee for the fight!
Cast useless loads away;
Watch through the darkest hours of night
Toil through the hottest day.

(8) To labour and to love,
To pardon and endure,
To lift thy heart to God above,
And keep thy conscience pure;

(10) If but thy God approve,
And if, within thy breast,
Thou feel the comfort of His Love,
The earnest of His Rest.

A civic society was formed to consider these problems and eventually it produced a plan for the bypass, now known as Rawdon Road, and the closing of Main Street to all but essential traffic. The setts are there still. Comparison of maps of Haworth before and after the construction of the bypass and its attendant car parks suggests that what has changed modern Haworth is not so much the Brontë antiques, Brontë tweeds, Brontë hotels, Brontë cafes, and Brontë fish and chip shops, but the insistence of so many Brontë enthusiasts on coming by car.[53]

As the car became dominant local bus services declined. Stanbury was particularly badly affected when the service from Keighley to Colne via Laneshawbridge was

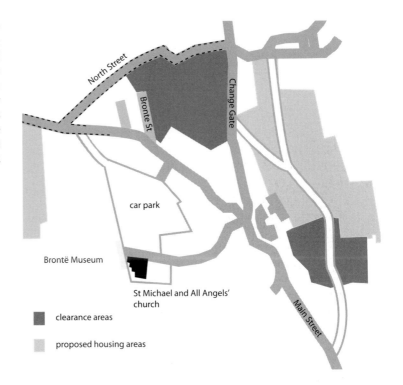

This plan of Haworth shows the Civic Trust proposals for traffic management and associated redevelopment within the village. A new car park is shown at the left of the plan. A new road (dotted) would by-pass the cobbled Main Street in one direction, while Main Street would be made one-way only.

North Street

Bronte St

Change Gate

car park

Brontë Museum

St Michael and All Angels' church

Main Street

clearance areas

proposed housing areas

withdrawn in 1955, and the Brontë Bus Company confined itself to tours after 1956.[54] But the chief victim was the railway. In 1954, when the cost of maintaining the old Great Northern line forced its closure, the Worth Valley Railway was still carrying a large number of passengers but did not cover its costs. In 1955 Oxenhope became an unstaffed halt and by 1958 British Rail was considering closure. A diesel service, introduced in 1960, increased passenger numbers but there was still no profit because goods traffic was declining. In 1961 the railway was closed.[55]

The idea of 'rescuing' the line was put forward by Bob Cryer, later MP for Keighley. In January 1962 a meeting in the Temperance Hall, Keighley, led to the formation of the Worth Valley Railway Preservation Society.[56] The financial obstacles were formidable, but in September 1964 British Rail finally agreed to sell the line for £6,000–7,000. The Society had £4,000 in the bank, and complex negotiations and fund-raising delayed the opening until the railway's centenary in 1967. A regular service began in June 1968.[57] In the meantime the society built up an impressive array of rolling stock, including 29 locomotives.[58] The Worth Valley Light Railway Company had to face commercial realities. The original aim had been to restore a full passenger service but it was soon clear that, for the foreseeable future, the service would be confined to summer weekends.[59] The achievement was a great credit to the voluntary and unpaid efforts of the thousand or so Society members. In the year of reopening steam traction ended on British Rail, so film makers wanting to simulate the steam age had to turn to preserved railways. The Worth Valley Railway was in an ideal position to profit, not least because it was the only one with a tunnel! The biggest success was the filming of the *Railway*

Gordon R. (Bob) Cryer, MP for Keighley, 1975–83 and for Bradford South, 1987–94. Best remembered for the leading role he played in the creation of the Worth Valley Railway Preservation Society, Cryer memorably described the Hartington Middle School in Keighley – attended by Haworth children – as looking rather like the German Prisoner of War camp, Colditz Castle. He was killed in a car crash in 1994.

Children, first broadcast in 1970. Society membership doubled to over 2,000,[60] and in 1971 the line carried 8,250 passengers during the four days of the Whitsun holiday, 50 per cent more than the previous year. The railway was thriving.[61]

In January 1973 a report revealed that of 541 visitors to Haworth questioned 90 per cent were day trippers and 342 were on a return visit. Most of the remainder expected to come again. Only 54 regarded it as a 'once in a life time' experience. Some 85 per cent came in a total of 484 cars. Fewer than half intended to visit a cafe or a restaurant. Many brought picnic lunches to eat in the park. For about one-third it was 'a day out'. Only half came specifically for the museum, and 12 per cent for the museum and railway. Haworth was no longer a miniature Manchester. It had become a tourist attraction instead.[62]

This air photograph shows Hebden Road running across the top. Below is the Haworth Brow estate. Running down from the top is the old turnpike which crosses the Hebden Road and continues down the east side of the Brow estate to the Bridgehouse mill complex. A third of the way down the picture Station Road crosses from Mill Hey on the left, meeting the turnpike by the Bridgehouse mills. Haworth station is just below Station Road. Bridgehouse Lane climbs up to the middle of the right hand edge. Then Main Street snakes across the picture from the middle right to the bottom. The triangle made by Changegate, West Lane and North Street can be clearly seen but the church is blurred. On the bottom left is Mytholmes Lane. Haworth Park is in the angle of Bridgehouse Lane and Main Street and on the left of it are the Central Schools and the Institute.

FROM THE COLLECTION OF STEVEN WOOD

Living in the past 20

The village community in decline

One of the features of old Pennine townships, such as Haworth, had been the way family and community had coincided. You would not have needed to go far to visit your uncles, aunts and cousins, while your grandparents would have been near at hand too. You would have attended the same church or chapel and got your education at the same Sunday schools and primary day schools. You and your friends would have worked within the village, often at the same textile mill. Most of you would have married within the community, too. Your leisure activities were similarly structured church or chapel choirs and entertainments, the local brass band, cricket and holidays dominated by the Christian year, except for the annual fortnight, but even then there was the likelihood that you would all turn up at Morecambe or Scarborough together because your employers forced you to take your holidays at the same time.

Later chapters have traced the gradual breakdown of this society due to the collapse of manufacturing, the retreat from organised religion, and the development of communications of all sorts from railways and buses to cars and aeroplanes. You could now work in one place while living in another. Your leisure interests were no longer bound to the community in which you lived, nor to its religious organisations. You could turn outwards and travel to neighbouring places which had facilities that your own village could not afford. Or you could turn inward to the radio, the TV and the internet. Relatives were widely scattered, even on different continents. Holidays changed from a communal affair to a family one.

Even the institutions that survived both shrank and changed. Hawksbridge Baptists were now reduced to services in the vestry because the congregation was so small that it could not afford to heat the entire chapel. Horkinstone Baptists transferred to a new chapel in Denholme Road, which then closed down in turn.[1] In Oxenhope Methodists fared rather better. They knocked down their old antiquated chapel and built a smaller, more up-to-date one. In Haworth in the late 1970s Hall Green Baptists were financially strong enough to renovate their chapel, but by the end of the century they were in low water again. The West Lane Baptists, on the other hand, managed to revamp their

Ivy Bank Mill was built in the 1870s, but it has been derelict since it was gutted in a fire in 1997 and the remaining walls are now dangerously unstable.

PHOTOGRAPH: CARNEGIE, 2009

premises, celebrating their 250th anniversary with a flower festival, a cheese and wine event with Juliet Barker as speaker and a concert,[2] something the Haworth Methodists could not afford. Only the annual Methodist Scartop Charity lived on unchanged, largely because it was a good day out.[3]

The Church of England has emerged as relatively the strongest religious denomination, which would have been unthinkable a hundred years earlier. St Michaels' Haworth was able to celebrate its 100th anniversary in 1981 in some style, and in April 1988 the full peal of bells was rung for the first time for 16 years after £20,000 was raised for their restoration.[4] St Mary's Oxenhope built an extension and reinstated some forgotten stained glass on its 150th anniversary. It too refurbished its bells and revived its reputation for bell-ringing.[5] But the Church of England is also feeling the financial strain of smaller congregations, with plans for amalgamating parishes in order to save on clergy stipends and pensions. Anglican churches are particularly affected by the greater mobility. Cars make it possible to 'shop around.' A 'feminist' Anglican might well be attracted to Haworth with its first female vicar, the Rev. Jenny Savage. A Haworth Methodist, who favoured union with the Church of England, on the other hand, might prefer to travel down to the 'shared' church in Keighley, while anyone seeking an evangelical approach could join St Mark's Utley.

The churches and chapels offer their premises for concerts, and the same trend is observable there too. Down to the Second World War they could mount them out of their own resources. Now the entertainment is likely to be supplied by groups coming from outside Haworth. When the Haworth Baptists celebrated their 250th anniversary, for instance, the concert was provided by the Cobbydale Ladies Singers of Silsden and the Aire Valley Male Voice Singers.[6] Even with societies that have their base in Haworth, the majority of their members do not live there. The Gilbert and Sullivan society, for example, still performs annually in the West Lane Baptist chapel, but most of its members come from outside the village. The Haworth Brass Band continued to have a high profile as long as John Moor was its conductor, but soon slipped out of the news once he left, with engagements locally few and far between.[7] Cricket continues to be played, but is experiencing a similar contraction. The West Bradford League collapsed, forcing Haworth and Oxenhope to join farther-flung leagues ,which was only possible in a car-borne society.

For many people this is a disorienting experience, even if they are aware of the beneficial sides to what has been happening and are not church- or chapel-goers or members of the societies that featured so strongly in the lives of the old villages. One result has been a movement to try to halt the erosion by an appeal to their historical significance. An Upper Worth Valley History group has been formed, based on the police contact point in Haworth, and there have been recent histories of Oxenhope by Reg Hindley and of Stanbury by Dennis Thompson, each protesting the uniqueness of where they live.[8] But the most powerful historical aid to the preservation of the status quo is still the Brontë legend.

The Brontë effect

When Bradford Metropolitan Council took over the running of the old Keighley borough in 1974 the Brontë Society was riding high with a steadily increasing membership and so many visitors to the parsonage that there was serious concern about the effect on the building's structure. The entrance fee was raised in the hope that it would stem the flood and the strategy seems to have had some success.[9] In 1986 there were reports of falling visitor numbers but by 1990 they were not far short of 200,000 again. The rise was temporary.[10] The following year saw a fall to 157,963. By 1996, when Jane Sellars resigned as curator, totals of a little over 100,000 appear to have been the norm, while in 1998 only 82,000 passed through the door.[11]

The financial implications were considerable and the 1999–2000 accounts showed a shortfall of £80,000. As 80% of the Society's expenses were staff salaries it must have become obvious that either the wages had to be cut or the number of employees reduced. Sharp disagreements appear to have taken place within the society's council with the result that the 'Director' at the time, Mike Hill, resigned and left to become the Director of Cleveland Arts. He was replaced by Alan Bentley who was designated simply as 'Museum manager'[12] The Society's outpost at 74 Main Street, which had doubled as a shop and meeting place for small literary groups, was sold in order to liquidate the outstanding debts and the marketing of museum tickets was transferred to the nearby tourist information centre.[13] Another economy was the hiving off of the society's journal, *Brontë Studies*, which would now only be sent to those who subscribed to it, instead of to all society members. The membership secretary, Jill Greenwood, accepted voluntary redundancy, and her former functions were divided among other members of the staff.[14] There was a further fall to 76,201 in 2002 which did not help either. Then, 2003 showed a recovery to the previously low figure of 82,000, while 2004 and 2005 both recorded further small increases but the 'ideal' figure that Mike Hill had posited on his appointment in 1997 of 120,000 now appears to have been unduly optimistic.[15]

While Mike Hill as 'Director' must bear some responsibility for failing to accept that the fall in visitor numbers required some belt-tightening, he did not cause them. Nor was it the quality of what was on offer. In 2001 the Museum won the Sandford Award from the Heritage Education Trust for its excellent educational work which caters for all from school groups to adults. Some of the poor attendance years were caused by temporary aberrations – bad weather and the foot and mouth outbreak for example.[16] Yet the failure of the considerable publicity from film and TV programmes about the family or adaptations of the novels like the BBC's serialisation of *The Tenant of Wildfell Hall*, to generate more than a small recovery suggests a deeper problem. Could Councillor Eric Dawson's contention that the drawing power of the Brontës was fading be the reason?[17] There was certainly more scepticism of the wilder claims of Brontë romantics. An attempt in 1994 to get Top Withens, then already in ruins, restored as the moorland farmhouse that Emily Brontë had in mind when visualising *Wuthering Heights* failed. In the end Yorkshire Water was persuaded to prevent it from disappearing altogether by taking measures to preserve it in its current state, but the plaque attached to the ruins drew attention to the belief of many scholars that Emily had no specific house in mind at all, borrowing elements from a wide variety of the different ones known to her.[18]

Similarly Bradford Council's enthusiasm for developing interest in the countryside and the creation of the Brontë Countryside Agency is difficult to evaluate. Did the conversion of George Merrall's old residence into a Youth Hostel at Longlands, and the setting up of a Country Park on Penistone Hill, turn visitors away by directing attention to the countryside rather than to the village? There were certainly plenty of walkers, and there was a clash between their interests and those of the farming community and Yorkshire Water, owner of Stanbury Moor. A further complication was the passage in 1979 of the Countryside Act, which extended the powers of the Nature Conservancy beyond the National Parks to areas of special scientific interest. One of these covered both Stanbury and Haworth Moors. The Pennine Way and a few other well-established paths crossed the area, and fears were expressed that the creation of any more could seriously damage the unique moorland wildlife.[19] In 1987 the Nature Conservancy and the Countryside Commission were asked to prepare a management plan, to which Yorkshire Water and North West Water were invited to contribute, that included greater access for ramblers and riders, but their efforts were repeatedly obstructed. The same year, for instance, the Nature Conservancy agreed a new circular route from Ponden Clough via Alconden Stones to Withens, but Yorkshire Water, on whose land most of it lay, expressed reluctance to allow access until the possible damage to wildlife could be assessed, a process it thought would take three years. In 2000, thirteen years later, the assessment was still in progress![20] Similar delaying tactics were experienced on

Top Withens farmhouse, 1869. Dating from the late sixteenth century it was once thought that Top Withens was the model for *Wuthering Heights*. This old photograph shows a whole line of weavers' windows in the upper storey. Textiles are never mentioned in Emily's book, so unless her artistic licence was extensive, we must conclude that the attribution is wrong. The farm is now in ruins.

Haworth Moor, where apparently endless scientific studies were conducted about the damage done to the environment by the use of moorland paths. The issue was finally forced by the Countryside and Rights of Way Act of 2000.[21] There was little doubt in the mind of the *Keighley News* reporter about its significance. Now ramblers and riders could roam the moors which had inspired the Brontë sisters![22] An interesting historical footnote is that agreement was reached to establish an out-of-doors centre at Heights Farm, which had previously played host to children evacuated from Keighley at the time of the 1926 smallpox epidemic.[23]

More significant may have been the change in leisure habits. The 1980s were a difficult period in which the engineering and iron industries went the same way as textiles had in the previous decade. For most people money was tight, and expensive holidays beyond their means. Days out in the immediate vicinity were cheap alternatives. By the late 1990s there had been a complete change. Prosperity was returning, and the exchange rate made foreign holidays relatively cheap. Another complication was the change in the structure of the family weekend. From the time of the Second World War church and chapel attendance on Sunday had declined, and leisure pursuits had taken its place, but the law still forbade Sunday trading except during the summer in tourist resorts. In 1992 a motion by the Welsh MP Ray Powell to remove this summer time exemption backfired, igniting a debate that ended in the abolition of most of the restrictions. In many families Sunday shopping replaced leisure activities and may well have adversely affected other alternatives such as day trips to places like Haworth.[24]

Despite these developments the Brontë effect could still exercise a potent influence in preventing change. One morning in March 1992 the people of Haworth awoke to see a 144-foot high glaring white wind turbine at Naylor Hill Quarry on Haworth Brow. There had been rumours for some time that Calderdale Council was planning a wind farm of up to 35 turbines at Flaight Hill on the edge of their district above Oxenhope and Haworth inhabitants should not have been surprised that the first one in the Bradford district appeared where it did. In the early twentieth century the quarry machinery had been operated by a wind pump, so it was natural for the present owner, Cedric Gillson, to lead the renewed interest in wind power. Nonetheless, there was outrage that Bradford had given him planning permission, and attempts were made to force him to dismantle it by pointing to the way the finished turbine departed from his original specification. The protesters failed and by the end of the year the turbine had become an accepted feature of the landscape, many of the inhabitants regarding it as an asset rather than an eyesore.[25]

Encouraged by Gillson's success and the appearance of the first batch of a 23-turbine wind farm on Ovenden Moor, clearly visible from Haworth, Calderdale increased the size of their proposed Flaight Hill farm to 44, and plans were submitted to Bradford Council for a considerable number of turbines in its own district, including 5 at Oakworth and 4 at Haworth in addition to the one already in operation. Fears were expressed that the turbines would cause environmental damage, and there was particular criticism of the Flaight Hill site. John Bewick, a senior lecturer at Keighley Further Education College, claimed that the 20 metre square foundations needed for each of the 200 foot high turbines would irreparably damage the drainage system of the moorland bog, drying out the peat and ruining it as a habitat for wildlife. There were also strong protests from Oxenhope, led by Reg Hindley, who spoke up for the many who regarded the moors as a haven for walkers. He claimed that the submissions breached Bradford's own guidelines.[26]

The most powerful opposition came from the Brontë Society, which feared that the enormous structures would dominate the skyline and alter forever the moors that inspired the works of the famous Brontë sisters. The Society's council had condemned Gillson's original turbine 12–1 and the worldwide membership of over 3,000 expressed strong concern at the subsequent developments. Traders and hoteliers, too, believed that tourism would be badly hit. Dr Juliet Barker, a former curator of the Parsonage Museum, led the opposition, declaring that 'the cultural and literary importance of the area is reason enough for turning down the Haworth applications'.[27] Bradford Council, which had initially looked with favour on the bids, executed a hasty U-turn and for one reason or another rejected all of the turbine proposals in its district, not just the ones that affected Haworth.[28] Appeals to the government inspector failed, and he also refused to sanction Calderdale's Flaight Hill development. So a comprehensive victory in which the Brontë Society played a leading role had been achieved. Wind farms had been seen off in the same way as electricity pylons.

Employment versus housing

If you talk to people from Oxenhope you will find that many of them have a noticeable inferiority complex, which takes the form of a belief that their village has always been the neglected poor relation of Haworth. 'We lived in the shadow of Haworth before the War,' 65-year-old Jack Feather, a life-long resident, told a *Telegraph and Argus* reporter in 1986. 'Haworth had a right good councillor [he is presumably referring to Thomas Duerden] in those days and he wanted everything for their park – we are in their shadow, though the railway has opened us up a bit.'[29] This curious piece of muddled historical reasoning – the railway opened in 1867, Haworth Park not until 1929 – expressed the belief of both life-long Oxenhopers and incomers that Haworth got too much publicity and Oxenhope too little.

This mild paranoia was not necessarily a bad thing because the result was a determination that Oxenhope's voice should be heard. Within Bradford Oxenhope had no independent representation but was part of the same ward as Oakworth, Haworth, Stanbury and Crossroads, whose interests were not necessarily the same as its own. Oxenhope quickly realised that a parish council could act both as an effective pressure group and as a focus for the sort of community cohesion that the churches were no longer able to provide. In the autumn of 1986 there was a poll in which 748 voted in favour of setting up a parish council with only 97 against and 76 undecided. Bradford also was supportive, with the result that inaugural elections for an 8-seat parish council took place in February 1988.[30]

The parish council had a right to be consulted and had its administrative costs funded by Bradford, but it had no legislative or money-raising powers, which led critics to write it off as a mere 'talking shop'. They proved to be quite wrong. Bradford consulted local opinion about plans for the village and took into account their views on the listing of protected buildings and conservation areas in particular. A community centre was built, a village green established and improved public toilet facilities provided.[31] The parish council also sponsored the annual Straw Race. In 2003 the powers of metropolitan parish councils were equalised with those in other types of authority. The administrative funding was withdrawn, but parish councils were allowed to set a precept for small items such as allotments, street lighting and playing fields. Oxenhope was in the forefront of the movement and was the first parish council in West Yorkshire to be awarded quality status by the National Association of Local Councils.[32]

Yet many of the pressures that affected Oxenhope were economic and social ones which could be limited but not stopped and which will be familiar to readers in similar villages throughout the Pennine area and beyond. Although its relative isolation enabled a range of local shops to survive, including a Co-op mini-market, the wish that Oxenhope should be preserved as an industrial working village was not realised. This was partly due to a rather romanticised view of the past. Quarrying had always been a feature of the 'industrial' period of Oxenhope's development, but it only needed Blackmoor Quarry to be listed for possible redevelopment for fears to be expressed about damage to a local beauty spot. Each nineteenth-century Pennine village had had its own abattoir, but the residents near the one belonging to J. and K. Meats on Hebden Road made repeated complaints about it, despite inspectors finding nothing wrong with the way the business was conducted. In the end the firm relocated to Bradford, and Oxenhope lost 11 jobs. George Hodgson, the chairman of the parish council at the time, regretted that the firm could not find an alternative site in Oxenhope but expressed relief that the noise and conditions which had led to the complaints were now at an end.[33]

Mixing residential housing with small businesses always leads to strains of this type, and what the Oxenhope council really wanted was that the 'industrial' element would be provided by the remaining textile businesses or, failing that, the establishment of new enterprises in the mills when they were sold. They were regularly disappointed. In April 1980 a downturn in the textile trade led Hields to close its operation at Lowertown Shed with the loss of 41 jobs. The council opposed the firm's plans to demolish the mill and in May 1981 the building was bought by Haworth Scouring Company which was planning to add the quality woollen market to its overseas carpet wool trade. In 1988 rising costs forced the company to relocate to Bradford. This time permission was given to knock the mill down, and it was demolished in August 1989. The chief factor in the calculations of the company was the price of land, which was rising sharply, so it found that by selling its Oxenhope property and buying in a cheaper area it could use the extra money to develop and modernise its business.[34]

The rising land values were due to the demand for housing, with developers willing to offer far more than small businesses. That is what had happened at Lowertown Shed, and it was repeated at the Sykes, Charles and Perseverance Mills, each being converted to flats or other residential units.[35] The pressure affected even Oxenhope's long-established Pawson engineering company which made springs, clips and fasteners for hundreds of different applications. In 1982 George Emmott Pawson sold out to a consortium of three, including the general manager and the works manager, but by 1999 it too was proposing to turn most of its Wadsworth House premises into 11 houses with three more on land nearby in order to raise enough money to expand elsewhere. If the plans are not approved the managing director warned bluntly 50 jobs will be lost.[36] The last textile firm, West Yorkshire spinners, ceased producing knitting wool at Lowertown (Bridge) Mill in 2003,[37] and Skipton Properties Ltd promptly applied for a licence to convert it into nine residential units and eleven dwellings. The chairman of the Oxenhope parish council, Derek Allen, attempted to delay a decision by suggesting that the site should first be assessed to see whether it could be used for employment, a vain hope if the fates of the other mills were anything to go by.[38]

Mill owners were not the only ones who stood to make a profit from selling to house builders. The original 1983 plan had been to convert the church infants' school into the new community centre. A government grant of £40,000 was available, but a 'mystery buyer' made a much better offer which the diocese of Bradford accepted instead. The money was badly needed to offset liabilities incurred in the purchase and rehabilitation of the former junior school, which had become the Church of England school for the district, so the community centre had to be built elsewhere. The Oxenhope Methodists' new chapel was also financed by the sale of surplus land for housing.[39]

In a way these changes enabled Oxenhope to at least put off the evil day when there would be house-building applications for greenfield sites. Even so with the population rising by 500 between 1981 and 2001 the council found itself having to fight plans for houses infilling between Leeming and Lowertown and an estate at Best Lane.[40] Yet the problems which bulked large in the imagination of Oxenhope's inhabitants were small compared with other places. Had all the houses proposed been built they would have been a fraction of the 1,500 planned for Silsden before the turn of the century floods forced a rethink. Between 1989 and 2003 house prices in Oxenhope rose by 64%, hardly more than the average for the Bradford Metropolitan district as a whole, while those in greater Keighley were 108% up and East Morton an astronomical 135%. This was despite all the census indicators showing that within the Bradford Metropolitan Council area only Ilkley had a more prosperous lifestyle.[41]

By 2007 Oxenhope was effectively a dormitory village. Arthur Smith remarked on how quiet it was in the middle of the day, with only retired people about because everyone else was at work in Keighley or Bradford. Indeed quietness is Oxenhope's chief virtue so there is not quite the same hostility to provision for the elderly as to housing in general. The proposal to establish a nursing home, retirement flats and a nursery at Perseverance with the prospect of 50 jobs was welcomed.[42] And there is the Sue Ryder home for the care of cancer patients established at Manorlands, the former home of J.P. Heaton, in 1974. The idea may have come from Professor Robert Turner, who lived at Moorhouse. He was consulting pathologist in chemotherapy at Bradford Royal Infirmary from 1956 and a pioneer in the treatment of breast cancer.[43] Though it does receive grants Manorlands relies heavily upon contributions from the public to keep it going, so there are charitable events and appeals for money every year which create considerable publicity. The inhabitants of Oxenhope have no need to fear. For as long as Manorlands flourishes their village will not be forgotten.

The other parts of the Haworth township did not take to the idea of parish councils with Oxenhope's enthusiasm. Haworth had its own village trust, so when one was belatedly created in 1997 covering Crossroads, Haworth and Stanbury, it was probably the result of pressure from the two smaller villages who felt left out.[44] This cobbling together of three somewhat disparate units was described at the time as having the effect of recreating the natural administrative unity of the past, but in reality it was more a new unity than the echo of an old one. Stanbury initially was part of the Oxenhope Board of Health district formed in 1864 which it then deserted for Oakworth in order to avoid paying a water rate. In 1894 Crossroads was forcibly united with Haworth despite a petition in which no one voted in favour of the amalgamation. In revenge its councillors obstructed any measure which benefited old Haworth, notably the library.

Ah, the library! In 1938 Keighley had provided the township with a branch library at long last which was open two mornings a week. In 1974 Bradford abandoned it in favour of a mobile library because the topography of the district made access to it difficult for many borrowers. Despite an eloquent plea on behalf of its revival by Ian Dewhirst, the former Keighley reference librarian, wit and lecturer extraordinaire, supported by Alan Bentley of the Brontë Museum, there proved to be little or no interest. Haworth was still the 'Strange, uncivilized little Place' depicted in Steve Wood's recent book.[45]

Many of the problems the three villages faced were the same as those of Oxenhope. The position with manufacturing jobs at Haworth was a little better than at Oxenhope. Chapter 16 listed Airedale Springs at Ebor, and there was another newcomer, Wydean, which took over its current premises in the Bridgehouse Mill complex in 1964. The firm has 50 employees and specialises in producing military items such as touch cords for cannon salutes, accoutrements for royalty and overseas heads of state, medal ribbons, bugle cords, sashes, revolver lanyards, epaulettes, gold braid, webbing, and laces etc.[46] Food-processing firms encountered difficulties. Some 93 jobs were lost when the Yorkshire Biscuit Factory closed in 1985. Brontë Foods, which had units in Bradford, Haworth and Cullingworth, flourished for a time, but its frozen chicken business failed in 2004 due to competition from Thailand.[47] As the last section indicated, there were still jobs available in quarrying, but the textile sector continued to shrink. What there was tended to concentrate on the retail side. The Edinburgh Woollen Mill Company which took over the former Townend Mill in Haworth, failed to interest local businesses in a centre for craft work and ended by turning it into a tea-bar and shop. The firm did employ a demonstration weaver, but there was little pretence that the goods it sold were made on the premises.[48] The result is that employment in Haworth itself is mainly in the service sector and heavily dependent on tourism.

A successful example of the textile trend represented by the Edinburgh Woollen Mill Company was provided by an enterprising businessman, Barry Brookfield, who took over Ponden Mill at Stanbury in 1976 as a mill cum restaurant, promising that he would sell fabrics actually manufactured on the premises. The scheme did not work and Brookfield was soon selling materials that had been made elsewhere. When Bradford discovered the change there was trouble, but in the end he was allowed to get away with it. His business flourished. He bought Darley Mill at Harrogate and then Brookes Mill off the M62. Perhaps his greatest success was realising the potential of the then largely unknown continental duvet. Ponden Mill fabrics are now sold throughout the entire region and the mill shop just outside Stanbury attracts customers from a wide area. When Brookfield finally sold out to Marston Mills Ltd in 2005 he had no fewer than 30 different outlets.[49]

Stanbury was largely unaffected by the housing boom for the simple reason that there was no room for expansion on its narrow ridge. In Haworth there was more pressure, and a struggle took place over the disused Haworth Central Schools. The result was a compromise covering the whole complex, including the institute building, in which a community centre shared the land with residential units.[50] Elsewhere the same issues

Modern Haworth: award-winning housing off West Lane on a road called, simply, Heathcliff.

PHOTOGRAPH: CARNEGIE, 2009

emerged as in Oxenhope. A proposal to build houses in the part of Bridgehouse Mill formerly occupied by Brontë Foods, was only frustrated by a fire on the site. West Lane Baptists imitated Oxenhope Methodists and financed the revamp of their chapel by selling the land on which the Sunday school had stood for housing for the elderly, and there was some infilling on Coldshaw and off West Lane. A combination of the terrain and the Brontë influence ensured that it would be kept to a minimum.[51]

Crossroads had no such protection but it tried its best to bang the history drum. There was a successful campaign to save the spire on the old Lees Primary School, and complaints that new developments would spoil the centre of Lees village. The area really has little claim to preservation on historical grounds, and a good case could be made that new housing would improve the look of the place, but this did not prevent anguished protests being made to the proposal to build 102 new homes there in 1996. Indeed the only plausible grounds for opposition was the extra traffic which would be generated and this is the real problem for Haworth as well, not housing.[52]

Road versus rail again

The traffic generated by visitors in the pre-1974 period has already been described. Since then the problem has got steadily worse, and one plan after another devised to solve it has failed. The chief tourist attraction is Main Street, which is both steep and narrow. Parking was banned in the street itself at an early stage, and off-street spaces provided for those living there, but access both to shops and dwellings still caused problems, and it was not until 1997 that those wishing to recreate the Victorian village street managed to get it pedestrianised. A similar clash developed over the new Health Centre which was built eventually in 2006 on what had been a car park, limiting further the parking available for visitors.[53] Most of the houses in Haworth are of the terrace type and without garages, so the only parking spaces are usually in the street. Bradford Council had to step in and provide dedicated spaces for the occupiers to prevent visitors monopolising them. New car parks were provided near the Parsonage Museum, where the 'new' Sunday schools had been, off Sun Street, at Weavers' Hill and at the Bankfield and Dimples quarries. There were so many coaches that they more or less blocked West Lane until a neighbouring field was appropriated for a coach park. Finally a scheme was drawn up for a large car and coach park on Penistone Hill, but in 2006 councillor Peter Hill was still complaining that on summer weekends the inhabitants found it difficult to get out, or in again if they were out.[54] It was not only in the summer either. In December 2006 29 coaches on their way back from St Nicholas Fair at York caused traffic chaos when they stopped off in Haworth.[55] The problem was getting to the car park. Penistone Hill was on the other side of Haworth from Crossroads, which was the usual point of entry, so it generated a constant stream of traffic along Mill Hey, Bridgehouse Lane, Rawdon Road and West Lane.

This chronic traffic problem needs to be borne in mind when considering the behaviour of Haworth's most notorious businessman, Ted Evans, or 'Clamp it' Evans as he became known from his practice of using the firm Carstoppers to clamp any cars or coaches he considered to be parked illegally on or around the private car parks he owned. In 1995 he banned coaches from his Changegate car park as a protest against the way he claimed Bradford Council had signposted only the public car parks. His action caused chaos when ten coaches, breaking their journey from the Edinburgh tattoo to allow their passengers to visit Haworth, had to disgorge them in the open street and then pick them up again later. This did have the positive effect of correcting the signs as Evans wished and forcing Bradford to provide the West Lane coach park mentioned above. Thereafter, his clamping activities burgeoned and there were few who escaped, ranging from the Prime Minister of Australia, Gough Whitlam, on a visit to the Brontë Parsonage (which caused some amusement) to disabled drivers (which caused no amusement at all). Even a clarification of the wheel-clamping laws in 2005 failed to stop the complaints, which began to affect the business of nearby traders, and in 2007 the local magistrates were asked to issue an Anti-Social Banning Order against George McDickens, one of the wheel clampers, which was suspended by the judge until the case being brought against Evans himself was heard.[56]

An 'Asbo' might bring 'Clamp it' Evans to heel, but it would not cure the traffic problems. There did seem to be an alternative to the car – the Keighley and Worth Valley Railway. The passenger figures do show an improvement *vis à vis* the Brontë Parsonage Museum, but the pattern is the same. A total of 151,000 travelled in 1982, and its peak year was 1988, with 168,515, after which they fell away to around 100,000 in 2000, rising again to 117,600 in 2006 which, like the parsonage, was well below the earlier peak.[57] As with the museum there were explainable bad years. The figures for

1998 were affected by the closure of the Ingrow tunnel for repairs during the autumn, and those of early 2002 by a landslide between Damems and Oakworth caused by that winter's heavy rainfall,[58] but the general performance of the company, like that of the museum, was excellent. In 1989 and again in 1999 it won the Ian Allan Heritage Award for the best independent railway in the country and the only one which ran all year round with staff who were entirely voluntary.[59] Damems station received an award as the best small station. When the Ingrow station was found to be beyond repair it was replaced by a disused one uprooted from Foulridge and transported whole to its new location. All the remaining stations were updated.[60] At Haworth the station bridge was repaired, and a picnic area established, so that the marshalling yard could be viewed in safety and comfort.[61] The fleet of locomotives was augmented, and there were visits from other societies. Perhaps most important of all a Vintage Carriage Museum was established at Ingrow which proved a hit both with visitors and the TV companies.[62] The railway had even more TV exposure than the parsonage; episodes of ITV's *Sherlock Holmes* and *Poirot* series involving rail travel and many other costume dramas of the Victorian and Edwardian periods were filmed on it.[63] Again, as with the parsonage, the influence on passenger numbers was limited. Chairman Graham Mitchell had no doubts. It was the change in the trading laws that had done it, passenger numbers on Sunday halving.[64] There is one rather sad note to record – the death of Bob Cryer, ironically, in a car crash in 1994. In 1999 his widow, Keighley's current MP, Ann Cryer, unveiled a memorial plaque in his honour.[65]

A 2004 book criticised those running the railway for failing to turn it into a fully commercial operation.[66] That option was had been explored in depth by Bob Cryer at the time of its foundation, and there is no evidence that, even if it had proved profitable, it would have made a greater contribution to solving Haworth's traffic problems. The space for car parking at Keighley station is very limited, so if you wish to reach Haworth by rail you have either to use public transport at the Keighley end or park at one of the stations further up the line, at Ingrow, Oakworth, or Oxenhope. Even then when you arrive at Haworth you would find that the station is down in the valley and that reaching Main Street requires a stiff climb up through the park. Attempts are being made to circumvent the problem. Ponden Mill has been persuaded to sponsor a 'hoppa' bus service running from the station to Ponden via top Haworth,[67] but the preference shown by visitors, who are not railway enthusiasts, for the family car over a community serving railway which includes two changes is not hard to understand.

There is an amusing tailpiece which illustrates the problem. A feature of recent years has been the campaign for fair trade. The *Keighley News* ran articles on the exhibition at the West Lane Baptist chapel and the campaign by Rita Verity of the shop 'Sonia's Smile.'[68] Children at Haworth primary school were told about the difficulties encountered by small coffee producers in the Andes. They began learning Spanish and were shown a video of the extraordinary temple site at Machu Picchu way up in the mountains. Haworth people were immediately struck with the resemblance between the problems there and those in their own village. Both were tourist hotspots; both suffered considerable degradation because of the large numbers of people flocking to see attractions; and both suffered from chronic traffic congestion. As a result an arrangement was made 'twinning' Haworth with Machu Picchu.[69] The resemblance was probably most apparent to the children from 'Bottom' Haworth. Until 2000 they would have been taught in the old Central Schools in Butt Lane half-way up the slope to 'Top' Haworth, but they now found themselves forced to struggle all the way up to a new school at the top of Rawdon Road. It must have brought home to them rather forcibly one of the difficulties that Andean children faced.

Parent power

Hitherto little or nothing has been said about secondary education because the township of Haworth is not big enough to have a school of its own, so its children have to attend institutions outside its boundaries. However, with the school leaving age nearing 18, no account of life there at the beginning of the twentieth-first century would be complete without a description of the main changes. From the later nineteenth century a favoured few from Haworth would have gone either to the Bradford Grammar School for Boys or to the Bradford High School for Girls, but for the overwhelming majority secondary education would have begun at 11 and in Keighley. Since 1872 Keighley had had both a boys' grammar school sited in the town centre, a technical college until 1961, when it moved to Oakbank up the Worth valley, and a girls' grammar school at Greenhead in Utley at the far north-west corner of the borough. Access to both for Haworth children was by passing the 11+ examination. The remainder would have gone to new schools created by the 1944 Education Act, some to the secondary technical school, which drew children from all over south Craven, but the vast majority to Hartington, one of the three secondary modern schools, which was housed in the buildings of the old free grammar school down Strawberry Street in the town centre.

In 1963 the borough went comprehensive and opted for what was known as the Leicestershire plan, the changeover being completed in 1967. This created a three-tiered system with children changing schools at 9 and 13. As in the full comprehensive system the schools were not selective, and they were co-educational; they preserved the wide range of courses which was considered one of the comprehensive schools' virtues and the reduced size removed what many thought was one of their drawbacks. The system was also more economical because many of the existing school buildings could be reused which obviated the need for large new expensive ones. Unfortunately it was these fiscal considerations, not educational ones, that determined the final Keighley pattern. Greenhead and Oakbank were to be the senior schools, but their existing accommodation was insufficient so the change was shifted from 13 to 14. The middle schools were to be housed in the technical school and the three modern schools but the extra year which they were now expected to take made their buildings in turn insufficient. Once again the borough shied away from the expense of building the extra accommodation they needed and decreed that the primary schools should remain as they were and the middle schools take children at 11. Under this revised school system children from the Haworth, Oxenhope and Stanbury primary schools would go first to Hartington as their middle school and then on to Greenhead. Experience was to show that the Leicestershire plan had inbuilt defects which made the schools within it inferior to all-through comprehensive schools, and which Keighley's bowdlerised version made very much worse. The problems of the under-funded educational system that Bradford inherited from Keighley in 1974 need to be taken into account when considering the changes which it introduced.

Measures were immediately taken to make the Keighley schools conform to the proper Leicestershire plan as in the rest of Bradford. New classrooms and facilities were provided at both Oakbank and Greenhead so that they could take the extra year. The middle schools were increased to ten in number and the oldest ones provided with long overdue new buildings. Hartington had been a particular target for criticism, being described memorably in 1976, by Bob Cryer, then the town's MP, as looking rather like the German prisoner-of-war camp, Colditz Castle. The new Hartington was to be in Haworth itself at the top of Rawdon Road.[70] Up to this point Bradford's efforts had much to commend them but the Council now made a decision that many would regard as disastrous. It seemed quite natural to the planners that the five northern middle schools should feed Greenhead and the five southern ones Oakbank. What they did not take into account was the location of the town's considerable Asian community. Under the old system Asian children attended both senior schools, with Oakbank taking relatively more than Greenhead. Under the new arrangements practically all the Asian children were transferred to the Greenhead pyramid. In 1986 roughly 20% of Greenhead's intake comprised Asian children; a decade later it was 65%.[71]

Once they were aware of the implications of Bradford's reorganisation, European parents became more and more restive and many tried to avoid at all costs having to send their children to Greenhead. Their efforts were powerfully aided by the actions of the Conservative governments of the day. Schools were instructed that if they had spare capacity when all the children within their catchment areas who wished to attend had been catered for they could offer places to children from other areas, and 'successful' schools were encouraged to build extra accommodation to take pupils who would otherwise have gone to 'unsuccessful' schools. The competitive pressure was then increased by allowing some schools to opt out of local authority control and become 'grant aided' by the government instead, which gave them more control over school policy and finance and access to extra funds. Oakbank's head teacher, John Roberts, seized the opportunity to go grant aided and successfully put in a bid for his school to be a specialist 'Sports College', which brought it an extra £800,000 for new classrooms and science laboratories. The school was 'swamped by its own success' with 1,200 pupils and bursting at the seams. Greenhead had 950 with a capacity for 300 a year but an average intake of only 230.[72]

Haworth parents could rest relatively content with what had happened. They had acquired a brand new middle school in Haworth itself, and the revised arrangements put them squarely within the Oakbank catchment area. The amount of travelling their children had to do was drastically reduced, and there was no longer any need to go down into Keighley itself to get a secondary education. Only 1% of the Worth Valley population was Asian, so Oakbank's overwhelmingly European intake also insulated them from Keighley's ethnic tensions, with John Roberts unashamedly making a pitch for the children of the European middle classes. Indeed by the late 1990s he had the excuse that his real rival was not Greenhead at all but the Cullingworth Parkside School, which was also grant aided.[73]

These changes had hardly been absorbed when there was a new twist of the educational wheel. The accession to power of the New Labour government in 1997 brought an emphasis on raising basic educational standards by means of the Standard Attainment Tests or 'Sats', which were to be taken by all pupils at the ages of 7, 11 and 14. Sats was designed to fit a system in which children changed schools at 11. The result was that Bradford found itself forced to alter its entire school system. In the Keighley area Oakbank and Greenhead were to become 11–18 comprehensives. Of the ten middle schools, seven were to be used as extra primary schools to accommodate the increase in pupils at junior level and the remaining three were to be closed. The undertaking was a massive one which needed an extensive school-building programme, the redeployment

Haworth from the Brow. Main Street rises up the picture from Hall Green chapel in the centre to the parish church, partly obscured by trees at the top right. Below the chapel and to the left is the Drill Hall. The ruined Ivy Bank Mill can be seen at the bottom left and the tracks of the Worth Valley railway come into the picture on the bottom as they pass the Bridgehouse Mill, which just squeezes onto the picture's right-hand edge.
PHOTOGRAPH: CARNEGIE, 2009

of the staffs of the now redundant middle schools and the reallocation to new schools of every child between 9 and 13. Bradford underestimated the time which would be needed to make the necessary changes and it was soon apparent that the target date of September 2000 was premature, but it pressed ahead despite repeated warnings. The resultant chaos attracted national attention, and in August 2001 the administration of all Bradford schools was put in the hands of a private company, Serco QAA.[74] Haworth children did not come through unscathed, but again they probably suffered less than most. The failure to complete the buildings at Oakbank on time caused severe difficulties there for over two months, and Haworth primary schoolchildren found themselves shuttling between the former Hartington middle school and their original school in Butt Lane for a time.

Would it really have mattered educationally whether Haworth's children had attended Oakbank or Greenhead? In the Keighley years when Haworth children went to Greenhead there was a general perception that it was much the better of the two upper schools, and its examination results were certainly superior, but closer inspection reveals a rather different picture. Greenhead's intake included the former technical school students who were of a higher calibre than those of the modern schools, so better results were to be expected. Even when these students had passed through the system the arrangement by which Greenhead took pupils from the peripheral regions of the Keighley borough gave them an in-built advantage over Oakbank because its intake from the central core had a lower initial attainment level. In the Bradford years the reverse was the case. The lower attainment levels at entry, particularly of Asian students, whose home language was not English, put Greenhead at a decided disadvantage, so the change to Oakbank again appeared to put Haworth children in the superior school. Yet when the value added system of assessment was used for the first time in 2003 Greenhead produced better figures than either Oakbank or the Roman Catholic comprehensive school, Holy Family, or the neighbouring South Craven comprehensive school.[75] There is little prospect that the evidence will sway many European parents. What they want are schools that reflect their own family values, not community ones which force their children to face the realities of multi-cultural Britain, and Asian parents left to themselves act in a similar way. In 2006 Haworth primary school was still receiving children from East Morton in the far north-east of the old borough whose parents were desperate to get them away from Greenhead and into the Oakbank pyramid.[76] Greenhead's intake has fallen further, and by 2007 Bradford were planning for only 180 a year in spite of the value added figures showing that Greenhead's lead had increased.[77]

Finally a school story with a nice historical twist to it. If you had been driving up to Haworth from Keighley during this turmoil you would have been assailed by placards exhorting you to 'Save Oldfield school'. This referred to Bradford's plan to close Oldfield primary school and send its children to an augmented Stanbury primary school which was to have a two-storey extension added to it to accommodate the extra pupils. There were good educational reasons for believing that both Stanbury and Oldfield children would have been better off in a school a hundred strong which could employ teachers with a variety of skills. Nonetheless, there was opposition from Oldfield, reluctant to lose its 'community' school, and from the inhabitants of Stanbury who believed that the extension would 'spoil their view.' More practically there was the transport problem. Although the two schools were not much more than a quarter of a mile apart, they were separated by the valley of the river Worth so that in order to get to Stanbury school the Oldfield children would have had to go down Pitcher Clough onto the Bradford–Colne turnpike, which had no pavements, and then up the steep hill past the Old Silent Inn into Stanbury. For young children, even in summer, walking would not be an option, so they would have to go by car which would cause serious traffic problems in Stanbury's narrow main street.[78] It was at this point that Tom Lee intervened.

Tom Lee was an American who lived in the state of Michigan. In December 1996 he bought the title of 'Lord of the Manor of Stanbury', at an auction, from Viscount Mountgarret, for £13,250. Mountgarret warned him that there was nothing left but the title; Lee was not so sure. In October 1998 he claimed that both schools were on land donated by the lord of the manor, and that if either were closed the land on which it stood would return to the donor. Bradford replied stuffily that it was aware of the position, but it did not affect the change from a three-tier to a two-tier system, which rather missed the point of what happened to the vacated site. In fact Lee's intervention gave Bradford an excuse for much needed second thoughts because there was a Schools Sites Act of 1841, confirmed as recently as 1977, which allowed *any* donor of freehold land to reclaim it if the use were changed, not just lords of the manor.[79] If Lee had any right to the land on which Oldfield school stood it was nothing to do with the 'manor of Stanbury', because Oldfield lay within the lordship of Oakworth which was anciently part of the manor of Keighley. Mountgarret was correct; it was just an empty title.[80] This too had been the experience of Frank Scholefield, titular lord of the manor of Oxenhope, when he lost his claim to waste land at Blackmoor Quarry which had been farmed for a period between 1943 and 1956 by Elliston Stirk of Earby and then left waste because the water supply had failed.[81]

There was no medieval manor of Stanbury because it was always part of the demesne of the manor of Bradford. What has happened is that that since the sale of the 1630s some subsequent lord of the manor of Bradford subinfeudated the hamlet on his own authority as a money making ploy, even though there were no rights left. This is typical of modern Haworth. It has turned into a sort of time capsule, peopled by Brontë romantics, mock feudal magnates, ghost story inventors, steam train enthusiasts, picnickers in the park and moorland walkers, but whose real industrial history is firmly in the past. Yet there are few who would wish that past back, with its grinding poverty, and in which Haworth's main asset was its abundance of cheap labour. There is a natural concern for a decline in community values, but this is countrywide, and there is unease that an area dedicated to leisure pursuits is somehow inferior to one with 'real' jobs in industry or commerce. However, for practically everyone in Haworth township, whether they are involved with the tourist trade or not, life has never been better.

Notes and references

Notes for Chapter 1: The Haworth area before the Norman Conquest

1. Talk by Arthur Raistrick at Keighley Girls Grammar School in the *Keighley News*, 22 March 1952; J. A. Gilks, 'Early Mesolithic Sites at Nab Water, Oxenhope Moor', *Yorkshire Archaeological Journal* (*YAJ*), vol. 66 (1994), pp. 1–20.

2. Steve Wood drew my attention to Armshaw Low. The geological survey casts doubt on whether the Silver Hill mound is actually a Bronze Age barrow. See also Raistrick 1952; M. L. Faull and S. A. Moorhouse, (eds), *West Yorkshire: An Archaeological Survey to AD 1500*, vol. I (West Yorkshire County Council, Wakefield, 1981), pp. 80, 82, 104.

3. The reference is to Chapter 12 in Emily Brontë, *Wuthering Heights* (Folio edn, 1997); 'Elf Bolts', *Keighley News*, 22 November 1963. For the Halifax remains see H. Ling Roth, *The Yorkshire Coiners 1767–83*, and *Notes on Old & Prehistoric Halifax* (Halifax 1906, reprint S. R. Publishers, Halifax, 1971), pp. 286–32.

4. N. J. Higham, 'Brigantia Revisited', *Northern History* (*NH*) XXIII (1987), pp. 1–19.

5. John James *Continuation and Additions to the History of Bradford and Its Parish* (Bradford 1866; reprinted E. J. Morten, 1973) p. 17; J. Horsfall Turner, *Haworth Past and Present* (Brighouse 1879; reprinted Olicana, Otley, 1972) p. 11.

6. For the Keighley Roman coin hoard see M. L. Baumber, *From Revival to Regency: Keighley and Haworth 1740–1820*, vol. I, *Industry and Communications* (Crabtrees printers, Keighley, 1982) pp. 15–16. The line of the Manchester to Aldborough road is traced in J. Norton Dickons, 'Roman Roads', *Bradford Antiquary*, (*BA*) vol. III (NS vol. I), pp. 240–54.

7. Faull and Moorhouse, *West Yorkshire: An Archaeological Survey*, p. 123.

8. For map see W. Kapelle, *The Norman Conquest of the North: The Region and its Transformation 1000–1135* (University of North Carolina Press, 1979), p. 4.

9. P. N. Wood, 'The Little Kingdom of Craven', *NH*, XXXII (1996), pp. 1–20. See map on p. 6 in particular.

10. A. Raistrick, *The Pennine Dales* (London, 1968; reprinted Arrow, 1972) p. 72 and n. 9.

11. For 'bury' names see Margaret Gelling, *Signposts to the Past* (1978; reprinted Phillimore, Chichester, 2000) p. 143.

12. M. L. Faull and Richard T. Smith, 'Three possible Dark Age ecclesiastical sites in Yorkshire', *Landscape History*, vol. 4, pp. 21–38. For the 1764 terrier see Borthwick Institute for Historical Research, University of York (BIHR) Records of Diocesan Administration Terriers E, Pontefract D. R. III xxxii E6.

13. M. L. Faull, 'Roman and Anglian Settlements in Yorkshire', *NH*, IX (1974), p. 24; Faull and Moorhouse, *West Yorkshire: An Archaeological Survey*, p. 182.

14. Kapelle, *The Norman Conquest of the North*, pp. 37–9 for Siward.

15. For articles on multiple estates see A. R. H. Baker and J. R. Harley, (eds), *Man made the Land* (David and Charles, Newton Abbot, 1973); G. R. J. Jones, *ibid.*, p. 28; See also G. R. J. Jones, 'Early Territorial Organisation in Gwynedd and Elmet', *NH*, X (1975), pp. 3–27; and G. R. J. Jones, 'Multiple Estates and Early Medieval Settlement' in P. H. Sawyer, (ed.), *English Medieval Settlement* (Arnold, London, 1979), pp. 9–34; Kapelle, *The Norman Conquest of the North*, pp. 65–85.

16. There is no study of the manor of Wakefield as a multiple estate. The deductions are mine based on Faull and Moorhouse, *West Yorkshire: An*

Archaeological Survey, pp. 216–18.

17. S. J. Chadwick, 'Notes on Dewsbury Church and Some of its Rectors and Vicars', Part I, The Church, *YAJ*, vol. 20 (1909), p. 370 gives a piece of doggerel verse by a Jacobean vicar which lists

them. See Faull and Moorhouse, *ibid.*, for more details.

18. There are many descriptions of this custom. The one I have used comes from a Haworth Ramblers report in *Nelson Leader*, 21 September 1934.

Notes for Chapter 2: Lords and manors in medieval Haworth

1. J. Le Patourel, 'The Norman Conquest of Yorkshire', *NH* VI (1971), pp. 1–21.

2. W. E. Wightman, 'The Significance of Waste in the Yorkshire Domesday,' *NH*, X (1975), pp. 51–71.

3. A. Raistrick, *The West Riding of Yorkshire* (Hodder and Stoughton, London, 1970), p. 40. For Skipton see Le Patourel, 'The Norman Conquest of Yorkshire'.

4. W. H. Wightman, W.H., *The Lacy Family in England and Normandy 1066–1194* (Oxford, Clarendon Press, 1994), pp. 48–9 and map.

5. For overstocked manors see Kapelle, *The Norman Conquest of the North*, pp. 166–75.

6. *Ibid.*, p. 198.

7. See map in Wightman, 'The Significance of Waste in the Yorkshire Domesday'.

8. Faull and Moorhouse, *West Yorkshire: An Archaeological Survey*, p. 296.

9. C. Whone, (ed.), 'Court Rolls of the Manor of Haworth', *Bradford Historical and Antiquarian Society*, *(BHAS)* Local History Series III (1946), p. vii; Faull and Moorhouse, *West Yorkshire: An Archaeological Survey*, p. 393.

10. W. Farrer, *Early Yorkshire Charters* (Ballantyne, Hanson & Co., Edinburgh, 1916–42), vol. III, p. 412; R. H. Skaife (ed.), 'Return of Knights' Fees in Yorkshire', *Surtees Society*, vol. xlix, (1867) p. 227.

11. The one-third fee of John de Horton clearly refers to Horton and Clayton, not Oxenhope which was only one-sixteenth.

12. J. James, *History of Bradford* (Bradford, 1842; reprinted E. J. Morten, Didsbury, Manchester, 1968), vol. I, pp. 49–50 gives the Inquisition. See vol. II, p. 254 for Bolling; p. 266 for Horton; p. 271 for Clayton; p. 294 for Allerton; and p. 298 for Heaton.

13. H. C. Maxwell-Fyfe (ed.), 'Calendar of Close Rolls 1307–13', PRO Rolls Series 1892, p. 315; *Surtees Society*, vol. xlix, p. 361.

14. By deduction from John Lister (transcriber), 'The Extent of the Manor of Bradford 1342', *BA*, vol. II, pp. 57–65.

15. Whone, 'Haworth Court Rolls', *BHAS*, p. viii. Jordan is first mentioned as a witness in 1209 and his latest appearance is in 1240.

16. Lister, 'Extent of the Manor of Bradford 1342', *BA*, vol. II, p. 64 for Roger and William, p. 73 for John; Skaife 'Return of Knights' Fees', p. 227 for Godfrey.

17. James, *History of Bradford*, vol. II, p. 298.

18. Lister, 'Extent of the Manor of Bradford 1342, *BA* vol. II, p. 64.

19. W. P. Baildon, 'The Early Pedigrees of the Copley Family', *Thoresby Society Miscellanea*, vol. xxvi, pp. 360–71; the 1339 is in Baildon (ed.) 'Yorkshire Deeds vol. II', *Yorkshire Archaeological Society Record Series* (*YASRS*) vol. xxxix, p. 130.

20. Baildon, 'Yorkshire Deeds', p. 202.

21. Bradford Court Roll Transcripts, (BCRT), Bradford Central Library (BCL), Local History Library, p. 137.

22. 'He gave nothing for relief because he was a purchaser.' BCRT, 1, p. 137.

23. BCRT, 3, p. 112.

24. Faull and Moorhouse, *West Yorkshire: An Archaeological Survey*, p. 393; Lay Subsidies of the West Riding, Co. York: Poll Tax second year of Richard II (1379), Wapentake and Morley, *YAJ*, vi (1879), pp. 289–90.

25. *Ibid.*, pp. 392–3; Whone, 'Haworth Manor Court Rolls', pp. ix–x.

26. Whone, Preface, p. x.

27. Baildon, 'Early Pedigree of the Copley Family Part II', *Thoresby Society Miscellanea*, vol. xxvii, pp. 195–211; Faull and Moorhouse, *West Yorkshire: An Archaeological Survey*, pp. 393–4.

28. W. Robertshaw, 'The Manor of Clayton', *BA*, vol. VIII (NS vol. vi), pp. 348–83.

Notes for Chapter 3: Fourteenth-century Haworth

1. For Horsfall Turner see *Yorkshire County Magazine*, vol. 1 (1891), p. 106; for Clifford Whone see 'Haworth Manor Court Rolls', p. 4n. I later refer to 13 similar tenements at Stanbury which

seems to suggest that there were 13 in each of Near and Far Oxenhope as well and that 4 oxgangs = 12 acres of arable land.

2. For Mill Hey see West Riding Deeds Registry at

Wakefield (WRDR), H465/575, 11/12 April 1716. Whether the woodland relates to 'Leecssheha' is disputed. Clifford Whone believed that it referred to the present Leeshaw reservoir area but the prior of Nostell had no land in Near Oxenhope. It probably refers to a wood near Lees on the Haworth/Far Oxenhope boundary, see W. P. Baildon (ed.), 'West Yorkshire Deeds', *Bradford Historical and Antiquarian Society* (*BHAS*) vol. II (1935), No. 120, p. 142, 139. For a discussion of the different interpretations of this document see R. Hindley, *Oxenhope: The Making of a Pennine Community* (privately published, Oxenhope, 2004), p. 15

3. WRDR, G147/155, 9–10 April 1714; Emmott Estate Plan 1769.

4. At Kildwick which was much better land the villeins lived on rye bread.

5. Lister 'Extent of the Manor of Bradford', *BA*, vol. I, p. 63.

6. *Ibid.*

7. James, *History of Bradford*, p. 49n; Denis Thompson, *Stanbury, A Pennine Country Village*, (privately published, 2002), p. 3.

8. WRDR, GG248/347, 20 December 1734; and KK45/58, 7–8 December 1736.

9. Lecture first reported in *Keighley News*, 11 February 1950 and repeated 8 December 1951. A further article in *Keighley News*, 13 February 1954.

10. K. Emsley, 'The Chapelry of Haworth,' in *Transactions of the Brontë Society* (*TBS*), vol. 20, pt 3 (1991), p. 165 gives the most up-to-date account. See also H. I. Judson's, 'The Early Clergy of Bradford', *BA*, NS vi p. 31; Horsfall Turner, *Haworth Past and Present*, p. 31; and W. T. Dixon and J. Lock, *A Man of Sorrows: The Life, Letters and Time of the Rev. Patrick Brontë 1777–1861* (Nelson, London, 1965) p. 209.

11. W. Brown (ed.), 'Yorkshire Deeds II', *YASRS*, vol. xxxix (1913), p. 198; Emsley, 'The Chapelry of Haworth'; W. Robertshaw, 'Notes on the Manningham Family', *BA*, NS vii, p. 108 gives *Inquisitions quod damnum 11th Edward III*, 239/25, as the source.

12. BCRT, Bradford Reference Library, I, p. 72 and 2, p. 92, for Haworth; 3, p. 91 for Oxenhope.

13. BCRT, 1, pp. 37, 42 and 51 for distraining; 1, pp. 74, 76 and 79 for Smith; 1, p. 134 for Couper.

14. BCRT, 3, p. 89.

15. BCRT, 3, p. 150 and 1, p. 94.

16. BCRT, 2, pp. 32 and 71.

17. Braving, BCRT, 1, p. 7 and 10; his wife, 1, p. 65; John's wife, 1, pp. 36, 82, 98 and 2, p. 1; and Beertasters, 1, pp. 37, 90 and 98.

18. BCRT, 1, p. 13 for John; 1, p. 89 and 2, p. 2 for tithes; 3, p. 92 for the plough dispute.

19. BCRT, 1, pp. 108–9 for Saltonstall; 2, pp. 16–17 for the bees; and 3, p. 97 for the horse and p. 113 for the stag.

20. BCRT, 1, p. 89 for the Smith case; 2, p. 131 for William; 3, p. 73 for sheep worrying; 3, p. 88 for waggon path; and 3, p. 122 for the ditches.

21. The three cases can be found at BCRT, 1, p. 49 and 72 and 3, p. 88.

22. For Margaret BCRT, 1, p. 20; Cecilia, 2, pp. 69 and 71; Avicia, 2, p. 98 and 121.

23. BCRT, 1, pp. 143–4; 2, pp. 7, 23, 24, 54, 62, 68–9 and 97.

24. A. E. Stamp (ed.), 'Calendar of Close Rolls 1259–61', PRO Rolls Series (1934), p. 20, m. 17.

25. Lister, 'Extent of the Manor of Bradford', *BA*, vol. I, pp. 57–65.

26. J. C. Holt, *Robin Hood* (Thames and Hudson, London, 1982; reprinted 1989) particularly pp. 103–5 and 128.

27. Article by JS (Joe Stobbs?) in *Keighley News*, 10 June 1967.

28. Ian Kershaw, 'The Scots in the West Riding 1318–19', *NH*, XVII (1981), pp. 231–9.

29. Maxwell-Fyfe, 'Calendar of Close Rolls 1307–13', PRO Rolls Series (1934), p. 315; *Surtees Society*, vol. xlix, p. 361. Philippa was still in possession when the Court Rolls begin.

30. Judson, 'The Early Clergy of Bradford', *BA*, NS vol. vi, pp. 31–40; *Surtees Society*, vol. 145, p. 157, No. 358.

31. BCRT, 1, pp. 116–17; and 3, p. 25.

32. BCRT, 2, pp. 140; and 3, p. 91–2.

33. BCRT, 1, p. 89; 2, p. 25, 27, 32, 38 and 39; 2, p. 8 and 58.

34. BCRT, 1, pp. 130, 134–5; 2, p. 140.

35. BCRT, 2, p. 61; 3, p. 63.

Notes for Chapter 4: The collapse of manorial authority

1. H. Heaton, *The Yorkshire Woollen and Worsted Industries* (Oxford University Press, 1965), p. 21; John James, *History of Bradford*, p. 32.

2. Heaton, *The Yorkshire Woollen and Worsted Industries*, p. 22.

3. *Ibid.*, pp. 71–4.

4. *Ibid.*, p. 133.

5. Borthwick Institute for Historical Research, University of York (BIHR) PR, vol. 15.1, fol. 101, 22 October 1556. Will of Richard Pighells, 1

October 1556. All the wills referred to come from these registers unless otherwise stated.

6. Richard Hoyle (ed.), 'Early Tudor Craven', *YASRS*, vol. cxlv (1987), Introduction.

7. For all except Haworth see B. Jennings (ed.), *Pennine Valley: A History of Upper Calderdale* (Smith Settle, Otley, 1992), p. 49. For Haworth see James J. Cartwright (transcriber) 'A Subsidy roll for the Wapentakes of Agbrigg and Morley of the 15th Year of Henry VIII', (1542), *YAJ*, vol. 2, p. 45; '1545', *Thoresby Society Miscellanea*, vol. xi (1904), pp. 333–7 and 360–8; '1546', PRO E179/207/185.

8. *Halifax Guardian*, 22 November 1856, p. 6.

9. James, *History of Bradford*, p. 39.

10. Lister, '1342 Extent', *BA*, vol. I, pp. 57–65; '1379 Poll Tax', *YAJ*, vol. vi (1881) pp. 289–90.

11. *BCRT*, 4, pp. 81, 89, 101–2 and 106.

12. C. Whone, 'Haworth Manor Court Rolls', *BHAS*, Local Series III (1946), pp. 1–2 and 12–3.

13. The numbers should be treated simply as indicators. Families present at the beginning naturally have more references than those which come later in the period covered and it is possible for a family having just one branch to be more important than those with many.

14. The locations are based on the work of George Redmonds, *Yorkshire Surnames Series*, Part One, *Bradford and District* (1990); Part Three, *Halifax and District* (2001).

15. William Shackleton, *Four Hundred Years of a West Yorkshire Moorland Family: The Heatons of Ponden* (Pudsey, 1921), p. 8, unpublished copy in West Yorkshire Archives, Bradford (WYAB).

16. PRO, E101/62/8.

17. Keighley Local Studies Library (KLSL), BK 10/223, 224, 225, 226.

18. Malcolm Birdsall, 'Vernacular Buildings of Haworth', in *Annual Conference Report of the West Yorkshire Vernacular Building Group* (2000), p. 8.

19. Whone, 'Haworth Manor Court Rolls', *BHAS*, pp. 2, 5, and 7.

20. Shackleton, *Four Hundred Years of a West Yorkshire Moorland Family*, p. 5.

21. *Yorkshire Vernacular Building Study Group – Ponden Hall Recording*, 28 June 2003, pp. 16–17. I do not think Ponden was occupied in the fourteenth century as the report tries to infer.

22. Alison Armstrong and Arnold Pacey, *High Bradley: Architecture and History*, (Addingham and Bradley, 2001), particularly p. 122.

23. R. C. M. Thornes, *West Yorkshire 'A Noble Scene of Industry': The Development of the County 1500–1830* (Wakefield, 1981), p. 7; Jennings, *Pennine Valley*, pp. 52–3.

24. K. MacCutcheon, 'Yorkshire Fairs and Markets', *Thoresby Society* (1940), pp. 67 and 110–1.

25. W. Collins (ed.), 'Yorkshire Tudor Fines I', *YASRS*, vol. II (1887), p. 266; 'Yorkshire Tudor Fines II', *YASRS*, vol. V, pp. 93, 102 and 124.

26. Collins, 'Yorkshire Tudor Fines II', *YASRS*, vol. V, p. 127 also WYAB, *Ferrand Papers*, B60; J. Lister, 'Elizabethan Halifax', *Transactions of the Halifax Antiquarian Society (THAS)*, xxi (1921), p. 44.

27. W. A. Brigg, (ed.), 'Yorkshire Stuart Fines I', *YASRS*, vol. LIII, p. 181.

28. Brigg, (ed.), 'Yorkshire Stuart Fines II', *YASRS*, vol. LVII, pp. 113–14. As noted earlier the brief information makes it difficult to reconcile the 9 messages sold with the 8 of 1579. One may have been a mortgage.

29. W. Collins (ed.) 'Yorkshire Tudor Fines', vol. iii, *YASRS*, p. 82.

30. *Ibid.*, p. 120

31. *Ibid.*, p. 82, 120 and 189.

32. *Ibid.*, 'Yorkshire Tudor Fines III, Michaelmas 1587', vol. VII, *YASRS*, p. 85.

33. *Inquisitio Post Mortem of Christopher Holmes 1614* shows Eltofts still Lord.

34. Preamble to the Jury's verdict 20 September 1629, WYAB, *Heaton Papers*, B121.

35. Joseph Craven, *A Moorland Village and its People: A History of Stanbury*, pp. 5–6; James, *History of Bradford*, pp. 118–9; H. F. Killick, 'The Duchy of Lancaster and the Manor of Bradford', *BA*, NS vol. iii (1912) particularly pp. 23–5.

36. WYAB, *Heaton Papers*, B123.

37. *Ibid.*, B127 has details of a legal opinion on the issue.

38. *Ibid.*, B122 specifically excepts them from the bargain.

39. Craven, *A Moorland Village* ..., p. 5 and 10. The Jury Verdict in *Heaton Papers*, B121 lists 20 different holdings, so Craven's schedules are not complete but you can see the process at work in them.

40. See the Borthwick probate registers as above.

41. Birdsall, 'Vernacular Buildings of Haworth', p. 7.

42. KLSL, *Brigg Collection*, 250, 254 and 257.

43. WYAB, *Heaton Papers*, B2.

1. Horsfall Turner, *Haworth, Past and Present*, pp. 32–4. Dates are based on them witnessing wills, and so are only approximate.

2. University of York, Borthwick Institute for Historical Research, (BIHR), proved 10 August 1536.

3. BIHR, Probate Register, 13B, fol. 869, 16 August 1543.

4. BIHR, Probate Register, 21B, fol. 433, 15 September 1580.

5. BIHR, Probate Register, 24A, fol. 277, 6 May 1590. The following analysis of the preambles is based on Anne Duffin, *Faction and Faith: Politics and Religion of the Cornish Gentry before the Civil War* (University of Exeter Press, 1996) pp. 43–4.

6. BIHR, Probate Registers, PR 40B fol. 333, for Naylor, not proved until 9 February 1629; PR 41B fol. 527, for Stansfield.

7. The date 1488 was given at hearings of the consistory court about the 1879 application for a faculty to knock the church down. See chapter 14.

8. BIHR Probate Register 15 fol. 207; Horsfall Turner, *Haworth, Past and Present*, p. 34.

9. Horsfall Turner, *Haworth, Past and Present*, p. 35.

10. BIHR, *Cause Papers*, H2452. Ambrose Sutcliffe estimated it was 55 years earlier, H2570.

11. *Keighley News*, 8 January 1955.

12. A. F. Leach, 'Early Yorkshire Schools vol. II', *YASRS*, vol. xxxiii (1908), p. 33. See also K. Emsley, 'Chapelry of Haworth', in *Transactions of the Brontë Society* (*TBS*) (1991), vol. 20, pt iii, p. 165. A. Holroyd, *Collectiana Bradfordiana* (Saltaire, 1873), p. 135 quotes an Ecclesiastical Survey from the reign of Henry VIII.

13. For the text see WYAB, MM 1/a/2, 18 December 1559.

14. W. Aveling, 'Catholic Recusants of the West Riding of Yorkshire', *Leeds Philosophical and Literary Society Proceedings*, vol. x, pt vi (1963), p. 300.

15. Doris and Arthur Greenwood, *St Mary's Church Elland* (privately printed, Elland, 1954), p. 47.

16. BIHR, *Primary Visitation of Archbishop Neile 1632*, fol. 155r, Haworth.

17. WYAB, *Heaton Papers*, B16. A Lay for money disbursed about Infranchising the Churchland.

18. *Ibid.*, B17. A lay for Tithes on the New Lands; Holroyd, *Collectiana Bradfordiana*, A Valuation of Bradford Rectory and Vicarage, pp. 136–7.

19. BIHR, *Cause Papers*, H3828.

20. Information unclear but the general consensus appears to be that John and Christopher were brothers not cousins. Turner, *Haworth, Past and Present*, p. 35 gives 1635 for the establishment of the free school.

21. W. P. Baildon, (ed.), 'Miscellanea vol. I', *YASRS*, vol. lxi (1920), p. 96, Knighthood Fines.

22. WYAB, *Heaton Papers*, B71.

23. K. Rock, (ed.), 'The Protestation of the Commons 1641' *BA*, NS, part 47 (1982), p. 145.

24. Yorkshire Archaeological Society, (*YAS*), Fawkes Papers. Typed copy of lay in possession of the author, originally provided by Sarah Fermi.

25. YAS, DD 146 Box 9 No.1 Marriage Settlement 19 February 1635/6.

26. H. P. Kendall, 'The Civil War as affecting Halifax and the surrounding Towns, Part III, (concluding)', *THAS*, vol. xi (1911), p. 84.

27. The exact date is unknown but it was after the execution of the deed in note 32.

28. WYAB, *Heaton Papers*, A160.

29. *Yorkshire Parish Register Society*, (*YPRS*), vol. 27 (1906); G. E. Lumb, (ed.), *Rothwell Parish Register, vol. I*, p. 102, 13 May 1613, bap. Henry, son of Thomas Casson; p. 112, 1 December 1622, bap. Henry, son of Peter Casson.

30. Background Notes for 1979 Yorkshire TV programme, *The Brontë Connection*, copy in the Library at Brontë Parsonage Museum, Haworth. I have so far been unable to find where Mrs Butterfield obtained her information.

31. WYAB, *Heaton Papers*, A108. John Parker of Extwisle; J. Midgley, Headley, 30 November 1640.

32. Will of Robert Heaton, 22 February 1641 lists his sons as Michael, Jonas and Joseph. And his natural sons as John, Robert, Peter, James and Nathan.

33. WYAB, *Heaton Papers*, A135, 23 August 1650.

34. Garforth and Currer deeds 1617–82. Photocopy in possession of author.

35. WYAB, *Heaton Papers*, B65 18 February 1650/1.

36. *Ibid.*, A164 and A160.

37. *Ibid.*, A149.

38. *Ibid.*, A152.

39. *YPRS*, vol. 82 (1927); W. A. Brigg, (ed.), *Keighley Parish Registers II*, mar. 20 September 1685; *West Yorkshire Archives Calderdale Halifax Register*, (microfilm) bap. 19 January 1687; BIHR, wills and inventories. Tombstone gives his age as 78.

40. WYAB, *Heaton Papers*, Quitclaim A446, Will A448.

41. BIHR, *Cause Papers*, H5982. Answers of Edmund Garforth reveals this man's existence. John James in his *History of Bradford* misdated the Commonwealth Church Survey of 1650 to 1655, an error

which Turner copied. They therefore assumed that Garforth preceded Towne as perpetual curate when it was the other way round.

42. Horsfall Turner, *Haworth, Past and Present*, p. 40.
43. Rev. Bryan Dale, *Yorkshire Puritanism and Early Nonconformity*, T. G. Crippen (ed.) (Congregational History Society, 1909), p. 157, prints his denial before the Bishop of Chester in 1640 and p. 158 quotes from his pamphlet on free grace.
44. Horsfall Turner, *Haworth, Past and Present*, pp. 40–1.
45. BIHR, *Cause Papers*, H2452. Evidence of Edmund Garforth.
46. KLSL, *Brigg Papers*. Transcript of the Keighley Quarterly Minute Book, 1717–20, pp. 89–90.
47. See the *Nelson Leader*, 21 July 1933 for Stanbury visit. See also *Keighley News*, 23 November 1905.
48. For a history of the Keighley Meeting see M. L. Baumber, *A Pennine Community on the Eve of the Industrial Revolution: Keighley and Haworth 1660–1740* (Crabtrees, Keighley, 1977), pp. 122–9.
49. BIHR, Visitation 1667 Pontefract gives date as 23 November 1660. *Cause Papers*, H5982 28 x pub. September 1660 for Collier's appointment; A. M. Gibbon, *History of Ermysted's Grammar School, Skipton* (Liverpool, 1947) for his period there. The rest of the background is from Robin Greenwood, *History of the West Lane and Hall Green Baptist Churches* (mss, London, 2002), p. 25 and note 34, pp. 138–42.
50. WYAB, *Heaton Papers*, B72 and B73 for Moore; Horsfall Turner, *Haworth, Past and Present*, p. 43 for Margerison.

51. J. Horsfall Turner (ed.), *The Diaries of Oliver Heywood 1630–1702*, 4 vols. (Brighouse, 1885), vol. IV, p. 194 and vol. II, p. 272.
52. Horsfall Turner, *Haworth, Past and Present*, p. 40, quoting the Haworth registers.
53. BIHR, Visitation 1662–63, Court Book 1, p. 69; and Turner, *ibid.*, p. 41.
54. 'List of Yorkshire Recusants', March 1665/6, *Surtees Society*, xl (1861), p. 137. Editor erroneously thought they were Roman Catholics.
55. BIHR, Visitation 1667, Pontefract, fol. 68v.
56. 'List of Yorkshire Recusants', *Surtees Society*, xl (1861) p. 166.
57. BIHR, Visitation 1674, Craven fol. 45a, under Keighley.
58. BIHR, Visitation 1682, Pontefract Court Book, p. 62. Widdop was presented in Keighley in 1674.
59. BIHR, Visitation 1684–85, Pontefract and Doncaster Court Book, fol. 42.
60. BIHR, *Cause Papers*, H2456.
61. Lay for the repair of Bradford parish church only lists for Stanbury and Far Oxenhope. Evidence of Richard Greene, clerk, was that the cost was £200. Haworth traditionally a fifth. Material about the case drawn from BIHR, *Cause Papers*, H2452, 2454, 2456 and 2570.
62. James, *History of Bradford*, p. 208.
63. BIHR, *Cause Papers*, H3828 Pollard v. Roberts, unless otherwise stated.
64. WYAB, 51D81/41, Rev. T. W. Story, *Notes from Old Haworth Registers*; reprinted from Parish Magazines, Keighley 1908, 26 January 1656/7.
65. BIHR, Visitation 1667, Pontefract under Haworth.

Notes for Chapter 6: The dual economy

All of the inventories except two come from Borthwick Institute for Historical Research (BIHR). Robert Heaton's can be found in the West Yorkshire Archive Bradford (WYAB), *Heaton Papers*, B5 and that of Richard Pollard in the BCL, Local History Studies Section Case 31, Box 3 Item 31. The date given is the appraisal date.

1. 1666 Hearth Tax, PRO, E179/210/3949. Inventory of Richard, 6 March 1702. John was the subject of a legal case during 1714–15, Gawkroger v. The trustees of the school and Appleyard. BIHR, *Cause Papers*, I, 250, 331 and 569.
2. Horsfall Turner, *Haworth, Past and Present*, p. 21. For the Midgleys of Oldfield see Baumber, *A Pennine Community on the Eve of the Industrial Revolution*, for example pp. 24–6.
3. *YAS*, DD146/19 Box 1.
4. *Ibid.*
5. WYAB, *Heaton Papers*, B21, 1 September 1704.
6. Inventory, 27 August 1735. Emsley, K. *Haworth Today*, Bradford Library Services. Bradford 1995

p91
7. George Taylor jun., 27 March 1702; Heaton, 29 March 1714; Crabtree, 29 June 1723.
8. Taylor, Heaton and Crabtree see note 7; William Rishworth 8 February 1695; John Heaton of Oldsnap, 26 March 1700.
9. George Taylor snr. 21 June 1694; John Smith, 8 April 1710; Michael Brigg, 7 November 1723; Richard Whitfield, 25 February 1726; John Hey 15 February 1737.
10. See note 7 for Taylor; Timothy Pighells, 20 July 1693; Barnard Hartley 22 February 1697; John Binns, 7 February 1719; Michael Hartley, 21 October 1720; WYAB, *Greenwood Papers*, 59 and

11. Heaton, see note 7, Rishworth see note 8; Jonas Denby 16 December 1719, John Fether, 5 July 1729.

12. 25 October 1708.

13. Ambrose Hey, 23 March 1693; John Sutcliffe, 6 April 1693; Thomas Fether, 2 January 1694; David Greenwood, 9 December 1696; John Rishworth, 30 October 1697; Robert Heaton, 27 October 1696; Jonas Wheelwright, 20 November 1696; James Rishworth, 27 July 1699; Sarah Wright, 21 April 1698; Jonas Briggs, 28 August 1701; William Heaton, 19 March 1708; Caleb Heaton, 27 November 1712; William Ogden (Sawood), 19 March 1714; Thomas Rishworth, 23 June 1719; John Sharp, 7 April 1742; William Ogden (S. Nab), 19 April 1742; William Sagar, 18 February 1743; Timothy Holmes, 30 October 1750.

14. John Rawson, 3 July 1702; John Crabtree, 29 June 1723; Isaac Dewhirst, 16 August 1730.

15. Adam Wright, 7 February 1735; Robert Craven, 30 June 1737.

16. 1666, see note 1.

17. From a transcript in (KLSL), Original PRO; Yorkshire Vernacular Buildings Study Group, Report No. 1666, 28 June 2003; Ponden Hall, Haworth, pp. 10, 16–7.

18. Ogden, see note 13; Heaton see note 7.

19. The revised Folio edition of 1997, c1, p. 12.

20. Robert Pighells, probate granted 2 April 1722; Jane Sutcliffe, 1 June 1692; Richard Pollard has a silver cup and spoon, John Holmes has 14 spoons, Timothy Pighells, 2 silver spoons.

21. John Smith and George Taylor see note 9; Sara Smith 30 December 1700.

22. See note 19

23. *Keighley News*, 2 February 1935.

24. Richard Pollard and Robert Heaton, see introductory note; George Taylor note 9; Christopher Holmes, 12 May 1963; John Heaton; Oldsnap, 25 October 1708; Joseph Midley, 12 June 1690.

25. Christopher Holmes see note 24.

26. Yorkshire Vernacular Buildings Study Group, Annual Conference 2000: *The Vernacular Buildings of Haworth*, pp. 5–6, 14–7.

27. Yorkshire Vernacular Buildings Study Group,

Ponden Hall, p. 19.

28. *Thoresby Society Miscellanea*, vol. xi (1904), pp. 333–7 and 360–81 for 1545 subsidy; Fairfax Lay 1643, *YAS*, Fawkes Papers; Stanbury Lay c.1640; WYAB, *Heaton Papers*, B22; 1662 poll tax, see n.1; 1666 hearth tax 1689 poor relief, *Heaton Papers*, B20; 1704 poor relief, *Heaton Papers*, B33.

29. H. P. Kendall, 'The Civil War as affecting Halifax and the Surrounding Towns', *THAS*, (1931), pp. 1–28. *Halifax Guardian* 29 November 1856, p. 6.

30. Baumber, *A Pennine Community on the Eve of the Industrial Revolution*, p. 107.

31. C. D. Rogers, *The Lancashire Population Crisis 1623* (Manchester University Education Department, 1975), see also P. Laslett, 'Did the Peasantry Starve?' in *The World we have Lost further explained* (Methuen, 3rd edn, 1983), pp. 122–53.

32. *Leeds Mercury*, 10 February 1784; E. Le Roy Ladurie, *Times of Feast, Times of Famine: A history of climate since the year 1,000* (Eng. Edn, George Allen & Unwin, 1972), pp. 129–227; T. W. Story, *Notes on Old Haworth Registers*, pp. 6–7 and 13–15, and Horsfall Turner, *Haworth, Past and Present*, pp. 37–40.

33. R. Scholfield and A. Wrigley, *The Population History of England 1540–1840* (Cambridge University Press, 1989), Appendix 9, pp. 638–44.

34. Gale's account is among his papers at KLSL.

35. R. W. Hoyle (ed.), *Lord Thanet's Benefaction to the Poor of Craven in 1685* (Friends of Giggleswick, 1978), p.xi. Poor burials calculated from the Keighley burial registers now in KLSL.

36. The original of pew assignations is in the Bradford Cathedral Archives; there are copies in Horsfall Turner, *Haworth, Past and Present*, pp. 46–8; Holroyd, *Collecteana Bradfordiana*, pp. 175–6; WYAB, *Heaton Papers*, B21 for Poor Rate Assessment.

37. Heaton, see intro.; Yorkshire Vernacular Buildings Study Group, Ponden Hall, p. 21; Wright, see note 15.

38. Daniel Defoe, *A Tour through England and Wales 1724–26* (Everyman edn, 1962; reprinted 1966) vol. ii, p. 193ff.

39. Horsfall Turner, *Haworth, Past and Present*, pp. 48–9. A more detailed analysis is not possible as Haworth was part of Bradford.

Notes for Chapter 7: The evangelical revival

1. Horsfall Turner (ed.), *The Journals of Oliver Heywood 1630–1702*, vol. I, p. 158. A comparison of dates confirms me in my conviction that Edmund Robinson, the notorious coiner, was never the perpetual curate of Haworth. For a detailed examination of the evidence see Greenwood,

History of the West Lane and Hall Green Baptist Churches, p. 28.

2. Bradford Cathedral Archives (BCA), *Bradford Churchwardens Accounts 1667–1728*. Lists of pewholders are in BCA; Horsfall Turner, *Haworth Past and Present*, pp. 47–8; Holroyd, *Collectiana Bradfordiana*, pp. 175–6.

3. BIHR, *Cause Papers*, I, 652 and BCA as note 2.

4. Horsfall Turner, *Haworth Past and Present*, pp. 45–6.

5. BIHR, *Cause Papers*, I, 250, 331 and 569. It may be the same as the nineteenth-century Balcony family.

6. G. H. Smith, 'The Smiths of Halifax', *THAS* vol. xlix (1949), pp. 74–9. Greenwood, *History of West Lane and Hall Green Baptist Churches*, p. 32–3 quotes James Ford, 'Bromsgrove: A Seventeenth Century Baptist Church', *Transactions of the Baptist Historical Society*, vol. 1, no. 2 (1909), p. 106.

7. WYAB, 51D81/02, quoted by Horsfall Turner, *Haworth Past and Present*, p. 49.

8. WYAB, *Heaton Papers*, B81, B84, B88, B92 for Stanbury farms 1704–13; Salterforth rents 1704–15 in B80–98 probably represent the rent charge bought with the Scott money.

9. BIHR, *Glebe Terriers*, dated 1698, 1716, 1727 and 1743 exist. None of them lists a parsonage house so Sowdens was clearly not adopted despite Smith's efforts.

10. For his lecture see *Keighley News*, 11 February 1950.

11. Lawrence Stone, *The Road to Divorce, 1530–1837* (OUP, 1991), pp. 96–110 for clandestine marriages.

12. Horsfall Turner, *Haworth Past and Present*, p. 49 is a year wrong; he has forgotten that until 1752 it began on 25 March.

13. West Yorkshire Archives, Wakefield (WYAW), Quarter Sessions (QS), Order Books 10/9 and 10/10; KRL, Quaker Minute Book (QMB), I, p. 3.

14. QMB, I, pp. 15, 16, 68.

15. QMB, I, pp. 9, 10–11 and 25.

16. QMB, 16 June and 18 September 1723.

17. M. L. Baumber, *A Pennine Community on the Eve of the Industrial Revolution*, pp. 122–9.

18. Greenwood, *History of the West Lane and Hall Green Baptist Chapels*, p. 32, quotes W. H. Whitley, *The Baptists of North West England 1649–1913* (Kingsgate Press, London, and G. Toulmin and Sons, Preston, 1913), pp. 72–3.

19. Greenwood, *ibid.*, p. 32–3, quotes James Ford, 'Bromsgrove: A Seventeenth Century Baptist Church', *Transactions of the Baptist Historical Society*, vol. 1, no. 2 (1909), p. 106.

20. WYAW, QS, Order Books 10/9 for John Rhodes and QS10/10 for North Ives in the name of Thomas Feather. See also Greenwood, *ibid.*, p. 33; also note 5 on pp. 151–2 for John Moore.

21. Evan Lewis, *History of the Bethesda Baptist Church Barnoldswick, Yorkshire* (Cwmavon, 1893), pp. 16–41.

22. S. L. Ollard and P. C. Walker (eds), 'Archbishop Herring's Visitation Returns 1743', vol. II, *YASRS*, vol. lxxi, pp. 39–41.

23. WYAB, *Heaton Papers*, B101, B102 and 51D81/02, p. 311. The dispute lasted nearly a year.

24. Frank Baker, *Life of William Grimshaw* (Epworth Press, London 1963), p. 72; Faith Cook, *William Grimshaw of Haworth* (Banner Press, Edinburgh, 1997), pp. 74–6.

25. J. W. Laycock, *Methodist Heroes of the Great Haworth Round 1734–84* (Wadsworth & Co. the Rydal Press, Keighley, 1909), pp. 39–43.

26. N. Curnock (ed.), *Journals of John Wesley*, 4 vols. (Robert Culley, London, 1909–16), vol. iii, p. 234, 25 February 1746.

27. Baker, *Life of William Grimshaw*, p. 106.

28. *Ibid.*, p. 131 & 177.

29. *Ibid.*, p 132.

30. Cook, *William Grimshaw of Haworth*, p. 139.

31. Ollard and Walker, 'Archbishop Herring's Visitation Returns 1743'. See also Cook, *ibid.*, p. 95; Baker, *Life of William Grimshaw*, p. 120; and J. Newton, *Memoirs of the Life of the late William Grimshaw in Six Letters to the late Rev. Henry Foster*, Letter Five, pp. 84–5 for the benediction story.

32. Baker, *ibid.*, p. 120, 124.

33. Cook, *William Grimshaw of Haworth*, p. 103.

34. Baker, *Life of William Grimshaw*, p. 214; Newton, *Memoirs of the Life of William Grimshaw*, pp. 92–3; Articles in *Keighley News*, 13 February 1954, 27 January 1962, and 23 June 1972.

35. Baker, *Life of William Grimshaw*, pp. 133–7; Laycock, *Methodist Heroes …*, pp. 53–9; Curnock, *Journals of John Wesley*, vol. iii pp. 369–72.

36. M. E. Snape, 'Anti Methodism in Eighteenth-Century England: The Pendle Forest Riots 1748', *Journal of Ecclesiastical History*, vol. 49, no. 2 (1998), pp. 258–81.

37. WYAW, QS Records 1751–55, fol. 120. The quotation is from Holroyd, *Collectiana Bradfordiana*, p. 25.

38. BIHR, *Cause Papers*, I, 1375, Faculty Book 1736–68, pp. 245–8. A list of pewholders in the new chapel is in BCL, Local History Section, Case 30,

Box 5, Item 1.

39. Lists of pew sales in Haworth Parish Registers for late eighteen and early nineteenth centuries under various dates when they changed hands.

40. Baker, *Life of William Grimshaw*, p.108–10 for typical movement patterns.

41. Laycock, *Methodist Heroes ...*, pp.149–51.

42. *Ibid.*, pp.185–91; Baker, *Life of William Grimshaw*, p.252–3.

43. Baker, *Life of William Grimshaw*, p.249.

44. *Ibid.*, p.270.

45. See Greenwood, *History of the West Lane and Hall Green Baptist Chapels*, pp.41–6 for a more detailed account.

46. BIHR, Drummond, *Primary Visitation Returns 1764*, vol.II, fol. 5r; Alec Charlton and

G. H. Richards, *Those Two Hundred Years: West Lane Baptist Chapel 1748–1948* (Haworth, 1948), pp.3, 6.

47. Newton, *Memoirs of the Life of the late William Grimshaw ...*, p.77. The others were John Fawcett and John Parker, later pastor of Barnoldswick.

48. Laycock, *Methodist Heroes ...*, p.276; Greenwood, *History of the West Lane and Hall Green Baptist Chapels*, p.47.

49. In 1764 Richardson was residing at Huddersfield, and Haworth was administered by a curate, Mr Bliss, see BIHR, Primary *Visitation Returns of Archbishop Drummond 1764*, vol.II, fl5v, but he was certainly there by 1781 when he exhibited his license, see BIHR, *Exhibit Book, Leeds 1781*.

50. Laycock, *Methodist Heroes ...*, p.299.

Notes for Chapter 8: The pace quickens

1. *Keighley News*, 8 February 1964.

2. BCL, Local History Section, WYAW, *Bradford Local Acts vol.I*. Unless otherwise stated the information is from minute books, Box 50, 1755–1782, and Box 8, 1804–23 and 1783–99.

3. Minute Book, 25 July 1755. In an earlier book I credited Grimshaw incorrectly with £500.

4. WYAW, Quarter Sessions (QSI), 38, fols 264r–v, Leeds; 5 October 1775.

5. WYAW, 35, fols 268v–9r, Bradford; and 1769–71, fol. 228r, Wetherby.

6. George Sowden, *Recollections of the Brontës* (Hebden Bridge Parochial Magazine Aug.-Nov.1894; reprinted Angria Press, Todmorden, 2005), p.5.

7. Minute Book, p.193.

8. Minute Books, 23 September 1773, 27 December 1781 and 2 September 1807. Sarah Fermi drew my attention to the Ramsdens and the sale to the Emmotts.

9. BCL, Local History Section, WYAW, B11, p.199, and A3 for the award itself. WYAB, *Greenwood Papers*, 82, 85.

10. *Leeds Mercury*, 14 September 1773 for final submissions' date.

11. Gary Firth, *Bradford and the Industrial Revolution* (Ryburn Publishing, Halifax, 1990), pp.30–1.

12. PRO, HO67/26, Crop Returns 1801, Haworth.

13. WYAB, F/T/7, has a coal lease of 4 January 1808. For South Dean see sale in *Leeds Mercury*, 18 February 1783.

14. WYAB, 94D85/10/6/2, for Copley's will; and Firth, *Bradford and the Industrial Revolution*, pp.120–2. See also Robin Greenwood, *History of the Greenwoods of Haworth*, vol.II, *Haworth*

Background (Mss, London, 1999), pp.49–50.

15. Unfootnoted details about the Greenwoods are in Greenwood, *ibid.*, vol.V, *The Bridgehouse Greenwoods*. See also Wakefield Deeds Registry, H465/574, 13 April 1716; and L412/544, 27 May 1717.

16. Deeds Registry, X423/546 and BB453/607. Also see Greenwood, *ibid.*, vol.IX, p.4.

17. Greenwood, *ibid.*, vol.V, p.18 for a description and discussion about the dating; WYAB, *Ferrand Papers*, B450, John Greenwood's will of 19 April 1770 for the lead mines; Greenwood, *ibid.*, vol.IV, *Haworth Families*, p.91.

18. See E. M. Sigsworth, 'William Greenwood and Robert Heaton: Eighteenth Century Worsted Manufacturers', in *Bradford Textile History Journal*, (1953), pp.61–72. Greenwood, *ibid.*, vol.X, Appendix III, pp.9–11, contains the inventory.

19. Greenwood, *History of the West Lane and Hall Green Baptist Chapels*, p.45 for West Lane Baptist Chapel.

20. WYAB, *Ferrand Papers*, B450, 19 April 1770.

21. Greenwood, *History of the Greenwoods of Haworth*, vol.V, p.26.

22. Mortgage of 23 November 1763 refers to the 'late' William Greenwood.

23. For the Helliwells and John Greenwood, see, for example, West Yorkshire Archives Calderdale (WYAC), RP1393 and 1632.

24. *Leeds Intelligencer*, 19 October 1773. William was the partner of John Rhodes; WYAB, *Ferrand Papers*, B454, 455, 459.

25. WYAC, SU D48/1, describes him as 'woolstapler'.

26. WYAB, *Greenwood Papers*, 53, 59, 78 and 93 for the Abraham Tillotsons.

27. Greenwood, *History of the Greenwoods of Haworth*, vol. VI, *The Old Oxenhope Greenwoods*, p. 9, quoting Greenwood's ledger. For Sarah's marriage see, *Leeds Mercury*, 1 May 1802; also Greenwood, *ibid.*, vol. VI, p. 22.

28. WYAB, *Heaton Papers*, A472.

29. WYAB William Shackleton, *Four Hundred Years of a West Yorkshire Moorland Family: A Brief Account of the History of the Heatons of Ponden House*, p. 44 mentions the tenant, Thomas Simpson.

30. Shackleton, *Four Hundred Years of a West Yorkshire Moorland Family*, p. 44. See Chapter Six for relations with the Northern Association.

31. Shackleton p. 44 is wrong. The renewal for only a year shows that he intended to return.

32. WYAB, *Heaton Papers*, B151 for his purchases between 1771 and 1790.

33. *Ibid.*, B147 for his dealings with spinners and B149 for weavers.

34. A list of pieces belonging to him at Halifax is in *Heaton Papers* B149

35. Sigsworth, 'William Greenwood and Robert Heaton', p. 67.

36. Figures worked out by Sigsworth, *ibid.*, see p. 72.

37. R. S. Fitton and A. P. Wadsworth, *The Strutts and the Arkwrights 1758–1801: A Study of the Early Factory System* (Manchester University Press, 1938), p. 93.

38. Mill details from George Ingle, *Yorkshire Cotton: The Yorkshire Cotton Industry 1780–1835* (Carnegie Publishing, 1997), pp. 162–4 unless otherwise stated.

39. WYAC, RP 2213, in 1792 he borrowed £460 from Peter Wilson of Methley Park gent.

40. WYAB, *Heaton Papers*, B150 gives details of bills of exchange.

41. Shackleton, *Four Hundred Years of a West Yorkshire Moorland Family*, p. 49.

42. WYAB, *Heaton Papers*, B154 for details; A499 describes the first mill; *Leeds Mercury*, 21 March 1795 for the fire. See also C. Aspin, *The Water-Spinners* (Helmshore Local History Society, 2003) p. 108–10.

43. *Yorkshire Vernacular Building Group: Ponden Hall, Haworth*, Recording 28 June 2003, identifies the rooms devoted to textiles and posits an extra bay. Their return to domestic functions in 1801 is my suggestion.

44. WYAC, RP1408 and 1410; Thompson, *Stanbury*, p. 115.

45. KRL, *Diary of John Kitson* (photocopy unpaginated). The diary proper only runs from 1854 to his death in 1865 and consists mainly of religious reflections on his infirmities but it is prefixed by an account of his early life.

46. See M. L. Baumber, *From Revival to Regency*, vol. I, *Industry and Communications*, pp. 35–6 for more details.

47. WYAW, QSI, vol. 45, fol. 145r, Bradford.

48. W. B. Crump, 'Ancient Highways of the Parish of Halifax: The Old Haworth Road', *THAS* vol. xxviii (1928), pp. 225–51; E. W. Watson and B. A. Gledhill, 'Wadsworth Highways Part I', *THAS*, vol. li (1951), p. 107; WYAB, *Greenwood Papers*, 87; WYAW, QSI, vol. 45, fols 305v–306r–v, Bradford, 18 July 1799.

49. *Leeds Intelligencer*, 11 July 1814; *Leeds Mercury*, 15 July 1815, 19 August 1815, 15 June 1816, 3 July 1819, 10 June 1820.

50. WYAB, 94D85/10/1/5.

51. *Leeds Mercury*, 20 June 1818, Hebden Bridge; Haworth TT Minute Book, 14 August 1805; *Leeds Mercury*, 14 August 1819.

Notes for Chapter 9: The textile revolution in Haworth

1. WYAC, RP 2127; Aspin, *The Water-Spinners*, p. 78. They appear to be the same as the three men supposed to be working 'secretly' on a machine mentioned on p. 34 but it is difficult to tell as his book has no footnotes.

2. John James, *History of Worsted Manufacturing* (Bradford, 1857, new edn Frank Cass Ltd, 1968), pp. 327–8; WYAB, *Heaton Papers*, B25 and 26 has Church lays which list him. Sometimes confused with the cotton mill at Midgehole, Hebden Bridge of 1783.

3. James, *ibid.*, p. 355.

4. Royal Commission for Historical Monuments (RCHM), H308.

5. Guildhall Lib. Royal Exchange Insurance policy, 9 January 1801, MS7253/32a, No.180991.

6. Greenwood, *History of the Greenwoods of Haworth*, vol. III, *Background on Haworth Textile Mills in Haworth*, p. 40; Horsfall Turner, *Haworth, Past and Present*, p. 140–1.

7. Greenwood, *ibid.*, vol. III, p. 41.

8. WYAB, 94D85/10/3/77; and Deeds in RCHM, H330, transcriptions by Mrs D. Kinghorn.

9. Thompson, *Stanbury*, pp. 145–50.

10. George Ingle, *Yorkshire Cotton: The Yorkshire Cotton Industry 1780–1835* (Carnegie Publishing, 1997), pp. 162–4; Aspin, *Water Spinners*, p. 112; Greenwood, *History of the Greenwoods of Haworth*,

vol. III, p. 35; Trade Directories: Baines 1822, Parsons and White 1830; *Leeds Mercury*, 16 October 1841.

11. RCHM, H330, RG III, p. 51; John Hodgson, *Textile Manufacture and other industries in Keighley* (1879, new edn Shaun Tyas, Stamford, 1999), p. 153; Trade Directories: Baines 1822, Parsons and White 1830.

12. RCHM, H311 and 324; Pigot Directories 1828 and 1834.

13. Thompson, *Stanbury*, pp. 151–3.

14. KRL, *Diary of John Kitson*; *Halifax Journal*, 12 February 1803; Aspin, *The Water Spinners*, p. 53 reproduces the advert in full.

15. Factories Inquiry commission, Supplementary Report 96, 97, 98; and 155 J. T. Ward, *The Factory Movement, 1830–55* (Macmillan, 1970), p. 25.

16. Juliet Barker, *The Brontës* (Weidenfeld and Nicolson, 1994), p. 218 and note 63; Sworn in Skipton Sessions, 28 June 1836; Justices' Qualification Oaths 1819, 37, mss.; WYAW, Prosecutions Greenwood, vol. III, *Textile Mills in Haworth*, p. 55; *Bradford Observer*, 9 October 1845; *Halifax Guardian*, 11 October 1845.

17. *Leeds Mercury*, 13 and 20 September 1834; *Leeds Intelligencer*, 4 May 1839; Ward, *The Factory Movement*, p. 215.

18. *Halifax Guardian*, 7 May 1842.

19. *Keighley News*, 15 September 1842; Robson Trade Directory 1840; KLSL, Poor Rates, September 1842 and April 1844; Pigot Trade Directory 1841.

20. *Bradford Observer*, 5 March and 2 April 1840.

21. *Ibid.*, 17 November 1842.

22. *Leeds Mercury*, 13 April 1839.

23. *Bradford Observer*, 18 August 1842.

24. *Halifax Guardian*, 20 August 1842.

25. *Keighley News*, 23 May 1927. Obituary.

26. *Ibid.*, 26 May 1928.

27. *Bradford Observer*, 25 August 1842 and *Leeds Mercury*, 27 August 1842

28. *Ibid.*, 8 and 25 September 1842; Barker, *The Brontës*, p. 402; George Sowden, *Recollections of the Brontës* (Hebden Bridge Parochial Magazine, 1894; reprinted Angria Press, Todmorden, 2005), p. 9 for when Brontë acquired the pistols.

29. RCHM, H320 says steam powered from 1844 but no boiler house listed in rates until 1854.

30. Hodgson, *Textile Manufacture and other industries in Keighley*, pp. 119–20; 1851 Census; RCHM, H332. KRL, Poor Rate, April 1844, Highways Rate 1847.

31. Greenwood, *History of the Greenwoods of Haworth*, vol. V *The Bridgehouse Greenwoods*, pp. 54–5 and vol. X, *Appendices*, pp. 57–71 for family details. There appears to be no foundation for the allegation that James Greenwood's bankruptcy was caused by railway speculation. Nor did he own Springhead. The mill there was owned by his brother, Joseph, and leased to the Merralls. See David Pearson, *How did Haworth get its Railway? A Study in Nineteenth Century Local Enterprise* (unpublished MA Dissertation, University of York), p. 19.

32. White 1847 and Slater 1848 directories; KRL, Poor Rates of April 1844 and May 1849, the Highways Rate, April 1847, and the Poor Rate Valuation of November 1851; WYAB, 94D85/10/3/98, 7 May 1850.

33. KRL, Highways Rate, April 1847, Poor Rate May 1849, October 1852 and December 1854, Poor Rate Valuation, November 1851; Directories: White 1847 and 1853, Slater 1854; *Leeds Intelligencer*, 22 November 1851; *Halifax Guardian*, 29 November 1851; Tithe Award, 1852–53 and 1851 census.

34. See Leather's allegations in *Bradford Observer*, 7 February 1856.

35. *Ibid.*, 3 June 1852; *Leeds Intelligencer*, 12 and 26 June, 7 August 1852; *Halifax Guardian*, 19 November 1853 and 7 January 1854.

36. Directories omit Lumbfoot Mill; KRL, Haworth Poor Rate, December 1854 lists it but there is no assessment.

37. *Halifax Guardian*, 4 May 1855; *Keighley News*, 18 January 1908 and note 26.

38. Despite claims of *Keighley News*, 27 January 1954, Hattersleys did not take Mytholmes until 1863.

39. *Leeds Mercury*, 31 August 1844; *Bradford Observer*, 22 August 1844.

40. *Bradford Observer*, 24 October 1844; *Halifax Guardian*, 26 October 1844; *Leeds Mercury*, 24 May 1845; Michael Baughan, *The Midland Railway, North of Leeds* (David and Charles, Newton Abbot, 1987), pp. 50, 53.

41. *Leeds Intelligencer*, 11 October 1845, Prospectus and supplement, *Leeds Mercury* and *Halifax Guardian*, same date.

42. *Bradford Observer*, 4 and 18 March 1847.

43. Barker, *The Brontës*, p. 92.

44. *Halifax Guardian*, 11 May 1861. Nine of Halifax's 22 districts showed decreases 1851–61.

1. Laycock, *Methodist Heroes* ..., pp. 194–5, 307; *Keighley News*, 28 June 1952, for Sawood.

2. *Ibid.*, p. 194.

3. N. Curnock, (ed.), *Journals of John Wesley* (Everyman edn from Robert Culley original, London 1909–16), vol. vii, p. 380n., 27 April 1788.

4. BIHR, *Faculty Book 1*, 1736–68, pp. 247–8, 22 March 1757; p. 449, 1 July 1768.

5. BIHR, *Cause Papers*, 1836, 28 January 1779.

6. KLSL, BK15/1/4c, Methodist Records, Keighley Circuit 1799–1820; *Keighley News*, 11 October 1961; *ibid.*, 28 June 1952 for return to Sawood.

7. KLSL, Methodist Records, Keighley Circuit, BK 15/1/4/c.

8. Steven Wood, *Haworth: 'A strange, uncivilised little place'* (Tempus, 2004), pp. 78–84 for Jack Kay.

9. *Leeds Intelligencer*, 25 September 1847; Margaret Smith, *Letters of Charlotte Brontë*, vol. II, 1848–51 (Clarendon Press, 2000), pp. 640–1.

10. WYAB, 3D77/23; Joseph Craven, *A Moorland Village and its People: A History of Stanbury* (Keighley, Rydal Press, 1907), pp. 40–2; *Keighley News*, 25 April 1953. See also Thompson, *Stanbury*, pp. 65–6.

11. *Keighley News*, 1 December 1928 and 22 June 1935; KLSL, BK/1/1/1/b, Sawood paid from March 1833. BK/1/1/1/c, 14 March 1836.

12. M. L. Baumber, 'Patrick Brontë and the Development of Primary Education in Haworth', *Transactions of the Brontë Society (TBS)* vol. 24, Pt. 1 (1999, pp. 66–81 for a more detailed account.

13. *Keighley News*, 18 September 1869 and 9 March 1929.

14. Rev. Henry Dowson, *A Brief Historical Account of the Churches in the Association, Circular Letter to the West Riding of Yorkshire Association of Baptist Churches* (Bradford, 1842), for Haworth see pp. 16–17; Alec Charlton and G. H. Richards, *Those Two Hundred Years: History of the West Lane Baptist Chapel 1748–1948* (privately published, Haworth, 1948), p. 3; Horsfall Turner, *Haworth, Past and Present*, pp. 113–23; *Leeds Mercury*, 17 July 1935.

15. Endowed Charities: West Riding II, 1897, pp. 189–90; KLSL, Anonymous, *Thirty-Four Years: A History of the Keighley Baptist Church* (Keighley, 1842), p. 1.

16. William Fawcett, 'Memoir of the Rev. Miles Oddy of Haworth, Yorkshire', *Baptist Magazine*, Fourth Series, vol. V (January 1842) pp. 1–5.

17. *Keighley News*, 1 December 1928 and 31 January 1942; Greenwood, *History of the West Lane and Hall Green Baptist Churches*, p. 170, n. 13.

18. Turner, *Haworth, Past and Present*, p. 123; Greenwood, *ibid*, p. 67.

19. KLSL, *Diary John Kitson*, p. 67.

20. WYAB, DB71, C7/2, *Minutes of Lancashire & Yorkshire Association 1787–1836*.

21. Juliet Barker, *The Brontës: A Life in Letters* (Viking, 1998), pp. 20–1; Barker, *The Brontës*, p. 178.

22. Andrew Elfenbein, 'The Argument between the Rev. Winterbotham and the Rev. Brontë', *TBS*, vol. 20 (1990), pp. 89–94. Relevant letters can be found in *Leeds Intelligencer*, 18 January 1834; *Leeds Mercury*, 25 January, 22 February and 18 March 1834. For the identity of Peter Pontifex see Greenwood, *History of the West Lane and Hall Green Baptist Churches*, p. 173, note 4.

23. *Leeds Intelligencer*, 6 January 1838, *Bradford Observer*, 8 and 15 February, 18 and 25 April 1844.

24. *Leeds Mercury*, 8 February 1813; *Leeds Intelligencer*, 15 and 29 January and 5 February 1829.

25. J. Horsfall Turner, *Brontëiana* (Bingley, 1898), pp. 220–32; and *Leeds Mercury*, 5 November 1836.

26. M. L. Baumber, 'The Haworth Church Rate Controversy', *YAJ*, vol. 75 (2003) pp. 115–28 gives more details.

27. WYAB, MM1/c/3–5; *Heaton Papers*, B106, 108 and 109.

28. See Barker, *The Brontës*, pp. 82–8; *Leeds Intelligencer*, 18 April 1857 for J. Hodgson Ramsbottom's Letter.

29. WYAB, 94D85/10/1/4.

30. See note 29.

31. *Bradford Observer*, 9 March 1837 and 20 April 1837.

32. KLSL, BK 217A, Chapel Admissions Register 1826–77; *Bradford Observer*, 7 July 1836.

33. *Keighley News*, 2 April 1932; *Bradford Observer*, 23 March 1837.

34. White's directory 1847, lists Cranmer; for Nicholls part see W. T. Dixon, and J. Lock, *A Man of Sorrow: Life, Letters and Time of the Rev. Patrick Brontë 1777–1861* (Nelson, London 1965), p. 328; *Nelson Leader*, 21 September 1934.

35. *Leeds Intelligencer*, 22 October 1836 and 13 July 1844; *Halifax Guardian*, 6 March 1847; Dixon and Lock, *A Man of Sorrow*, p. 327–8.

36. *Bradford Observer*, 28 December 1843; *Leeds Intelligencer*, 27 July 1844; *Bradford Observer*, 29 February 1844; *Keighley News*, 18 March 1911.

37. Horkinstone see Greenwood, *History of the West Lane and Hall Green Baptist Churches*, p. 82; and Slater Directory 1854.

38. Greenwood, *ibid.*, p. 77.

39. KLSL, BK217A, Baptist Church Meeting Book 1826–77; *Bradford Observer*, 27 March 1845 for the chapel opening; Wesleyan chapel *Leeds Mercury* 3 October 1846; organ openings 13 December 1845 and 25 June 1857; for Stanbury see *Bradford Observer* 3 and 24 July 1845, *Leeds Mercury* 22 November 1845 and 3 October 1846.

40. PRO, HO129/494. BIHR have a microfilm copy.

41. Greenwood, *History of the West Lane and Hall Green Baptist Churches*, p. 110.

42. *Leeds Intelligencer*, 18 January 1834, Brontë-Editor.

43. *Bradford Observer*, 20 November 1834; *Keighley News*, 2 July 1921, 23 July 1932, 6 July 1933, 28 July 1934 and 6 July 1935.

44. Barker, *A Life in Letters*, p. 75.

45. *Bradford Observer*, 8 February 1844 for Scoresby's letter; see also Baumber, 'Patrick Brontë and the Development of Primary Education in Haworth', *TBS*, vol. 24, Pt.1 (April 1999), pp. 66–81.

46. *Leeds Mercury*, 27 June and 4 July 1846; Concert, *Bradford Observer*, 23 July 1846.

47. *Leeds Intelligencer*, 20 October 1849; *Keighley & Haworth Argus*, 1 February 1855; Obituary, *Keighley News*, 29 November 1879 and *Keighley Herald*, 5 December 1879; *Keighley News*, 19 October 1935 and 7 February 1959.

48. Symington and Wise, *The Brontës, Their Lives, Friendships and Correspondence*, vol. I, pp. 168–9

49. *Leeds Mercury*, 29 March 1834.

50. Smith, *Letters of Charlotte Brontë*, vol. I (1829–47), p. 547, 7 October 1847; Recollections of E. P. Evans in Charles Lemon, (ed.), *Early Visitors to Haworth* (Brontë Society, 1996), p. 109; George Sowden, *Recollections of the Brontës* (1894; reprinted Angria Press, 2005), p. 2–3.

51. Barker, *The Brontës*, p. 724; *Keighley News*, 17 October 1908; Symington and Wise, *The Brontës, Their Lives and Friendships and Correspondence*, vol. IV, 833 (622) 10 March 1853 and 840 (626), pp. 57–9; Sowden *Recollections of the Brontës*, p. 2.

52. *Leeds Intelligencer*, 16 May, 6 June 1857; *Leeds Mercury*, 23 May 1857; *Halifax Guardian*, 23 May, 6 June, 4, 11 July and 18 July, 1 August 1857.

53. Sir T. Wemyss Reid, *Memoirs 1842–85* (Cassell, 1905), p. 230. I am grateful to Sarah Fermi for drawing my attention to this reference.

54. Symington and Wise, *The Brontës, Their Lives, Friendships and Correspondence*, vol. IV, pp. 242–3. Mrs Gaskell to W. S. Williams, 20 December 1860; *Halifax Guardian*, 12 May 1855.

Notes for Chapter 11: New bottles for new wine

1. WYAB, 33D80/5/2.

2. *Times*, 27 February 1837.

3. J. T. Ward in Norman Gash (ed.), *W. B. Ferrand, The Working Man's Friend 1809–89* (Tuckwell Press, East Linton, 2002), pp. 39, 44, 63–8, 69, 70, 85, 87.

4. *Leeds Intelligencer*, 2 July 1842.

5. See note 1; KRL, Union Minute Books, KU1/3,1/4, 1/5 and 1/6 from which the 1848–59 figures were calculated.

6. *Leeds Mercury*, 10 April 1841; J. T. Ward, *The Factory Movement 1830–55* (Macmillan, 1970), p. 276; KRL, KU3/3, Letters 1854–62, 14 July 1858.

7. Memorial of Keighley Union Guardians, *Leeds Mercury*, 23 October 1852.

8. KRL, KU 1/5, p. 150.

9. WYAB, *Heaton Papers*, B50.

10. WYAW, QSI 45, fols 203r–v, 290r–v, 291r.

11. Whone, 'Court Rolls of the Manor of Haworth', *BHAS*, Local History Series III (1946) gives examples.

12. WYAW, QSI 30, fols 169r, 170r–71v; 32 fol. 190r; 33 fols 67r–v; 38 fol. 257v.

13. WYAW, QSI 42, fols 49–50r, Pontefract.

14. For example, Jane Akeroyd, *6d.* and whipping; Susan Brooke, *4d.* and 2 months, QSI 38 fol. 195v; 41 fol. 250v.

15. Marie Campbell, *The Strange World of the Brontës* (Sigma, Wilmslow, 2001), p. 78. Steve Wood identified the grave. Robin Greenwood still has William's weapons.

16. WYAB, *Ferrand Papers*, C237; *Bradford Observer*, 12 February 1835; *Leeds Intelligencer*, 16 November 1852.

17. *Keighley News*, 25 September 1954.

18. Brontë's letters see Juliet Barker, *The Brontës*, pp. 167–8; Dixon and Lock, *A Man of Sorrow*, pp. 318–19.

19. *Leeds Intelligencer*, 20 June 1840; *Halifax Guardian*, 17 November and 29 December 1855; White Directory, 1861.

20. Lemon, *Early Visitors to Haworth*, pp. 4, 32, 42–3, 45.

21. *Bradford Observer*, 30 March 1843; *Halifax Guardian*, 9 February 1849.

22. Lemon, *Early Visitors to Haworth*, pp. 4–5, 16, 19; Horsfall Turner, *Haworth, Past and Present*, pp. 149–52.

23. *Leeds Mercury*, Supp.1, November 1845, 3 October

1846; *Bradford Observer*, 6 November 1845; *Leeds Intelligencer*, 22 September 1849.

24. *Bradford Telegraph & Argus*, 25 October 1932.

25. B. H. Babbage, *Report on a Preliminary Inquiry into the Sewage, Drainage and Supply of Water and the Sanitary Condition of the Hamlet of Haworth* (1850), pp. 11, 16–17.

26. Dixon and Lock, *A Man of Sorrow*, pp. 432–4.

27. Babbage *Report on a Preliminary Inquiry into the Sewage, Drainage and Supply of Water ... of Haworth*, pp. 26–7.

28. Dixon and Lock, *A Man of Sorrow*, p. 435.

29. Babbage *Report on a Preliminary Inquiry into the Sewage, Drainage and Supply of Water ... of Haworth*, p 11; *Ibid.*, p. 437.

30. KLSL, BMT/HA 1/1/1 fol. 71.

31. *Ibid.*, fol. 116.

32. *Ibid.*, fols 172, 174.

33. Calculated from ages in the parish burial register 1788 to 1812.

34. Babbage, *Report on a Preliminary Inquiry into the Sewage, Drainage and Supply of Water ... of Haworth*, p. 10.

35. G. H. Wilmore, *Public Health Reform in Haworth 1851–81* (unpublished MA dissertation, Huddersfield, 1996), pp. 24–6.

36. Ward in Gash (ed.), *W. B. Ferrand*, p. 111, 197.

37. *Halifax Journal*, 16 November 1805; *Leeds Intelligencer*, 17 September 1821; *Bradford Observer*, 21 August 1843.

38. *Keighley News*, 6 August 1866; M. Hagerty, 'Bradford Friendly Societies in the 1790s', *BA*, NS, Part 46 (1976); p. 49 for Greenwood.

39. Hagerty, *Bradford Friendly Societies in the 1790s*, p. 64.

40. *Keighley News*, 29 August 1931 and 23 February 1846.

41. *Bradford Observer*, 9 July 1840; *Leeds Intelligencer*, 6 June 1846.

42. *Bradford Observer*, 16 April 1846; *Leeds Mercury*, 11 January 1859.

43. *Leeds Mercury*, 7 September 1833, sermon by Rev. Brother Brontë. For Branwell see Barker, *The Brontës*, p. 230, 247.

44. WYAB have a photocopy at 48D82.

45. *Keighley News*, 23 October 1965; article by Ian Dewhirst, also *Keighley News*, 16 January 1954; Barker, *The Brontës*, p. 905 n.83 for Branwell's poems.

46. *Keighley News*, 29 August 1925, article on Brontë connections with the old Mechanics Institute.

47. *Bradford Observer*, 13 November 1834 says it has been meeting for more than half a century.

48. For example *Bradford Observer*, 10 April 1834, 5 January 1843, 8 February 1844, 24 October 1844; *Leeds Intelligencer*, 27 July 1839.

49. Emily Brontë, *Wuthering Heights*, Chapter 7, (Folio edn), p. 56; *Leeds Mercury*, 28 February 1852 for the move. Barker, *The Brontës*, pp. 210–1 states that the orchestra was connected with Merrall's mill in 1833. I can find no evidence for this and it must be doubtful whether he had enough adults to form one at that time, most of his employees being children. She may be confusing this orchestra with the later Springhead Brass Band and Hartley Merrall senior with his son Hartley junior.

50. Symington and Wise, *The Brontës, Their Lives, Friendships and Correspondence*, vol. I, pp. 130–1, 6 July 1835.

51. *Ibid.*, vol. II, p. 48A.

52. Barker, *A Life in Letters*, p. 263.

53. *Keighley News*, 24 June 1916 reproduces the poem.

54. School Prize Giving Programmes and Magazines, *Greenhead School Records* examined by the author when writing his unpublished mss. *History of Keighley Girls Grammar School 1872–1967*.

55. *Keighley News*, 'The Brontës and Haworth', 30 March 1935.

Notes for Chapter 12: The Worth Valley railway and the late nineteenth-century textile industry

1. R. Povey, *A History of the Worth Valley Railway from 1861 to the Present Day* (Worth Valley Railway Preservation Society, 1968).

2. PRO, Rail 331/1 fol. 1r.

3. PRO, Rail 331/1 fol. 3r.

4. PRO, Rail 331/1, pp. 5, 6, 16.

5. *Keighley News*, 13 February 1864, 9 April 1864.

6. *Ibid.*, 22 April 1918.

7. Povey, *A History of the Worth Valley Railway*.

8. PRO, Rail 331/1, p. 84; Povey, *ibid*.

9. *Keighley News*, 5 November 1866.

10. *Ibid.*, 27 April 1867.

11. *Keighley News*, 20 April 1867.

12. PRO, Rail 331/1, pp. 4, 8 and 36; *Keighley News*, 1 February 1868.

13. See the appropriate Haworth rate books in KRL.

14. Shed D in RCHM, Mill Survey Map H319 Ebor; KRL, Haworth Supplementary Rate Valuation (SRV), 1863–79.

15. KRL, see appropriate Keighley rate books.

16. KRL, Haworth SRV, 1863–79.

17. KRL, Keighley Poor Rate Books, 1867 and 1869.

18. John Hodgson, *Textile Manufacture in Keighley* (Keighley, 1879, new edn Shaun Tyas, Stamford, 1999), p. 51.
19. KLSL, Haworth SRV, 1863–79, p. 197.
20. KLSL, Oxenhope Rate Book, 1867; RCHM, H330.
21. KLSL, Rate Valuation (RV) rise in Rate Books, 1858 and 1865; RCHM H327.
22. KLSL, SRV, 1863–79, p. 19 for rise in valuation.
23. KLSL, Far Oxenhope Rate Book, 1869; Haworth RV, 1870, RCHM, H308.
24. Analysis of 1881 Census.
25. *Keighley Herald*, 3 July 1875.
26. *Ibid.*, 15 July 1876, 16 January 1886.
27. *Ibid.*, 25 May 1878.
28. Analysis of 1881 Census.
29. *Keighley Herald*, 26 April 1879.
30. *Keighley News*, 11 May 1957; 1881 Census analysis.
31. For more details see David Pearson, *How Haworth got its Railway: A Study in Nineteenth Century Local Enterprise* (Unpublished MA Dissertation, University of York, 2003). For newspaper comment see *Keighley News*, 5 October 1872, 22 February 1873, 23 July 1881 and 19 May 1883; *Keighley Herald*, 20 May 1876.
32. *Keighley News*, 20 June 1885 for the fire.
33. RCHM, H320. Rebuilding complete by 1887.
34. *Keighley News*, 13 August 1949, for article on the firm's centenary.
35. KLSL, SRV 1882–84, Sykes rates rise £196; Dewhirsts, Haworth, RV, 1885, SRV 1886–94; RCHM, H308.
36. RCHM, H330; KRL, valuation rises in Haworth, SRV 1863–79, p. 25 and RV 1881.
37. KLSL, Haworth, 1885 RV, Rate rise; SRV 1886–94; RCHM, H311, for engine.
38. *Keighley Herald*, 1 November 1882; KRL, Haworth, SRV 1882–84; SRV 1886–94, RCHM, H326.
39. PO directory 1861; KLSL, Keighley Poor Rates 1862, 1867, 1868, and 1869; *Keighley News*, 7 October 1871.
40. *Keighley News*, 9 January 1864, 9 December 1865, 30 November and 7 December 1878; RCHM,

H310; Thompson, *Stanbury*, pp. 119–22.
41. Thompson, *Stanbury*, pp. 141–2, directories and rate books.
42. *Keighley News*, 28 May 1864; KRL, Haworth Rate Books; Thompson *ibid.*, pp. 130–1.
43. Thompson, *ibid.*, pp. 161–8, unless otherwise stated.
44. *Keighley News*, 29 May 1954.
45. *Ibid.*, 14 June 1884 was a little premature.
46. *Ibid.*, 17 November 1888, 25 January 1890 and 1 February 1890.
47. Thompson, *Stanbury*, pp. 156–8.
48. *Keighley News*, 5 May 1866.
49. *Ibid.*, 1 February 1873
50. From a talk by David Cant to Haworth Historians in October 2002.
51. *Keighley News*, 19 November 1964, memories of George Selby; 17 April 1970 has a photo of the old wooden viaduct (see photo p150).
52. *Ibid.*, 26 July 1884; Thompson, *Stanbury*, p. 126.
53. *Keighley News*, 21 March 1891.
54. *Ibid.*, 26 December 1891; Worth Valley Trade article.
55. *Ibid.*, 1, 8, 15 July and 23 September 1893.
56. KLSL, Haworth, RV 1881, RV 1885; Trade directories Slater 1887, 1891, Kelly 1889, 1893.
57. *Keighley News*, 26 December 1896 on Worth Valley Trade article.
58. *Ibid.*, 21 April 1894 and 4 January 1896; Thompson, *Stanbury*, pp. 110, 132–3.
59. *Keighley News*, 23 April 1898, 21 December 1901, 24 September and 10 November 1900, 21 December 1901.
60. *Ibid.*, 15 July and 12 August 1905; KLSL, Haworth Rate Books, 1905 and 1910; Kelly directories, 1908 and 1912.
61. *Keighley News*, 19 September 10, 17 October, 7 and 28 November 1908, 8 May 1909, 23 April 1910, 11 March and 15 July 1911, 15 June 1912, 30 March and 8 June 1912; KLSL, Haworth, SRV 1914; Thompson, *Stanbury*, p. 142.
62. RCHM, H327; Worrall trade directory, 1910–11.

Notes for Chapter 13: An industrial community

1. Unless otherwise indicated the figures are from the author's analysis of census data.
2. *Keighley Herald*, 8 March 1879, *Keighley News*, 9 April 1881, 13 May 1889, 6 February 1897. Figures for Haworth LBH district until 1894 when a new UDC formed which includes Lees and Crossroads.
3. *Keighley News*, 1 February 1873 and 1 March 1930.
4. Mine details from R. Burt, M. Atkinson, P. Waite and R. Burnley, (eds), *Yorkshire Mineral Statistics 1845–1913* (Department of Economic History, University of Exeter, 1982).
5. Based on the street names in the censuses.
6. *Keighley News*, 12 November 1870, Oddfellows Lodge Visit, Eboracum to Woodlands.
7. *Ibid.*, 27 March 1869.

8. *Ibid.*, 6 May 1871 for plans but first referred to as 'new' in medical officer's report; 9 April 1881.

9. *Ibid.*, 1 November 1890, Ackroyd's letter.

10. *Ibid.*, 2 April 1887.

11. *Ibid.*, 11 January 1890.

12. *Ibid.*, 21 January and 27 June 1891, 29 April 1893.

13. *Ibid.*, 19 March and 15 October 1904; KLSL, UDC minutes, BMT/OX 1/1/10, p.83.

14. *Keighley News*, 21 January 1865 and 15 September 1866, 11 March 1871 and 4 October 1872; KLSL, copy of the act and BMT/HA1/1/2, p.205 and 368.

15. *Keighley News*, 16 January 1875; *Keighley Herald*, 8 January 1876 for complaints.

16. *Keighley News*, 9 April 1887 and 4 January 1890.

17. *Ibid.*, 16 July 1887.

18. *Ibid.*, 11 July 1874, March 1875 for retorts; for rise in coal prices, 11 January 1873.

19. *Ibid.*, 3 June 1876; 40. 15 February 1879.

20. *Ibid.*, 16 July 1887.

21. *Ibid.*, 11 January 1890.

22. *Ibid.*, 10 December 1892 and 8 August 1903;

23. *Keighley News*, 3 February 1878 and 8 March 1879.

24. *Ibid.*, 9 July 1892 and 22 October 1892.

25. *Ibid.*, 9 May 1896.

26. *Ibid.*, 31 August 1895.

27. *Ibid.*, 18 March 1899.

28. *Ibid.*, 3 February 1900.

29. KLSL, BMT/HA 1/1/9 7 February 1902, pp.91–3, 25 and 27 February 1903, pp.213–4; *Keighley News*, 15 February 1902.

30. *Keighley News*, 3 October 1903.

31. This and what follows is again the author's own analysis.

32. 1887 rate from figures in *Keighley News*, 7 April 1888; 1893–94 from quarterly reports in *ibid.*, 19 February, 11 May, 10 August and 16 November 1894; 1902 rate from *ibid.*, 22 February 1902.

33. *Ibid.*, 16 June 1894 gives foundation date.

34. *Keighley Herald*, 28 July 1877.

35. *Ibid.*, 16 April 1898.

36. *Ibid.*, 20 January 1968.

Notes for Chapter 14: Church and chapel

1. See M. L. Baumber, '"That Vandal Wade": The Rev. John Wade and the Demolition of the Brontë Church', *TBS*, vol. 22 (1997), pp.96–111; *Keighley News*, 27 December 1902, 7 March 1903 and 20 February 1904.

2. *Keighley News*, 20 November 1867, 3 September 1892, 12 July 1893; *Keighley Herald* 4 May 1883; KLSL BK115/1/2/1a Bridgehouse; BK115/1/2/1b Lowertown.

3. *Keighley News* 8 April 1871, 15 December 1882, 18 September 1909; KLSL BK115/1/1/4b.

4. *Keighley News* 24 January 1863; KLSL BK115/1/2/1a and 1b.

5. KLSL BK115/2/13a; Lowertown waited until £3–4,000 subscribed.

6. *Keighley News* 10 September 1864, 10 August 1867 and 7 June 1884.

7. *Ibid.*, 18 September 1909

8. *Ibid.*, 9 December 1882 and 26 October 1889.

9. *Ibid.*, 31 March 1899, 19 April 1873, *ibid.*, 11 and 25 October 1902, Mill Hey's in 1890 allowed by the circuit; *Keighley Herald* 8 January 1876, 7 April and 30 June 1877, 9 April 1897.

10. *Keighley News* 22 October 1870 and 1 July 1871.

11. *Ibid.*, 25 June 1927. His memory was at fault. They were at Oxenhope not Haworth.

12. *Ibid.*, 10 April 1869.

13. *Ibid.*, 18 February and 20 May 1899.

14. *Ibid.*, 11 May 1907 and 10 October 1908; *ibid.*, 16 March 1946 for 1903 peal.

15. *Ibid.*, 13 December 1862 and 12 November 1864.

16. See *Ibid.*, 17 April 1929 and 19 December 1931, Obituaries of S. O. Hands and James Riley.

17. *Ibid.*, 19 October 1895 and 24 April 1897.

18. *Keighley Herald*, 16 June 1882 and 5 January 1883; *Keighley News*, 26 February 1881, 24 May 1884 and 9 May 1885.

19. *Keighley News*, 6 October 1900, comments of Alderman W. A. Brigg.

20. *Ibid.*, 23 May and 4 July 1908.

21. *Ibid.*, 10 October 1896.

22. *Halifax Guardian*, 6 April 1861; *Keighley Herald*, 13 May 1876, 30 March 1883 and 12 April 1930.

23. *Keighley News*, 18 March 1865 and 10 September 1904; KRL, BMT/HA 1/1/10, p.14, 7 February 1905.

24. *Keighley News*, 17 August 1889, 5 July 1890.

25. *Ibid.*, 18 April 1891, 16 April and 10 December 1892; KRL, BK 115/1/2/1c, 14 September 1907.

26. *Keighley News*, 28 August 1879 for Hall Green; KRL, BK115/1/2/1b and 1c, Wesleyan Methodist Circuit Records for the others.

27. Bryan Hughes, *John Laycock* (Music Opinion Ltd, St Leonards, East Sussex, 2003), pp.52, 55. All three were built by Laycock and Bannister of nearby Crosshills.

28. *Keighley Herald*, 12 February 1897; *Keighley News*, 18 August 1900 etc, 29 April 1905 and 29 August

1908.

29. *Keighley News*, 15 February and 20 September 1913.

30. *Ibid.*, 6 May and 25 November 1911, 2 and 23 November 1912.

31. *Ibid.*, 9 April 1898, 1 April 1899, 11 April 1903 etc.

32. KLSL, Lees Methodist Records, BK115/2/5/3a, 27 January 1905, 2 February 1906; *Keighley News*, 28 April 1910.

33. WYAB, 62D81/1; Greenwood, *History of the West Lane and Hall Green Baptist Churches*, pp. 92–3, 111–12.

34. See n.34 and Alec Charlton, G. H. Richards, *Those Two Hundred Years: West Lane Baptist Church 1748–1948* (Haworth, 1948), p.11.

35. *Ibid.*, and Alec Charlton, G. H. Richards, *Those Two Hundred Years: West Lane Baptist Church 1748–1948* (Haworth, 1948), p.11.

36. *Keighley Herald*, 23 June 1883, 16 April 1886.

37. WYAB, 62D81/1 and 2, Society Numbers in the Haworth and Oakworth Wesleyan Methodist Circuit 1889–1912 and 1912–70 for Individual Society returns.

37. *Keighley News*, 13 March 1875; *Keighley Herald*, 26 January 1883.

39. *Keighley Herald* 23 June 1883.

40. *Keighley News*, 6 December 1873 has Holden's address on these lines.

41. KRL, BK115/1/2/1a, 21 March 1876.

42. *Keighley Herald*, 3 July 1875.

43. *Ibid.*, 10 May 1879, from a long report of the 'unsectarian' meeting.

44. For fuller accounts of the disputes see *Keighley Herald* and *Keighley News* for 26 April, 5, 10 and 17 May 1879.

45. *Keighley News*, 23 April 1881; *ibid.*, 14 March 1964 for Abraham; *Keighley Herald*, 11 August and 24 November 1882; Eunice Skirrow, 'Upper Worth Valley Schools', *TBS*, vol. 20, part 3 (1991), p. 159.

46. *Keighley News*, 16 October 1886, 12 November and 17 December 1887, 31 March, 7 April and 18 August 1888, 17 December 1892.

47. *Ibid.*, 18 Sept. 1885, 7 Nov. 1891

48. *Ibid.*, 15 Sept. 1888, 19 Jan. 1889 Letters from a Browsider.

49. *Ibid.*, 27 July 1889

50. *Ibid.*, 16 Apr.1892; KRL, BK115/1/2/1b, 19 March 1895.

51. *Keighley News*, 6 May 1893. For Hirst see 16 April 1949.

52. *Ibid.*, 26 April 1879.

53. Letter in *ibid.*, 7 June 1890.

54. *Ibid.*, 23 April 1881; *Keighley Herald*, 18 August 1883.

55. See *Keighley News*, 15 July, 12 August and 14 October 1893, 3 August 1895.

56. *Ibid.*, 14 November 1896.

57. Skirrow, 'Upper Worth Valley Schools', p. 159; Peggy Hewitt, *Brontë Country: Lives and Landscape* (Sutton, revised edn, 2003), p. 11; *Keighley News*, 27 February, 6 March, 15 May, and 4 September 1886. Letter from Robin Greenwood about Marion.

58. *Keighley News*, 10 May 1879. Redman pooh-poohed the Anglican forecast.

59. *Ibid.*, 2 March 1901. Letter from James Smith for rate; 14 November 1903 gives loan total.

60. *Ibid.*, 28 April 1868 says it was founded the previous July.

61. KRL, BK15/1/1/4c, 3 March 1887.

62. *Keighley News*, 6 May 1893.

63. *Ibid.*, 4 December 1897; KRL, BK15/1/1/4c, 24 March 1893.

64. *Keighley News*, 30 July 1870 and 19 April 1879.

65. Exceptional; parish church collections averaged between £70 and £75.

66. *Keighley News*, 19 June 1897.

67. KRL, BK115/1/2/1b and 1d, 2251 in 1900, 1717 in 1914. Baptists see Greenwood, *History of the West Lane and Hall Green Baptist Churches*, app., pp. 111–12

68. See note 67.

69. *Keighley News*, 15 January 1898. Obituary.

Notes for Chapter 15: That's Haworth!

1. M. L. Baumber, '"That Vandal Wade"', pp. 96–112. The Sowden quote is from his *Recollections of the Brontës*, p. 10.

2. *Keighley News*, 28 January, 17 June and 8 July 1871, 8 February 1873, 23 October 1875, 21 October 1876; *Keighley Herald*, 12 May 1877, 23 October 1886.

3. *Keighley News*, 9 July 1898, in UDC report.

4. Limited space in reading room was mentioned by Rev. David Arthur.

5. *Keighley Herald*, 21 July 1877. Notice to quit previous premises. No one seems to know where they were. Loan on new ones took years to pay off.

6. *Keighley News*, 22 September 1906, for Ladies physical culture at Lees; *Keighley Herald*, 16 June 1877, for Billiards.

7. *Keighley News*, 19 October 1878; 8 February 1873,

Oxenhope had had a church institute for some time.

8. For example, meagre, *ibid.*, 17 September 1892; 14 in 1895, *ibid.*, 11 May 1895; 12 in 1896, *ibid.*, 5 September 1896.

9. *Keighley Herald*, 15 February 1879 for foundation. By 1886 there were complaints of lethargy and then silence. As Stanbury had to be revived it too must have disappeared.

10. See *Keighley News*, 13 November 1897, 21 January 1899 and 28 January 1911 for Oxenhope Young Men's Reading Room; *ibid.*, 2 June 1906. The chief attractions of the revived Stanbury M.I. were a plentiful supply of newspapers and a billiard table.

11. *Ibid.*, 9 July 1898.

12. *Ibid.*, 8 November 1902.

13. *Ibid.*, 4 February 1899 and 30 November 1901.

14. *Ibid.*, 19 July and 25 October 1902.

15. For the formal debates BK/HA 1/1/9, pp. 158, 171. For furore in the press see *Keighley News*, 19 July, 9 August, 13 September (Letter JS), 20 September (Letters James Rushworth and ABC), 11 October (debate on the site), 25 October (Letter from Story), 1 November (letter supporting M.I.) and 8 November 1902 (Story again).

16. KLSL, BMT/HA 1/1/9, 6 October 1903 The committee could only suggest a further approach to Carnegie though the letter never seems to have been sent. For unsuitability see letters from Old Ratepayer in *Keighley News*, 17 October 1903; Onlooker, *ibid.*, 1 October 1904; and Old Inhabitant, *ibid.*, 14 January 1905.

17. *Keighley News*, 19, 26 May and 2 June 1906 cover the issues at length. 2 June gives poll result.

18. For quotes see *ibid.*, 13 May and 22 July 1905, 19 March and 19 May 1906.

19. *Ibid.*, 20 March 1869, 7 January 1871. For an analysis of the significance of dialect see Patrick Joyce, *Visions of the People* (Cambridge University Press, 1991), pp. 279–305. For its persistence in Haworth see John Waddington-Feather's note in 'Charlotte in Kentucky: Coaching Haworthese', *Brontë Studies*, vol. 29, part 3 (November 2004), pp. 260–3; See *Keighley News*, 27 August 1904 for Sutcliffe on 'Haworth People'.

20. *Keighley News*, 23 October 1875. Wade's address to the Mechanics' Institute.

21. *Ibid.*, 6 August 1932 recalls the triumph.

22. *Ibid.*, 26 July 1862.

23. *Ibid.*, 21 October 1899 and in 30 January 1970.

24. *Ibid.*, 24 August 1912 in an entertaining dialect letter.

25. *Ibid.*, 20 July 1912 and 10 May 1913.

26. *Ibid.*, 28 February 1953. Stories of the Haworth Brass Band.

27. *Ibid.*, 18 August 1917. Obituary.

28. *Ibid.*, 7 June 1913. Reminiscences at the opening of the Oxenhope Cricket Pavilion.

29. *Ibid.*, 24 September 1881.

30. *Ibid.*, 11 September 1909.

31. See *ibid.*, 7 June 1913. 3rd to Haworth's 6th. For changing arrangements.

32. *Ibid.*, 16 April 1949. Obituary.

33. *Ibid.*, 8 January 1949 celebrating his 80th birthday.

34. *Keighley Herald*, 3 November 1882; relationship from 1891 census.

35. For Lees see *Keighley News*, 11 March 1911 and 15 April 1961; *ibid.*, 8 December 1866 for Haworth.

36. *Ibid.*, 8 December 1866.

37. KLSL, Minute Book 1868–1938, 43D83. Renumbered as BK12/1 and 12/2.

38. *Keighley News*, 18 May 1872. Building approved by Oxenhope LBH.

39. Thompson, *Stanbury*, p. 223; *Keighley News*, 23 January 1892.

40. *Keighley News*, 1893 half-yearly reports, Haworth 759 and Stanbury 134, 23 July; Uppertown 310. No figures available for Oxenhope Industrial but *c.* 300.

41. *Keighley News*, 30 April 1898.

42. *Ibid.*, 25 November 1911 has a letter about milk competition with local farmers.

43. *Ibid.*, 23 January 1893 and 19 January 1901, Half Yearly Reports. The Merrall strike played a part too.

44. For these details see the Oxenhope and Stanbury Minute Books in KLSL.

45. F. Hartley, *The Jubilee History of the Lees and Crossroads Co-operative Industrial Society 1861–1911* (Co-operative Wholesale Society, Manchester 1911); also see Ox. Industrial Minute Book.

46. *Keighley News*, 24 June 1933 shows that it started in 1885.

47. *Ibid.*, 19 August 1899 and 3 February 1912.

48. *Ibid.*, 17 July 1909 gives 289 depositors.

49. *Ibid.*, 22 July 1905, 14 and 21 September 1907 and 17 July 1909.

50. *Ibid.*, 30 August 1895 and 1 February 1896.

51. *Ibid.*, 29 January 1887 for the distinctly cool attitude of the speaker at the Ox. Co-op. Festival.

52. *Ibid.*, 21 October 1899.

53. David James, 'Our Philip: The Early Career of Philip Snowden', *Bradford Antiquary*, 3rd Series, vol. 3, pp. 44–6.

54. *Keighley News*, 16 July 1898, 11 March 1899.
55. *Ibid.*, 2 February 1907.
56. *Ibid.*, 13 September 1906; 16 and 23 January 1909

57. *Ibid.*, 26 March 1910 for letters.
58. *Ibid.*, 27 January 1912.

for report and Smith's letter.

Notes for Chapter 16: Armageddon

1. *Leeds Intelligencer*, 3 December 1860; *Halifax Guardian*, 1 June 1861.
2. *Keighley News*, 10 and 31 March, 5 May, 14 and 27 July 1866, 6 July 1867.
3. *Ibid.*, 2 June 1866, Adjutant's remarks; 30 January 1869 and 12 February 1870, government returns.
4. *Ibid.*, 30 April 1870, 5 August 1871.
5. *Ibid.*, 20 July 1867 and 6 September 1873 the annual competitions reported regularly by the *Keighley News*.
6. *Keighley Herald*, 8 September 1888 for Nan Scar; *Keighley News*, 8 December 1900 gives the Bingham wins.
7. *Keighley News*, 17 September 1904, 17 December 1910, 6 January 1912; 8 January 1916, Lord Derby's scheme.
8. *Ibid.*, 12 September, 17 October and 7 November 1914. For garments see, for example, 12 and 19 September, 6 and 31 October 1914.
9. *Ibid.*, 6 February 1915.
10. *Ibid.*, 12 September 1914 and 13 February 1915 for letters; 10 October for death.
11. Background from articles in *ibid.* for 11 January, 15 February, 15 March, 29 March and 14 June 1919. Judgements on the war in general follow B.H. Liddell Hart, *History of the First World War* (Cassell, 1930, BCA edn reprint, 1977). It is often difficult to tie casualties to individual actions as they appear in the paper some time afterwards.
12. *Keighley News*, 8 January 1916.
13. *Ibid.*, 27 March 1915; on enlistments see 8 January 1916.
14. *Ibid.*, 29 March 1919.
15. *Ibid.*, 21 April 1917, Casuality list; 7 September 1918, Casuality list.
16. Fears of a similar mutiny prompted draconian measures in the British Army. Occasionally innocent men were executed. There was no Haworth victim but a Keighley Private Henry Macdonald has subsequently been given a posthumous pardon.
17. *Keighley News*, 7 July 1917, originally listed as missing on Messines ridge.
18. *Ibid.*, 22 December 1917 says it was at Cambrai.
19. There is a long list of soldiers missing and taken prisoner for this regiment.
20. *Keighley News*, 30 November 1918, 13 July and 24 August 1918; 25 January 1919 for Hodgson.

21. *Ibid.*, 28 August 1915, for Beasley; 29 March 1919, for Laurie Bell.
22. *Ibid.*, 28 September 1918, for John Finan's war.
23. WYAB, 62D81/4/9/6.
24. *Ibid.*, 2 October 1915, Commissions Arthur; 2 June 1917, Robinson and Scarborough; 14 September 1918, Maude described as second lieut. when POW; 28 September 1918, Scarborough listed as killed, and on 5 October 1918, Robinson.
25. *Ibid.*, 29 December 1917 for Lewis Barnes; 2 November 1918 for Joe Bates; 16 June 1917 for Sam; 4 January 1919 for Ratcliffe; 25 January 1919 for Hodgson.
26. *Ibid.*, 26 August 1939, ARP need volunteers; 15 November 1941, presentation to chief warden; 6 July 1940, Fire fighting; 1 March 1941, Home Guard; 19 May 1945, Observer Corps.
27. *Ibid.*, 6 January 1940, Bradford; 23 March 1940, new plans fall flat; 12 April 1941, Guernsey-success of Guernsey boys at Lees Junior; 7 June 1941, letters from parents; 6 December 1941 concert; 16 December 1939 comforts; and many more.
28. Greenwood, *History of the Greenwoods of Haworth*, vol. VI, *The Old Oxenhope Greenwoods*, p. 115 quoting *Yorkshire Post* and *Leeds Mercury*, 30 June 1943.
29. Many issues publicise the penny a week collections. *Keighley News*, 11 Nov. 1944, Boxes mentioned; 7 June 1941, clothes rationing is mentioned; 30 November 1 940, Dig for Victory; National Savings mentioned on numerous occasions.
30. Haworth is subsumed under Keighley so it is difficult to find specific local references.
31. Greenwood, *History of the Greenwoods of Haworth*, vol. VI, p. 115.
32. *Keighley News*, 20 November 1943, Oxenhope total; 1 June 1940, Clay.
33. *Ibid.*, 7 February 1942, Toothill; 24 April 1943 Pigott; 1 July 1944, Wormald.
34. *Ibid.*, 3 January 1942, Martin; 4 July 1942, Denby and Peacock; 29 December 1945, Smith.
35. *Ibid.*, 23 Jun.1945, Edmundson; 20 January 1945, Webb.
36. *Ibid.*, 18 December 1943, Jack Finding; 30 June 1945, Taylor and Dutton; 17 November 1945, McCracken-Hamilton; 24 March 1945, Jarvis; 17 July 1943, Peacock and Cox.
37. *Ibid.*, 3 July 1943, Bentham-Binns meeting.

1. *Keighley News*, 17 March 1923.
2. *Ibid.*, 29 May 1943, for his obituary.
3. *Ibid.*, 8 January 1916, Haworth's Blessings.
4. *Ibid.*, 10 January 1925 Duerden's comments; 8 October 1927, Haworth's Improvement.
5. *Ibid.*, 13 October 1923, 17 Febrary 1923 and 29 January 1927 respectively.
6. *Ibid.*, 7 July 1923 and 8 May 1926; KLSL, BMT/ HA 1/1/19, p. 87.
7. *Keighley News*, 3 May 1919, 11 October 1919, 11 February and 11 March 1922.
8. *Ibid.*, 21 November 1925, for revised agreement; 11 July 1925, Dry seasons; 9 June 1928; 6 July and 7 September 1929, 8 March 1930 and 6 January 1934; 10 October and 5 December 1931, Growing demand.
9. *Ibid.*, 19 June 1915, Keighley scheme opposition; 19 September 1925, Oxenhope.
10. *Ibid.*, 10 and 17 April 1926, items on its opening.
11. *Ibid.*, 5 September 1925 and 28 March 1931.
12. *Ibid.*, 11 February 1928 for Duerden comments; 10 March 1928 and 9 February 1935 for unit costs.
13. Greenwood, *History of the Greenwoods of Haworth*, vol. VI, p. 98.
14. KLSL, BMT/HA 1/1/17, p. 35, 9 January 1927 and p. 159, 5 January 1928; 1/1/18, p. 18 and p. 28 application p. 28, 5 November 1929. The playground and paddling pool 1/1/20, p. 185 and 1/1/21, p. 255.
15. KLSL, BMT/HA 1/1/15, pp. 67, 103, 124; *Keighley News*, 7 May and 9 July 1921 and 7 February 1926. For later details see BMT/HA 1/1/16, pp. 90, 195, 230, 1/1/18, p. 138 and 1/1/20, p. 244, 339.
16. *Keighley News*, 29 August 1925 carries a long article. For pre-war beginnings see 13 December 1913.
17. *Ibid.*, 20 March 1920, 21 February 1925 and 17 April 1926.
18. *Ibid.*, 6 May 1885, 3 July 1897, 13 June and 11 July 1925; KLSL, BMT/OX1/1/11, pp. 113, 176, 204, 213, 220, 224; 1/1/2, pp. 28, 39, 57, 69, 83, 98, 115; 1/1/13, pp. 103, 130, 141, 146, 163; 1/1/16, pp. 57, 62, 185.
19. *Keighley News*, 5 June 1935.
20. *Ibid.*, 8 December 1928 and 22 June 1929; 17 Aug. 1929, Worth Valley Assessment Committee; Guardians comments, KLSL, KU 1/40, p. 53 and 1/41, p. 189.
21. Where there is no footnote information from a File on Reorganisation in KLSL.
22. *Keighley News*, 21 April 1934, for Hill's views.

23. *Ibid.*, 20 July 1929 and 12 March 1932, for the educational difficulties.
24. *Ibid.*, 2 April and 17 Dec. 1932, 7 Jan. and 25 Feb. 1933 and 5 May 1934, and UDC minutes.
25. *Ibid.*, 15 December 1934. UDC still votes 6–4 for Keighley; KRL, BMT/OA 1/1/17, p. 202.
26. From the Reorganisation file. Cuttings appear to come from the *Yorkshire Observer*.
27. *Keighley News*, 14 July 1928.
28. *Ibid.*, 20 March 1920, article on Oxenhope's water supply.
29. *Ibid.*, 12 January, 2 and 9 February 1889, 29 April 1916 and 13 December 1958.
30. *Ibid.*, 19 May 1933, Dr Scatterty's report. National ones from A. H. Halsey, (ed.) *British Social Trends since 1900* (2nd edn, Macmillan, London, 1988).
31. Kelly directory 1922 lists for Sykes; Thompson, *Stanbury*, p. p. Griffe, pp. 134–5; Lumbfoot, p. 143–4; Emmott, Kelly directory 1927; *Keighley News*, 14 April and 20 October 1928, Hields; 20 December 1930, Unemployment.
32. For example, *Keighley News*, 18 September 1954, only two unemployed at Haworth; 17 September 1955, no one at all.
33. *Ibid.*, 21 March 1953, 18 September 1954, female labour; 22 October 1960, 3 February 1968, vacancies.
34. *Ibid.*, 6 October 1962; Old Oxenhope and Brooks Meeting Mill Greenwood, *History of the Greenwoods of Haworth*, vol. VI, pp. 114–19.
35. *Keighley News*, 12 March 1960, for Bridgehouse.
36. See *ibid.*, 25 March 1964 for Merralls modernisation; 18 January and 6 February 1965 for the fire; 29 January 1966 for Jerome.
37. See *ibid.*, 3 September 1966 and 15 October 1971 for Hields.
38. *Ibid.*, 11 June 1966 Mytholmes Mill fire; 8 October 1971, final closure.
39. RCHM, Dunkirk H308 and Charles H330. Thompson, *Stanbury*, pp. 111–13, Ponden; Greenwood, *History of the Greenwoods of Haworth*, vol. III, *Background on Haworth*, *Textile Mills in Haworth*, p. 47.
40. Greenwood, *ibid.*, vol. III, p. 31. Dates for Ivy Bank and Ebor supplied to the author orally.
41. *Keighley News*, 18 November 1967, Cullingdale; 13 August 1966 Holmes; 16 February 1963, Ashmount.
42. Census figures have been re-arranged because before 1921 raw figures include Lees and Crossroads but not Stanbury and after 1921 Stanbury but not Lees and Crossroads.

1. *Keighley News*, 9 July 1927.

2. *Ibid.*, 19 November 1927 and 19 May 1928.

3. *Ibid.*, 3 July 1926 and 23 May 1927.

4. *Ibid.*, 28 April 1917 and 30 December 1922.

5. WYAB, BK115/1/2/1/d-f, for circuit figures 1909–44; 62D81/1 and 2 for individual societies.

6. *Keighley News*, 14 May 1892, 7 January, 16 September, 23 December 1893 and 27 January 1894.

7. *Ibid.*, 16 December 1911.

8. WYAB, 62D81/4/11, has programmes; *Keighley News* carried reports; *ibid.*, 30 March 1929, Willie Moore.

9. *Keighley News*, 12 February 1927 and 11 February 1928.

10. *Ibid.*, 28 October 1922, Long Lee advert.

11. *Ibid.*, 23 October 1926, 22 October 1927, 13 October 1928, 19 October 1929, 25 October 1930.

12. *Ibid.*, 22 August 1931.

13. *Ibid.*, 22 February and 13 December 1930 for the shows; 4 November 1933, Marsh orchestra 11 Annual Report.

14. Baptist membership figures from Greenwood, *History of the West Lane and Hall Green Baptist Churches*, Appendix B, pp. 111–12. See also *Keighley News*, 14 January 1928, Alec Charlton, and G. H. Richards, *Those Two Hundred Years, West Lane Baptist Church 1748–1948* (Haworth, 1948), p. 11 and Marion Day, *The Hall Green Story* (Crosshills Typing Agency, 1994), p. 30–2.

15. *Keighley News*, 16 March 1946 and 29 November 1947 West Lane; 12 July 1947 Oxenhope; 18 February 1950, Lees.

16. *Ibid.*, 12 May 1945 and 3 May 1947.

17. *Ibid.*, 22 December 1945, 11 May 1946, 15 March 1947, 27 March 1948, 9 April 1949, 1 April 1950.

18. *Ibid.*, 24 March, 26 May and 6 October 1951.

19. *Ibid.*, 27 January and 17 March 1951.

20. *Ibid.*, 4 September 1954.

21. *Ibid.*, 21 April 1956, Lees; 3 September 1960, death of Margaret; 16 January 1960, decline in G&S.

22. *Ibid.*, 11 October 1958.

23. *Ibid.*, 26 May 1956, down from 165 in 1945 to 108 in 1956.

24. *Ibid.*, 19 February 1927, 28 February 1959.

25. *Ibid.*, 21 May 1932 comment; 30 May 1953, last walk; also article 9 June 1962.

26. *Ibid.*, 30 March and 6 July 1946, 20 March 1948, 1 March 1958.

27. *Ibid.*, 28 November 1955, Oxenhope; 1 May 1965, Haworth.

28. *Ibid.*, 4 October 1947 and 17 September 1949.

29. *Ibid.*, 2 October 1954, Mill Hey; November 1952, 4 April 1953 and 28 March 1964, Bridgehouse; 3 June 1950, 12 May 1951 and 21 June 1952, West Lane; 16 October 1970, Oxenhope; 14 June 1952 Sawood; WYAB, 62D81/9/8; *Yorkshire Post*, 24 November 1973, Stanbury.

30. *Keighley News*, 1 February 1947, Grace's obituary; 28 August 1920, Keighley contest.

31. *Ibid.*, 31 January 1925, Wood; 30 May 1925, Sugden; 10 November 1928, Jackson.

32. *Ibid.*, 5 September 1931, 1931 contest; 21 January 1950, 3 February 1951, Casson.

33. *Ibid.*, 12 March 1955; 5 October 1973 about decline and recovery.

34. *Ibid.*, 24 May and 14 June 1952, Lees; 22 September 1961, Haworth; 28 August 1965.

35. *Ibid.*, 23 May 1953, the Shepherds troubles. The Oddfellows still exist.

36. From *Keighley News* reports on the twice yearly meetings. Detail was often a little unpredictable.

37. *Keighley News*, 1 July 1933, Lees details; 1 July 1933, Haworth; 24 January 1925, Old Hall farm.

38. *Ibid.*, 13 August 1927, 18 August 1928 and 20 August 1938; WYAB, 58D/1/18/1–3, minute books 1928–58.

39. See *Keighley News*, 15 June 1929 for new store; WYAB, 58D86/1/19/13, merger papers.

40. For the Industrial see the minute book in KRL and WYAB, 43D83 (BK) 12/1.

41. For Haworth see the minutes WYAB, 58D86/1/18/3 and half yearly report *Keighley News*, 2 June 1962.

42. *Keighley News*, 18 October 1958, Lees 1,000; 14 April 1962, Bocking problems.

43. *Bradford Telegraph and Argus*, 15 September 1967. For the merger papers see WYAB, 58D86/1/19/13.

44. *Keighley News*, 9 March and 19 October 1963 for self-service; 4 September 1970 and 19 November 1971, for sale.

45. *Ibid.*, 31 January, 7 and 14 February 1959.

46. *Ibid.*, 5 June 1920 and 22 January 1955.

47. *Ibid.*, 30 April 1921, 20 October 1923, 13 April 1929, 30 April 1932 and 8 April 1933; Robert Grillo, *Chasing Glory: The Story of Association Football in Keighley*, vol. I, *Down to 1940* (Empire Publications, Manchester, 1997).

48. *Keighley News*, 24 May 1947 and 14 May 1955.

49. *Ibid.*, 2 May 1959, 29 April 1961, 5 May 1962, 11 May 1963, 14 May 1966. No final tables for 1957 or 1958.

50. For more details about the local leagues see

Robert Grillo, *Glory Denied: The Story of Association Football in Keighley*, vol. II, *1940–98* (Empire Publications, Manchester, 1999).

51. *Keighley News*, 30 September 1922, 15 September 1923, 26 September 1925, 25 September 1926, 24 September 1927, 15 September 1934, 7 September 1935, 17 September 1938, 2 September 1939.

52. *Ibid.*, 15 September 1945, 27 September 1947 and 25 September 1948, also won the Keighley charity cup 1944–46.

53. *Ibid.*, 12 October 1963.

54. *Ibid.*, 2 April 1949 and 18 February 1950.

55. *Ibid.*, 17 September 1960, 16 September 1961, 22 September 1962, 21 September 1963, 11 September 1965.

56. See *ibid.*, 18 September 1970, Haworth West End

in 1970; 29 September 1972, Meths win.

57. *Ibid.*, 26 November 1968, 14 May 1971, 17 March and 18 August 1972, 5 and 12 October 1973.

58. *Ibid.*, 24 October 1964, West Lane first show; 25 January 1964, Oxenhope first show.

59. *Ibid.*, 31 August 1912. See also 11 January 1913, 25 January 1913; KLSL, BMT/HA 1/1/12, p. 264.

60. *Ibid.*, 13 October 1956 and 30 March 1957. WI and Old Age Welfare groups reported regularly.

61. *Ibid.*, 28 November 1959, report on St James gives this condition; 1 February 1964, Oxenhope ditto.

62. *Ibid.*, 24 April 1948, 3 June 1961, 5 April 1969, for dispute between Hughes and Garland.

63. Greenwood, *History of the West Lane and Hall Green Baptist Churches*, p. 113.

64. *Keighley News*, 13 April 1973, Oxenhope survey.

Notes to Chapter 19: The new Haworth

1. *Keighley News*, 9, 23 and 30 December 1893; Mabel C. Edgerley, 'History of the Brontë Society 1893–1943', *TBS*, vol. x, part 53 (1943), p. 144; W. H. Black, (ed.) 'Early History of the Brontë Society,' *TBS*, vol. xiv, part 72 (1962) p. 38; C. H. Lemon, *A Centenary History of the Brontë Society* (Brontë Society, 1993), pp. 1–4.

2. See note 1; also Claude Meeker, 'Haworth, Home of the Brontës', *TBS*, vol. i, part 3, (1895), pp. 19–21; *Bradford Observer*, 16 May 1895; Lemon, *A Centenary History of the Brontë Society*, p. 5 for the reduced committee.

3. Black, 'Early History of the Brontë Society,' pp. 38–9.

4. Edgerley, 'History of the Brontë Society' *TBS*, vol. x, part 53 (1943), p. 147.

5. *Keighley News*, 7 September 1895; *Yorkshire Weekly Post*, 22 January 1898.

6. Edgerley 'History of the Brontë Society', p. 145, 146; Lemon, *A Centenary History of the Brontë Society*, p. 13.

7. C. M. Edgerly, 'The Building and Purchase of the Old Parsonage', *TBS*, part 37 (1927), pp. 25, 106–8; *Keighley News*, 20 March 1926, 16 July 1927, 7 July 1928; 21 September 1901 for Roberts; *Bradford Telegraph*, 1 January 1936.

8. *Keighley News*, 17 February 1912, 18 and 25 April 1936.

9. *Ibid.*, 1 August 1953.

10. *Ibid.*, 14 May 1955.

11. See *ibid.*, 27 January 1956, 8 June 1957, 4 January, 17 and 24 May and 7 June 1958, 6 June 1959.

12. *Bradford Telegraph and Argus*, 8 December 1962; *Times*, 25 February 1963; *Keighley News*, 2 and 30 March 1963; also Lemon, *A Centenary History of*

the *Brontë Society*, pp. 65–6.

13. *Yorkshire Post*, 10 February 1964; *Keighley News*, 18 April 1964.

14. Lemon, *A Centenary History of the Brontë Society*, pp. 66ff.

15. *Keighley News*, 15 January 1971.

16. *Ibid.*, 16 May and 28 August 1959, Reviews.

17. *Ibid.*, 14 July 1928, 2 May 1969; Lemon, *A Centenary History of the Brontë Society*, pp. 28–9.

18. *Keighley News*, 2 July 1949 and 8 May 1954.

19. *Ibid.*, 7 January 1956, 5 February 1971.

20. *Ibid.*, 1 October, 18 August and 5 November 1892, Oxenhope; *Keighley Herald*, 5 January 1878, Stanbury.

21. WYAB, 30D86/7; *Keighley News*, 23 and 30 August 1862, 18 May 1895.

22. *Keighley News*, 28 August 1965, on pigeon shooting; 10 December 1904, first show of 'homers'.

23. *Ibid.*, 5 September 1863 and 18 August 1866 (2nd Show).

24. *Ibid.*, 18 August 1917, Haworth; KRL, BMT/OX 1/1/11, Oxenhope UDC minutes.

25. *Keighley News*, 20 September 1941.

26. *Ibid.*, 1 January 1949, his career; 25 August 1923, early wins; 9 February 1957, closure.

27. *Ibid.*, 31 May 1902.

28. *Ibid.*, 4 June 1904, 23 July and 6 August 1910.

29. Reg Hindley's investigations have shown that the number of hill farms in 1881 was little different from what it had been in 1851 before the combing revolution but that there was a sharp decline in the early twentieth century.

30. WYAC, HEP: 254; *Keighley News*, 10 May 1930 recalls the lst walk; see 27 August 1932, for Tom

Stell's seat.

31. *Keighley News*, 13 June 1903 and 9 January 1904, nature studies; see also 23 March 1929, and obituary 19 June 1943.

32. *Ibid.*, 9 July 1927.

33. Peggy Hewitt, *Brontë Country: Lives and Landscape* (revised edn, Sutton, 2003), p. 115; *Keighley News*, 26 September 1931, Guides; 17 August 1935, Bancroft wedding report; 28 September 1935, Naylor.

34. *Ibid.*, 19 May 1962.

35. *Ibid.*, 31 March 1951 and 29 March 1958.

36. For example, *ibid.*, 16 March 1929.

37. *Ibid.*, 29 August 1953 for 2nd Haworth Show.

38. *Ibid.*, 1 October 1960.

39. *Ibid.*, 30 April 1960, 15 August 1969, 23 June 1972.

40. For example, *ibid.*, 19 May and 23 June 1972.

41. Whiteley Turner, *A Spring-Time Saunter: Round and about Brontë Land* (Halifax Courier, 3rd edn 1913; reprinted M. D. T. Rigg publications, 1991). No less than six chapters are devoted to the Brontës.

42. For example, Sutcliffe's *Man o' the Moors* and Heaton's *Greed Shadows*.

43. *Keighley News*, 18 April 1931, 28 September 1963, 22 May and 23 July 1965, 25 June, 2 and 9 July 1966, 20 May 1967.

44. *Ibid.*, 24 May 1930, 22 July 1933, 29 January 1949, 27 April 1957, 21 May 1960, 8 June 1973.

45. *Ibid.*, 18 August 1928, 6 February 1970.

46. *Ibid.*, 25 February 1961, on closure of Worth Valley Line.

47. *Ibid.*, 3 September 1910; KLSL, BMT/OX 1/1/9, p. 88, 9 September 1910; BMT/HA 1/1/13, p. 214, 4 January 1916 for pole positions; BMT/OX 1/1/11, p. 39, 8 December 1916, for speed restrictions.

48. *Keighley News*, 10 September 1910.

49. *Ibid.*, 7 February 1925 in the UDC report; KLSL, BMT/HA 1/1/16, p. 110, 145–6, 290; 1/1/17, p. 45, 174, 203, 293 and n. 47; Hewitt, *Brontë Country*, pp. 31–6.

50. *Keighley News*, 16 July 1949.

51. *Ibid.*, 24 November 1906, 2 February and 2 March 1907.

52. *Ibid.*, 30 December 1962 and 5 January 1963.

53. *Ibid.*, 31 July 1970, final plan.

54. *Ibid.*, 31 December 1955, 7 January 1956, 11 and 25 February 1956; Hewitt, *Brontë Country*, p. 35–6.

55. *Keighley News*, 3 July 1954 and 10 October 1955; 30 June 1962, a nostalgic special ran in June 1962.

56. *Ibid.*, 20 January 1962.

57. *Ibid.*, 2 November 1963, 12 June 1965; 5 April 1969, AGM; *Daily Express*, 26 September 1964.

58. *Keighley News*, 7 January 1967, AGM; 3 July 1970.

59. *Ibid.*, 26 February 1966, 25 March 1967, weekend service referred to.

60. *Ibid.*, 16 October 1969, 15 May 1970, 17 September 1971, 20 October 1972, 1972 AGM.

61. *Ibid.*, 3 July 1970, 4 June 1971.

62. *Ibid.*, 12 January 1973

Notes to Chapter 20: Living in the past

1. *Keighley News*, 13 July 1935; *Bradford Telegraph and Argus*, 18 December 1996.

2. *Keighley News*, 19 May 1978 and 28 June 2002.

3. *Ibid.*, 23 July 1995.

4. *Ibid.*, 20 May, 18 September 1981 and 14 April 1988.

5. *Ibid.*, 22 November 1985, 21 June 1991, 6 November 1992 and 8 October 1999.

6. *Ibid.*, 28 June 2002.

7. *Bradford Telegraph and Argus*, 20 October 1979, 20 June 1995 and 26 January 1996.

8. Reviews in *Keighley News*, 29 November 2002 and 1 January 2005.

9. *Bradford Telegraph and Argus*, 21 November 1975; *Keighley News*, 11 June 1999.

10. *Ibid.*, 21 November 1986; *Bradford Telegraph and Argus*, 6 December 1991.

11. *Keighley News*, 10 January 1992; *Bradford Telegraph and Argus*, 21 October 1996 and 4 February 1999.

12. *Keighley News*, 31 March, 20 April, 19 May 2000, 9 June 2000, 4 May and 27 October 2001; *Bradford Telegraph and Argus*, 7 February 2001.

13. *Ibid.*, 12 November 2001.

14. *Keighley News*, 2 November 2001.

15. *Ibid.*, 9 January 2004, 13 January 2006 and 11 June 1999.

16. *Ibid.*, 3 and 17 August 2001; 3 May 2002.

17. *Bradford Telegraph and Argus*, 18 September 1998.

18. *Yorkshire Post*, 21 February 1994; *Bradford Telegraph and Argus*, 4 March 1994; *Keighley News*, 23 August 1996, *Bradford Telegraph and Argus*, 13 February 1999.

19. *Ibid.*, 31 January 1979 and 2 August 1995; *Keighley News*, 29 September 1978 and 9 January 1987.

20. *Keighley News*, 9 October 1987; *Bradford Telegraph and Argus*, 20 January 2000; *Keighley News*, 30 November 1992.

21. *Ibid.*, 16 November 2001.

22. *Ibid.*, September 2004.

23. *Ibid.*, 24 March 2003.
24. *Ibid.*, 16 October 1992 and 29 October 1999.
25. *Bradford Telegraph and Argus*, 26 March 1983 and 31 March 1992; *Keighley Target*, 2 January 1991; *Bradford Telegraph and Argus*, 18 August 1992; *Keighley News*, 6 November 1992 and 14 May 1993.
26. *Bradford Telegraph and Argus*, 22 February and 11 March 1994.
27. *Keighley News*, 19 November 1993; *Bradford Telegraph and Argus*, 10 and 11 March 1994.
28. *Ibid.*, 22 February and 8–9 December 1994.
29. *Yorkshire Post*, 14 August 1985.
30. *Keighley News*, 7 November 1986 and 12 February 1988.
31. *Ibid.*, 14 May 1999.
32. *Ibid.*, 5 November 2004 (19 months ahead of Keighley Town Council!) and 30 July 2006.
33. *Ibid.*, 25 May 2001; *Bradford Telegraph and Argus*, 8 February 1989.
34. *Ibid.*, 17 April 1980, *Keighley News*, 1 May 1981, 25 September 1981, 26 February 1988 and 7 April 1989; *Bradford Telegraph and Argus*, 8 August 1989.
35. Sykes, *Keighley News*, 14 March and 16 October 1981, was fought over for over four years. Perseverance see *Bradford Telegraph and Argus*, 2 October 1989; Charles is mentioned indirectly in connection with the sewage problems created by extra houses in the mill complexes, *Keighley News*, 3 December 1988.
36. *Ibid.*, 29 January, 5 February 1982 and 2 July 1999.
37. Hindley, p. 90.
38. *Keighley News*, 24 March 2003.
39. *Ibid.*, 31 March 1983 and 15 September 1987.
40. *Ibid.*, 17 November 1995; *Bradford Telegraph and Argus*, 16 September 1996, 26 November 1999 and 7 December 2001.
41. *Keighley News*, 9 June 2004. Census 1981 1,995. Comparative figures for 2001 are difficult to come they are given only for the Worth Valley ward as a whole. Hindley p. 81 gives 355 (14% with long term illness) which works out at c 2,500 total.
42. *Keighley News*, 18 October 2002.
43. There are references too numerous to itemise but see especially *Ibid.*, 6 April 1979. For Turner see his obituary *Ibid.*, 14 December 1990.
44. *Ibid.*, 10 September 1997.
45. *Ibid.*, 6 July 2001; *Bradford Telegraph and Argus*, 27 September 2001; *Keighley News*, 14 May 2005 contains a review of his book. This is now not just a Haworth disease. As I write a report has been published showing that Britain has slipped from 34d to 19th in the literacy stakes.
46. *Ibid.*, 17 September 1993 and 29 April 2002.
47. *Ibid.*, 29 November 1985; *Bradford Telegraph and Argus*, 23 February 2004.
48. *Keighley News*, 28 December 1985 and 11 March 1988.
49. *Bradford Telegraph and Argus*, 4 March 1980; *Keighley News*, 18 March 1980 and 19 February 2005.
50. *Ibid.*, 23 August, 18 October and 20 December 2002; 21 March 2003.
51. *Ibid.*, 2 July 2004 for the fire; 16 February 1996 for Baptists.
52. *Ibid.*, 9 September 1983, 13 January 1994, 25 March 2005 for spire campaign and protests; *Keighley News*, 16 February 1996 for housing scheme.
53. *Ibid.*, 20 January 1997 and 3 March 2006.
54. *Ibid.*, 18 May 2006.
55. *Ibid.*, 7 December 2006.
56. *Ibid.*, 12 August 1995, 15 December 1995; *Bradford Telegraph and Argus*, 23 August 2002; *Keighley News*, 13 May 2005; *Bradford Telegraph and Argus*, 26 May 2007. 'Evans himself was unabashed. He claimed that the receipts from his Changegate Carpark had increased every year since 2000 and 5% in the current year as evidence that his activities could not be the cause of the traders' problems.'
57. *Ibid.*, 4 January 1982, *Keighley News*, 26 January 1990; *Bradford Telegraph and Argus*, 27 April 2000, *Keighley News*, 13 January 2006.
58. *Ibid.*, 16 October 1998 and 15 February 2002.
59. *Keighley Target*, 23 March 1989; *Keighley News*, 29 January 1999.
60. *Keighley News*, 14 December 1987; *Bradford Telegraph and Argus*, 10 May 1988.
61. *Keighley News*, 12 November 1992 and 8 January 1998.
62. Refs too numerous to list. Won Railway Heritage Interpretation Award in 2003 (*Ibid.*, 7 February 2003).
63. TV credits see *Ibid.*, 12 February 1988, 8 November 2002, 3 October 2003 and 30 July 2004; *Bradford Telegraph and Argus*, 14 December 1990, 12 August 1993, 5 February 1996, 26 January 2006; 8 January 2003.
64. *Keighley News*, 8 October 1999.
65. *Ibid.*, 29 October 1999.
66. *Ibid.*, 21 May 2004.
67. *Ibid.*, 31 January 2003 and 11 January 2007.
68. *Ibid.*, 23 August 2002, 13 February 2004, 28

January and 10 June 2005.

69. *Ibid.*, 14 and 28 October 2005.

70. *Bradford Telegraph and Argus*, 23 November 1983.

71. *Keighley News*, 5 October 1996; *Bradford Telegraph and Argus*, 21 October 1996.

72. *Ibid.*, 30 September 1992.

73. *Keighley News*, 14 December 2001.

74. *Ibid.*, 3 April 1998, 10 December 1999, 4 February 2000, 1 September 2000 and 3 August 2001.

75. *Ibid.*, 24 June 2003.

76. *Ibid.*, 23 October 2003 and 10 February 2006.

77. *Ibid.*, 12 October 2006 and 11 January 2007.

78. *Bradford Telegraph and Argus*, 11 December 2000.

79. *Keighley News* 16 October 1998. The early history of Oldfield school can be found in Baumber, M.L., *A Pennine Community on the Eve of the Industrial Revolution, Keighley and Haworth 1660–1740* (Keighley: privately published, 1977), pp. 151–2.

81. *Bradford Telegraph and Argus*, 27 January 1978; *Keighley News*, 20 February 1981.

Bibliography

Manuscript sources

Bradford Cathedral Archives
Churchwardens' Accounts 1667–1728.
List of Pewholders 1705.

Bradford Central Library
1755 Bradford-Colne Turnpike Act, *Bradford Local Acts vol. 1.*
Local History Library, Case 30, Box 5, Item 1, *List of Pewholders* (1756).
Local History Library, Case 31, box 3, Item 5, *Inventory of Richard Pollard of Hob Hill.*
Oxenhope Enclosure Award (1779).

Borthwick Institute for Historical Research, University of York
Primary Visitation of Archbishop Neile, 1632.
Visitations of 1662–63 Court Book vol. 1; 1667, Pontefract; 1674 Craven; 1682 Pontefract Court Book; 1684–85 Pontefract and Doncaster Court Book; Court Exhibition Books 1716, 1719, 1722.
Primary Visitation of Archbishop Drummond 1764.
Exhibit Books of 1764 and 1781.
Cause Papers H2452, H2454, H2456, H2570, H3828, H5982, I250, I569, I652 I1375 I1836.
Faculty Book 1736–68.
Probate Registers 13–41.
Wills and Inventories 1689–1750.

The Guildhall Library, London
Royal Exchange Insurance policy 9 Jan 1801, MS7253/32a, No. 180991.

Keighley Local Studies Library
Brigg Collection 250, 254, 257.
Papers of the Rev. Miles Gale.
Transcript of the Keighley Quaker Quarterly Meeting Minute Book.

Photocopy of the Diary of John Kitson, Woolcomber 1854–65, with an account of his early life.
Wesleyan Methodist Circuit Records, Todmorden Stewards Quarterly Book, 1748–93.
Quarterly Minutes of the Keighley II Primitive Methodist Circuit, BK 15: 1/1/4/b, 1875–85; 1/1/4/c 1885–94; 15/1/1/4/d 1895–1910.
Keighley Wesleyan Methodist Circuit Records BK15/1/4/c.
Quarterly Minutes of the Haworth & Oakworth Wesleyan Methodist Circuit, BK 115: 1/2/1a 1871–88; 1/2/1b 1888–1900; 1/2/1c 1900–09; 1/2/1d 1909–20; 1/2/e-f 1920–44.
Minutes of the Meetings of the Lowertown Wesleyan Methodist Trustees, BK 115/2/13a; Lees 115/2/5/3a; Stanbury 115/2/10/1a.
West Lane Baptist Chapel Admissions Register, 1826–77, BK217A.
Minutes of the Haworth Local Board of Health, BMT/HA 1/1/1, 1/1/2, 1/1/9.
Minutes of Haworth UDC BMT/HA: 1/1/10, 1/1/12, 1/1/13, 1/1/15, 1/1/16, 1/1/17, 1/1/18, 1/1/19, 1/1/20, 1/1/21.
Minutes of the Oakworth UDC BMT/OA 1/1/17.
Minutes of the Oxenhope UDC BMT/OX: 1/1/9, 1/1/11, 1/1/12, 1/1/13.
Book of Local Acts.
File of Press Cuttings on the Local Government Reorganisation, 1929–38.
Poor Law Union Minute Books: KU1/3, KU1/4, KU1/5, KU1/40, KU1/41 and Letter Book KU3/3, Letters, 1854–62.
Rate Valuations and Assessments: Poor Rate Valuation 1851, 1881, 1885; Supplementary Valuations 1863–79, 1882–84, 1886–94, 1914.
Assessments: Poor Rate, 1842, 1844; Highways Rate, 1847; Poor Rates, 1849, 1852, 1854, 1858, 1865,

1882, 1905, 1910; Oxenhope Rate, 1867; Keighley
    Rate, 1862, 1864, 1867, 1868 and 1869.
Censuses for Haworth Township 1841–1901 (microfilm
    and microfiche).

The National Archives, Kew
E101/62/8, Flodden Muster, 1513.
E179/207/185, 1546 Haworth subsidy.
E179/210/3949, 1666 Hearth Tax.
HO67/26, Crop Returns 1801, Haworth.
HO 129/494, Religious Census 1851, Haworth and
    Oxenhope (microfilm copy at BIHR).
PRO Rail 331/1, Minute Book of the Worth Valley
    Railway Company, 1861–83.

Royal Commission for Historical Monuments, Swindon
Textile Mill files: C1 Ponden; H305 Griffe; H307
    Lumbfoot; H308 Dunkirk; H310 Hollings;
    H311 Brooks' Meeting; H316 Springhead; H319
    Ebor; H320 Lee Syke; H322 Bridgehouse; H324
    Roydhouse; H325 Oxenhope; H326 Holme; H327
    Lowertown Shed; H328 Bridge or Lowertown;
    H330 Charles; H331 Wadsworth House; H332
    Sykes; H338 Spring Row; H340 Fishers' Lodge;
    H343 Mythomes.

West Yorkshire Archives, Bradford
Ferrand B60, Manor of Haworth; B450, Greenwood
    interest in lead mines; B454, 455, 459; C237.
Greenwood 53, 59, 78, 82, 85, 87, 93.
Heaton Papers, A108, A135, A149, A152, A160, A164,
    A446, A448, A449, A472, B2, B5, B16, B17, B20,
    B21, B22, B33, B50, B52, B65, B71, B72, B73,
    B80–98, B106, B108, B109, B143, B147, B149,
    B150, B151, B154, and *Michael Heaton – Robert
    Heaton 6 Sept. 1819.*
Haworth Parish Registers, 1788–1812.
Keighley Parish Registers.
F/T/7, Coal Lease, 4 Jan 1808.
Deeds, MM series, 1/c/3–5;.
30D86/7, Rejected Haworth Enclosure, 1860.
33D80/5/2, Haworth Poor Relief Figures, 1819–34.
43D83/12/1, Minute Book of Oxenhope Uppertown
    Co-operative Society, 1868–1938.
51/D/81/1, 51D/81/2, 51D81/41.

58D86/1/18/1–3, Haworth Co-operative Society
    Minutes, 1928–58.
58D86/19/13, Merger of the Oxenhope Co-operatives
    with Keighley.
58D86/1/25/1, Minute Book of the Stanbury Co-
    operative Society, 1895-.
62D81/1 and 2, Society Numbers in the Haworth &
    Oakworth Wesleyan Methodist Circuit, 1889–1912
    and 1912–70.
62D81/4/11, Programmes for oratorios at West Lane
    Methodist Chapel.
62D81/9/8.
94D85/10/6/2, Edward Copley's 1716 will;
    94D85/10/1/4, 94D85/10/1/5, 94D85/10/3/77,
    94D85/10/3/98.
Shackleton William, Photocopy of his diary for
    1793–94.

West Yorkshire Archives, Calderdale
HEP: 254.
RP1393, RP1408, RP1410, RP1758, RP1632, RP2127,
    RP2213.
SU48/1.

West Yorkshire Archives, Leeds
Tithe Awards for Haworth, Near Oxenhope, Far
    Oxenhope and Stanbury, 1852–53.

West Yorkshire Archives, Wakefield
Former Craven Water Board deeds.
Turnpike Records: Box 8, Minutes of Bradford-Colne
    Turnpike, 1755–82 and 1783–99; Box 50, 1805–23.
Quarter Sessions Records QSI: 30, 32, 33, 35, 38, 42
    and 45; Skipton Sessions June 1836. Justices'
    Qualification Oaths, 1819, QSI 37.
Oxenhope Enclosure Award 1779 with two pages of
    sketch maps at B11 (p. 199), and a further map at
    A3.
Deeds Registry H465/574, L412/544, X423/546,
    BB453/607.

Yorkshire Archaeological and Historical Society, Leeds
Fawkes Papers.
Currer and Garforth Deeds.
DD 146, Box 9, No.1.

Printed sources

'1545 subsidy Wapentakes of Agbrigg and Morley',
    Thoresby Society Miscellanea vol. xi (1904),
    pp. 264–6, 333–7, 360–81.
Anon., Typescript Copy of the Minutes of the
    Lancashire and Yorkshire Baptist Association
    1787–1836, with annual lists of affiliated chapels.

WYAB DB71 C7/2.
Babbage, B.H., Report on a Preliminary Inquiry into
    the Sewerage, Drainage and Supply of Water, and
    the Sanitary Condition of the hamlet of Haworth
    by Benjamin Herschel Babbage, Superintendant
    Inspector (April 1850).

Baildon, W. P. (ed.), *Yorkshire Deeds vol. ii*, YASRS, vol. xxxix.

Baildon, W. P. (ed.), *Knighthood Fines, Miscellanea vol. i*, YASRS, vol. lxi (1920).

Baildon, W. P. (ed.), 'Early Pedigrees of the Copley Family', *Thoresby Society, Miscellanea vol. xxvi*, pp. 194–211.

Barker Juliet, *A Life in Letters* (Viking, London, 1998).

Bradford Court Roll Transcripts (Local History Library, Bradford Central Library).

Brigg, W. A. (ed.), *Yorkshire Stuart Fines* (2 vols), YASRS, vols liii (1915), lviii (1919).

Brigg, W. A. (ed.), 'Parish Register of St Andrew's Keighley vol. II', *Yorkshire Parish Register Society, vol. lxxxii* (1927).

Brown W. (ed.), *Yorkshire Deeds vol. II*, YASRS, vol. xxxix (1913).

Calendar of Close Rolls 1259–61 and 1307–13, the latter in *Surtees Society vol. xlix*.

Collins, W. (ed.), *Yorkshire Tudor Fines* (3 vols), YASRS, vols ii (1887), v (1888), vii (1889).

Curnock N. (ed.), *The Journals of John Wesley* (Everyman edition) from original four vols (Robert Culley, London, 1909–16).

Extent of the Manor of Bradford 1342 printed in *Bradford Antiquary (BA)*, II, p. 57–65.

Farrer, W. (ed.), Early Yorkshire Charters, printed for the editor by Ballantyne, Hanson & Co. Edinburgh (12 vols 1916–42).

Hartley, James, *The trial of two opinions tried, wherein the false reasonings of Mr Johnson and his friends are exposed and refuted* (Keith, 1767).

Hearth Tax for Haworth 1672. Transcript in the Keighley Reference Library.

Holroyd, A., *Collectiana Bradfordiana*, privately printed (Saltaire, 1873) pp. 175–6.

Hoyle, R. W. (ed.), 'Lord Thanet's Benefaction to the Poor of Craven in 1685', *Friends of Giggleswick* (Giggleswick, 1978).

Hoyle, R. W. (ed.), *Early Tudor Craven*, YASRS vol. cxlv, introduction (1987).

Keighley Girls' Grammar School, Selections from the School's Prize Giving Programmes.

Kitson, John, Diary for 1854–65 prefixed by an account of his early life (unpaginated), Photocopy KRL.

Lemon, Charles (ed.), *Early Visitors to Haworth* (Brontë Society, 1996).

Lumb, G. (ed.), Registers of the Parish of Rothwell Part I 1638–89 *Yorkshire Parish Register Soc. vol. 27* (1906).

Newton, John – *Memoirs of the Life of the late William Grimshaw in Six Letters to the late Rev. Henry Foster* (Letter 5).

Poll Tax List 1379 in *YAJ, vol. vi* (1881), pp. 289–90.

Ranger, William, *Report to the General Board of Health on the Boundaries to be adopted for the purpose of the Public Health act 1848 in the parish of Haworth, Eyre and Spottiswoode*, HMSO (1853).

Rock, K. (ed.), 'The Protestation of the Commons 1641', *BA*, New Series, part 47 (1982), p. 145.

Skaife, Robert (ed.), 'Return of Knights' Fees for the Wapentake of Morley', *Surtees Soc. vol. xlix*.

Smith, Margaret, *Letters of Charlotte Brontë, vols I (1829–47)* (Clarendon Press, 1987) *and II (1848–51)* (Clarendon Press, 2000).

Symington, A. S. and Wise T. J., *The Brontës, Their Lives, Friendships and Correspondence, The Shakespeare Head Brontë* (4 vols) (London, 1932).

Turner, J. Horsfall (ed.), *Brontëiana* (printed for the editor, Bingley, 1898).

Turner, J. Horsfall (ed.) *The Diaries of Oliver Heywood 1630–1702* (4 vols) (printed for the editor, Brighouse, 1885).

Visitation of Archbishop Herring 1743 vol. 2, YASRS vol. lxxii.

West Yorkshire Vernacular Buildings Group: Report of the Annual Conference held at Haworth 19–21 May 2000; Recording of Ponden Hall 28 June 2003.

Whone, C. (ed.), 'Court Rolls of the Manor of Haworth', *Bradford Historical and Antiquarian Society, Local History Series vol. III* (1946).

'Yorkshire Recusants, List for March 1665/6', *Surtees Soc. vol. xl* (1861).

Newspapers

Bradford Telegraph and Argus.
Halifax Guardian.
Keighley News.
Keighley Herald.
Keighley and Haworth Argus.
Keighley Visitor.
Leeds Mercury.
Leeds Intelligencer.
Nelson Leader.
The Times.
Yorkshire Observer.
Yorkshire Post.

Trade directories

Baines 1822, Pigot 1828, Parsons and White 1830, Robson 1840, Pigot 1841, White 1847, Slater 1848, White 1853, Slater 1854, White 1861, Post Office 1861, Kelly 1861, Slater 1887, Kelly 1889, Slater 1891, Kelly 1893, Kelly 1908, Worrall 1910–11, Kelly 1912, Kelly 1927.

Parliamentary papers

Factories Inquiry Commission, Supplementary Report 1834: 96, J. & J. Greenwood; 97, William Greenwood; 98, Jonas Hird; 155, Hartley Merrall.

Rivers Pollution Commission (c.3471), 1871 (pub.1873), PP XXVI, 127.

Endowed Charities: *Administrative County of the West Riding and the County Borough of Bradford vol. II* (North West Division London, 1897).

Books

Anon., *A Brief Historical Account of the Churches in the West Riding Association of Baptist Churches* (Baptist Association, 1842).

Anon., *Thirty Four Years – History of the Keighley Baptist Church* (privately printed, Keighley, 1842).

Anon., *Elland: A Review of the Origin and History of the Elland Clerical Society, 1767–1868* (privately printed, Huddersfield, 1868).

Armstrong, Alison and Pacey, Arnold, *High Bradley: Architecture and History* (privately published, Addingham and Bradley, 2001).

Aspin, Chris, *The Water Spinners* (Helmshore Local History Society, 2003).

Baker, A.R.H. and Harley, J.R. (eds), *Man made the Land* (David and Charles, Newton Abbot, 1973).

Baker, F., *Life of William Grimshaw* (Epworth Press, London, 1963).

Barker, Juliet, *The Brontës* (Weidenfeld and Nicolson, London, 1994).

Baughan, Peter E., *The Midland Railway, North of Leeds* (David and Charles, Newton Abbot, 1987).

Baumber, M.L., *A Pennine Community on the Eve of the Industrial Revolution: Keighley and Haworth 1660–1740* (printed by Crabtrees for the author, Keighley, 1977).

Baumber, M.L., *From Revival to Regency: A History of Keighley and Haworth 1740–1820, vol. I One Industry and Communications* (printed by Crabtrees for the author, Keighley, 1982).

Brontë, Emily, *Wuthering Heights*, revised Folio edition (London, 1997).

Burt, R., Atkinson, M., Waite P., and Burnley R. (eds), *The Yorkshire Mineral Statistics 1845–1913* (Department of Economic History, University of Exeter, 1982).

Campbell, Marie – *The Strange World of the Brontës* (Sigma Press, Wilmslow, 2001).

Charlton, Alec and Richards, G.H., *Those Two Hundred Years: West Lane Baptist Church, Haworth, 1748–1948* (privately printed, Haworth, 1948).

Cook, Faith, *William Grimshaw of Haworth* (Banner Press, Edinburgh, 1997), pp. 74–6.

Craven, Joseph, *A Moorland Village and its People – A History of Stanbury*, copy at West Yorkshire Archives, Bradford, 3D77/23.

Dale, Rev. Bryan, *Yorkshire Puritanism and Early Nonc onformity, Illustrated Lives of the Ejected Ministers*, T.G. Crippen (ed.) (Congregational History Society, 1909).

Day, Marion, *Hall Green 1824–1974* (Crosshills Typing Agency, 1974).

Defoe, Daniel, *A Tour through England and Wales 1728*, (2 vols) (Everyman edition).

Dewhirst, Ian, *History of Keighley* (Keighley Corporation, Keighley, 1974).

Dixon, W.T. and Lock, J., *A Man of Sorrow: The Life, Letters and Time of the Rev. Patrick Brontë 1777–1861* (Nelson, London, 1965).

Duffin, Anne, *Faction and Faith: Politics and Religion of the Cornish Gentry before the Civil War* (Exeter, 1996).

Faull, M.L. and Moorhouse S.A., *West Yorkshire; An Archaeological Survey to AD 1500* (West Yorkshire County Council, Wakefield, 1981).

Feather, W., *A History of the Three Graces Lodge 408, Haworth 1792–1987* (privately printed, Keighley, 1988).

Firth, Gary, *Bradford and the Industrial Revolution* (Ryburn, Halifax, 1990).

Fitton R.S. and Wadsworth, A.P., *The Strutts and the Arkwrights 1758–1801, A Study of the Early Factory System* (Manchester University Press, 1938).

Gelling, Margaret, *Signposts to the Past* (1978, reprinted by Phillimore, Chichester, 2000).

Gibbon, A.M., *The Ancient Free Grammar School of Skipton: A Study in Local History* (Liverpool University Press and Hodder & Stoughton, Liverpool, 1947).

Green, S.J.D., *Religion in the Age of Decline: Organisation and Experience in Industrila West Yorkshire, 1870–1920* (Cambridge University Press, 1996).

Greenwood, Doris and Arthur, *St. Mary's Church Elland, Yorkshire* (privately printed, 1954).

Greenwood, Robin, *Mss History of the Greenwoods of Haworth II: Haworth Background* (1999).

Greenwood, Robin, *Mss History of the Greenwoods of Haworth III: – Background in Haworth: Textile Mills* (1999).

Greenwood, Robin, *Mss History of the Greenwoods of Haworth IV: Haworth Families* (1999).

Greenwood, Robin, *Mss History of the Greenwoods of*

Haworth V: The Bridgehouse Greenwoods (1999).

Greenwood, Robin, Mss History of the Greenwoods of Haworth VI: The Old Oxenhope Greenwoods (1999).

Greenwood, Robin, Mss History of the Greenwoods of Haworth IX (1999).

Greenwood, Robin, Mss. History of the Greenwoods of Haworth X: Appendices (1999).

Greenwood, Robin, Mss. History of the West Lane and Hall Green Baptist Churches, Haworth (London, 2002).

Grillo, Robert, Chasing Glory, The Story of Association Football in Keighley, vol. 1: Down to 1940 (Empire Publications, Manchester, 1997).

Grillo, Robert, Glory Denied, The Story of Association Football in Keighley vol. 2: 1941–98 (Empire Publications, Manchester, 1999).

Halsey, A. H. (ed.), British Social Trends since 1900 2nd edition (Macmillan, London, 1988).

Hartley, F., The Jubilee History of the Lees and Crossroads Co-operative Industrial Society 1861–1911 (Co-operative Wholesale Society, Manchester, 1911).

Heaton, H., The Yorkshire Woollen and Worsted Industries (Oxford University Press, London, 1965).

Hewitt, Peggy, Brontë Country: Life and Landscape (Sutton, Stroud, 2003).

Hodgson, John, Textile Manufacture and other Industries in Keighley (Keighley, 1879, reprinted by Shaun Tyas, Stamford, 1999).

Holroyd, A., Collectiana Bradfordiana (printed for the author, Saltaire, 1873).

Holt, J. C., Robin Hood (Thames and Hudson, London, 1982, reprinted 1989).

Hughes, Bryan, John Laycock (Music Opinion Ltd, St Leonards, East Sussex, 2003).

Ingle, G., Yorkshire Cotton, The Yorkshire Cotton Industry 1780–1835 (Carnegie, Preston, 1997).

James, John, A History of Worsted Manufacturing (Bradford, 1857, new edition, Frank Cass, 1968).

James, John, History of Bradford (Bradford, 1842, new edition, E. J. Morten, Didsbury, Manchester, 1968).

James, John, Continuation and Additions to the History of Bradford and Its Parish (Bradford, 1866, reprinted by E. J. Morten, Didsbury, Manchester, 1973).

Jenkins, D. T., The West Riding Wool Textile Industry 1770–1835 (Pasold Research Fund Ltd, Edington, 1975).

Jennings, B. (ed.), Pennine Valley, A History of Upper Calderdale (Smith, Settle, Otley, 1992).

Joyce, Patrick, Visions of the People (Cambridge University Press, 1991).

Kapelle, W., The Norman Conquest of the North: the Region and its Transformation (University of North Carolina Press, 1979).

Ladurie, E. Le Roy, Times of Feast, Times of Famine, a history of climate since the year 1,000 (ed. Allen and Unwin) (London, 1972).

Laslett, P., The World We have Lost – Further Explained (original edition, Methuen, London, 3rd edition reprint, Cambridge University Press, 1983).

Laycock, J. W., Methodist Heroes of the Great Haworth Round (Wadsworth & Co., the Rydal Press, Keighley, 1909).

Leach, A. F., Early Yorkshire Schools vol. II (Yorkshire Archaeological Society, Record Series vol. xxxiii, 1908).

Liddell Hart, B., The First World War (Cassell, London 1930, reprinted by Book Club Associates, 1977).

Lemon, Charles, A Centenary History of the Brontë Society (Brontë Society, 1993).

MacCutcheon K., Yorkshire Fairs and Markets (Thoresby Society, 1940).

Pearson, David, How Haworth got its Railway: A Study in Nineteenth Century Local Enterprise (MA Dissertation, University of York, 2003).

Povey, R, History of the Worth Valley Railway from 1861 to the present day (Worth Valley Railway Society 2nd edition, 1968).

Raistrick, A., The West Riding of Yorkshire (Hodder and Stoughton, London, 1970).

Raistrick, A., The Pennine Dales (Arrow, London, 1972).

Redmonds, George, Yorkshire Surnames Series, Part One – Bradford and District (1990); Part Three – Halifax and District (privately printed, 2001).

Reid, Sir T. Wemyss, Memoirs 1842–85 (Cassell, London, 1905).

Rogers, C. D., The Lancashire Population Crisis 1623 (Manchester University Education Department, 1975).

Roth, H. Ling, The Yorkshire Coiners 1767–83 and Notes on Old & Prehistoric Halifax (one vol.) (Halifax, 1906, reprinted by S. R. publishers, Halifax, 1971).

Sawyer, P. H. (ed.), English Medieval Settlement (Arnold, London, 1973).

Schofield R. and Wrigley A., The Population History of England 1540–1840 (paperback edition, Cambridge University Press, 1989).

Shackleton, William, Four Hundred Years of a West Yorkshire Moorland Family. A Brief Account of the History of the Heatons of Ponden House, Pudsey (1921, unpublished, mss copy at West Yorkshire Archives, Bradford).

Sowden, George, Recollections of the Brontës (Hebden Bridge Parochial Magazine, Sept. – Dec. 1894, reprinted by Angria Press, Todmorden, 2005).

Story, Rev. T. W., Notes from Old Haworth Registers (reprinted from parish magazines, Keighley, 1908).

Stone, Lawrence, *The Road to Divorce 1530–1837* (Oxford University Press, 1991).

Thornes, R. C. M., *West Yorkshire 'A Noble Scene of Industry' The Development of the County 1500–1830* (Wakefield, 1981) p. 7.

Turner, J. Horsfall, *Haworth, Past and Present* (printed for the author by J. S. Jowett, Brighouse, 1879, reprinted by Olicana, Otley, 1972).

Thompson, Dennis, *Stanbury, A Pennine Country Village* (privately printed, Stanbury, 2002).

Ward, J. T., *The Factory Movement 1830–55* (Macmillan, London, 1970).

Ward, J. T., *W.B. Ferrand The Working Man's Friend 1809–89* (ed. Norman Gash) (Tuckwell Press, East Linton, 2002).

Wilmore, G. H., *Public Health Reform in Haworth 1851–81* (unpublished MA dissertation, Huddersfield, 1996).

Whitley, W. H., *The Baptists of North West England 1649–1913* (Kingsgate Press, London, and G. Toulmin & Sons, Preston, 1913).

Wightman, W. H., *The Lacy Family in England and Normandy 1066–1194* (Clarendon Press, Oxford, 1994).

Wood, Steven C., *Haworth, 'a strange, uncivilised little place'* (Tempus, Stroud, 2004).

Yorkshire Vernacular Building Study Group, *Ponden Hall Recording* (Leeds, 2003).

Articles

Anon., 'History of the Barnoldswick Baptists', *Baptist Quarterly* (1969), pp. 16–41.

Anon, 'Purchase by Brontë Society of the old Parsonage', *Transactions of the Brontë Society (TBS)*, vol. xii, part 37, pp. 107–8; 'report of the Opening of the Brontë Parsonage Museum by Sir James Roberts', vol. xii, part 38, pp. 138–50.

Aveling, W. – 'Catholic Recusants of the West Riding of Yorkshire', *Leeds Philosophical and Literary Society Proceedings*, vol. x, part vi (1963).

Baumber, M. L., 'That 'Vandal Wade' The Reverend John Wade and the Demolition of the Brontë Church', *TBS*, vol. xxii (1997), pp. 96–111.

Baumber, M. L., 'Patrick Brontë and the Development of Primary Education in Haworth', *TBS*, vol. xxiv, Part 1 (1999), pp. 66–81.

Baumber, M. L., 'The Haworth Church Rate Controversy', *Yorkshire Archaeological Journal (YAJ)*, vol. 75 (2003), pp. 115–28.

Birdsall, Malcolm, 'Vernacular Buildings of Haworth', *Annual Conference Report of the West Yorkshire Building Group* (Leeds, 2000).

Black, W. H. (ed.), 'Early History of the Brontë Society', *TBS*, vol. xiv, part 72 (1962).

Cant, David, 'Spring time Saunter in the footsteps of Whiteley Turner', *Talk to Haworth Historians* (Oct. 2002).

Crump, W. B., 'Ancient Highways of the Parish of Halifax; The Old Haworth Road', *Transactions of the Halifax Antiquarian Society (THAS)* (1928), pp. 225–51.

Dickens, J. Norton, 'Roman Roads', *Bradford Antiquary (BA)*, vol. iii (NS I), pp. 240–54.

Edgerley, C. Mabel, 'History of the Brontë Society 1893–1943' *TBS*, vol. x, part 53 (1943).

Elfenbein, Andrew, 'The Argument between the Rev. Winterbotham and the Rev. Brontë', *TBS*, vol. xx (1990), pp. 89–94.

Emsley, K., 'The Chapelry of Haworth' *TBS*, vol. xx, part 3 (1991) p. 165.

Faull, Margaret, 'Roman and Anglian Settlements in Yorkshire' *Northern History (NH)*, ix (1974).

Ford, James, 'A Seventeenth-Century Baptist Church', *Bromsgrove Transactions of the Baptist Historical Society*, vol. 1, no. 2 (1909), p. 106.

Gilks, J. A., 'Early Mesolithic Sites at Nab Water, Oxenhope Moor', *YAJ*, vol. 66 (1994).

Hagerty, J. M., 'Bradford Friendly Societies in the 1790s', *BA* (NS), part 46 (1976), pp. 49ff.

Higham, N. J., 'Brigantia Revisited', *NH*, xxiii (1987).

James, David, ''Our Philip': The Early Career of Philip Snowden', *BA*, (3rd Series) vol. iii (1986), pp. 44–6.

Johnson, David, 'Publish and be Damned; Hardwicke's Marriage Act', *History Today* (November 2003), pp. 38–44.

Jones, G. R. J., 'Early Territorial Organisation in Gwynedd and Elmet', *NH*, x (1975).

Jones, G. R. J., 'Multiple Estates and Early Medieval Settlement', *Sawyer* (1979), pp. 9–34.

Judson, H. I., 'The Early Clergy of Bradford', *BA*, (NS) vol. vi, p. 31–40.

Kendall, H. P., 'The Civil War as affecting Halifax and the Surrounding Towns', *THAS* (1931), pp. 1–28.

Kershaw, Ian, 'The Scots in the West Riding 1318–9', *NH*, xvii (1981), pp. 231–9.

Killick, H. F., 'The Duchy of Lancaster and the Manor of Bradford' *BA* (NS) vol. iii (1912), pp. 23–5.

Le Patourel, J., 'The Norman Conquest of Yorkshire', *NH*, vi (1971), pp. 1–21.

Lister J, 'Elizabethan Halifax', *THAS*, xxi (1921) p. 44.

Meeker, Claude, 'Haworth, Home of the Brontës', *TBS* vol. i, Part 3 (1895), pp. 19–21.

Oddy, Miles, 'Obituary of', *Baptist Magazine*, vol. v, Fourth Series (January 1842) pp. 1–5.

Robertshaw, W., 'Notes on the Manningham Family', *BA*, (NS) vol. vii, pp. 105–12.

Robertshaw, W., 'The Manor of Clayton' *BA*, (NS) vol. vi, pp. 348–83.

Saunders, Moses, 'A Memoir of', *Strict Baptist Handbook* (1875) pp. 296–8.

Smith, G. H., 'The Smiths of Halifax', *THAS* (1949).

Stanley, B. E., 'Patrick Brontë's Notebook', *TBS*, vol. xiv, part 72 (1962), pp. 17–19.

Sigsworth E. M., 'William Greenwood and Robert Heaton: Eighteenth Century Worsted Manufacturers', *Bradford Textile History Journal*, (1953), pp. 61–72.

Skirrow, Eunice, 'Upper Worth Valley Schools', *TBS*, vol. xx, part 3 (1991), p. 159.

Snape, M. E., 'Anti-Methodism in Eighteenth Century England: The Pendle Forest Riots of 1748', *Journal of Ecclesiastical History*, vol. 49, no. 2 (1998), pp. 258–81.

Waddington-Feather, John, 'Charlotte in Kentucky: Coaching Haworthese', *Brontë Studies*, vol. 29, part 3 (2004).

Watson, E. W. & Gledhill B. A., 'Wadsworth Highways Part I', *THAS* (1951), p. 107.

Wightman, W. E., 'The Significance of Waste in the Yorkshire Domesday', *NH*, x (1975) pp. 51–71.

Yorkshire TV, 'The Brontë Connection', Background notes to 1979 TV programme (copy at Brontë Parsonage Museum).

Index

Index entries in *italic* type refer to illustrations or to their accompanying captions.